Was That Thunder?

A Memoir
Of Pro-life Rescue,
1988-1997

James H. Trott

... It is not light that is needed, but fire; it is not the gentle shower, but thunder. We need the storm, the whirlwind, and the earthquake. The feeling of the nation must be quickened; the conscience of the nation must be roused; the propriety of the nation must be startled; the hypocrisy of the nation must be exposed; and its crimes against God and man must be denounced.   – Frederick Douglass, 4 July 1852

And when the seven thunders had uttered their voices, I was about to write : and I heard a voice from heaven saying unto me, Seal up those things which the seven thunders uttered, and write them not.   –The Book of Revelation 11:4

Oak and Yew Press

Was That Thunder?

A Memoir
Of Pro-life Rescue,
1988-1997

James H. Trott

Copyright 2015
James H. Trott

First published edition 2015

Philadelphia

"Bright, Shining Moments" -- by Joe Wall

    Sometimes, in the evening of our lives, we look back with regret, with sadness – reflecting on what a muddled business it has been. The wasted opportunities, the false starts, the confusion, the stupidity of much of what we have done. We think about the lack of charity and commitment, of our selfishness, of our narcissistic devotion to our own 'interests.'

    But if we have rescued, if we have tried to save our unborn brothers and sisters by placing our bodies in the way of those who sought to kill them, we know that, at least a few times, we did something that was utterly selfless. Something that was good and decent, pure, holy and noble.

    Anyone who has rescued, who has sat in front of a clinic door. . . , knows that high, exultant feeling, "hey, this time I got it right, this time I have it all together, this time I did the RIGHT thing!"

    These, in our otherwise humdrum lives, were our "bright, shining moments" that we can look back on with a kind of awe, knowing that our loving God has reached down and chosen us – with all of our weaknesses, with all of our failings – to save those He loved best, the least of His brethren, the unborn children.

CONTENTS

	page
Title Page	
Copyright Page	
Prefatory Reflection – Bright, Shining Moments	
Contents	
Introduction: A Memoir?	1
Chapter One – At The Beginning	15
Chapter Two - The Seige Of Atlanta	41
Chapter Three -- Recruiting The Masses (1989)	95
Chapter Four – The Decisive Decade (1990)	159
Chapter Five -- Moving Onward (1991)	195
Chapter Six – Developments (1992)	249
Chapter Seven - Counter-Attack (1993)	267
Chapter Eight - Choke Holds (1994)	305
Chapter Nine – Dispersed, Disbanded (1995-6)	339
Chapter Ten – Englewood And Allentown (1997)	357
Chapter Eleven – Writing Paul Hill (11/97 – 12/98)	395
Chapter Twelve -- Easing Off (1998)	443
Afterword 1999 – 2007	453
Appreciations	473
Bibliography	477
Sources of Illustrations	482

Was That Thunder?

A Memoir of Pro-life Rescue

Introduction: A Memoir?

A Memoir. Farmboys don't write memoirs. At most they record humorous or nostalgiac anecdotes. Yankees don't write memoirs, either, just diatribes. Hippies? Roofers? Carpenters? ... Poets? ... Presbyterians?

My wife and I have occasionally said a narrative of our lives would make fine reading – if we billed it as adventure fiction. But we also say that some people write about life and some people live it. That's no doubt unfair and meant primarily to justify ourselves. Nonetheless, many important and dramatic things can't be recorded – some involve things too private for us to publicize, while some concern the private secrets of others. Furthermore the journey seems to use up the creative energy which might be used to record it.

Nevertheless, despite all this, I seem to be writing a memoir, self-conscious and uneasy as it makes me. I believe I can blame three important men in my life, three kinsmen.

The first is my eldest son, Joshua, who persuaded me to begin it. A writer himself, he saw a great deal of the rescue movement as he was growing up. He says this is a project that needs doing, and that my range of experience qualifies me. I might add that he told me this while we were working on a particularly difficult roof in not particularly good roofing weather, which circumstances may have inspired both his suggestion -- and my susceptibility to it.

The second kinsman is my father-in-law, Cecil John Miller, now gone to glory. "Jack" (he didn't tolerate being called Cecil!) often told anecdotes involving himself very much in the memoir genre.

For the same reasons that I am not naturally inclined toward "memoir," I sometimes balked at listening to Jack's stories, particularly those in which Jack came off rather well. Since for many years (1975 to 1983) we were not only in the same family but in the same congregation and community, we saw a lot of each other. One time, sitting on his back porch, I summoned my courage to point out my difficulty.

Was That Thunder?

Jack and Rosemarie Miller

"Dad," I said, "Don't take this wrong. I am asking you this question, because I really want to understand. But it seems to me that when you speak publicly of various incidents and events you have been involved in, you could just as well tell them in the third person – you know, like the Apostle Paul, 'I once knew a man' . . . – but when you tell about what you did and what you said, and what you thought, and the effects you had on others, it seems to me at times to sound like bragging. "

Summoning his own distinctive manner of responding to difficult questions, Jack grew quieter and thought a moment before he replied, "Perhaps there is something to what you say. It is certain that my heart is no less desperately wicked than others. As Calvin says, our hearts are "idol-making machines." My heart is always ready to use an occasion for its own idolatry. However if there is pride in what I say openly, others are liable to correct me, whereas no one rebukes my pride when I am silent."

Boomerang! That was and continues to be quite a rebuke to me – for "silent" false humility, and the raging pride of private self-congratulation are among my more active sins. To make myself vulnerable by telling my own story is thus also an act of repentance.

And third, my brother-in-law, Paul, encouraged me to write something like this seven years ago. He wondered if an account of my times in prison might not be of special interest to the contemporary church.

My son suggested this memoir, for which my wife's father had given me the apologetic thirty years earlier, and my brother-in-law helped prepare the ground. Three generations of kinsmen – blame them!

But even taking seriously the idea of writing such an account I was up against another barrier. For not only do my inclinations tend away from the "personal memoir," I have a positive tendency toward history – and that creates other dilemmas for me. I don't feel qualified, nor do I know anyone who is qualified, to write a fair history of the "Rescue Movement" (1983-1999 or so).[1] It was far too big and far too diverse. It has been estimated that it resulted in about 50,000 arrests.[2] Since there was no central coordination, planning or reporting center, except perhaps some hapless clerk cubbyholed in the depths of the Justice Department central offices, there is therefore no person or group of people who knows about all the separate rescues.

For a few of the early years "Operation Rescue" (OR) in Binghamton, New York, which had fifteen "staff," at its peak[3] did keep records of all the rescues reported to them – but those files can not have been complete, even during the three or four years before the proaborts succeeded in shutting

---

[1] Bob Brothers tells me Richard Cowden Guido has written a history which has not been published. Our own Joe Roach wrote up his account of Philly rescue under the title *Rescuing During the Cultural War*. And in 2012, Monica Migliorino Miller published *Abandoned*, her autobiographical account of midwest pro-life activism.

[2] I think Pat Mahoney says 70,000 in his Bridgehead radio interview. (Youtube)

[3] OR staff included for a time a fulltime lawyer at whose house I once stayed.

Was That Thunder?

OR down. A full and true history will probably never be written.[4]

Nevertheless, my inclination is to collect the tidbits of history, the data, rather than record the experience and memories of living it. I have tried to exercise self-restraint in this regard, but the result is still perhaps an uneasy marriage of chronicle or journal, as it were, and memoir.

So much for this memoir's *raison d'être*. But a few more prolegomena might be helpful. Who is the guy doing the talking, for instance?

Born in 1949, I am the son of a Yankee and a Montanan. My father grew up in small town Andover, Massachusetts; my mother in smaller town Fort Benton, Montana. My father graduated from Harvard College with a Fine Arts degree in 1942, just in time to go into the Army Air Corps, where he served as an aerial photographic specialist, mostly in Italy. When he got out, so he told us, he felt he was too old to go back to school for architecture, his original plan, so he got a job making models of insects for the Chicago Natural History Museum, AKA: Field Museum. There he met my mother. Eight years younger, she was at Antioch college [5] on a work/study program, which involved sorting birds eggs at the museum where Dad worked.

Dad claimed that his first trip to Montana was like entering a world he had dreamed of. He loved it along with one of its daughters. After getting married and spending a brief time back in Chicago, the two of them returned to Montana where Dad entered into the farming business, the occupation of almost all of my relatives there.

I lived most of my first eighteen years between our small farm and the small town where we lived. I never thought of myself as anything but a Montanan, until years later I began to realize that bred in my bones was a strong set

---

[4] They were estimating 40,000 rescuers had risked arrest in the first years, before Operation Rescue folded up.

[5] She was at Antioch at the same time as Coretta Scott (later King) and her sister, as witnessed by an all-school photograph my brother Jon found.

of New England values. I early imbibed the great western mythology, through movies, books and phonograph records, and was deeply gratified when I got my first set of six-guns (firing roll caps) for Christmas. When I got my first 22 rifle at age eleven, I thought I was Natty Bumpo.

James Edwards and Lucille Hanford Trott & son, 1949

My parents loved books, and read a great deal to us. They were also great lovers of the outdoors, of camping, and "nature". My dad was particularly knowledgeable about insects and my mother, about birds. We grew up with the idea it was great fun eating wild plants and identifying wild creatures. In contrast to my uncles, however, my Dad never liked hunting. He had more of a Thornton Burgess view of animals, and hated to hurt them.

High standards of moral behavior were maintained verbally, and where necessary through punishment. As often as not these were modern, enlightened punishments – like spending the afternoon in our rooms. I think Dr. Spock had too much to do with our upbringing, but on a diminishing scale. Certainly there were some notable spankings along the way.

We were active church goers: Methodists. We sang in

choirs and my parents served in many other capacities. We did not drink – although my father smoked a pipe, often late into the night in his little second story office near my bedroom.

Early on, partly through cousins and partly through exploring my parents' library, I discovered sex, and by the age of eleven was fairly obsessed with it. Anybody who suggests this obsession was "normal" or "healthy" hasn't the slightest idea. Without saying much more about my lust, I will say it seems to me there were "sins of the fathers" at its foundation, going back perhaps for generations, along with my own strange combination of hyper-imagination and outward conformity.

For the purposes of this memoir, I emphasize that in my imagination from early on, woman was treated primarily as an "object," rather than a person, in the same way the "fetus" is regarded in much contemporary feminist and legal rhetoric.

I did very well in school, despite never learning to study very hard. In a small school and a small community, one excels more or less because one is expected to, and because there are, relatively speaking, very many opportunities to do so. I was class president, a football captain, and a member of bands, choirs, drama productions, various clubs and organizations.

The level of conformity in fashion and behavior was very high in our school and town. This translated into a high standard of public ethics and a uniform enforcement of public morality. I caught just a few glimpses of an undercurrent of hypocrisy when it came to private morality, but hardly knew how to interpret them.

Much later I learned some highly respected people were playing some very dirty games. For instance, at least one leading citizen was quietly seducing a string of high school girls. I did not register that then, however, not at least in any form that made it part of my world-view or expectations. By the last few years of high school I was self-consciously religious and thought the only serious hypocrite was myself.

The summer after my graduation, through friends and kindred who were part of a revival in a rural church, I became a Christian, that is to say, no longer just religious, but one who believed in Christ and the Christian message in its historical, spiritual, and personal ramifications.

My grades in high school had been good, largely because the subjects all interested me. I had applied to, and was accepted at Harvard, Dartmouth, and the University of Montana. "Two roads diverged in a yellow wood..."

I went to Harvard. I told others I made that choice because I wanted to see the other half of my heritage – Massachusetts. Indeed, I did get to know and enjoy all the living members of my father's family, most of them still in Andover, his old home town. But I also went because it was expected of me – as much by my community as my family. 'Small town boy makes good,' has a certain imperative to it. Saying 'I don't want to make good, thank you,' didn't seem like an option.

Striking students meeting at Harvard stadium

Am I glad I went? At one point I tried to transfer back to Montana – and for years I complained a lot about Harvard. I had perhaps three brilliant professors, for whom I am very thankful. I learned to study during my freshman year, motivated by a desperate conviction that I was the stupidest guy there.

And I got to see the complete breakdown of the liberal institution – in the Vietnam student strikes of 1968-9. I learned that the smartest people in the country are not necessarily all that bright, and are among those most easily misled. I saw civil disobedience up-close for the first time and it was ugly – hostile, aggressive, and the farthest thing from something I wanted to be part of.

And I met my wife! So yes, I'm glad I went. Roseann Miller, was going to Wellesley, twelve miles west of Cambridge. When I arrived at Harvard Square in 1967, I was horrified at the drab, dry, dusty place to which I had been lured by trickery. I soon learned that all the photographs in the admissions materials were taken at graduation in the spring, after millions of dollars had been spent annually planting, watering and cultivating the Yard to please the returning alumni.

Following graduation each year all this was abandoned and let go to wrack, ruin, drought, and desert – until the next spring. 1967 was a dry summer. Wellesley, on the other hand, was not only more or less out in the country, but maintained its beautiful grounds year round. Therefore, at least the first few times I went out there, seeing the girls was just an excuse.

But a couple of years later, I met Roseann at a joint Harvard, Radcliffe, Wellesley Christian Fellowship retreat on Cape Cod. Our romance grew quickly, and to the bewilderment of many of our mutual friends, who saw us as very different types, we slipped into love. Nonetheless, we might have progressed much more slowly, were it not for the inspirational effects of Selective Service. Under the pressure of my low draft lottery number, we decided to get married sooner rather than later – in the middle of my senior and her junior year. I will leave the account of how hard marriage was at first to Roseann's own memoirs.

Seven months later I was in the army. We were together much more than most army couples, eventually going to Japanese language school together in California. We were sent to Japan, where we lived "on the economy" (rather than on base) and attended a Japanese church for a year and a half. Our eldest daughter was born there, and we named her "Kimiko" which means "child who sees Christ".

In Japan after Kimiko's birth

Getting out of the army, the GI bill attracted me with its offer of four years schooling. Up to that point I had no formal Bible training, and thought I might get it at the seminary where Roseann's father taught, Westminster, in Chestnut Hill, near Philadelphia. Thus our move East. Although seminary proved rather a deadend for me (I left after a year and a half), we got established in a church,[6] and gradually found ourselves settling as Philadelphians.

I used most of the remaining GI bill for some technical training, and within a few years was making my living as a roofer/carpenter, as I still am.

Our second daughter, Adriel, was born, and we moved from the suburbs into the city despite dire predictions

---

[6]My spiritual evolution was such that I had gone from being a pious, though liberal Methodist to a loosely charismatic evangelical to a conservative Presbyterian.

about our safety from people we otherwise respected. Joshua was born. Tobiah Loren came along, via C-section. And Jedidiah joined us by the same method. Our youngest child, Victoria, was yet to be born as we enter the time-frame proper of this memoir.

One more bit of prolegomena – and then we will get on with it. I suppose for the sake of those who never saw a "rescue" take place, I ought to give a general idea of what was involved. From the standpoint of an objective observer (and there were none) a rescue usually consisted of a number of people going to an abortion clinic on a particular day and sitting or standing in front of its doors.

To the casual observer it would have been unclear what they were doing, except at those points where someone, a doctor, an employee or a "client" tried to get into the clinic. At that point it became obvious the people were passively but definitely blocking the doors, since they would not move out of the way to allow clinic staff and pregnant mothers to get into the clinic.

They appeared to be rather ordinary people, except for this blocking behavior, which included the fact they did not respond to police warnings to leave.

They were not aggressive, nor were they verbally offensive. They might have a few signs which said various things affirming the humanhood of the unborn or the evil of abortion.

They were quiet and sometimes even silent. During some of the time they spent in front of abortion clinics, they were singing or praying, or listening to one of their number speak or preach. A pedestrian coming upon the rescue or someone driving by saw a compact group of inactive people in front of a building, usually with a number of police present.

If you asked any of the people involved, "Why are you doing this?" they would have replied "to prevent babies from dying here today". They were usually accompanied by some others, moving around on the periphery, whom they called "sidewalk counselors." These walked about, pursuing the specific purpose of speaking to the "moms and dads" who came for abortion appointments.

Many sidewalk counselors came regularly to the clinics anyway, but when there was a "rescue," they took special advantage of the "sit-in" or "blockade" (both terms were used by reporters and police, especially in the early days) to offer alternatives to the wouldn't-be parents who showed up for appointments.

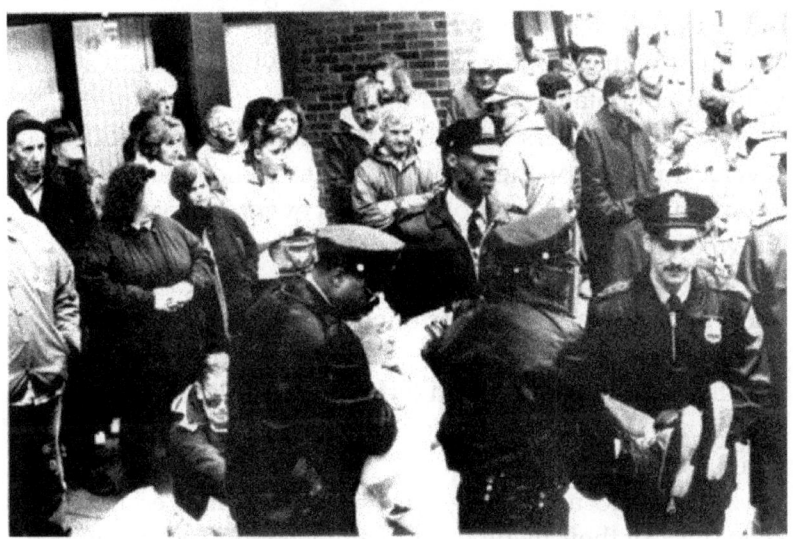

Rescue at Blackwell abortion clinic, April 1991

The rescue movement was self-consciously peaceful and prayerful. Nonetheless, there were a few kinds of hostile encounter that sometimes took place during a rescue.[7] On some occasions, an abortionist or member of his staff, a boyfriend, a parent, or a pregnant mom herself, upon finding that the rescuers would not move out of the way, would yell, threaten, and even strike out at the rescuers. At some rescues "pro-choice" demonstrators along with "escorts"[8]

---

[7] I will leave the discussions of police violence until later. In rare situations -- rare at least in Philadelphia -- but not in places like Pittsburgh, East Hartford or Los Angeles, police would be rough or even brutal toward rescuers.

[8] Rescuers usually referred to abortion clinic escorts as "deathscorts"

from the abortion clinic, would raise a ruckus.

In most jurisdictions police would be on the scene shortly after the rescuers showed up. In general, the Philadelphia police were quite professional. The Civil Affairs Unit was usually in charge at a rescue, and their approach was to separate proaborts and prolifers, and to carry on some sort of liaison with rescue leaders. The object from the police point of view was to expedite their own goals without too much strain on their own ranks. Of course they had to be careful how they handled the situation, which was always a political hot potato.

The "rescuers" stayed in front of the doors until one of several things happened: 1/the clinic cancelled its day's appointments, or 2/the police moved everyone away and allowed access to the clinic again, or 3/the police arrested the rescuers and transported them away to be processed under a wide variety of charges as criminals. The third alternative resulted in an official record being kept, but the other two usually did not, so it is often difficult to speak with much precision about how many rescuers participated where and when.

Some local rescue groups were organized enough to keep track of their members and any legal procedures which involved them, but others were more ad hoc and did not keep tabs, even on official matters very well. When there was a "national" event, it was even harder to keep track of who and even how many were involved.

Rescuers agreed to promises to be peaceful, prayerful and to submit to leaders during particular rescues. They were often asked to sign a pledge to that effect. Nonetheless there were said to be some places where there was not enough leadership authority to strictly enforce proper conduct. Philadelphia leaders were some of the best, and therefore our conduct was kept to high standards.

There were not any primary or official theoreticians for the rescue movement, although the earliest rescuers gained and transmitted much practical wisdom. The movement was not fundamentally ideological – and therefore it was not united primarily by ideology. The only central idea was that human life was precious enough and therefore abortion was wrong enough to justify risking arrest in an effort to stop it.

There were many speeches given at rallies over the years – and these did indeed repeat certain basic themes – but they were neither mindless mantras nor radically new. They were rather sermons on themes that did not originate with the speakers or the movement.

The rescue movement owed a great deal to the Civil Rights movement, for instance. The stark words of Frederick Douglass on the title page of this book apply as well to abortion as to slavery. Dr. King was frequently quoted by pro-lifers, especially in his statements concerning the divine basis for doing what was right in the face of what was "legal" and wrong.[9] Many of the songs we sang came via the civil rights movement.

The rescue movement further owed something to various labor and peace movements in American history – which in turn owed a good deal to English and European history,[10] out of which were formulated doctrines of just submission, passive resistance, and Christian martyrdom, ultimately going back to the Gospels and the Book of Acts.

I cannot speak as an appointed representative of the movement, nor as an authoritative general historian thereof. I am not a credentialed theologian or theoretician, but I can record my own experience: what I heard and thought, and what the rescuers I knew believed and said. Since I knew a few who were involved early, I can share tidbits of history I picked up from them, together with details from published accounts. One can also perhaps recall some of what leaders and speakers said or did at particular rescues or meetings. This ought to make for good memoir material – although it will only be one out of fifty thousand memoirs that could be written on the subject.

Among my own recollections, I have tried to pick and

---

[9] See his *Letter from the Birmingham Jail*.

[10] As a daughter points out, something was also owed to Gandhi.

choose in order to avoid describing too many similar events, and too much mere detail. I have also tried to restrain myself from too many trips to the soapbox upon which I naturally climb.[11]

Since rescue itself was always accompanied by song, and there were many songs, I was at first inclined to incorporate a lot of lyrics. Since my own serious meditations tend to end up in poetry, I thought I'd incorporate a number of my poems, too. Stew de memoir anyone? Wiser critics, indeed all the readers of the first draft agreed the hymn lyrics had to go – and most of the poetry, too. What's left is a small sample with direct relevance to the particular reminiscences of which they remain a part. [12]

One perceptive reader of my manuscript commented that a theme seems to emerge: the rescue movement had a hand in rescuing me. I believe that is so. Perhaps one day we will be able to say it was instrumental in helping to rescue the American church. I believe it will prove a significant divide in our nation's turn toward the ultimate repeal of Roe v. Wade. That event for which we pray will mark the greatest repentance from idolatry since our founding. May it come soon.

---

[11] Some of my reviewers wish there was a little less history, but I feel I owe those passages to posterity.

[12] Any reader who wishes to read more poetry can find my pro-life poems, *Conceptions and images*, online at the Createspace eBookstore and other book sites.

CHAPTER ONE – AT THE BEGINNING

Is it such a fast that I have chosen? A day for a man to afflict his soul? Is it to bow down his head as a bulrush, and to spread sackcloth and ashes under him? Wilt thou call this a fast, and an acceptable day to the Lord? Is not this the fast that I have chosen? To loose the bands of wickedness, to undo the heavy burdens, and to let the oppressed go free, and that ye break every yoke? Is it not to deal thy bread to the hungry, and that thou bring the poor that are cast out to thy house? When thou seest the naked, that thou cover him; and that thou hide not thyself from thine own flesh? Then shall thy light break forth as the morning, and thine health shall spring forth speedily; and thy righteousness shall go before thee; the glory of the Lord shall be thy rearward.   Isaiah 58:5-8

As I open this narrative, I am going to try to fuse two trains of events, one personal and the other historical. The one may be illustrated by five snapshots of me and my wife; the other by freeze-frames of a nascent "rescue movement".

The Process of Getting Involved

First snaphot: Roseann and I sit in a military medical waiting room, waiting. (As per the universal motto of all military activities: Hurry up and wait.) A radio news program is describing a US Supreme Court decision [13] which makes abortion legal throughout the nine months of pregnancy, provided it is "for medical reasons." The guy in the PFC's uniform (me) responds internally with a vague sense of regret, as though some revered person in his life had proved petty and less reliable than he had thought. However,

---

[13] Doe v. Bolton, companion case to Roe v. Wade, January 1973.

he hasn't enough knowledge or conviction to discuss the court decision or the feeling with his wife, who also listens silently. The only personal knowledge he has of abortion comes from vague rumors he heard in high school about a hometown girl who went to New York for that purpose.

Second snapshot: me, minus the uniform and military haircut, and sporting a beard, about 1984. In the interim Roseann and I have had five children. I hear of a pro-life demonstration being held in downtown Philadelphia. With undefined purpose, I ride down on the subway to participate, taking my ten year old daughter, Kimiko, along. Among my mixed motives is a sense that I have a statement to make – in the form of an oak wood-carving I had made, a sculpture of a hand with a child emerging from its palm.[14]

"Behold I have graven thee upon the palms of my hands"

---

[14] My wife commissioned it, based on a favorite scripture: "Can a woman forget her sucking child, that she should not have compassion on the son of her womb? yea, they may forget, yet will I not forget thee. Behold, I have graven thee upon the palms of my hands; thy walls are continually before me." (Isaiah 49:15-16)

A Memoir of Pro-life Rescue

That demonstration, across the street from Planned Parenthood, has a sub-set of snapshots, including one of me and a few others angrily chanting some loud but ineffectual chant like "Stop the killing! and "Murderers"while pro-life leaders try to quell us.

In another snapshot, a newswoman refuses her cameraman's suggestion that they interview Kimiko with the words, "she's too young." My chief feelings as we rode home again on the subway were a sense of satisfaction at having done something, and a sense of relief that probably we wouldn't ever do anything like that again. It seemed too remote from everyday life, an alien activity, and it left me uneasy.

I could not articulate it, but I had an instinctive feeling that if I formally signed on to take a stand for justice, I implicitly made a commitment to pursue it until justice was established. That was an overwhelming prospect.

Furthermore, "demonstrating" felt futile and frustrating to me – I had no sense of doing something constructive or effective, even when I broke ranks and chanted slogans.

Third – a freeze-frame: a year or two later, in March, my wife Roseann, and our two oldest daughters are participating in another demonstration, this one is a picket near an abortionist's home in suburban Cheltenham. No one involved had any expectation of arrest. They were just "demonstrating". They did not go on private property, or even stand still in one place. Rather they went along a public sidewalk carrying signs. Vaguely reminiscent of the First Amendment? However an unconstitutional ordinance had been passed, which became the basis for arrests. Others involved included our good friends Bill Devlin and Pat Stanton, and Orthodox Rabbi Yehuda Levin. [15]

The Cheltenham police had anticipated the picket It

---

[15] Several Orthodox Jewish rabbis were active in pro-life events over the years, including several who regularly came to the March for Life in Washington. I believe they were all from New York City.

Was That Thunder?

wasn't the first in front of Dr. Klebanoff's home. With what motives none of us ever knew, the police had brought in a long string of trailers containing stadium lights with which to illuminate the scene of the expected crime. Cables ran back

Rabbi Yehuda Levin from New York

and forth along the street to power these. It looked like the set of a big movie. The handful of pro-lifers who were there to picket were astounded. The police, for their part, also looked a bit sheepish, especially when the expected picketers were few, and none of them looked even moderately criminal.

Next freeze-frame – the following year (1987) -- me with a bewildered face, staring at the wall of our small Philadelphia row house. I have just heard that three of our friends from church have been arrested as part of a pro-life "sit-in" in front of an abortion clinic in New Jersey. I feel ambivalent about this news, having unreserved respect for the three, and at the same time an unreserved commitment to "law-and-order". I am unable to come to any judgment about what they've done, which is itself an unusual and uncomfortable state of affairs for me.

The last of the camera shifts brings us to the opening of this memoir proper. The camera descends and zooms, coming to focus on the bearded fellow with a little more forehead, standing in the kitchen door of the same row house and listening to the phone. On the other end is Chuck Depoy, one of those from our church arrested the previous year. Chuck is inviting us to a pro-life rally to be held on the 4th of July 1988 at Valley Forge National Park.

That rally at Valley Forge was to be a turning point in a campaign that had gone on since before Roe v. Wade, but which had begun in earnest five years earlier, which takes us back to another stream of historical snapshots.

The Early Rescue Movement – Philly and the Nation

Catholic pro-life efforts began in the late 60s, when a few states began to loosen their laws against abortion. Protestants were much slower to get aboard, partly because the pro-abortion rhetoric had been effective in making most think it was "a Catholic cause".

The first pro-life "sit-in" took place in June of 1970 in Washington DC, where six or seven prolifers went into the vestibule of a facility performing illegal abortions. They were arrested and roughly handled by police, but charges were dropped.

In 1975 Dr. Harold O.J. Brown, Ruth Bell Graham[16], and Dr. C. Everett Koop founded the Christian Action Council (CAC) to inform and motivate Evangelical Protestants against abortion.

In August 1975, John Cavanaugh O'Keefe[17] and his sister Lucy were arrested after several hours of counseling women in a Rockville, MD abortion clinic. Several similar events took place in 1976 in Washington DC, Maryland, Virginia, and Ohio. In the next two years "sit-ins" took place at abortion clinics in fifteen states, including Alaska.[18]

---

[16] Ruth was the wife of evangelist Billy Graham.

[17] In an interview, Bill Calvin described John Cavanaugh-O'Keefe as the "leading intellectual of the movement". Bridgehead Radio, Youtube

[18] Much of the information in this and the next three paragraphs is courtesy of Joe Wall, from his "A Brief History of Rescue". The actual name of the activity and the organization, "Operation Rescue" is said to have been coined by Joe Wall, a

In 1976, one of the first pro-lifers ever arrested was Donna Rozewski, a Chicago sidewalk counsellor who had to resort to counter-charges against a clinic worker to stave off false accusations of assault. Donna herself had suffered an abortion.[19]

In March 1977, John P. Stanton,[20] at the invitation of Elder Charles McConnell, showed a filmstrip to six couples from Maple Glen Bible Fellowship, north of Philadelphia. The filmstrip was by Dr. Wiltke of the National Right to Life organization.[21] Charles McConnell was already stirred up about the issue. After seeing the filmstrip, several others were also deeply moved, including Phildelphia residents, Lou and Lynn Prontnicki. A few months later Lou and Tom Seelinger began to seek avenues for pro-life activism. For example they attended the fourth *March for Life* in Washington in 1978. [22]

In 1978, Joe Scheidler,[23] Monica Migliorino and twenty-five others staged a "sit-in" at a Chicago abortion clinic, Concord Medical Center.[24]

That year Lou Prontnicki and Tom Seelinger founded the Philadelphia CAC and representatives from many area evangelical churches began to attend monthly meetings. Some of these whom I knew or came to know included Bill Devlin, Jim O'Brien, Michael Smith, Ben Sheldon, Barry Traver, Robert Godfrey, and Mike Hardin.

A group from these churches went to Washington under the banner "Evangelicals for Life/PCAC" in the 1979

---

veteran rescuer from Philadelphia, although I didn't get that information from Joe.

[19] Monica Migliorino Miller, *Abandoned*, p. 31-33.

[20] John Stanton was universally known as the "Father of the Pro-life Movement in the Delaware Valley".

[21] Both Dr. Wiltke and John Stanton were Roman Catholics.

[22] *A Brief History of the Beginning of the Pro-Life Movement among Evangelicals in the Philadelphia Area*. . .Lou Prontnicki, May 2008.

[23] Joe Scheidler is among the earliest, best-known, and most committed of pro-life activist leaders -- again a Catholic.

[24] M.M.Miller, *Abandoned*, p. 33.

March for Life. Several of the CAC leaders were from Fleischman Memorial Baptist Church in Hunting Park under the care of Pastor Jim Correnti. The CAC undertook a campaign to educate churches and Christian schools about abortion, since most Protestants were still ignorant about it.

Also in 1979, Francis Schaeffer and C. Everett Koop launched their nation-wide film series, *Whatever Happened to the Human Race?* at Philadelphia's Academy of Music.

In 1980, an activist group in St. Louis included John Ryan and Joan Andrews. This group did "sit-ins" at clinics for several years until the local Catholic Archbishop, John May, discouraged his flock from participating.

That year, under the oversight of Tenth Presbyterian church, Alpha Pregnancy Services, a crisis pregnancy center was founded. All over the country many other such organizations were started by by both Catholics and Protestants to provide alternatives to abortion, with a wide range of services for women in crisis pregnancy.

Also by 1980, CAC was providing pro-life voter's guides. By 1981, Protestant churches began to hold annual *Sanctity of Human Life Sundays* near January 22, the anniversary of Roe v Wade.[25]

In 1983, a group of pro-lifers from around the country gathered to discuss appropriate responses to the horror that abortion had become – a million and a half babies dying yearly in the United States alone. Their principle interest was to promote "direct action tactics" designed to hinder and impede the bloody business of abortion clinics. They decided to call themselves PLAN (Pro-life Action Network).

Joe Scheidler wrote a book *Shutdown: 99 Ways to Close Abortion Clinics*. It catalogued many of the methods prolife activists were to actually use, although some of his suggestions were scrapped as unwise or impracticable.

In May 1983 with the backing of a number of pastors, including James Boice (Tenth Presbyterian), Joseph Ross (Deliverance Evangelistic) and Ben Sheldon (Bethany Collegiate Presbyterian) the CAC organized an "Operation

---

[25] Maple Glen Bible Fellowship began this tradition in 1977.

Was That Thunder?

Trumpet " campaign to put a full page pro-life ad in the *Philadelphia Inquirer*.

In May 1984, as a result of an inspiring visit by John Cavanaugh O'Keefe, about 40 people from the Philadelphia area joined more than a hundred others to "sit in" at an abortion clinic in Gaithersburg, Maryland. Only two people were arrested.

John Cavanaugh O'Keefe, intellectual and activist

Next, at the first "sit-in" in our area, on 3 July 1984, 19 pro-lifers went inside the Women's Suburban Clinic in Paoli, where they are arrested. This tactic relied on surprise and relatively low levels of security at abortion facilities. Those involved usually went in and locked doors behind them where possible as they occupied various rooms. In some cases they deliberately de-sterilized the facilities and the equipment, to further delay their use later, even after police took them away.

From 1984-1987, there were approximately 22 "sit-ins," which gradually came to be called "rescues," a term older then "operation rescue" and credited to Jack O'Brien. Jack was another veteran who, along with his wife, Pat, came to be deeply respected as a leader. Most of the early events involved going inside clinics, including the one on Roosevelt Blvd. in Philadelphia and those at Paoli and Bridgeport.

During the July '84 rescue, Lou Prontnicki was shocked to see the name of Dr. Steven Allen listed as one of the Paoli clinic's abortionists. Dr. Allen had saved Lou's wife's life at Bryn Mawr Birth Center when her blood pressure dropped dangerously during the birth of their second child two years earlier. This was on top of the same kind of experience at the Salvation Army's Booth Maternity Clinic where, after they had their first child, they learned Dr. Franklin, who delivered him, was also one of the most outspoken abortionists in the Delaware valley. This was the sort of painful "crucifixion" rescuers went through again and again as they found themselves involved in a deeply schizophrenic world. [26] Most began to research their doctors, and to boycott those who were associated with killing babies.

Another "sit-in" was carried out in September of that year at the Women's Medical Center in Bridgeport, where 26 pro-lifers were arrested. On that occasion police officers paid by the clinic for "security" pretended to be friends of the rescuers, and only revealed their real affiliation in court.

The Prontnicki's brought others from their church, including Eunice and Stanley Kalbach. [27] Stan was one of those arrested at the July 3 rescue.

Another "sit-in" took place in December 1984 at the Northeast Women's Center. As was the case in other locales, most of the early rescuers here were Catholic. Among the Protestants at this rescue were Lou Prontnicki, Bruce Rathburn, a Westminster Seminary student [28] and Stanley Kalbach. A Westminster professor, Dr. Roger Greenway wrote an article printed in the *Presbyterian Journal* entitled "I Saw My Students Arrested". [29]

---

[26] Conversation with Lou Prontnicki, 2 Sep 2015.

[27] The Kalbachs became our good friends after they began attending our church in 1990.

[28] Bruce Rathburn wrote an article for *the Presbyterian Journal* , 24 Apr 1985, entitled"A Weekend Witnessing in Jail"

[29] *Presbyterian Journal*, 26 Dec 1984.

Was That Thunder?

Bill Devlin[30] was involved first as a CAC church representative from Lansdale Presbyterian church. As early as 1984, he led a prayer march in Lansdale.

My friend, Stanley Kalbach, one of the early Protestants among Philadelphia area pro-life rescuers

The CAC put together a prayer and protest march of 200 people at the three center city abortuaries in January 1985.

The next month 47 were arrested inside the Bridgeport clinic, while 200 others protested and prayed outside.

Then again in March, 150 pro-lifers returned to Bridgeport, where 61 were arrested for "sitting-in".

In April, 1985, the as-yet-unknown Randy Terry from Binghamton, New York, communicated with Philly area prolifers and asked for help doing a demonstration in Elkins Park at the Ob-Gyn practise of Dr. Jeffrey Stowe. The Binghamton pro-lifers had succeeded in tracing Dr. Stowe

---

[30] Bill Devlin moved into Philly in 1985, and later became head of the Philadelphia CAC, which went through a couple of re-organizations under his leadership.

back to this practice. He flew to Binghamton twice a week to do abortions in the only abortion facility there.

The Philly activists together with Randy and Cindy and a few others from New York, arrived in Elkins Park with signs, but there was no need to go inside the clinic, or indeed to stay there all day. The clinic staff was so chagrinned at being publically associated with an abortionist, that they nearly ran into each other in an effort to vacate the premises and close up business for the day.[31] This may have been Randy Terry's first venture into pro-life "direct action".

Bill Devlin invited a fellow nurse, Bill Free, who took his son to participate for the first time in a "sit-in" about 1986 at the Northeast Women's Center.[32]

It was about this time Joe Foreman became active in Philadelphia. In June 1986 he was spokesman for the Valley Forge Citizens for Life, when the Norriston Suburban General Hospital announced it would quit doing abortions. This was after pro-lifers had been carrying on monthly prayer gatherings there.[33]

The early Catholic pro-life leaders included John Stanton, Jack and Pat O'Brien, Earl and Kathleen Essex, and Mike McMonigal, with many other stalwarts, most of whom it was my privilege to get to know later.

In May of 1986, Philadelphia rescuers staged a "sit-in" at Northeast Women's Center, then located at 9600 Roosevelt Blvd., and for the first time, they received stiff jail sentences handed to them by Judge Conroy. In turn the rescuers appealed. News accounts suggest that some of them had

---

[31] Lou Prontnicki's brief history notes that the building used by that facility is now a Korean church. Lou and family went into overseas missions in Jordan and Egypt from 1985 through 1989.

[32] Bill and Dottie Free also became members of our church, and thus were among the earliest activists we were acquainted with. With Kim Bennett of Alpha Preganancy Services, and Colleen Ryan, Dottie began post-abortion Bible studies/ prayer groups for women in the early 90's.

[33] Along with Philly's Mike McMonigal, Joe came to be numbered among the national leaders of Operation Rescue a couple years later.

been arrested 15 times by then.

Also in 1986, Randall and Cindy Terry, who had continued protesting outside the abortion clinic in Binghamton, attended a PLAN convention, sponsored by Joseph Scheidler. [34]

A "youthful" Randy Terry, founder of Operation Rescue

Later that year a number of PLAN people met in Pensacola, Florida, for a "sit-in" inside an abortion clinic. Randy Terry and Joe Scheidler were there with Joan Andrews, who disabled an abortion suction machine [35] For this she was jailed, ultimately for nearly three years. Her long prison sentence stirred up considerable protest among other pro-life people, including many that had no "direct action" involvement. Pro-life sentiment around the country was greatly stirred at Joan's treatment, and her firm refusal to

---

[34] Lynn Mills of Detroit, and Monica Migliorino with her future husband John Miller, were also early PLAN activists. Monica was one of the thinkers of the movement. Lynn (who also helped shut down Jack Kevorkian, "Dr. Death") is interviewed in the rescue history with Jonathon Van Maren of Bridgehead Radio, available on Youtube.

[35] I'm told she detached/pulled out an electric cord from it's permanent mounting to the wall socket.

agree to cease such activities if she were released.

In March 1987, Joe Schiedler, Randy Terry, and others formulated plans to blockade clinic doors from the outside instead of going into the buildings and offices.[36] This had the advantage of making their actions open and public. Randy promoted a vision of a nationwide movement among those already active, but extending far beyond them, to involve many more evangelical Protestants, as well.

Joan Andrews, an inspiration to many early rescuers

In November 28, 1987, Operation Rescue sponsored one of its first rescues under that name in front of the abortion clinic at Cherry Hill, New Jersey.[37] It is estimated 300 people were there, with 211 of them arrested. This was the event and place where people from our own Presbyterian congregation

---

[36] Lynn Mills in her interview on Bridgehead Radio (2015 – see Youtube) says PLAN undertook a "We Will Stand Up" campaign in 1987, in which they vowed to shut down the abortion clinics in every town that the Pope visited. Many clinics closed on their own in anticipation of these "demonstrations".

[37] This "trial" rescue was under the Operation Rescue banner, but the New York events were the first official OR rescues.

first became involved.[38]

The next Operation Rescue event was a week-long series of rescues in New York City in May 1988, during which over 1600 protesters were arrested. The first rescue was at the clinic run by Dr. Herbert Schwartz.

Lou Prontnicki's recalls that the groundswell of antiabortion sentiment and activity, at least within Philadelphia area Protestant churches, occurred from about 1978 through 1988. But on the national level it seemed as though a ground swell began in 1988, with the advent of Operation Rescue.

Randy Terry (behind pole) at 1st New York Rescue.
At bottom right is John Ronning, a Philadelphia friend,
who was to meet his wife in the Atlanta jail exercise yard.

---

[38] I believe the first involved were Sue Laurito, Chuck Parker and Chuck Depoy. Joy Fesi, Don Ranck, Jeannie Kelly, Kimiko and I followed, with many others. Devlins, Kalbachs and Frees had been active before this, but not as part of our church.

Crossing the Line

As Operation Rescue got off the ground, those involved in sacrificial leadership envisioned abortion grinding to a halt as millions of Christians crowded in front of every "abortuary" door around the country.

In that phone conversation with me in 1988, Chuck Depoy did a masterful sales job. He did not ask me to come to the rally, he asked me to pray about coming. There was no pitch or spiritual arguments. He trusted I had heard those already.

Where, I wonder now? I suppose I had heard them from several of my respected friends as they discussed their arrests at the first events sponsored by "Operation Rescue". Yet these arguments were implicit in scriptures I was already familiar with, based for the most part on principles I was already committed to.

Chuck left the persuasion to my conscience. He also asked me if I would be willing to call ten or twelve others in the church and tell them about the rally.

We had made other plans for those dates. At first this was a great relief. Roseann and I discussed it and agreed that getting away for a couple of weeks was the highest priority for our family. We hadn't had a genuine vacation for a number of years. Besides... Roseann and I have different modes of self-justification, my favorite is... 'What difference can we possibly make anyway?'

I did not want to think too much about anything, especially if that thinking was going to result in more effort and discomfort. I did not know I was poised very near the edge of a precipice, over which I would soon descend in an avalanche of self-searching, study, and personal revolution.

As the date drew nearer, both Roseann and I found an increasing uneasiness over our plans. At last, *tete a tete*, we came to the conclusion we could do both things merely by putting off our departure for three or four days. We decided to attend the rally. I took our five kids, and a picnic lunch Roseann had prepared.

Was That Thunder?

The people streaming into the Valley Forge Rally formed a crowd like none I had ever seen. They were not the pious evangelical Protestant crowd of say, a Bill Gothard seminar or a Billy Graham crusade. They were not revivalists, nor academics – not like the groups of Pentecostals or Presbyterians I was familiar with. They were not the schizoid All-in-The-Family/Rebel-Without-A-Cause crowd of the sort we were part of during a Bob Dylan (Saved era) concert. There was nearly as wide a variety of age and type among them.

They were not a patriotic crowd in the sense I had hitherto known the word. I grew up a "Goldwater Republican," although it is a term I no longer enjoy and an association I no longer embrace.[39] While sharing a fundamental national loyalty, the people at this gathering seemed to have another loyalty more central, and to agree America had considerable need for change before we could expect God to "shed his Grace on thee, and crown thy good with brotherhood from sea to shining sea."

The best way to describe them, in terms of people I had known thitherto, would be that they were from outer space. There was about them an intention to act, to pursue a cause into events, which was alien to most of my experience in the evangelical Protestant church or in conservative political circles. But there was also a principled simplicity and pious demeanor which was alien to my experience either in ivy league academia or the army.

The speakers were also as varied a crew as one could imagine. One speaker was Adele Nathanson, the wife of the one American doctor who probably contributed most to the propaganda which led to the Roe v. Wade decision.

---

[39] Back then it meant to me: 1/ as little government as possible, 2/ that America was the most just place on earth, and 3/ its history, values and traditions so sacrosanct as to be impossible to improve upon. However, Barry Goldwater,"Mr. Conservative," turned out to be pro-abortion himself and shared that with his political ally, Justice Sandra Day OConner.

Adelle Nathanson

For the first time I saw and heard Randall Terry, a very young Pentecostal, would-be stand-up comedian from upstate New York. Bishop Austin Vaughn spoke, a Roman Catholic bishop-at-large and President of the Catholic Theological Society. Other speakers included several curiously competent voices for whom the ideas being discussed were obviously not new, nor primarily theories.

Adele Nathanson told of her husband's conversion from avid promoter of legalized abortion to defender of the child in the womb as fully human and in need of the full protection of the law. [40]

Bishop Vaughn spoke of growing up among urban Americans who felt the Democratic party could always be relied upon. "We believed the Democratic party was the party of the down-trodden, the little man, the man who had no voice. It saddens me deeply to say that is no longer true!"

Randy Terry spoke winsomely, albeit in an almost boyish voice, about the passage in Proverbs which tells us

---

[40] Bill Devlin had invited Bernard Nathanson to come and speak for the CAC at Chelten Baptist church a couple years earlier. At the end of his description of how he had helped get abortion legalized, and had not only aborted ten thousand babies, but his own child, he said, "I am plagued with guilt over what I have done." Bill asked Lou Prontnicki to come up and pray to close the meeting. Lou prayed for Dr. Nathanson that he would find and experience God's forgiveness. That prayer was eventually to be answered.

that God will not accept the excuse that "we did not know," but rather calls us to "hold back those being dragged to slaughter."

Nellie Gray spoke, the venerable Gibraltor who headed the March for Life in Washington over the many years since Roe. She minced no words in calling for Christians to take a stand against the liberal elite in control of the nation's capitol.

Randy had two messages that came through to me, although I'm sure he had more points than that. These were: 1/if abortion is murder then we ought to act like it, and 2/the Bible says Christ saved us by identifying completely with us. We are told to love one another as Christ loved us. Therefore we ought to identify with the unborn as fully as possible, making the legal system that condemns them deal with us. [41] The second point was a major basis for pro-life action cited by

---

[41] Pat Mahoney, in his Bridgehead Radio interview said the two new emphases which Randy introduced were: 1/its our fault, therefore repentance must be out keynote; and 2/this particular action is appropriate, because merely kneeling in front of a clinic will save lives. Pat says rescuers were motivated by a desire to do something that would concretely be effective, that would save lives.

Joan Andrews.[42]

Mike McMonigal, an Annapolis graduate and one of the most dedicated of our local leaders, spoke matter-of-factly and in careful understatement. [43]

Molly Kelly, also local, gave an energetic and dynamic speech. Our family was to get to know her later in tandem with Roseann's efforts to fight the public schools' libertine sex ed programs.[44] Molly, one of those people who was genetically incapable of being boring, was one of the pioneers of abstinence education and very active in promoting it.

Father McFadden and Bob Lewis spoke, two clergymen much respected in Delaware Valley rescue circles. Father McFadden is outstanding as a gentle and compassionate man with a pastoral heart toward everyone he meets. Bob Lewis, a tall military veteran, become a visionary Baptist pastor, preached boldly with a zeal for national revival and renewal.

And finally, the practical plans were announced. The next several days were to feature "rescues," gatherings in front of local abortion clinics to which we all were invited. We were told it was likely arrests would take place – that those participating would probably be charged as law-breakers.

I'm not sure if Randy Terry or Mike McMonigal said it then – certainly it was said innumerable times before and after that -- but most of us there were beginning to wrestle with the inevitable conclusion that where man's law is directly contrary to God's law, the man of God has to choose which to break. Action in one sense or the other is inevitable.

During the rally I found myself looking around and wondering how many were there to oppose the cause represented. One fellow seemed to be patrolling the crowd watching people. I decided he must be a cop, possibly FBI.

---

[42] She had spent at that date more than two years in jail for disabling the suction abortion machine in Florida.

[43] Mike was to become famous, among other things, for writing letters to Delaware Valley rescuers averaging six to eight pages!

[44] See Chapter Five

Was That Thunder?

In the ensuing months I learned he was a college professor.

Doug Nagy (with beard) in front of Northeast Women' Center [45]

Quite a few of the people at the rally had flown in from around the country and were staying at the nearby Valley Forge hotels. After the rally, there was a river of humanity flowing back to the hotels. As we drove out, we picked up a lady who was obviously having a hard time walking. She had a cheerful and determined face. As we drove her to her hotel she told us the doctors said she had only three months to live, but that she wanted to make her days count for something.

My First Rescue

The next day, having made my decision during and after the rally, I joined perhaps a thousand other people sitting around Suburban Women's Center in Paoli.

I do not recall the weather. Was it hot? Probably. But it could have been unseasonably cool and even lightly raining. I do not remember.

---

[45] Doug Nagy and his Owenna were respected rescue leaders and members of the Church of Latter Day Saints.

I don't even have a very distinctive memory or arriving at the clinic and approaching it. Despite the fact that it was located in a suburban residential neighborhood, there was hardly a place to park within half a mile. We parked way up a residential street and walked. As we drew near, we saw that most of those who had arrived in all those cars were indeed gathered around the sprawling one story building. It had three or four entrances, but every one of these had more than a hundred people standing or sitting close together in front of it.

Most were dressed informally, but the range of dress was wide. The age range was even greater – from teenagers to others in their eighties. And their affiliations were also diverse. That was obvious from the moment I walked over and joined a group at the central door facing the parking lot.

To my right were several people reciting the Rosary. "Hail Mary, full of grace, the Lord is with thee . . . etcetera," which decidedly non-Protestant prayer was to be burned into my memory over the years [46], while to my left were several people praying in tongues. Others read from the Bible.

There were several "marshals"[47] standing in front of our group. I think they were wearing armbands as their badge of office. Sometimes they led in hymns, or scripture songs. There was even a guitar player. I heard some of the rescue songs for the first time. The activities were not formal or rigid, but neither were they chaotic, rather there was a great deal going on at once. There were many levels of order, and obviously of affiliation, but no conflict [48] – not even with

---

[46] There was one line of the rosary I never recited with my Catholic brethren. I always "cut out the middleman" and went straight to Jesus when I said "pray for us".

[47] Thus we designated those appointed to direct us at rescues.

[48] I heard a few leaders who decided not to say the Rosary from the front of our group, but told those who wished to recite it together within the group to feel free to do so. Over the years, I was saddened to hear of several instances where Protestants and

the police, apart from the fact that we did not leave when they warned us of imminent arrest.

There seemed to be quite a few leaders, and although they varied a good deal in personality and style, decisions were made by consensus among them. I don't think there was anyone I was acquainted with in front of the particular door where I was placed. It turned out our group was not arrested until fairly late in the day.

I had no knowledge of the negotiations that took place, but I watched as eventually the police began to arrest people and carry them away on stretchers to vehicles waiting to transport them – all participants on either side continued to be civil and orderly.

Now the point approached for the first of many "crucifixions" I was to undergo in the rescue movement. I had never deliberately broken any law more serious than a speed limit and never, ever, disobeyed a police officer.

Tredyferin Township officer reading warning at Paoli abortion clinic during first Operation Rescue event there.

I believed that law enforcement and the cooperation of all good citizens were near the very foundations of safety and

---

Catholics split over being unable to find a working solution on this or other differences.

order. I believed that those who did not respect law enforcement and its officers – those who deliberately disobeyed laws and officers – were the very lowest and most destructive of people.

While I could offer certain theoretical affirmations for those who engaged in civil disobedience against clearly unjust regimes -- say that of Nazi Germany or the Jim Crow South -- I thought of these things as far enough from normal human experience that it never crossed my mind I might do it myself.

Yet I was about to be arrested. I was refusing to heed the warning being read to us. I was disobeying a policeman. I could stand up and walk away – hundreds were standing off to the side "in support," and not "risking arrest". But no, I had already commenced on a journey of consideration and conviction, I had reached a place where I knew and believed the simple principles upon which I acted.

Yet it was not the principle, nor even the action that was in question – it was the emotional and spiritual dimension where this crucifixion was taking place. I was crossing into a forbidden area – that of deliberate civil disobedience – crossing the clear line which was defined by the law and by law enforcement officers. This behavior had hitherto always been taboo -- so close to that other thing called "crime," that I made few distinctions between them.

The officers had worked their way around the building, arresting people one by one – giving warnings, lifting unresisting, but limp persons onto stretchers and carrying them away. When they carried away the lady to my right, I began to shake. I was literally trembling with contrary emotions [49] while they lifted me onto the stretcher and carried me away from the abortion clinic.

We were loaded into cars, then driven to the nearby police station where a continuous stream of us were processed and released.

---

[49] And perhaps nicotine withdrawal – I had been a tobacco chewer. One effect of my rescue involvement was that I gave up tobacco.

Was That Thunder?

The next day we left on our family vacation, aware that another eight hundred to a thousand people were going to be doing the same thing that day at Northeast Women's Center in Philadelphia – but confident we had done our share for the cause -- for the moment.

I found out a few weeks later that one of our good friends, who rescued at Paoli with us -- whom I will call Dolly – made another kind of sacrifice that day. As she stood in front of the doors, she saw a woman she recognized come out and talk to the police officers. Another rescuer said this woman was the administrator of the abortion clinic. But Dolly knew her through an academic association and up to that point had thought of her as a colleague and even mentor. The two of them had been in each others homes and discussed abortion, so that the administrator knew Dolly was a Christian and opposed to abortion – even respecting her for having thought seriously about it.

The administrator apparently didn't see Dolly at the rescue, but later found her name on a list of those arrested. Whereupon she called Dolly and said that they could no longer be friends or associates. Dolly replied with some confusion –"You mean that I don't have the right to express my opinion according to my conscience?" The administrator replied, "In general, yes, but not at my clinic."Over the following weeks Dolly tried to make further contact with this woman, but was rebuffed at every turn. The sad end of a relationship.

This was one example of the fact that most of us rescuing, although we had listened hard and thought hard about the "doing" of rescue, had not yet given a great deal of thought to the consequences and costs. Those who had been active longer (perhaps a hundred from our area had some prior involvement between 1984 and 1987) had a little more sense of the cost. We all knew about Joan Andrews' two year plus sentence in Florida. But locally, the highest cost we heard of was when Judge Guarino of Philadelphia Common Pleas Court had sentenced the May 1986 rescuers to 45 days in jail. Nevertheless, most of us who got involved in 1988, had yet to see legal consequences.

A Memoir of Pro-life Rescue

Instead we had seen women talking to sidewalk counselors because our efforts had rendered them unable to get into clinics. Soon we saw mothers changing their minds, and indeed heard from some of them about the changes of mind our small sacrifices had facilitated. Better yet, as the months went forward, we began to see pictures of the babies saved!

On our family went vacation following that first rescue we went to Maine, where we camped and hiked with good friends Rich and Lynette Robertson and their sons. We picked blueberries and wild strawberries. We camped on Warren Island where we ate mackerel and clams, and listened to Richard's wonderful campfire stories. After dark there, on her way to her tent, one of our daughters discovered some "foxfire," fungus-infected wood that glowed in the dark. A persistent little light in the midst of a lot of darkness.

Some of the Philly faithful in the rain, including my good friend Mike Doyle

Was That Thunder?

Right foreground: Chuck Depoy; Center background: Joy Fesi

CHAPTER TWO - THE SEIGE OF ATLANTA

...Thus saith the Lord God unto Jerusalem : thy birth and thy nativity is of the land of Canaan; thy father was an Amorite, and thy mother an Hittite. And as for thy nativity, in the day thou wast born thy navel was not cut, neither wast thou washed in water to supple thee; but thou was not salted at all, nor swaddled at all. None eye pitied thee, to do any of these unto thee, to have compassion upon thee; but thou wast cast out in the open field, to the lothing of thy person, in the day that thou wast born. And when I passed by thee, and saw thee polluted in thine own blood, I said unto thee when thou was in thy blood, Live: yea, I said unto thee when thou wast in thy blood, Live.   Ezekiel 16:3-6

Despite all the trepidation that came upon me at my first actual arrest, I saw nothing during that rescue (and I watched carefully!) to cause me to doubt my own actions or those of other at Paoli. I was therefore committed to two things: to continuing to rescue at least on a limited basis, and to continue examining what I was doing.

Stronger Foundations

I am not just politically, but temperamentally conservative. I don't like to act without a substantial foundation. Both my temperament and my Presbyterian theology support this. I am sort of a natural Calvinist. I believe that although God made man in his image, He also made him in complete dependence on Him, --- and that Adam pulled the plug, so to speak. Traditionally we say man is fallen in sin. So far as behavior goes, sin is both an attitude and a universal, though alien, instinct. Yet sin has infected every faculty of man. In one sense, a Calvinist believes one can never trust anything human one hundred percent – not mother, not apple pie, not ones church, not ones own thoughts and feelings. So my theology supports an inclination to constantly double check my own motives and those of others – principally against scripture.

But on the other hand, when I find a good thing I enjoy involving others. I like to "share," I like to talk, and I like to teach. In order to teach, you must analyze, order, and double-check things. A teacher has an instinct for self-preservation. Thus he does his homework in order not to be shown up as a fool. In order to teach I want to be sure I understand the subject myself.

Brother Andrew, respected Christian law-breaker

I began to read whatever I could find about abortion and its history in America. I began to research embryology (biology is my first academic love). I looked for more resources about civil disobedience, and the historical situations which challenged Christians' relationship to civil authority. Some things I'd read years before came into a new focus. Corrie ten Boom and Brother Andrew were two 20th century heroes of the Christian faith known to all my generation through the book (and movie) *The Hiding Place* and the book *God's Smuggler*.

Corrie ten Boom, another Christian law-breaker

Somewhat less well known was Brother Andrew's other book *The Ethics of Smuggling*. But as I re-read it, I realized this man was far ahead of us in thinking through many things. Both Corrie and Andrew found themselves in situations where they had to choose between being "law-abiding" and godly. While there were variations of interpretation concerning how the ethics worked out even within Corrie's family, all agreed that obeying God was a higher priority than pleasing the civil authorities. I found the apostles of the New Testament in similar circumstances on a number of occasions – Peter before the Sanhedrin ("Whether it is better to obey God or man, you must decide, but as for us, we will obey the Lord") and Paul wrestling with the proper response to the Governor of Damascus who has sent law enforcement officers to arrest him. [50]

Paul and Peter are often quoted to the effect that the Christian ought always obey the civil authority,[51] whom God gives the "sword" to punish wrong-doing and

---

[50] See II Corinthians 11.
[51] See Romans 13, Titus 3, and I Peter 2.

reward/protect the righteous, but their own practical exceptions to that dictum are often overlooked.

A remarkable number of respected theologians speak to the issues of civil disobedience. For instance, Melody Green quotes Charles Finney:

> Chapter 17 of Finney's *Systematic Theology*... gives guidelines regarding civil law:
> In what cases are we bound to disobey human governments?
> 1) We should obey when the thing required does not involve a violation of moral laws and obligation.
> 2) We must obey when the thing required has no moral value in itself; upon the principle that obedience in this case is a less evil than resistance and revolution. But -
> 3) We must in all cases disobey when human legislation is contrary to moral law or violates your conscience. [52]

I found even John Calvin, though seldom cited as an advocate of civil disobedience, giving foundational principles for it toward the end of his *Institutes*. After a strong reminder of the importance of submission he writes:

> ... But in that obedience which we hold due to the commands of rulers, we must always make the exception, must be particularly careful that it is not incompatible with obedience to Him to whose will the wishes of all kings should be subject, to whose decree their commands must yield, to whose majesty their sceptres must bow. And, indeed, how preposterous were it, in pleasing men, to incur the offence of Him for whose sake you obey men!... We are subject to the men who rule over us, but subject only in the Lord. If they command anything against this let us not pay the least regard to it, nor be moved by all the dignity which

---

[52] Melody Green, *Why I Got Arrested in Atlanta*, 1988.

they possess as magistrates -- a dignity to which no injury is done when it is subordinated to the special and truly supreme power of God. [53]

I found tremendous support in the man I think of as the most influential individual of the twentieth century, Alexander Solzhenitsyn. I'd read everything of his that appeared in English, and found him doubly significant – as a prophet and as a literary artist.

His books, particularly his *From Under the Rubble,* resonated in my mind as I rescued. This book, prophesying the end of the Soviet Union many years before it indeed came, teaches the method and the mindset of those who would oppose tyranny – as well as prescribing the attitude of forgiveness mandatory for healing after the end of an evil institution. Solzhenitsyn recommends what he himself practices in his writing – a combination of courageous and open resistance with a heart of charity. I continue to be astounded that he could write of such suffering and evil – even of Lenin and Stalin – with a softness of heart that refuses to hate. But resist he and millions of his fellow-citizens did. Here is a brief section where he commends grassroots-level resistance to "the lie":

> Oh, people will object at once and with ingenuity: what is a lie? Who can determine precisely where the lie ends and truth begins? "In every historically concrete dialectical situation,. . ." and so on -- all the evasions that liars have been using for the past half century. But the answer could not be simpler: decide yourself, as your conscience dictates. And for a long time this will suffice. Depending upon his horizons, his life experience and his education, each person will have his own perception of the line where the public and state lie begins: one will see it as being altogether remote from him, while another will experience it as a

---

[53] John Calvin, *Institutes of the Christian Religion*, Book Four, chapter 20, section 32.

rope already cutting into his neck. And there, at the point where you yourself in all honesty see the borderline of the lie, is where you must refuse to submit to that lie. You must shun that part of the lie that is clear and obvious to you. And if you sincerely cannot see the lie anywhere at all, then go on quietly living as you did before.

What does it mean, not to lie? It doesn't mean going around preaching the truth at the top of your voice (perish the thought!). It doesn't even mean muttering what you think in an undertone. It simply means: not saying what you don't think, and that includes not whispering, not opening your mouth, not raising your hand, not casting your vote, not feigning a smile, not lending your presence, not standing up, and not cheering....[54]

The rescuer might add "and not walking away".

Aleksandr Solzhenitsyn, twentieth century prophet

---

[54] *From Under the Rubble*, Aleksandr Solzhenitsyn, Collins and Harvill Press, London 1975. pp. 274 & 276.

Road to Atlanta

I had been out of town during the July 6th rescue at Comly Road in Northeast Philadelphia. It is estimated a thousand people were on hand there, although police only arrested 253 before the clinic (one of the oldest aborturaries in our area) closed for the day. We were still away on vacation when 117 were arrested on the 9th of July during another rescue at Cherry Hill, New Jersey.

My good friend, "Chuck" now Dr. Charles Parker spent a couple days in jail for that rescue along with two women from our church. They were jailed at Camden County prison, where the uniform was orange jump suits and the conditions overcrowded to say the least.

Chuck Parker and one of his daughters

When Chuck went into a cell that another prisoner was just leaving, he got a top bunk. A little later a third guy came in and put his mattress on the floor. Later in the day a big prisoner came into the cell and took the bottom bunk away from the guy there, so the third guy was demoted out of the cell. The big guy turned to Chuck and said, "You're one of them Christians aren't you?" When Chuck said yes, he said, "Good thing, otherwise I would have kicked you out, too." This pattern continued – that pro-lifers were almost always treated with respect and even "watched out for" when they were behind bars.

In mid-July, the Democratic Convention opened in Atlanta, Georgia, featuring Michael Dukakis as the presidential candidate. On the 18th, more than a hundred rescuers were arrested in front of an abortion clinic there, including more than a dozen from Philadelphia. Among them were a number of people I would come to respect. Although they were few in numbers, the media coverage was good in those early days. Mayor Andrew Young was initially ready to release the rescuers, but Marjorie Pitt-Hames, the attorney who had argued Doe v. Bolton before the Supreme Court, brought her full political influence to bear, and the rescuers stayed in jail. [55]

From Joe Roach's account of the first Atlanta rescue, I learned that the 134 "Baby Doe" rescuers succeeded in getting Ms. Pitt-Hames kicked out of their hearings. Perhaps there was an element of revenge in her later effort to block the release of rescuers with no other penalty than "time-served".

In response, Randy Terry, young and perhaps impetuous, issued a "call" to pro-lifers around the country to come and join "the siege of Atlanta". That language and title were poorly chosen from the standpoint of wooing the brethren from Atlanta. But Christians came from around the country. In August 1988, Jerry Falwell appeared in Atlanta and publicly gave a check for $10,000 to Operation Rescue toward legal expenses. Dr. James Dobson also expressed

---

[55] Later, I listened to a third hand account from one of our representatives who was sitting in the mayor's office as the high official there was agreeing to release the rescuers on time-served. Just then a phone call came through from Ms. Pitt-Hames. The negotiations came to an abrupt end, and the game was back to "hard-ball".

support for the rescuers. By the end of August, 752 rescuers had been arrested in Atlanta in 16 rescues since the 18th of July.

Mayor Andrew Young, former "trespasser" and inmate like the Atlanta rescuers he jailed.

In the second week of September, Philadelphia area rescuers blocked the doors at the abortuary in Stanton, Delaware, a jurisdiction without a local police force, and therefore under the authority of the State Police. Ninety-eight of us were arrested, each given two charges.

That was the first place I experienced a gratuitous bit of police "meanness". Three or four officers picked me up to carry me to the police vans, but one of them apparently could not resist trying to inflict some pain. He grabbed my moustache and pulled as hard as he could. Now I say he "tried" to cause pain and he pulled "as hard as he could," but his error, given his purpose, was that he did not pull far enough. In other words, he gave it quite a yank, but he only pulled it abut four inches, and as those who have moustaches will not doubt invite you to demonstrate for yourself, all that does is jerk the head sideways and stretch the upper lip to a slightly grotesque degree.

When the state police got me to the van, it was already fairly full, so they had to lift and push and generally get up close and personal. This was also a mistake, because I was wearing my old work boots, which had taken on a fragrant life of their own. One cop assured the others that I must have had a nervous accident!

At the state police troop headquarters where we were processed, I saw Joe Roach, hitherto a vice president in Philadelphia's largest bank, function as a leader for the first time. During a "prayerful preparation" meeting held at our church, more experienced leaders had asked for a volunteer to lead. Joe had tentatively gone forward. At the State Police barracks he was in charge of "negotiations," and despite being obviously nervous, he did a great job. Over the years I watched Joe grow to be a good leader, and one of our best negotiators and communicators.

Pro-life leaders worked hard at maintaining communications and reasonable information exchanges with law enforcement officials wherever possible. This was fraught with a certain amount of tension. We were unable to regard ourselves as malefactors in the situations where we were arrested. The police felt obligated to regard us as such. Nonetheless, there were many practical concerns on both sides, and these could be negotiated to a various degrees.

For instance, the expense in labor, time and resources spent on arresting a couple hundred people was considerable. If the police could persuade the clinic to close for the day, then we were generally willing to walk away from the doors and render it unnecessary for the police to go through all that.

Or for another instance, should they decide they must arrest us, a small police force might end up doing quite a bit of physical labor in moving a hundred limp bodies, loading and unloading them from their vehicles. We on the other hand, regarded every minute of our time in front of the doors as important, since the longer we were there the more time counselors had to speak with mothers.

These two diverse concerns might come together in negotiation, as we agreed to be carried only ten feet toward a bus, after which we would walk on – in exchange for another half hour before arrests began, and a reasonably careful pace for arrests to be carried forward. If they would not agree to close the clinic for the day, we might ask that the clinic not be reopened until the last arrest had taken place.

To plunge into this sort of thing which obviously required good communication and diplomatic skills was a rather daunting prospect. Yet Joe Roach did "dive in" and the rest of us admired him for it. Within a few years he had become very skilled at it. Later the police were to occasionally mistake him for a lawyer!

I was struck then and increasingly later, that God uses ordinary people to lead, so that the principle trick in leadership is not to forget you are ordinary. Joe never did, nor did the other Philly leaders. They had a spirit of service and humility which I still find remarkable each time I reflect upon it.

Also at that rescue was Father Robert Pearson from New Jersey, who was married with a substantial family. My understanding was that he had been a Lutheran, then an Episcopal, before becoming a Catholic priest. His roots may account for the fact that while we were in custody he suggested we sing "A Mighty Fortress Is Our God".

> A mighty fortress is our God, a bulwark never failing,
> Our helper He amid the flood, of mortal ills prevailing.
> For still our ancient foe doth seek to work us woe;
> His craft and power are great, and armed with cruel hate,
> On earth is not his equal.
>
> Did we in our own strength confide, our striving would
>   be losing,
> Were not the right man on our side, the man of God's own
>   choosing.
> Dost ask who that may be? Christ Jesus, it is He:
> Lord Sabaoth His name, from age to age the same,
> And He must win the battle. . . .

At many points in the nine years I rescued we sang hymns and songs like that during the rescue and after being arrested. Frequently as we sang, I would experience a measure of awe at realizing we stood in a very old tradition. I was a pre-schooler in the academy which had graduated the martyrs, and such living heroes as Solzhenitsyn, Corrie ten Boom and Brother Andrew.

Persecution seemed so distant to most American Christian in 1988, and evangelicals may still be heard regularly giving thanks that they are in a "free" country where there is none. To be arrested for doing what is right and opposing what was wrong had always seemed to me as unlikely as becoming president. Up until then. Now I had no doubt that I had been in that honorable position – twice.

While we were still in custody, Joe Foreman, whom I first talked to on this occasion, shared a short pep talk with us, in which he commented that rescue was one of the few places you found Catholic priests leading hymns written by Martin Luther.

A little earlier during our time in custody, Joe had sauntered over and sat beside me, while "casually" asking who I was and how I got there. When he discovered I was a Presbyterian, and in his own denomination, with several acquaintances in common, he seemed a little more genuinely casual. [56] Until then, he had suspected I was a pro-abort

---

[56] I was excited to find out one of my wife's best friends in high school and college was related to his wife.

plant.[57]

We were released that afternoon, with hearings scheduled a month or two later, and trials only a remote idea so far as I was concerned. As it turned out the first six tried asked for jury trials during which they were not allowed to say much about the real reasons they "trespassed". All refused to pay the stiff fines levied against them, to the result that the rest of us were tried on lesser charges and given only light fines – which we, too, refused to pay.

For the next few weeks the rescuers in jail in Georgia were constantly on our minds. We exchanged news daily about additional rescues and arrests and about the politics of what was going on. A number of us began to talk about going down there. Finally three or four from our church decided to go, if we could raise the money for tickets.

The first thing I did was write eight letters, addressed to men I held in high respect as godly and biblically informed. I desired first to solicit their prayers and support. I hoped to follow up with phone calls soliciting financial help, as well. That letter gave the biblical-theological context in which I found rescue compelling. It also reflected what my hopes were for rescue. It ended thus:

> The more people who join us in rescue and the more quickly they do it, the more babies will be saved and the more quickly national leaders will take our cries for the helpless seriously. On the other hand, if you leave us on the front lines alone, we will be picked off, sooner or later. Serious civil suits and potential criminal suits are already being brought against the best-known leaders in this movement.
>
> Pray for the babies, pray for those already doing rescues, pray for grace to join them.
>
> Through the Grace of our Lord and Rescuer Jesus Christ, . . .

---

[57] As Walker Percy points out, a great mystery for each of us is our own appearance – I suppose an unknown bearded guy with wire-frame glasses did fit a pro-abort profile.

Was That Thunder?

I called around after the letters had been received and found three of the recipients very supportive both in prayer and financially, with several others encouraging though insolvent. One, however, was dead-set against rescue.

It is hard to describe what I felt as I listened over the phone to this brother's angry statement that our "civil disobedience" was not only unwise but sinful, and not something he could either encourage or support. The degree to which I felt "blind-sided" by this was not just due to the fact he was a respected teacher, but also that I had known him for many years. At many junctures in his own life he had taken active and even radical stands against evil. He had been one of a few men in my life about whom I knew nothing but good. Indeed, I guess I had placed his image on a pedestal. Suddenly he toppled from it.

He did not have anything particularly reasonable or persuasive to say. I came to wonder if he identified civil disobedience with the ugly hypocrisy that characterized much of the Vietnam war era "peace movement," which he and I experienced first hand at Harvard. In any case this was another cross experience for me, as well as a further call to self-examination. We bought the airline tickets. But just before we left, I sent a "follow-up" letter containing these paragraphs:

> Dear Brother,
> Many in the church of Christ hold you in deep regard. I have had great respect for you myself and desire to go on honoring you for you dedication to the Lord and his kingdom, but your stance of opposition to the rescue movement leaves me with significant reservations.
>
> I would like to think your position against civil disobedience in the cause of saving babies was due, as it was in mine until recently, to not having thought through the issues. If such was the case, however, you would hardly be likely to say you didn't want to discuss the question further. Since you did say that, I am left

with an empty sense that your leadership is failing, that you are not applying God's word accurately.

If you in good conscience can read Ezekiel 16, Psalm 82, Isaiah 58, Proverbs 24:5-12, Matthew 25:31ff, or James 1:27 and the biblical-theological train which these are part of – if you can read these declarations of God's overwhelming concern for the helpless who are being slaughtered and still regard trespass laws as more important than saving lives, you are deceived. The passages which support submission to the civil authorities are indeed important. All those leading and most of those following in the rescue movement are committed to respecting civil laws and authorities <u>as far as possible</u>. But we are equally committed to serving God in his demands for protecting the helpless. When these two commitments reach a juncture and a choice, we choose to serve God rather than man. How do you regard the Old and New Testament faithful who ignored constituted civil authority?

. . .I hope I have misjudged you and can ask your forgiveness for so doing, but if I understood you correctly, I truly mourn. I mourn and I call you back to Christ. <u>We</u> are the unborn whose abortions he died to prevent. As he loved us so ought we to love one another.

You are highly respected in the church. Your words are given tremendous weight. You open doors and you close them. People will participate or avoid participating in rescues because of your words. People will live or die because of your words.

Rescued by His Grace –

Atlanta Gathering

On the 3rd of October we flew to Atlanta, and rode the public transport system (MARTA) to the Motel One on Chamblee-Tucker Road, where most of the OR people (thus we referred to both Operation Rescue "staff' and participants in activities they sponsored) were staying. I can't remember if I had a sleeping bag or was given a bed, but in any case I was given space in a room with two or three other men, one of whom was Chet Gallagher, a wonderful Christian brother, whom I came to know well over the next weeks.

Chet Gallagher, of Las Vegas, dedicated rescuer.

Although thousands of people "descended" on Atlanta that weekend and during the next week, it didn't seem to me that there were many people around the motel when I arrived. I wondered if the whole thing was going to fall flat. Randy Terry in his national call for people to come to Atlanta to rescue had more or less vowed to "shut Atlanta down." Perhaps that rhetoric was a little highflown.

The first two people in our church who had gotten involved in "the rescue movement" had been Sue Laurito and Joy Fesi, the wives of a police officer and a fire fighter, respectively. (Strictly speaking, there were three other people who were involved earlier in the Roosevelt Boulevard and Bridgeport "sit-ins". However these, Stan and Eunice Kalbach, and Bill Devlin, had not joined our church at that point.) Soon two men followed: Chuck Depoy, a truck-driver,and Chuck Parker, one of our pastors. All these were involved before I was. I think Don Ranck and I got involved about the same time as a number of others. [58]

Chuck Depoy had already gone to Atlanta. Don and Joy and Sue and I went to Atlanta together.

Rallies took place at St. Jude's Catholic Church the evening before rescues commenced in earnest. There were many speakers from many parts of the country and many denominations. But the three speakers I most remember were Joe Foreman, Mike McMonigal, and the priest who was pastor of that church. I remember the priest, because I got the strong impression that it was difficult for him to "stick his neck out" in this way. I could relate to that and it made me admire his courage.

Randy Terry had been arrested before the meeting, just outside the church, on charges of inciting to commit a crime. [59] As the rally started that night, Police officers marched in and served the other leaders with injunctions against blocking Atlanta clinics. The pastor of that church, St. Jude, welcomed everyone and announced that no arrests would take place there that night. In light of two recent invasions of the church by law officers, this may have had overtones of bravado, but we all applauded.

Mike reminded us that Mayor Andrew Young, fighting job discrimination aimed at Black Americans in 1968, said "even if it means tying up the country, we'll have to do it." At a demonstration at Bethesda Naval Hospital, Andrew Young had said they would be "tying up" the hospital "so no one can get in or out." Apparently Mayor Young and the rescue movement agreed on some important principles. At least the younger Andrew Young had agreed with us.

I had gotten to know Joe Foreman a little bit since meeting him at the Delaware rescue. Joe is a slight and modest-looking individual with dark hair, glasses and a

---

[58] Joy Fesi says Don's mother always reproached Joy as the woman who was responsible for getting her son arrested.

[59] Randy was back with us the next morning when the rescues commenced. I've read elsewhere that a local family put up a property bond for his release.

moustache, at first glance bearing a resemblance to the old emperor of Japan in his younger days. Indeed he was often inscrutable, and always understated, although his sense of humor and wry mode of speech were also trademarks. His parents had been missionaries in Korea.

During Atlanta, Joe was one of the leading tacticians. He introduced us to the "Atlanta crawl," which Jeff White of California calls "The Foreman crawl". We were asked to agree we would do nothing that looked like aggression or physical opposition to police officers, but rather, if approached, to drop to all fours and move slowly on hands and knees toward our objective, like a baby. "Be willing to suffer," Joe said.

"If a policeman touches you, stop!" he said, "and so long as he is touching you, don't move. But if he moves away, go ahead crawling toward the doors." After a demonstration, Joe quipped, "You see the dilemma posed by hundreds of crawling people." Joe told us not to go OVER the bicycle-rack-like barriers the police would probably place around the perimeter of the clinic in any circumstances. He said nothing against going UNDER them.

Dr. Martin Luther King, Jr., Christian law-breaker

Another priest spoke about Martin Luther King, Jr., and his *Letter from the Birmingham Jail*. Eight prominent Alabama bishops and clergymen wrote to him in 1963, urging him to wait and let the legal processes take their course. Dr. King responded from his jail cell, "Wait always meant never ... Justice too long delayed is justice denied."

That speaker went on to say it is easy for this city and this nation to say "wait" when they don't show the aborted fetuses on television, and continue to speak of children as "tissue". He compared today's "moderates" with those in the 1960s, who were more devoted to order than to the justice of the civil rights movement.

Bishop Austin Vaughan spoke, he whom I'd first heard at Valley Forge in July. He said "I came down here to save the babies – and I came down here to support dedicated people." He compared the 25 million babies aborted since Roe v. Wade with the 11 million people who died in the Holocaust, and the 1.1 million fatalities resulting from all American wars.

I'm not sure if it was in Atlanta or Valley Forge where Bishop Vaughan said something that continues to resonate in my mind, "To the best of our understanding, there is only one on-going kind of creation today. That is, at the moment of conception of each and every child, God creates a human being with an eternal soul." To the best of my understanding that is solid theology, and a powerful inspiration to protect life.

That evening a number of us were asked to stay for a few minutes. We had been selected by the who-knows-who methods that were standard in the rescue movement. We were asked to be "marshals" or team-leaders, and given more detailed instructions about how we were going to proceed the next morning. I felt both honored and nervous about participating as a leader. It seemed to me there were far too many unknown factors in what we were about to do. I only like to lead when I feel competent.

The next morning most of us rose early and ate no breakfast. [60] We gathered in the Motel One parking lot and it was quite incredible how many people were there. Randy called the marshals into a little office with picture windows giving onto the mob-scene. He gave us some last minute directions including the day's objectives. Looking back and seeing twenty or thirty faces plastered to the picture windows, I asked him if it wouldn't be wise to be careful of lip-reading cops. He looked at me (whom he didn't know) incredulously and said, "You aren't serious." Actually I was, which shows he was not yet nearly as paranoid as I was. [61]

Somehow – I don't remember the process – each of the marshals was assigned a team of twelve or so, whom we were to lead. The others didn't know which clinic we were going to, but they expected us to get them there. Among my crew were Chet Gallagher, and a fellow from Colorado named Coke, as well as the parish priest from the church where the rally had been held, and maybe seven others. Joy was also a marshall. Bishop Vaughan was one of the members of her

---

[60] Fasting in the Christian tradition was part of many rescuers' practice. But there was also the practical fact that coffee has a way of coming back to haunt you.

[61] In the army I was assigned to military intelligence. Between my native paranoia, my Calvinism, and that training, yes, I'm often inclined to suspect people are up to something shady.

crew.

Randy went out with a bullhorn and addressed the crowd. "We're not going down there as the heroes," he said. "We are going down there in a spirit of repentance . . . we are 15 years late. There are no heroes here today." After relatively few words he prayed.

With TV cameras all over the place and police helicopters overhead providing a throbbing bass counterpoint, we began to disperse, many of us going to the commuter rail (MARTA) station and back toward the airport. Along in the capacity of a sort of general supervisor was Susan Odom, a respected OR leader from Philadelphia. Our object in going out to the airport was merely to spend time and perhaps divert anyone trying to make sense of our movements. At a given time we were supposed to get back on MARTA, head back into town and the stop nearest the clinic we were going to.

Some of us wandered around the airport shops until we lost track of time and Susan rushed about trying to hurry us on to the train. I remember she got some official to open the turnstile so she could load us on and then she paid for the whole crew.

Was That Thunder?

Atlanta Rescue

When we arrived at our stop, the station was already packed with rescuers. Several leaders led in prayer and song, and then we filed out of the station and walked the two or three blocks toward the Hillcrest clinic.

When we got near, we could see long cordons of uniformed police officers standing shoulder to shoulder perhaps seventy yards back from the clinic front entrance and around the side. I suspect we had taken an unexpected approach, since the cordon that faced us seemed to have only just formed up – and not in the very best of formations. As we approached them, true to our instructions, hundreds of rescuers went down on their knees. However, soon the crawling rescuers were stopped before the police line and were piling up three or four deep.

Although I had been supposed to be leading my little squad, I had completely lost track of all but a couple of them. I hope the others were following me, but I wasn't sure. Frankly, the unrolling of events had all my attention, and I was thinking more like a one man "hero" than a leader – despite Randy's exhortation back at the motel.

Seeing the relative uselessness of rescuers crawling three deep, and hearing Chuck, who was serving as sort of a lieutenant, urging people at the back to get up and go around the end, I wasted no time in hurrying on to where, sure enough, the cordon ended, and a wide gap allowed anyone so minded to walk around toward the clinic. Seeing a few of us moving around, several officers peeled off the cordon to try to stop us, but that of course freed up others kneeling in front of them, and these once more began their crawl forward. We stayed on our feet until officers approached us, and then dropped, but they were too few for us at that point, and those of us not directly stopped at any given moment, went on.

In this way the first few of us soon came to the "bicycle rack" barriers, arranged in a three-sided corral about thirty feet from the doors. There were a few officers manning these, but not many. We dove under the barriers, and were immediately set upon by the officers. I did not know it at the time, but soon found that Major Kenneth E. Burnette, head of the Atlanta police, was there. I believe there were only two or three other officers with him, the rest being employed in the cordon. For the first ten minutes these officers were busier than one-armed paperhangers.

All I had heard about Major Burnette previous to this was that he had interrupted a news conference Randy Terry had held on the courthouse steps in Atlanta. As the reporters gathered around Major Burnette he said, "I guess I read the same Bible as Mr. Terry, and I don't see in my Bible where Jesus every physically intervened for anybody." The pro-lifers present stood in shocked amazement at this statement, since to the best of our understanding, the whole Incarnation and Passion of Christ were precisely that – though certainly more than that.

Pain compliance --without anything to comply to – Peter, from Canada, treated to Atlanta's hospitality

Not entirely dissimilar to Pilate's soldiers, Major Burnette's approach at the clinic was to employ pain compliance methods – to what end we never could figure out. He was not giving us any orders to which to comply. It seems as though he had just been itching to inflict some pain, and now had the opportunity. Or maybe he'd been reading up on these techniques and was anxious to get in some practice. I still bear some (small) scars of his ineffectual efforts.

I believe the first four under the barricades were Chet Gallagher, Art Tomlinson, a fellow named Peter from Canada, and myself. I remember several cops holding Peter while one of them did something to him. My impression at the time was that he hollered like he was being murdered, but seeing a tape much later I learned he was crying out in praise to Jesus. My reaction at the time was strenuous disapproval toward Peter because we had been told not to cry out or yell during the rescue. The rule-keeper in me is not buried very deep. The reaction of my heart was wonderfully hypocritical and judgmental.

Soon hundreds of others filtered through the police cordons and at intervals two or three would crawl under the barriers (usually one or two others helped by lifting them) to be immediately set upon by a squad of police officers, and carried or dumped back outside the corral.

As the morning went on, the police numbers greatly increased. They were concentrated inside the barricades and supplemented by officers from all over the city. There were riot crews complete with helmet and face masks. There was one crew, the "Red Dogs," a special narcotics squad, with distinctive hats and insignia, as well as a bunch of very young officers from the academy. I remember speculating about how close these were to graduating.

The next two hours or so segues into kind of blur for me, with snapshots and short dialogues or tableaus. I continued to crawl slowly to the barricades and under, only to be carried back over and toward the waiting police buses each time, where I was dropped, and left. But we were not loaded, probably because the buses were already jam-packed with rescuers.

Nor were we kept in anyone's custody, so most of us turned to crawl back again. After a few such trips, I was bleeding from four places, two each side of my neck from

Major Burnette's [62] thumbnails, where he had practiced pain compliance. I was also bleeding from my elbows, the bridge of my nose, and other places I don't recall.[63] My white and green shirt looked rather macabre.

I believe I made this crawling trip six or seven times, but it could have been as few as four or as many as fifteen. At one point I looked at the police officers and recognized in their faces how frustrated many of them were. They were used to dealing with criminals and they knew we were not criminals. Some of them no doubt agreed with our principles – and yet here they were being required to defend a practice and an institution many thought was evil.

The "Atlanta crawl" – nonthreatening --like babies

I also remember a new spin on an old insight: that when people are deeply frustrated there is a tendency to "vent" or "act out" that frustration in the direction of least resistance – which in this case was our direction! In other

---

[62] According to a Southern Baptist newsletter, which reported 14 of its members were involved in the Atlanta rescues, Major Burnette, a deacon at First Baptist Church in Redan, Ga., said his officers did not use any unnecessary force!

[63] With more leisure and a certain degree of heroic complacency, I counted eleven wounds the next day in jail.

words some of the roughness with which we were being treated originated in something like sympathy for us! We were the dog being kicked for looking so sad!

You may ask why the police did not load me or many others on the buses the first time they carried us away. I don't know for sure. Perhaps the original intention was to avoid arresting any but the leaders. I remember seeing a few buses full. Perhaps they had filled up their available transport, and were saving the few paddy wagons they had left for the worst "criminals" among us.

I recall looking over to my left as I went forward among fifteen or twenty others doing the same almost penitential crawl, only to see the priest who I had led so poorly that morning (I think he was Father Hoffman), kneeling to the side and praying. "Keep praying, Father!" I asked, and truly meant it. It was clear that in terms of any immediate objective, our efforts were otherwise futile.

Looking across the barricades during the morning I had seen perhaps three men make it to the doors of Hillcrest clinic, from which they were immediately dragged away.

Major Burnette, Southern Baptist deacon.

One man had almost crawled to the doors when Major Burnette stepped in front of him. The fellow, a big guy, stopped and waited. Major Burnette (not a big fellow in either sense) put his foot against the rescuer's shoulder, and pushed him over and down on the ground. This sequence was caught by a network cameraman, and run many times on TV over the next few days. It came close to winning some network sympathy for rescuers – but only close. The pro-abort slant of the networks soon reasserted itself.

Perhaps just after I spoke to the priest, or perhaps two or three crawls later, I got within about eight feet of the barricades, when a young policewoman stepped in front of me. She knew what she was about. I don't think she was "just doing her job". I think she had seen how dogged I was, and perhaps how exhausted. By getting in my way, she knew she was forcing me to "give it a rest". She said nothing, however, but just stood there.

Since I couldn't move, I stopped and sat back on my heels. I looked obliquely to my right beyond the barricades at our objective, the doors of the clinic – the once place we could be briefly effective in our tiny, almost insignificant way: the portals of death. Yet even that goal was unreachable. To my left were many pro-lifers crowded, most of them on their knees and behind them, full police buses. I looked immediately to my right where bystanders, newspeople, some sympathizers, and watchers of all sorts stood. I listened to the sounds of policemen mumbling and radios crackling.

And suddenly, at lightning speed, I made a transition from intense activity to profound introspection. 'What was I doing here? Am I here to confront "them" the evil-doers, the anti-God, anti-child destroyers of life? Am I here to call *them* to account, to repentance? Whose doors are those? This doesn't seem primarily about *them* – it seems to be about us: not *their* sin, but something bigger and wider -- our sin – *my* sin.' All at once I suddenly saw myself in a different light[64] – and was quite undone by it. I began to sob loudly. Like old faithful at the appointed hour, a great rush of subterranean sorrow came welling up out of me.

I remember my very first thought in the midst of that

---

[64] Which is one way of translating *metanoia*, "repentance".

emotional outpouring: "oh no – not in public – I hope there's no camera on me". But I could no more hold back or stifle it into a respectable little weep than I could then-and-there stop abortion. I sobbed and heaved, on and on. I cried until my eyes were absolutely dry, holding my face in my hands. I can't say I knew all of what this was about right then. But after a day in jail, I knew the most part of it.

It was metanoia and a catharsis indeed – I was "beside myself" seeing myself anew, not as solver of a problem, not as the prophet confronting the erring nation, but as part of the problem, the one whose repentance was most needed, the one who most needed Jesus. The purification came with my knowledge of myself, and my part in it. Abortion became "our sin" that morning. I asked Jesus for forgiveness. I repented. I believed again and better.

But when my heart and eyes were completely cried out, I held my head up and saw that the policewoman had moved. (What she thought of my crying jag, Lord alone knows.) So I dropped down on my hands again and crawled to the barricades, where one last time I dived under, to be immediately grabbed. This time, however I was "bag-tied" with flexi-cuffs around my wrists, behind my back. I was then dropped back over the barricades – onto a pile of others who were similarly shackled. [65]

A few minutes later, I was picked up by two or three policemen and carried to a paddy wagon (delivery-truck style), into which I was tossed without ceremony.

Apparently this flying entrance was captured on network film and showed up on the evening news and the 700 Club, with commentary that I appeared to be unconscious – which I may have been, but only after the cops bounced me off the wall of the paddy wagon (one more purple heart – this time a cut on my forehead) – and only briefly, if at all. I think I saw that footage once while we were in jail, but others said

---

[65] "Bag ties" or "flexi-cuffs" are plastic handcuffs constructed on the same principle as bag ties, only many times heavier. I was to wear them on quite a few other occasions. They can only be removed by being cut off, to the best of my knowledge.

it was aired fairly regularly for several days.

Apparently the police had decided to put apparently hardcore types in paddy wagons. No doubt this was an honor. Within a few minutes, I became aware that there was another slightly younger guy in the paddy wagon. He was asking if I was OK, and I said I was. I vaguely recognized him as from near Philadelphia. He had a lot more energy left than I did or maybe he was at a different stage of repentance than I was just then. When they opened the doors to throw in the third guy, he made a break for it, bag-ties and all. He jumped out the doors and tried to get by the officers, but they grabbed him and tossed him back in.[66]

The third guy who had joined us meanwhile was Father Norman Weslin, subsequently famous in rescue circles as the founder of "The Lambs," a bunch of dedicated rescuers who began purposefully to rescue in the toughest jurisdictions, often refusing to identify themselves except by their "rescue names," pseudonyms, by which they were often known "outside" as well as "inside".

Father Weslin was a retired army major, and widower. He was another of those apparently indefatigable people one met among rescuers. I don't think any others were added to our van, but after a while we began moving.

The vans carried us to the new central police headquarters, where, at first, we were put in a separate room. Soon, however (I suspect through the sympathy of many police officers) we and the other "hardcore" people were mixed up among the other three hundred and forty-some rescuers in various rooms, so that no one knew who had been arrested where or in what peculiar circumstances.

In a crowded room I looked across and was greatly surprised to see an old acquaintance, Glen Kaiser, from Chicago. I wormed my way across to him, and we embraced. "I needed you to be here," I told him. What I meant tied in to

---

[66] Network coverage focused on this man's second arrest. He cried out that he couldn't breathe because of the knee in his back – but, hey, when you attempt escape, you can expect to be treated a little rough.

the repentance I had been brought to, but in particular it tied in to my brother Jon who, with Glen, belonged to Jesus People USA in Chicago.

Glen Kaiser of Jesus People USA, Chicago.

My brother had gone through a very painful marital break the previous year, which led to divorce. I had been selfishly, but severely disappointed with the JPUSA leaders, whom I thought should have been able to prevent this. I had felt and expressed a level of judgment and alienation since. Having Glen there made me feel like God was bringing sinners together with one mind again.

But such is the hardness of sin, that as soon as we were mostly gathered together in the large gymnasium of the police headquarters, I found another object for judgment and pride. I saw Peter the Canadian, and went over to chastise him for shouting and struggling when the police had first grabbed him. He denied that he had, so a little later (very full of myself) I took a leader aside and expressed my "concern" about this brother's conduct that morning. The leader went over and talked to him. (I still would like to crawl in a hole when I think of it!) Nothing more came of it, I'm glad to say.

In fact I believe this man went back to Canada and continued rescuing, proving he was a better man than I. There the numbers were far fewer and the jail consequences much more severe.

We were mostly "housed" in a gymnasium at first, sleeping on gym mats or the floor. There was only one telephone, and a line for it where you could wait for a couple hours. At one point I waited in line behind Melody Green, whose husband Keith's songs had been an important part of our church worship over the years.

Although I didn't see any of it as it was aired, national news focused for several days on the rescues in Atlanta. My parents in Montana copied some of the coverage to videotape and sent it to us later.

Melody was one of many well-known Christians from around the country who were in jail together in Atlanta.

It was interesting to watch some events I had seen first hand and many people I knew fairly well as they appeared on national news programs. There were brief periods during these broadcasts when we felt rescue was being fairly treated, for instance in the accurate portrayal of the harsh treatment some rescuers received at the hands of Atlanta police. The network segments were given titles like "Battlelines" and "Under Seige" and "Choices and Fear".

Was That Thunder?

John Stoessel narrated a program which focused a lot on Randy Terry, "a 29 year old used car salesman from Binghamton, New York". This program went out of its way to find "redneck" blue collar and fundamentalist spokesmen, depicting them as typical rescuers.

The network prejudices were evident, and quickly came to dominate. Melodramatic and lengthy treatment was given to sympathetic (always white) women who were seeking abortions amidst the rescues going on in Atlanta. Molly Yard, NOW's chief battleaxe, was given airtime to recite her rhetoric: "I accuse the leaders of so-called Operation Rescue of immoral behavior. . ." Clinic administrators were given long and sympathetic interviews, their rhetoric unedited.

For instance the administrator at the Surgicenter told the interviewer that the people on the street were her enemies, the "right to lifers". The morning of the rescues the Midtown Hospital administrator was shown going around inspecting his premises to make sure there were "no devices, no bombs," while he spoke of "these terrorists," referring to the pro-lifers. He spoke of "a showdown -- a war".

Excerpts from Randy Terry's brief speech to the rescuers at Motel One were given. His disarming opening, "How many of you are scared?" at which point he raised his own hand, and most of the rest of us did too. "Good," he said," that's a good sign".

Randy also said, "You might experience bodily pain today. If you do, you need to do nothing wrong." He went on to emphasize that our witness and purpose would be contravened by any sort of retaliation.

The networks showed the police lines and the arrival of rescuers at Surgicenter and Hillcrest, where I and my team went. They showed us crawling on hands and knees. They showed police cordons. They showed police using "pressure holds" as they arrested rescuers. They showed rescuers being dragged and carried by deliberately bent limbs.

The tapes included footage of Peter the Canadian and I got to hear what he said again, for my humility. His speech was praise to Jesus, "I praise you Lord, I worship you," as four officers picked him up and deliberately hurt him.

Later in the day, Major Burnette was interviewed. He said, "We used the necessary force to arrest them and we did not use any unnecessary force. And I regret we had to use any." He also said, "They brought hundreds of people here in an attempt to siege Atlanta. Somebody's been seiged, but it isn't Atlanta."

John Stoessel did catch Major Burnette in a whopper. Major Burnette said, "We had people who assaulted our police lines this morning." Stoessel said, "they weren't assaulting." Major Burnette answered, "I said they assaulted our lines." Interesting use of the word "assault" for a police chief. Major Burnette also complained, "They wouldn't get up and be arrested."

But Stoessel was not sympathetic to rescuers. He insinuated that we at times appeared to regard the whole thing as a game. In particular he showed Randy answering a cell phone, brand new technology then, with the words, "Maxwell Smart," which seemed to illustrate this point. Most of us however, saw it as Randy keeping his sense of humor in difficult circumstances.

Randy Terry's mentor for the "Maxwell Smart" line

Was That Thunder?

The TV news indicated that 343 people were arrested in the first three hours of the "Seige of Atlanta" rescues.

A network interviewer spoke with Randy back at the motel. He began by saying the "choice" people were tolerant of various views, "but you people aren't tolerant at all."

"No," Randy answered, "we are not tolerant of people murdering little babies and exploiting mothers, and when the nation grows tolerant of child-killing, it's dead. This is a holocaust. We've killed more people by a factor of four than Hitler killed Jews. 25 million people are dead because of abortion."

"Your critics would say, are you really comparing grown people with ungrown?"

"I absolutely am. They're still human beings. Where do you draw the line?"

"That's precisely the question..."

"Right. A human is a human is a human."

"They draw the line at a different place than you draw the line."

"Yes, and so did the Nazis and so did the slave-owners. If you want to kill an entire class of people just dehumanize them by using a name like 'Nigger,' use a name like 'Kike,' or use a name like 'fetus,' or 'uterine contents,' and suddenly you can accept the greatest atrocities in the world."

Campaign Continues

The second day (when I was already in police custody) the networks ran programs deliberately intended to move the sympathy toward the abortion side – although they really had no significance as "news". One program was about a woman wrestling with a supposed problem pregnancy in which the doctors told her they could not find a kidney or bladder in the fetus. She and her (white) husband were portrayed as wanting to have the baby but wrestling with the very difficult decision whether to abort their child. It was obviously thrown together quickly because it ended with the doctors finding a kidney and bladder! Oops, no abortion.

They also featured a 15 year old with a late second term pregnancy who came to Midtown from another state. They interviewed her and her parents. The pregnancy was supposed to be the product of a rape. The father said, "anything of this nature has no rights because it was the product of a rape" and as a second thought, "and you can't have a child having a child." The child was supposedly near 26 weeks gestation, that being the cutoff age for Midtown's abortions.

However the ultrasound showed the child was actually 31 weeks, which news caused the young mother to begin crying. The viewers were supposed to be sympathetic. But it struck me that a five week difference in the age of a child supposedly the product of a rape raised other significant questions – which may have been the cause of the 15 year old's tears, or the father's protestations.

A "hotline" group was interviewed, teenagers who counseled peers over issues of sexuality and parental misunderstanding. Again a careful listen left one with questions the programmers did not intend. For instance one of the teenagers said, "people choose an abortion because you can hide that from your parents. That isn't right." It sure isn't!

Joe Foreman was given a brief interview on national TV, during which he pointed out that there had been 7000 rescuers arrested since May, an indication that the movement was just beginning to roll.

Barbara Walters and Stoessel ended their segment discussing the awful effects of the pressure brought by the ignorant anti-abortion people. The cited the French abortion pill which Barbara told us was "safe and effective." Stoessel said antiabortion groups pressure had caused the manufacturer to cease production, until the French government ordered the company to keep making the pill.

Dan Rather waxed eloquent pointing out that four cases were presently before the Supreme Court any one of which could be used to overthrow Roe. He quoted the

Was That Thunder?

infamous Justice Blackmun "the next question is will Roe v. Wade go down the drain. I think there is a very distinct possibility it will. You can count the votes."

On the second day of rescues, the clinic escorts bringing supposed abortion patients through the battlelines were given extensive TV airtime. Featured were the cries of some of the rescuers calling to the mothers, as well as a few attempts by rescuers to hinder the mothers' progress toward the clinic.

Some news coverage also showed the police harassing rescuers, singling out and stopping cars and giving tickets to the drivers, for equipment or seat belt violations, etcetera.

Mike McMonigal was the focus of a brief segment in which he publicly asked the police why they were still twisting wrists when they made arrests. The police then turned on him, took away his mini-bullhorn and arrested him.

Joe Foreman, self-sacrificing Presbyterian minister

According to the news there had been 462 arrests by the end of the second day. Some ironic repartee was inspired among those of us who were in jail when the news commentator spoke indignantly of those arrested who were refusing to provide their identities and post bail, thus deliberately staying in jail! Thus far, none of us had been given an opportunity to give our identities or post bail!

Key Road Prison

Gradually, over the next few days, all the pro-lifers were bussed over to Key Road Prison, a famous old Atlanta prison once connected to the prison farm system, I'm told. Someone said it was the same place where Martin Luther King, Jr. spent a night in jail in 1960. Apparently Mayor Andrew Young had been held there, too! History is never without its dramatic ironies!

Upon arriving there we were marched into the central hallway, and told to strip. About the time two thirds of us were stark naked, a female guard came walking through and there was quite a scramble to cover up.

Finally we were indeed processed and then we gave our names as Baby Doe – with numbers supplied by them. I used to know which Baby Doe I was, but now I've forgotten.

The first thing I saw upon being taken over to our barracks-style ward, was an impromptu evangelistic service going forward, with three or four non-rescue inmates being baptized in the showers.

That began an eight day retreat which no church could ever reproduce. Among the many songs sung there was this favorite – borrowed from the Civil Rights movement:

>Paul and Silas went to jail,
>Had no money for their bail-
>
>CHORUS: Keep your eyes on the prize - hold on.
>Hold on, hold on!
>Keep your eyes on the prize - hold on.
>
>Mr. Policemen tell me why,
>Unborn babies have to die?
>CHORUS

Was That Thunder?

Be a hero - save a whale,
Save a baby - go to jail.
CHORUS

Y'know the one thing we did right,
Was the day we started to fight.
CHORUS

Y'know the one thing we did wrong
Was we waited far too long.
CHORUS

Oh, that cockroach on the wall
He don't bother me at all.
CHORUS

Civil rights leader Hosea Williams

On the one hand it was certainly not the most comfortable week of my life. My neck was swollen from Major Burnette's ministrations, and my injured glands susceptible to a severe sore throat that came on within two days. But that, too, was God's grace – to make me lie still, to pray, to rest, to think about what he had done and was doing – and to do more listening than talking.

Joe Roach's written reminiscences repeat a quote from the respected Civil rights leader, Hosea Williams[67], given at this time in an article in the *Atlanta Journal-Constitution* about the rescues there:

Hosea Williams. In conference with MLK in Selma in the '60s.

> I think what is happening in Atlanta right now is just terribly anti-American. It hurts me so bad that we who were the leaders of the movement in the 50's, 60's, and 70's, are now political leaders, [here he was particularly referring to Mayor Andrew Young] and we are doing the same things to demonstrators that George Wallace

---

[67] A Freedom Rider in the Civil Rights movement, Hosea Williams, with John Lewis, led the march across the Edmund Pettus Bridge in Selma Alabama on March 7, 1965 when peaceful protesters were violently attacked by state troopers. SCLC veteran Hosea called Andrew Young the "House Republican" of Dr. King's organization.

and Bull Connor did to us. When I saw the police twisting arms and bending fingers and using pressure points, well that's the way Adolf Hitler got started. I was very hurt and surprised at the way the anti-abortion demonstrators were mistreated.

In jail we had constant fellowship, worship, and prayer together, and were involved in ministry to the other inmates at mealtimes and other occasions when we were allowed to mix with them. We talked over the events of the rescue and speculated about the effect of the media coverage on national perspectives. I heard others speak of seeing young, Black police officers from the academy in tears as they arrested us.

One rescuer had a heart attack on a police bus after which he was rushed to a local hospital. There an iron-jawed female nurse had pounded on his chest as they rushed him in, shouting angrily, "Don't you die on us, you bastard!" Apparently there are some circumstances where it's useful to have your enemies opposed to your martyrdom.

Key Road prison was a sprawling, one story affair like an old army building, arranged in blocks that were wings off a central corridor. The mess hall, where we went for all our meals, was to one side of the center of this corridor.

I recall two events in particular from the mess hall. The first was that George Krail and I both had the same idea after we went through the line and, with full trays in hand, looked around for a place to sit.

George and Tina Krail, from New Jersey, are two of the best-known pro-lifers in the Delaware Valley. George, bearded, with a drooping handle-bar moustache and long, blond hair, is a gruff-voiced former "biker". He still looks and sounds the part. Tina, attractive, but remarkably strong, used to go into bars full of other crazy bikers and tell the half-loaded occupants, "My old man can take all of yas!" George recounts one occasion on which he stumbled out of the bar and tried to get his bike started before he was mobbed by angry men in black leather. Another time at a rival bar he met with more opposition than he could handle, so he went home and got his 4x4 pickup, came back and plowed through the parking lot, knocking over the bikes of the rival faction inside. He now says it was miraculous that he was not killed during those days.

George and Tina had their own involvement in abortion, which became one of the factors that drove them to Christ. George trusted Jesus as Savior first, after which Tina persecuted him mercilessly for many months, sometimes actually pounding on him with her fists. He didn't fight back. Finally she gave in, too.

The two of them, primarily evangelists by their own assessment, went frequently to rock concerts and the streets of Center City Philly where they witnessed to the lost. But abortion clinics were also among their regular mission fields. Both Tina and George worked as roofers and carpenters to support their extended family, which included their own and adopted children.

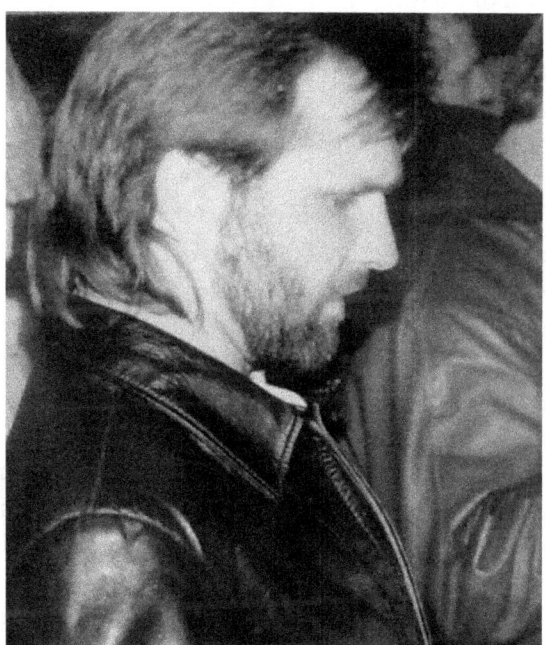

George Krail, former biker, now defender of babies

In the Key Road mess hall both George and I headed for the inmate that was obviously most in need of the gospel. By which I don't mean he looked worse than anyone else –

only that his need was more obvious than most others. This was a Black "transsexual," who had provided himself with "breasts" beneath his prison jersey. George and I went over and sat down across the table from him.

But when George reached out his hand across the table and said "Hi, I'm George, and I love Jesus," our table-companion exploded. I do not mean with anger, or any other obvious emotion. I mean he had his mouth completely full of food and he choked or coughed with as much force as one could, spraying the food across the table, our trays, our food, and even our faces.

George and I are apparently crazy in some of the same ways. As we sat in there in surprise, I'm sure we were both tallying all the incurable diseases that we had just acquired. Nevertheless, we both stayed in place. (Maybe we both were claiming the promises at the end of Mark about miraculous preservation of health.) Not only that, but George asked the guy if he was all right and we went on to eat what was on our trays, including no doubt a good deal that hadn't been there a moment before. We went on to have a good conversation with the fellow, during which George shared the gospel with him.

The second incident I remember from the mess hall was a brief event a few days later, which was more deeply disgusting to me. On this occasion I was barely able to finish everything on my lunch tray – not because the quality was poor, but because the quantity was great. (The food there was remarkably good, including greens cooked with bacon and buttery grits, which two foods have been on my personal favorites list dating back to that time). As I walked up to the trash barrel where we scraped our trays before turning them in, I found an old white inmate performing a ritual that haunts me still.

We were fed substantially three times a day at Key Road. Nothing short of a nuclear war could possibly keep us from being fed regularly, yet here was this old hobo picking through the garbage can for a morsel scraped off another prisoner's tray. I saw and see my soul and my nation there, full and sated, yet scrabbling with our fingers in the jailhouse garbage – for what?

    This man was another represetive of the spiritual poverty I wrote about a few years earlier [68] :

APPALACHIA IN SUBURBIA

We ain't never had nothin', don't know what it means
To own a home, be happy on our own piece of land.
The old man scrapes by, night ridge-runnin' man,
Drunk most the time on eighty-hour dreams

Of makin' it, while the kids grow wild :
Barefoot-souled and hungry for executive love
That I can't give 'em, don't have enough of
To even mean "precious" to my littlest child.

Ya, we got the big mortgaged split-level shack.
Sure, three cars and a place at the shore,
But you're always hungry if you have to have more,
You're always dirt-poor when you live out lack.

In her pinch-cheeked, hollow, self-starved eyes,
In the grim-faced smoothness of her moonshine man,
There is poverty deep as a dream that lies:
Appalachia surrounds us -- give if you can.

    Back in our barracks-style prison block, we had a string of sermons – at least two per day, from the many "clergy" among us. As an ordained Presbyterian elder I counted myself among the "clergy" when someone asked for a show of hands. This was partly because several months earlier I had submitted my resignation to our elder board or "session" only to have it refused. I took that refusal as an affirmation,

---

[68] Originally published in *Prisoners Pardons*. Now available online in: *Conceptions and images* :Pro-life Poems of James Howard Trott.. Createspace, 2015.

and decided to take it seriously. Our preaching at Key Road came from a pretty wide range of theological backgrounds. One of the best sermons I heard there was from Father Weslin.[69] The prison authorities expressed considerable ambivalence about our having services and sermons at all, but we kept it up, and they interfered very little.

Outside evangelists sometimes came in on Sundays, and we went to these services when allowed. At one, we were able to encourage several other inmates to go up front and commit (or recommit) themselves to Jesus as their Lord.

I got to know Chet Gallagher better, although he was gone for three days. The story was this. Major Burnette or one of his cohorts had bent back two of Chet's finger in "pain compliance" – so far as to do him real injury. The fingers were quite swollen and perhaps broken. Chet went on sick call and was sent out to a hospital, which turned out to be a ludicrous exercise in hurry up and wait in out-of-the-way locked rooms amidst bureaucratic wastelands. I wish I had him here to tell the story. When he came back and told us the saga he had us laughing in the aisles between bunks.

Chet, blonde and athletic and Robert-Redfordish in demeanor, had been a Las Vegas motorcycle cop until a few months before this. Although a rising star in a crack department, he had come under the conviction that abortion was a great evil. In response to this growing sense, he went out one day to an abortion clinic where rescuers stood before the doors. In uniform, he nonetheless crossed the line and turned and stood with the rescuers. I'm not sure how much warning his fellow officers had of this event, but it must have shaken them. In any case, the officer in charge approached him and asked him to surrender his badge and pistol, which he did. He then was placed on suspension, and eventually lost his job.

Chet and his wife had been struggling with their marriage, and there in Key Road Prison we prayed that God would restore it. From all I've heard since, it appears God

---

[69] A little later he preached what from a Protestant perspective was one of the worst sermons we had.

restored it indeed – with bells on. [70]

There were many wonderful men in that prison ward. I met several who knew people I knew, including one character, Marty Barrett, who it turned out had met an old friend of mine, Dick Kaufmann, there in July! I had no idea Dick a Presbyterian leader and teacher, was involved until then. It gave me a sense of restoration from the disappointment I had felt toward other leaders before coming to Atlanta.

Others from our church continued to rescue through the week, along with many hundreds from around the country. They were frequently "arrested," insofar as they were taken into custody, but most of them were released without charges a few hours later. The police knew they hadn't the capacity to hold them all. Don Ranck was finally taken into custody and showed up at Key Road after three or four days.

Don has a wonderful reminiscence about the day he was arrested – the third or fourth day of rescues. Adelle Nathanson had come down and decided to risk arrest that day. All of those arrested were taken to the central police headquarters and kept, as we had been, in the big gymnasium there. During one of the times of worship and sharing, Adelle asked the other rescuers to pray for her husband, Bernard, that he would come to Christ. At that time, although he had become an outspoken opponent of abortion, this seemed a remote possibility. Nonetheless, Don remembers praying then for Dr. Nathanson's conversion -- and again from time to time over the years.

Imagine Don's joy eight years later, upon listening to Charles Colson's 1996 broadcast report of seeing Bernard Nathanson baptized by Cardinal O'Connor in St. Patrick's Cathedral in New York. Assuring his evangelical audience, Colson said that Nathanson's confession of faith was as good as any he'd ever heard in a Baptist church.

---

[70] In 2005, I heard from my good friend Mary Ann McGuire that she saw Chet down in Florida where many pro-lifers gathered in their unsuccessful attempt to save the life of Terry Schiavo from "legal" starvation.

Was That Thunder?

Sue and Joy kept on rescuing every day until the end of the week, along with many others from Philly, including Grace Kuhar, who lived two blocks from us. Getting up every morning and going out to rescue was much more difficult than our life in jail. On several occasions proaborts punched and kicked them.

Joy recalled that mounted police were regularly used that week. The leaders advised everyone just to be careful to keep their hands close to their bodies, since the horses would not willingly step on them – but might step on a stray finger. Early in the week, at some point when Joy was not standing in front of clinic doors, a mounted officer and his horse stood next to her. She reached out and stroked the horse's nose for a while.

The next day, the same officer was on the scene of a rescue where she was blocking the door. As they passed by her, the horse turned its head and whinnied. With considerable surprise, the officer said "He remembers you!"

At the end of the week, weary with the daily grind at the clinics, Sue and Joy decided to fly home again.

Atlanta – Fellow Prisoners

Among the men at Key Road was Jim Kopp[71], known as "Atomic Dog," after a hyperactive comic book character. The chief thing Jim was renowned for during that time in Atlanta, and later through much of the rescue community, was his use of "Kryptonite" bicycle locks to make a small group of people a bigger "barrier" in front of an abortion clinic. By locking themselves together or locking themselves to the undercarriages of vehicles or concrete structures, "lock rescues" required quite a bit of police time and equipment to remove, thus keeping clinincs closed longer. The technique was controversial, however, insofar as it took attention away from the human side of things, and in some cases magnified

---

[71] See Chapter Thirteen: Afterword, concerning Jim Kopp's arrest and conviction for murdering an abortionist in 1998.

the physical danger to rescuers. I was to be involved in a few rescues where others locked in, although I never did myself.

Many rescue leaders from Vermont, upstate New York, California, Pennsylvania, the southwest, and from across the south were represented. Melody Green, widow of Keith Green, of the Last Days Evangelical Society, was arrested with us. Gary Leber of OR staff was there. I believe C. J. Mahaney from People of Destiny (PDI) was there. Both Glen Kaiser and Denny Cadeaux were represented Jesus People USA (JPUSA) in Chicago. Mike McMonigal was our principle leader from Philadelphia.

Pat Mahoney, Christian Defense Coalition

There I first met and heard Pat Mahoney, an incredibly energetic and expressive fellow with a lightning sense of humor. He was one of several rescuers who could be described as naturally high. No doubt contemporary educators would label him ADHD, and put him on Dilantin.

Eric Holmberg, a film-maker, from American Portrait Films was with us. His abortion videos became powerful teaching tools. Bob Jewitt from Atlanta was there. I think it was Tim Dresty from St. Louis, a courageous gentleman from one of the first rescue groups in the country, who smuggled in a camera with which he recorded some of the more egregious wounds that had been inflicted on rescuers.

Mike McHugh[72], a dedicated leader from Vermont was there. And many other men I did not have time to get to know. I think there were thirty-some ministers and priests, plus hundreds of others.

Parallel to our barracks but sixty yards away was the prison wing in which the women were kept. We had very little communication with them except once or twice when both groups were allowed out into the yard surrounding the prison.

From what they told us then, we learned their activities were more strictly regulated than ours. We were able to do little for them, but we could encourage them by our singing. We sang "My Eyes Are Dry" by Keith Green, not only because it is a beautiful hymn of repentance, but in hopes it would encourage Melody if she was still in the woman's wing. We held two or three worship services a day.

There were three priests who some humorist referred to (at least once) as "the unwed Fathers," because all three had children but no longer wives – Fr. Norman Weslin, arrested with me, was a widower who after retiring from the army went into the priesthood. The other two were also widowers, one a former Episcopal turned Catholic, and the last, a "late vocation".

After a great deal of soul-searching toward the end of our stay at Key Road, the dozen or so Catholic clergymen there decided to share their communion elements with the Protestant brethren, specifically some consecrated wine they had smuggled in. This was obviously a difficult and emotional thing for them and only agreed to after they had talked and prayed together for hours. We did not actually

---

[72] An online obituary indicates Paul Michael McHugh died in Virginia in 2014 at the age of 61. "He dedicated his life to pastoral and pro-life work, as well as the defense of constitutional liberties."

take communion together, but rather serially – according to our different approaches to that sacrament – but they supplied us with the wine, which was a serious act of trust.

Father Norman Weslin, later leader of The Lambs

After a few days we were allowed out in the "yard" around the prison to walk and enjoy the fresh air. The pro-life women were released into the yard at the same time.[73] Since we had the communion wine available, a zealous priest decided to take the opportunity to celebrate mass with some of the Catholic women, but a guard saw this and called his boss, the man in charge of prison activities, who came out and read the riot act to the priest. The priest responded by reading the riot act back, so the officer cancelled our yard-time and sent all of us back inside.

When I got back to the ward, I remember this same priest was there in the corner with his head in his hands. A little later, among his brother clergy, I heard him say, "Pray for me, I sinned out there."

---

[73] John and Linda Ronning, who became our Philly rescue friends, met and began their romance earlier that summer in that prison yard at Key Road!

Was That Thunder?

Not too long after that, he was "busted" by the prison authorities and taken away to solitary confinement.

The next night I got to preach – on Ezekiel 16 – in which sermon I declared that which God had shown me in front of the clinic – that we are like the unborn or "untimely born," found on an ashheap by the merciful God. But we are also those who have forgotten what we were and what he has done for us, so that as a nation and a national chuch we pursued idols and other gods, even to the point of being willing to sacrifice our own children.

In Atlanta I found, as I found over and over again in other prisons, that there was a blessedness in the forced "time-out," as parents now label the sit-in-the-corner form of discipline. Knowing we did not "deserve" to be behind bars, we nonetheless found the forced inactivity a call to meditation, Bible memory, renewed prayer, more thoughtful fellowship, and evangelism. The peculiar combination of repentance, worship and rest experienced there seemed somehow appropriate -- as I wrote in these verses:

LINES IN JAIL

Where but in this place
Might I digest the grace
You have heaped upon my plate ;
Locked up in me, its unjust fate.

How else might you contain such awe
And awesome glory beyond the law :
Shekinah-powered pulses that betray
And break upon this jail of clay.

For grace too free may be worse
Than (best for Adam's race) the curse ;
And as rhyme and meter help make verse
Poetry, here grace I best rehearse.

Bound tightly before willing to be bound,
Once free and lost -- now prisoner found.

The following lines, on the other hand, were merely minor irony aimed at the officious oversight of our guardians:

CRICKETS AT KEY ROAD

In an orderly world where silence is cleanliness
The stridulations of the crickets are an offense ;
The well-provided birds never obey lawful orders.

Then, two days after I preached, we were released on bail. Between the 18th of July and the 8th of October, 1265 people had been arrested in Atlanta. As mentioned above, during October the police made a point of NOT arresting hundreds of rescuers they hauled away from the clinics. The July rescuers were held as long as forty days, while some of us from the recent rescues were held for as little as four. From that series of events in Georgia, local rescue movements all over the country were started or strengthened.

I was processed out with Mike McMonigal, at which point I stubbornly tried to take a principled stand by refusing to give my social security number. Mike told me not to be silly. We had negotiated for a negligible bail-bond, and we had agreed to cooperate with the processing. The bail-bondsman's office across the street from the jail was straight out of a "B" movie. We signed for a five thousand dollar bond (I think) over against our 50 dollar bail, and were on our way. [74]

Back in Philly, our church reception was tremendously encouraging. Some of our letters from jail had been read from the pulpit. My family had been praying for me. My daughter Loren, recalls, "when you came walking down Palethorp (our side street), a glassless and skinnier version of yourself, I knew that you were a changed man, even from my eight year old perspective."

Also that month, Joan Andrews was freed in Florida

---

[74] It would be interesting to know if the bailbondsmen ever had to hunt down any of the rescuers to collect.

after two and a half years in jail. This was a great encouragement to the movement. Joan was to continue to serve as an example of perseverance against judicial pressure over the following decade.

At the end of the month, Kimiko and I rescued again in front of Elizabeth Blackwell Center (named for the eighteenth century herbalist whose name was never associated with abortion in any other context). The day began at Northeast Women's Center – and I started our day by driving to the wrong Comly Road! We eventually got there, then went to a church service, and on downtown. This was a "National Day of Rescue". We learned later that about 10,000 people participated nationally, with approximately 4300 arrested.

On 10 Dec 1988, Kimiko and I "risked arrest"[75] at the abortion clinic in the Chester Crozer Hospital complex. It was a bitterly cold day. Two heavy-set brothers from Delaware stood in the freezing cold wearing nothing but t-

---

[75] As mentioned earlier, "risking arrest" was a term used by rescuers to distinguish ones convictions and intentions on a particular occasion. There were always a considerable number of "prayer supporters" and "sidewalk counselors" at a rescue who did not risk arrest. Those "at the doors" after police warnings were said to be "risking arrest".

shirts! Over the years there were many rescues in extreme cold, and quite a few in extreme heat. Standing still in freezing cold for a number of hours is quite an enlightening experience. It gives one the opportunity to reflect on ones values as few other things do, particularly ones own love for comfort. Veteran rescuers often brought a newspaper with them to stand or sit on.[76] Since I often worked outdoors in winter, I knew how to dress for it, but standing still in it was outside my previous experience. It was good for my prayer life.

    On that occasion, after considerable enjoyment of the cold, we rejoiced that there were no arrests – or rather that as long as the police threatened to charge our leader, Joe Roach, alone, the rest of us said we would stay there. We kidded him that at least he got to wait inside a heated police cruiser!

    It was a fitting end of the year for me. I had been locked up in the Atlanta jail where Rev. Martin Luther King, Jr. was also said to have been incarcerated. I had studied his letter from the Birmingham jail which all the more confirmed for me that rescue stood in a well-established tradition of Christian civil disobedience – or rather divine obedience, as that letter makes clear. And now I stood in front of the old library building, formerly part of Chester Crozer Baptist Seminary, where Dr. King had gone to school. Now, however, that building was being used to put babies, and mostly Black babies, to death in their mothers' wombs.

    Also in December 1988, District Judge Newcomber found Randy Terry, Joe Foreman, Tina Krail, and Mike McMonigal in contempt of his injunction, for the rescues of July 4th and 5th. He handed down a sentence which included more than $2000 in "damages, the abortionist attorney's fees ($72,000 was what they asked) as well as a fine of $5000 for each violation (times two, in other words)." These were incredibly punitive measures.

---

[76] I always encouraged people to stand on frozen ground rather than sidewalks where possible, since I read in farm magazine that cold concrete takes the heat out of livestock much faster than standing on ice.

Was That Thunder?

Rescue at Crozer-Chester abortion clinic, former library of the Baptist seminary where Martin Luther King, Jr. studied.

But rather than allow such judgments to have the effect the court desired (to stifle the rescue movement with fear of crippling fines), the leaders chose to go ahead as though no such injunctions, sentences, or fines had been heard of. Their courage inspired the "rank and file" to go into 1989 taking the smaller risks which our own involvement entailed.

CHAPTER THREE -- RECRUITING THE MASSES (1989)

Then shall the King say unto them on his right hand, Come, ye blessed of my Father, inherit the kingdom prepared for you from the foundation of the world; for I was an hungred, and ye gave me meat; I was thirsty, and ye gave me drink; I was a stranger, and ye took me in; Naked, and ye clothed me; I was sick, and ye visited me; I was in prison, and ye came unto me. Then shall the righteous answer him, saying, Lord, when saw we thee an hungred, and fed thee? Or thirsty and gave thee drink? When saw we thee a stranger, and took thee in? or naked, and clothed thee? Or when saw we thee sick, or in prison, and came unto thee? And the King shall answer and say unto them, Verily I say unto you, Inasmuch as ye have done it unto one of the least of these my brethren, ye have done it unto me. . . .   Matthew 25:31-40

When I was in college, under the inspiration of an inestimable friend from West Virginia, I became interested in Jack Kerouac. Steve "Fuzzy" Williams and I wandered in the rain through a cemetery in Lowell, Massachusetts, where that icon of the "Beat generation" lay freshly buried – so freshly, in fact, that there was not yet any marker to be found. I read all of Kerouac's more popular works, and so was surprised in the 90s when I came upon his first book called *The Town and The City*. It is unique among his works -- more of a traditional 50's small-town novel, and apparently by someone with quite a different "persona" than the *Dharma Bum* who seemed to be ever *On the Road*. But all of his books give evidence of a writer who is more observer than "actor". I resonate to that.

No matter how "involved" I was in the rescue movement, in some sense I felt I was more an observer than an actor. I followed, watched, listened and reflected. There were always many others who seemed much more dedicated than I – but neither could I turn away. As Kerouac seemed to believe about the "Beats," so I believed of the rescuers, that they were at the very heart of American vitality, or more

Was That Thunder?

accurately, the only hope for a revival of American life.

Rescuers – Peculiar Saints

I had also come to believe every Christian in America should be "doing rescue" and that an important part of our job was to recruit those others. I had already witnessed resistance to rescue among Christians, and I was to see much more: some close at hand. But meanwhile the rescuers I knew were a tremendous encouragement to me and to one another. Nor were the leaders unique in this. Among the people who stand out in my memory are many "ordinary" ones like Patty McNamara, and Howard Walton, Barry Howell, Bob and Anita Brothers, Brian Woznicki and Jack Klotz. There were hundreds more I should name with them.

I rode down with Howard, Patty and several others to the hearings for the first Delaware rescue. I remember this trip partly because dealing with legal institutions was so new to me. But I also remember an event on the way.

When we exited Route 95, we passed over a bridge where a prison van was parked with only one man sitting in the driver seat. He appeared to be slumped forward over the wheel. We were on the way to our own criminal hearing, nevertheless Howard says, 'Hey, what's going on there?'

Howard is a cheerful, grizzled, and amazingly even-tempered Philadelphian. During the time I knew him he had surgery for cancer, and never seemed to have a downbeat minute through it all. He was mischievous but never malevolent – not even toward the abortionists.

Of course, none of us knew 'what was going on' with the prison van, and the road patterns were too complicated to get back to see, but as we drove along, we saw a man walking by himself, apparently in a prison uniform. So Howard says, let's follow him until we get to a phone. So we drove slowly ahead, keeping an eye on the guy, until we came to a town office of some kind, and pulled in to make a call. But Howard says, 'Jim, you come with me and we'll watch this guy until someone official can check him out. So Howard and I set off on foot "tailing" this supposed escaped prisoner, while others went in to make the phone call.

Howard Walton, persevering through thick and thin

After about ten minutes of this, the rest of them pulled up in the car and said they hadn't been able to get anyone very interested, although a local police dispatcher said he'd send someone around, so we piled back in the car and drove on to our hearing.

I suppose if this was the only description you ever heard of Howard, you would think he was unusual. He is unusual – but not in the way you mean. He is actually one of the calmest, most compassionate, and single-minded people you could meet. He is an activist, but not hyper-active. Rather his thoughts lead to action. His life is active. And in this case, he thought there might have been a crime, and he felt personally obligated to pursue justice. That was also how he felt about abortion, except he had no doubt about there having been a crime. In many of these things he was a typical rescuer.

Was That Thunder?

Patricia McNamara "Patty Mack"

Patty worked for Sears-Roebuck in their big Philadelphia office complex at Adams and the Boulevard. She had put in nineteen years with them, but her rescue involvement (rescues and court dates) caused her to miss some work. With less than a year to go to retirement, she was fired. Furthermore she saw this coming! Even so she did not flinch in her commitment, or back off in her involvement. What an incredible contrast with the way most American Christians live.

Barry Howell had been a longshoreman and a hellion. He lived a life of drugs, alcohol, and violence, until one day he fell from a high crane and smashed himself up. He always said it was a miracle he lived. In the midst of the ruin of his body and his life, he met Jesus, and began to live a life of faith. In large part he recovered his health, although his drug days left him with serious liver problems. His involvement in rescue began as a natural outgrowth of his quiet boldness. His ministry in jail was particularly fruitful.

A Memoir of Pro-life Rescue

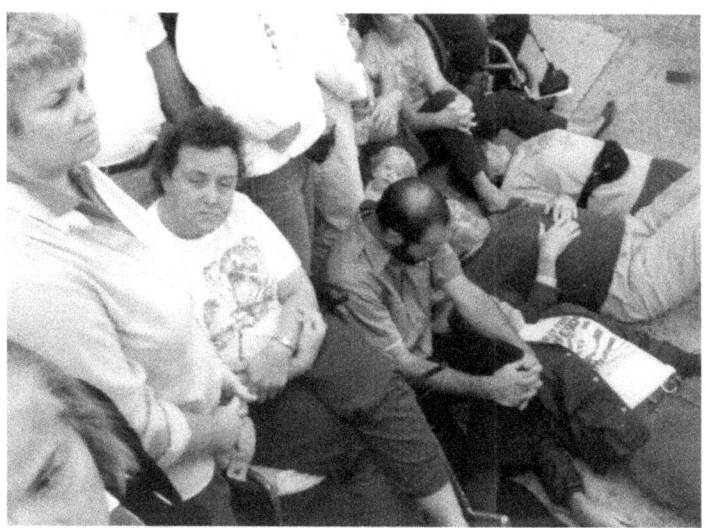

Maryann in her wheelchair, with other rescuers.

Years later, during sentencing at our Allentown trial, the prosecutor singled out Barry, showing the judge his long "rap-sheet," which included serious crimes like assault, etc. But our lawyer, Jim Owens, used the occasion for one of the most winsome presentations of the gospel I have ever heard in a courtroom, pointing out that Barry had indeed been a hardened criminal, but that his rap sheet ended abruptly in the 80s at the point where he had trusted Jesus Christ as his savior. Like Howard and Patty, Barry was all that's best about Philadelphians – good humor, a certain dry irony, and a whole cheesesteak worth of accent.

Brian Woznicki is rightly famous as the man who rescued regularly in a wheelchair, although he was not the only one who did it. (Maryanne was another regular) A genetic disability effects his speech and motor control, but Brian has a mind like a Swiss watch, and a heart of gold. He once recounted the time he met Surgeon General C. Everett Koop, the celebrated Philadelphia neonatologist, who, learning of Brian's own pro-life commitments, referred to the fact that Roe v. Wade rendered live births of others in his condition more and more unusual. Brian and I had several opportunities to hang out, including a few rides to rallies together. I particularly enjoyed hearing him recount his experiences as a boy scout being packed back into the woods by his fellow scouts.

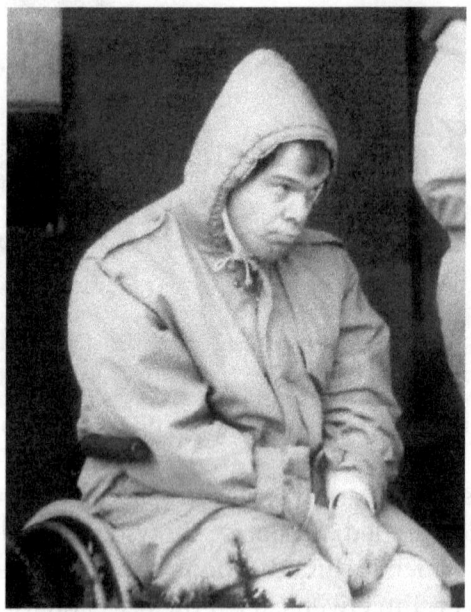

Brian Woznicki, rescuer on wheels

Jack Klotz was often Brian's "partner" at rescues. The giant former NY Jets tackle would gently load Brian in and out of the car and push his wheelchair up in front of the doors of a clinic. When the police began to arrest us, however, Jack was not as much use to Brian as he had been to Joe Namath. In fact it was Brian who often made the more spectacular plays. When the police came to get him, expecting to wheel him away, he would often dive out of his chair, so that they had to carry him just as they had to carry the others.

Jack, for his part, would quietly make a deal with the cops: if they would send three officers to escort him (since it would have taken that many to carry him) he would walk in a slow and dignified manner to the bus. Jack did this out of compassion for the officers, whose backs he wanted to save. Jack's compassion and faith also led him to work in an addictions ministry in Chester, and to help out with the Eagles team Bible studies.

A Memoir of Pro-life Rescue

Jack Klotz, one of several pro-football players who rescued

Jack was a friend of Reggie White, and encouraged "The Minister of Defense's" pro-life commitment. Reggie, is remembered, among many other things, for started homes for unwed mothers. Jack would often deprecate his own intelligence, claiming he "practiced too much without a helmet," but he was respected by all of us for both his heart and head.

Bob and Anita Brothers are West Philadelphians, living in a three-story "twin" home that has been in the family for generations. Bob worked his whole life as an editor, but the two of them became active pro-lifers before I did. Bob and I also share an interest in genealogical research. But these two have been far more "active," more faithful than I, not only in rescues,[77] but in picketing and sidewalk counseling at abortion clinics around the Delaware Valley. They were out every week, like perhaps a hundred others, offering alternatives to abortion-bound mothers and dads.

---

[77] Bob was with me at the last rescue I was involved with in 1997.

Was That Thunder?

Anita Brothers, Bob's steadfast helpmeet.

Two men from Delaware who stand out in my memory are Van Johnson and Earl Essex. Van was a vacuum cleaner salesman, who was as ordinary though as friendly a guy as you could ever meet. Why was Van out in the heat and cold, going to jail, while so many men like him were comfortably going about their daily self-indulgent rounds?

Earl was one of only two attorneys I ever knew to risk arrest. He was a pioneer, along with his wife Kathleen, who continued forward on many fronts after Earl was gone. I remember being arrested and loaded on the same bus with Earl, who lay in his seat silently, but to all appearances in pain. "Are you OK, Earl?" I asked him. "Oh yes," he said, then with some irony mixed into his expression, "as well as the circumstances permit. It's these adhesions" he added. In fact he was in very poor health, with unhealed surgeries, yet kept up his sacrifices to the last.

Two other men out of the hundreds of people I came to admire were Tyrone Malone and Chuck Matson, two quiet, gentle, but determined rescuers from Jersey who often came out with George and Tina Krail. Tyrone and George were two victims of the worst police "atrocities" I saw firsthand in my years of rescue, an episode I will describe at its proper place in the chronology.

Rescuers were peculiar people. They came from all walks of life and all sorts of backgrounds. There was an all-Black rescue in Michigan in 1989.[78] Our Philly rescues included Baptists, Catholics, Methodists, Mennonites, Jews, Presbyterians, Independents, Agnostics, and Atheists. We had ten year olds and eighty year olds. We had doctors, lawyers, carpenters, and housewives. Yet they all had a perspective in common. The peculiar perspective of rescuers was well illustrated by Linda Speir's account of how she got involved. It still sticks in my memory.

Linda, from New Jersey, had a growing burden that she needed to get involved in opposing abortion. (I think she'd seen something on TV that first made her sit up and take notice.) She called up a nearby pro-life office and asked what she could do. "Well," the woman on the phone answered, "you could come in here and help us stuff envelopes."

"No," Linda said," I was hoping to do something that had a little more direct effect."

"Well," the patient lady replied, "you could help out with a political campaign."

"What else have you got," Linda asked.

"You could help man a hotline for a pregnancy center, talking to women in crisis pregnancies," the woman answered.

"No," Linda said, 'I don't think I'd be much good at that."

"You could go out to abortion clinics and offer alternatives to women there as they come for appointments."

---

[78] Led by a former police officer, Greg Keath, who said, "One of our main goals is to expose Planned Parenthood because (it's founder) Margaret Sanger was a eugenist who believed that minority races should be eliminated. She had a Negro Project and had ministers and prominent blacks involved so she could penetrate the black community," he said. "Most of the major clinics today are in inner cities."

Was That Thunder?

"That's more what I had in mind," said Linda, "but I don't know if I would be much good at talking. Isn't there anything else?"

"Well," said the woman, getting a little weary, "you could go out with the crazy people that are blocking clinic doors and get arrested."

"Yes," Linda said, "that's what I'm looking for. How do I start?" The woman had no idea, but she gave her a phone number that eventually led to rescuers, and Linda remained active for six or seven years, often serving as a marshal.

Pro-life Education in Our Own Churches

January 22, 1973 was the infamous date of the Roe v. Wade decision. Therefore pro-life groups and churches around the country mark out the month of January as a time of special activities, publicity, and education, the biggest national event being the annual March for Life in Washington DC.

In 1989 the pro-lifers in our own congregation petitioned the elders for the opportunity to hold special Sunday school classes on the biblical view of the unborn child and our responsibility to oppose abortion and provide alternatives. This became a regular part of our church calendar except for a few years when the church leadership became preoccupied with other things. But in the many years of pro-life Sunday School classes, we covered a great range of topics related to abortion or the culture which led to its legalization through Roe v. Wade. Other events usually included a rescue or two during the weeks surrounding that date each year.

Also in 1989, I had the opportunity to speak to an adult Sunday School class at New Life Presbyterian church of Glenside, our "mother church". I talked about 'The Great American Dream versus Christian social involvement,' and suggested what I was only beginning to understand – that we as a nation and a national church had commitments to idolatry which fed the very evils we formally abhorred. Our desire for "security" had eclipsed the gospel in many dimensions of our lives.

ADEQUATE COVERAGE

> In case of catastrophe . . .
> . . . Like a thief in the night
> To provide for the future . . .
> . . . Walk by faith not by sight
> Some measure of comfort . . .
> . . . She gave her last cent . . .
> Who cares not for his own . . .
> . . . Having these be content . . .
> Use wisely the mammon of unrighteousness . . .
> . . . Sell all and follow me . . .
> We must be good stewards . . .
> . . . Tonight 'tis required of thee.

I spoke in our own adult Sunday School on "The Sleeping Church;" repenting on our feet; described a ordinary rescue day; and encouraged people to take the next steps to which God was calling them.

New York Rescues

On January 13, Kimiko and I went to New York City where Randy Terry led rescues in front of the national headquarters of Planned Parenthood.[79] Many of our friends from Philadelphia and Glenside were involved in these rescues, as well as a group of Orthodox Jewish rabbis. If I'm not mistaken, Nat Hentoff, jazz enthusiast, atheist and well-known writer for the *Greenwich Village Voice*, also participated. He definitely was involved in a number of rescues.

---

[79]"Planned Barrenhood" or "Banned Parenthood" as pro-lifers alternately called it. International headquarters are in London, UK.

Was That Thunder?

Nat Hentoff was noted for addressing Christian pro-lifers, to this effect, "It's all right for you people to oppose abortion – at least you think there is some hope after death for the baby even if it is killed. But we believe this life is all there is, so it's all the more important that anyone even remotely human be allowed to live it."

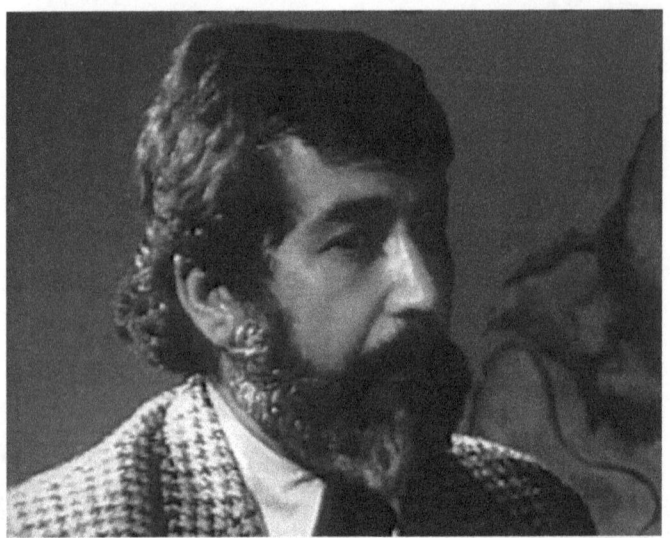

Nat Hentoff, noted Civil liberties advocate, novelist and writer for the *Greenwich Village Voice*. After 1986, strongly pro-life.

I remember a number of things clearly about those events. The first was the great parade we made as we set out the morning of the rescue with hundreds of people going down into the subway station together, walking through a long platform, and coming back up again through a different street entrance. A large contingent of plain-clothed police officers accompanied us, sticking as close to Randy Terry et al as possible. But something important came through on their radio communications, so they stopped to try to sort it out over the radio while the hundreds of pro-lifers filed by, and I don't think they ever quite caught up to the leadership again.

However, once we were back on the street and walking the several blocks we had to go to get to Planned Parenthood, I recall coming around a corner of a block and seeing four or five people standing there. One of them was a giant, bearded man with a black leather jacket – wearing a red miniskirt. He was sort of daring anyone to look at him funny. "Where but in New York?" someone asked.

We formed up in front of Planned Parenthood, where the leadership including the rabbis were already in place with a couple hundred others. Bull horns were used on this occasion, but I don't recall much of what was said. The police brought in a big squad of officers, with lots of decorations on their uniforms. They were merciless in an assault intended to get between us and the building. They walked all over those in their way, and succeeded in their goal, despite crushing quite a few rescuers, including both grandmothers and young teens.

After that, hundreds of other officers were brought in to cordon off the building. They arrested a few of us, but for the most part maintained the cordon throughout the day. I recall a few rescuers lying down in front of the buses that were taking the others to be booked. My friend and fellow church member, now pastor, Bill Slack later described that part of the days activities. There were a few such occasions over the years when enthusiasm may have exceeded wisdom!

In mid-afternoon, Randy led all of the rescuers away from Planned Parenthood. After we had walked two or three blocks, he stopped to pray, then led us back. We arrived just as the police cordon was beginning to disperse, but they quickly reformed, a few more of us were arrested, and the rest of us spent the next few hours kneeling and praying in front of the cordon. I recall one officer cheerfully telling us we should have waited another fifteen minutes and they all would have been gone. To keep off the cold, someone passed out new wool blankets obtained from a local church rescue mission.

Riding back on the subway after the rescue, I recall a stop at which a blind man got on with a tape player hanging at his side. As soon as the doors closed, he turned on the player and began to sing into a mike – his voice almost angelic in a crooner-style tune. He had a tin cup hung on his rig-out, too, and people dropped in coins as he walked through the car singing.

Was That Thunder?

After the rescue that night we went back to the cheap hotel where most of us were staying.

I did not stay that evening, but those who did were invited by the hotel owner, who was Thai I believe, to a free smorgasbord dinner that night. Many pro-lifers showed up at the prospect of free food. It turned out it was a funeral feast, and the body of the deceased, the hotel owner's mother, was dressed up and seated at the head of the table. It is said appetites were more subdued than usual.

In an evening rally at a large evangelical church, I was struck with the tremendous variety of people represented: rabbis, Easter Orthodox priests, Catholics, Pentecostals, and all other manner of Protestants. There were thousands of people present.

Neither Kim nor I was arrested on the 13th. I had to get back to Philly that night, so with fear and trepidation I left Kimiko with friends in order that she might rescue the next day. She was indeed arrested that day, and unlike most of the other juveniles, was actually processed as a juvenile, which required some time and hassle later. [80]

In early '89, one of the local leaders invited me to an OR meeting in Binghamton. I found being among these dynamic people rather intimidating. Randy Terry, Mike McMonigal, Jesse Lee, Keith Tucci, Joe Foreman, Pat Mahoney, Susan Odom, Janey Bray and various other leaders from New York, Buffalo, Albany, Boston, St. Louis, Florida, Nevada and I don't know where else. I was somewhat preoccupied with the sense that for lack of credentials I didn't belong there.

The meetings consisted chiefly in listening to speakers – and the speakers were powerful. George Callahan, an Episcopal pastor from Florida, addressed the dangers of burn-out and the symptoms thereof. He basically was saying what other leaders would repeat over the years during which the movement flourished – if you find you can't keep Christ-

---

[80] She was mostly miffed at 'looking young,' a complaint that is getting a little more muted now that she's in her forties.

centered, back off and get Christ-centered again.[81] Paranoia, anger, and vengeful thinking are not fruits of the Holy Spirit. If you begin to experience them, get back to the cross.

Note: His name spelled wrong in the OR video!

Pat Mahoney gave a talk with the arcane title, "Why the Media are Our Best Friends". I'm still not sure exactly what he was saying, but I think it was that: 'the media are always compelled to report – and, although they tend to report with a strong bias, even that can be counted on. At bottom they do want to appear the purveyors of the truth and the truth is what we want told.' He spoke of building relationships with media people, who, according to polls, had practically no acquaintances who were Christians.

Cindy Terry spoke of the peculiar burdens of rescue wives, and exhorted rescue leaders to give special consideration to and make special provisions for the special burdens of their wives and families. I remember her saying "You can't sacrifice your wife and kids for somebody else's wife and kids." Cindy was a mother and foster mother as well as a rescue wife, and what she said had the credibility of the suffering servant.

---

[81] Callahan's church in Florida came under the heavy guns of pro-abort civil suits – merely for allowing rescuers to meet in their facilities. First Amendment – what First Amendment!

Was That Thunder?

Rev. Daniel J. Little

Janie Bray, whose husband spent several years in jail for attempting to destroy an abortuary, may also have spoken, and perhaps Susan Odom, also. I think it was there that I first heard Susan Odom's oft-repeated motto – "The safest place on earth to be is in the will of God."

After Cindy spoke, Randy emphasized her point, saying we needed to put some of our rescue energy into our wives. Art Tomlinson added to this saying it was important we did not come walking in the door of our houses, thinking we had earned a rest, when our wives and children were sacrificing as much as we.

Rev. Jesse Lee

Randy's pastor, Dan Little, shared with us. His church was later to be pursued by the Clinton administration for taking a "political" stand and thus violating the "separation of church and state".

Jesse Lee spoke fervently in his winsome Virginia accent. Someone told me he was a descendant of Robert E. [82]

I remember another man there who may have been associated with Chet Gallagher. At any rate he was a police chief or a just-retired police chief, and his presence seemed ironic, as well as a blessing.

There was also another speaker, a lawyer with one of the nascent Christian legal organizations which sprang up about that time. In any case I remember him speaking and saying something that I found peculiar – that he felt funny trying to inform or inspire a group of people like us, because in his mind, those of us risking arrest in front of abortion clinics were the real warriors of our times. Along the lines of Randy's exhortation in Atlanta, I certainly didn't feel like a warrior -- only a rather confused sinner with a strong sense that we must do something about this evil.

I have often reflected on something Keith Tucci said at this conference, which struck me forcibly:

> Many of us have been prophesying that we need to come out of the stained glass churches, but many of us need to come out of our stained-glass families as well.

---

[82] Robert E. Lee was the young American officer who arrested John Brown at Harper's Ferry after that would-be revolutionary had shot a number of innocent people in his efforts to capture the Armory. Not too many years later, Lee was the head of another revolutionary army, himself. Curiously, his ?great-uncle, "Light Horse Harry" Lee, had been the first man to stand in the Continental Congress and propose that the colonies revolt and declare themselves independent. When he first spoke of it, the entire body objected saying his proposal was out of order. A month later, they not only entertained it but voted in favor of it. The sinews of history are people. And people always have connections to people. It is they who keep the themes – and the ironies -- alive.

Was That Thunder?

We try to raise our kids as good little Christians and when they backslide they are lost. But if we raise our kids to be activists, they backslide and they're good little Christians.

-- a dollop of irony on some food for thought.

The Babies Testify

Back in Philly, Chuck Depoy had been trying to "raise support" as a full-time pro-life activist. He had worked very hard at it, and unbeknownst to most of us who knew him, despite his chipper demeanor and usually smiling face he was getting discouraged. But his efforts at raising support and recruiting more rescuers included an evening meeting at New Life Glenside, which congregation had already provided fifteen or twenty rescuers. This meeting stands out in my mind, because it was the first time I saw the aborted babies at first hand.

Chuck Depoy, an early rescuer from our church

Chuck spoke well and clearly describing what rescue was all about. He ended by saying that, on the subject of seriousness of abortion, he had decided to let the babies speak for themselves. He invited us to observe a period of silence while those who wished to could come up front to see the remains of some children who had been aborted. He invited us, if we wanted to, to hold a tiny arm or leg in our hands.

One of the strongest and most incontrovertible witnesses which brought people to oppose abortion was the remains of babies. Thousands of babies from every stage of pregnancy had been pulled from dumpsters and trash containers over the years. There was no arguing with a dead baby. The pictures of these children are still a powerful witness to the reality of what abortion is. For that reason, such pictures always make the proaborts see red. [83]

A few years earlier, a trailer-sized storage container was discovered near the offices of a coroner in California. It contained thousands of aborted babies at all stages of growth, most of them in jars of formaldehyde. No one would take responsibility for it, so pro-lifers sought permission to hold a funeral service and bury the children. The state interposed and disallowed the service. They took over and finally buried them in a mass unmarked grave. Nonetheless, prolifers succeeded in getting many photographs of the remains.

Especially in the early years, many remains were discovered on loading docks in Chicago,[84] and in dumpsters near abortuaries all over the country. I was to hear rumors of

---

[83] From Monica Migliorino Miller's book, I learned these were most likely some of the thousands of babies whose bodies were taken from a Chicago loading dock by Monica and other pro-lifers. She describes how they ended up buried with memorial services all over the country, including one group of bodies her to-be husband Edmund Miller transported to Joe Foreman here in Philly. Chuck must have gotten them from Joe before the memorial burial.

[84] A special cemetery was dedicated as a burial place for more than a hundred of these babies west of Philadelphia.

remains collected from local trash containers.[85]

I went up and stood in awe before the extremely small, but perfect little arms and legs, the hands and feet upon which the fingers and toes were only eighths of an inch long. From the clean white table cloth, I picked up the arm of an anonymous "fetus" and held it in my hand, where it weighed barely more than a feather. The little thumb curled up at right angles to the curl of the four little fingers. The tiny bones and joints were unmistakable, although the child was probably only 10 weeks old or so when he died. No one could deny this came from a person. I felt awe. But I also felt awful.

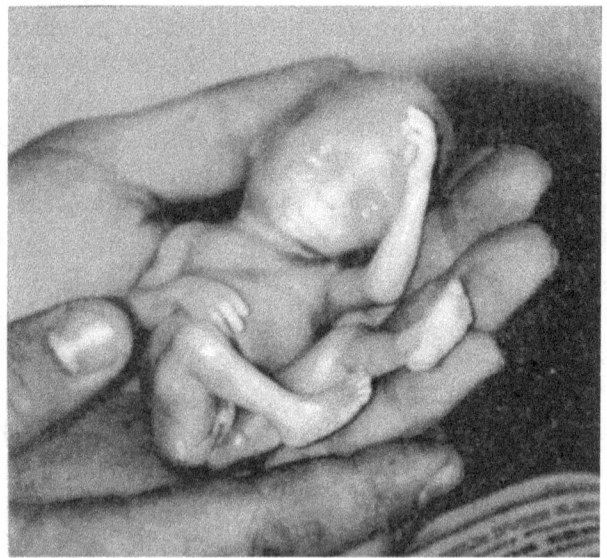

One of the innocent people who legal abortion killed.

A few years later, my youngest daughter, Victoria helped me butcher a deer. As we finished a good day's work, I loaded the innards into a sawdust-filled garbage bag, but

---

[85] Some places, like the Northeast Women's Center (NEWC) at Comly Road, used giant garbage disposals by which they eliminated this potential "danger" – the danger of the remains being recovered, that is. Soon high-security, locking dumpsters appeared at some aborturaries.

since she had shown interest, and was studying science, I first showed her the various organs. When I came to what I had thought was a full bladder, and punctured it expecting it to drain, I found it was something else – one, then two, tiny deer popped out. They measured no more than four inches from head to tail, yet even their hooves were picture perfect. Their tiny heads were clearly the head of deer, their legs perfect, each joint like clockwork. One more demonstration: the myth that a creature in the womb is "a blob of tissue" is a straight-out lie.

The hope Chuck and we others had was that we would not only stir up a considerable number of rescuers from that congregation, but eventually motivate the whole Protestant community to a greater awareness and involvement at some level. Other Protestant churches in the area gave promise of considerable involvment, including Church of the Savior in Wayne, Newtown Square Baptist, New Life Presbyterian of Philadelphia, and other churches in Montgomery County. Even a few UCC (United Church of Christ) congregations had members regularly involved. One in particular, Leidy Memorial Church, the oldest congregation in the area, had many members involved in rescue. [86]

But we did not succeed in recruiting large numbers or even in expanding into many of the evangelical churches in the area. The Catholic faithful were more than the Protestants, but they too testified to the problem of recruiting. I can only speculate beyond my own experience, but if my experience is a measure of the "why," then it was because of opposition among church leaders.

As a parent, former elder, and sometimes construction boss, I realize the "conservative" inertia that leadership inclines toward. I respect the operating engineers' desire to "go slow" in order not to wreck the train. But there is something else in established leaderships which is not

---

[86] This congregation eventually withdrew, since they had considerably more respect for Bible authority than the rest of the denomination..

commendable – it is fear of man, unbelief, and the desire to preserve control and self-respect. In fact, leaders are in some ways most susceptible to that old fleshly triumvirate: personal reputation, comfort and prosperity.

It was this to which Martin Luther King, Jr. responded in his Birmingham Jail Letter. Like the Civil Rights Movement, Rescue challenged these idols. Church leaders tend to be more interested in what bankers and lawyers tell them than what biblical logic would lead them to do. Come to think of it, the religious leaders in Jesus time were inclined to the same wrong priorities.

Bushwhacked Again!

A pastor of a Presbyterian church called and invited me to a meeting where the "session" (the board of elders) were going to discuss "civil disobedience" and rescue in particular. I went expecting to be asked questions about my involvement, my understanding of the biblical issues, and the ethical difficulties raised by rescue. Instead I was bushwhacked!

Those coming to the meeting seemed to have diametrically opposite sets of expectations about what was supposed to happen there. Up until about noon of the day of the meeting, my expectations were as I stated. But after lunch, I got a special delivery envelope containing a "paper" addressing the subject of abortion rescue, by none other than the individual who had expressed strong opposition to it back in August 1988 before Atlanta!

Although not a member of that church's session, this brother was part of the discussion, and he opened with all his guns blazing. The paper was a diatribe against rescue – I can think of no other fair description of it. It condemned rescue with much more heat than the substance of its arguments could warrant. In fact, it contained precious little biblical argument. The classic line that remains etched into my memory was this, "If I was a child not yet born, I wouldn't want anyone saving my life by illegal means." I never have been able to decipher that one.

My blood pressure as I read it could have inflated a bowling ball, but I sat down at my desk and tried to address the paper. After a couple of frustrating hours, I resigned myself to a debating meeting where I was going to have a very serious opponent.

However, the meeting itself was anything but a debate. Perhaps the moderator vastly overestimated my maturity and sang froid, or the other fellow's brevity. But he opened the meeting by asking the opposing brother to state his case! And there really was never any other case seriously considered. After we all listened to perhaps 45 minutes of reasons why rescue was foolish, ungodly and sinful, someone asked me what I thought!

I now see my self-pity crippled me – I took it all very personally and lost perspective entirely.

All I could say was that the whole meeting thus far had felt to me like a personal attack and condemnation. I explained that I not only thought rescue was a good idea, but I had come to feel a strong sense of "calling" to rescue. I asked the gentlemen gathered there how they would feel if other Christian brothers declared their callings sinful. I said it was well and good to say we ought to do something else about abortion. However, I asked "what are you doing?"

The opposing brother said, "I pray!" I answered, perhaps too hastily, but I think with validity – "and what good have your prayers done? Do you pray instead of teach your classes? Do you pray instead of counsel your clients? Do we pray instead of sharing the gospel or ministering to those we know to be in need?"

One brother expressed the high respect they all had for the man who spoke against rescue. In light of that opposition he was convinced they needed to give more careful thought to the objections. Strike one.

Another said that he supposed there was as much biblical support for blocking nuclear weapons sites as there was for abortion clinic rescue. Strike two.

Another spoke of the suffering he had seen working with a mission in an African country, and asked why we had more right to disobey our government than the Christians there did, when their suffering was so much worse. Strike three.

Dr. and Mrs. King, Dr. Frederick Reese, and Hosea Williams, Civil Rights leaders in Selma. They, too, were castigated by church leaders for "breaking the law"

Plainly there was a lot of emotion aroused, but not much evidence of sustained thought. Perhaps one out of fifteen men spoke neutrally or encouragingly about my involvement, but it was clear opposition to rescue carried the day.

After the meeting I got a chance to tell the opposing brother I thought the intensity of his reactions to rescue might come from his negative experiences of the "peace movement," but he said that was not the case. To be frank, I still have no clue what motivated him. [87]

I left the meeting with a deep sense of betrayal, and

---

[87] Much later a mutual acquaintance, who was also a rescuer, told me that this man had expressed something like regret over his opposition.

very little hope that this congregation would contribute much more to rescue. The moderator called me and apologized for how he managed the meeting, but what went on there was not purely a matter of management!

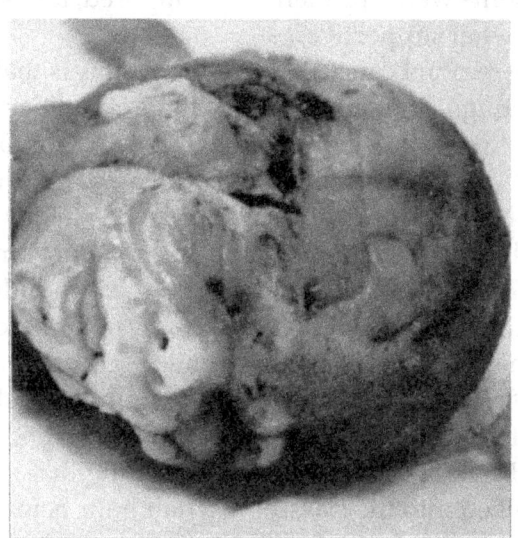

"Baby Face"-- Would this child rather have died than have someone trespass to save him? [88]

When the next election came around, I called every elder on that session and asked them if they knew who the pro-life candidates were. Not one of them had any idea. Not surprising. "Do something else about abortion" to many meant do nothing.

The drama wound on in that church. As I have said, some fifteen to twenty members had already been involved in rescue. I had spoken to a morning Sunday School class, and Chuck Depoy had an evening recruiting meeting there. In a subsequent evening meeting, the elders met again to discuss

---

[88] One of those Monica Migliorino found in a loading dock in Chicago. "Another fetal child, whom I called "Baby Face" was a five-month old who, from skin tones and facial features, appeared to be black. He or she was killed by the D& E method. But unlike most of the fetal children, the face of this baby was almost entirely intact. Although the baby's lower jaw was gone, and one eyeball was missing from its socket, this was a beautiful, well-formed face.

the question of their congregation being involved in rescue.

Due to an ironic coincidence, I can reliably report that during this closed meeting the fifteen or so elders split into several "camps" on the issue. Several were completely opposed, some were "prudentially" opposed, and a very few were somewhat supportive.

The reason I can accurately report this is that I "spied" on the meeting. After all, I was in Military Intelligence during my three years in the army! But no, I did not "spy" intentionally or in any of the conventional ways. No mechanical or electronic eavesdropping, no paid or ideologically-motivated informant, no stolen documents or photographs. In fact, my spying was quite by accident!

Both Roseann and I taught classes in homeschool co-ops over the years. After our own children went on to public high schools, we continued to teach as contract teachers in several different settings. That year, I was teaching two classes on Fridays, which met at the building that church used. I walked into the classroom a half hour before class to find a large poster covered in mysterious scribbles. My genetically devious mind immediately set about de-coding this, and when I realized what it was, I was unabashed in paying close attention!

In essence, it was a systematic representation of the "continuum" of opinions about rescue among the elders of that church! Apparently they had met the night before and inadvertently left this evidence of their deliberations. To make it complete, a helpful scribe among them, no doubt trying to facilitate the meeting had polled each elder and jotted his initials next to the "position" each took. Thus I knew I had three firm opponents among those elders, one firm ally, and whole lot of wish-washy guys in between.

But the saddest thing was that rather than work through the issues and come to a genuine consensus, they took this unresolved split to the congregation. In subsequent congregational meetings they announced their conclusion on the subject -- it was that they could not agree! The congregation was left to flounder. The trumpet call was not just indistinct, but two separate and contrary notes!

Although several members remained active in rescue for a time, there were few new recruits and only one elder who ever rescued from their midst, and he but once. In contrast, I was very thankful that many of the elders from our own church rescued, and many of their wives and children.

Circle of young people praying during
Center City Philadelphia prayer vigil

Delaware Court Room

During 1989, I was involved in fourteen or so rescues and spent weeks in court and several days in jail. Memorable to me was the April trial in Wilmington for the rescue on 28 January at the Stanton, Delaware abortuary. Kimiko and Adriel, my second daughter, had been along for the rescue, but did not risk arrest. I discouraged them because I was unsure how rough the state police might prove.

Was That Thunder?

Those rescuers who had been arrested were tried in Wilmington in groups of five or six. Although most of the trials took only one day, ours took two. Judge Bailick presided. We went "pro se," that is we defended ourselves. Most of us had little experience at such things – and in fact those with the most experience were perhaps a little too flashy and thus less effective, but overall the trial was an awesome and sobering experience.[89]

We did not start off with a particularly well-planned defense. The judge more or less disallowed the primary defense any rescuer would like to offer, "the justification defense," which says that one commits no crime when he breaks a lesser law in order to prevent a greater harm.[90] So our secondary strategy became simply to put ourselves on the stand. Rather than carry out the cumbersome and artificial process of questioning ourselves or each other, the judge allowed each of us to explain what we did and why we did it.

Brenda Caley and Susan Odom, true feminists

---

[89] I have often wished I could afford the cost of a copy of the transcript, but they say it must be re-transcribed from the reporter's shorthand record – which process is expensive.

[90] For example, breaking down some ones front door to rescue them from a fire; or trespassing to rescue a drowning person.

The defendants were Brenda Caley, her brother Jim, Ted Meehan, John and Joe Coffey, Jack Klotz, Annette Shusko, Janet Fraliciardi, Father Pierson (former Lutheran, former Episcopal, married Catholic priest), his wife Nancy, and myself. Father Pierson examined the arresting officers.

Ted gave an erudite presentation of the biological facts and the legal logic which had put him in his present position. He appealed to the judge on the basis of the "justification defense".

Janet spoke of the devastating after-affects of abortion. She showed a picture of her niece who was born as a result of George Krail's intervening by offering alternatives to the girl's mother.

Jim Caley, saw a "tissue sample" and became a pro-life activist

Brenda and Jim gave an account of how each of them got involved. Jim spoke of working in a lab where one day he was sent into a storage room to get a tissue sample and there saw a perfect baby in a jar of formaldehyde – another "tissue sample". That event affected his heart and thinking to where

Was That Thunder?

he was drawn to oppose abortion more actively.

Brenda, who worked with retarded children, told how precious these "imperfect" human beings were, and how their humanity made her want to act to protect others like them.

I was given the honor of wrapping up our defense. I referred to the powerful oath we each took before we testified, "I promise on the Holy Word of Almighty God, to tell the truth, the whole truth and nothing but the truth, so help me God."

I suggested this oath illustrated that all human authority relies on a higher authority. I mentioned the Centurion of the New Testament who described himself both as a man with authority and as one set under authority. His submissive understanding of how authority worked gave him an understanding of who Jesus was and what he could do. I talked of how all civil law from time immemorial recognized that people sometimes found themselves caught in a conflict between two authorities.

I pointed out it was uniformly recognized that in such a dilemma one ought always to obey the greater authority. If the authority of this court was based on the Bible and the God of the Bible, then the court itself was built around a recognition of God's higher authority. We, too, took that authority very seriously – so much so that when lesser laws which were contrary to it (such as Roe v. Wade and trespass laws) were brought to bear on us, we had no choice but to obey God. I challenged the court to take seriously its own profession.

I was both exhilarated and humbled by a sense that God had indeed given us words to say – knitting the testimonies together into a whole that was quite complete and potentially persuasive. The judge found us guilty of disorderly conduct and trespassing, but there were no repercussions.

Well, there was one repercussion. Because the trial was held over an extra day, I missed jury duty in Philly, so I had to have the Delaware judge write me a note to that affect – in order not to be found in contempt of court in Philly!

First Prison Sentence

We did not go to jail on that occasion, but nearly all of us did eventually. Philly arrests often resulted in many hours "in custody" each time, but usually we were released by the end of the same day. Chester County Prison was the first place I was officially incarcerated – for my first rescue at the Paoli abortion clinic. Eventually nearly six hundred of us received two day sentences there. We actually spent more like four days in prison.

One of Joe O'Hara's baby models sitting on the perimeter fence at Chester County Prison

During that stint, my first taste of jail, I was waiting in the "tank" (the holding cell where prisoners in transit are held together) before being processed into the prison. There a fellow started talking to me who was being processed out – probably to trial. As we talked I realized I knew his family.

Was That Thunder?

They were fairly well known Christians in the Delaware Valley. It turned out he was the "black sheep" of the family, who had been running from the Lord for some time. I said it was quite a coincidence bumping into him like that, and he agreed maybe Jesus wasn't done with him yet. I promised to pray for him. I had the privilege of seeing him again "inside" the same facility on a later occasion.

I first noticed something at Chester County which I saw repeated in other jails. Each block or ward had an unofficial "boss" among the prisoners, not, as one might suspect, the meanest guy on the block, but usually a fairly big, and benevolent "daddy," as it were. He arbitrated important questions like which television show we were going to watch in the dayroom, and maintained a kind of fairness among the prisoners on the block. Justice is built into the image of God.

I remember another small example of this. One time we were incarcerated in Philadelphia's House of Corrections, and when we got there we found a sign posted in the bathroom, "Please clean up after yourself. We may be criminals, but we don't need to be slobs."[91]

Although I don't remember much detail, I retain a deep impression we had a blessed time. I recall that on the day we were released, one of the rescuers broke down in tears. I later learned he had been directly involved in an abortion himself, and on top of that had a grandchild aborted.

---

[91] Here's another rescue jail story. When the first sentences were meted out to rescuers in the mid-80s, a group of Philly women arrived in their barracks-style block only to find an unusual sign posted in the bathroom. There were four toilets against one wall – two of them china, and two of them stainless steel. The sign said "White women to use white toilets only." Though shocked by this strange case of racial discrimination, the rescue women, who were indeed all white on that occasion, used only the white toilets. It was not until they were released that they found out the other prisoners had got word of their imprisonment, and come up with the logical explanation for why fifteen or twenty white women would be part of a single arrest. They assumed they were prostitutes – thus the effort to quarantine any infections they might carry.

He became an active minister to other men who had been involved in abortion. I saw profound healing in several men's lives through his ministry.

The Cheltenham Free Speech Case Goes to Court

In February, Roseann, Kimiko, and Adriel sat in a suburban courtroom, prosecuted with several others for their part in the picket back in March 1988, along a public street in front of a Cheltenham abortionist's home. As I mentioned in an earlier chapter, this was not a rescue, it was pure First Amendment activity. However a local ordinance had been passed, which became the basis for arrests. The other "defendants" included our good friends Bill Devlin and Pat Stanton, and Rabbi Yehuda Levin (from New York).

John Stanton at a rescue -- Father of the Pro-life Movement in the Delaware Valley

Rabbi Levin hadn't quite realized what he was getting into when he answered the invitation of some Philly Gentiles

Was That Thunder?

to picket a Jewish abortionist's home in the Philly suburbs. But neither did the Gentiles. The charges were insubstantial to say the least. They chiefly had to do with the highly questionable ordinance and transgressions thereof and the idea that those picketing there had "conspired" to do this evil.

The prosecutor tried various gambits. He attempted, for instance, to establish "conspiracy" between Pat Stanton and his father, John. John was often referred to as the father of the pro-life movement in the Delaware Valley. There was no doubt that Pat was acquainted with him! It was even fairly safe to suggest they shared views on abortion, but exactly what degree of conspiracy this constituted remained to be seen. Since Pat's brother Joe was the defending lawyer it was quite a family affair!

First the prosecutor asked Pat if his father had influenced him. Pat said his father had spent long hours praying in front of abortion clinics and offering alternatives to women there. He said his father had taken pregnant women into his home and seen to it that there financial and medical needs were met, as well as those of their children. He said his father had raised a large family, always working to provide for all of them. He concluded by saying, "how could I help being influenced by a man like that." Roseann says she was practically in tears after hearing his testimony.

But then Joe, the defense attorney, asked Pat if he agreed with his father on everything. Pat said no. Joe asked if they had ever disagreed on important matters. Pat said he remembered that when he was eighteen he couldn't wait to get out of the house.

Joe Stanton's further defense consisted in such things as getting Adriel on the stand and asking her a few germaine, legal questions, having to do with her understanding of the "injunction" she was charged with breaking. He read portions of it and asked here what she thought that meant. Unfortunately, precocious Adriel knew a lot more than her attorney suspected! But the thirteen year old defendant was a factor because the prosecution ultimately did not want publicity about prosecuting someone that young. Case dismissed.

A Memoir of Pro-life Rescue

Pat Stanton –"How could I help being influenced by a man like that!"

Another Case Dismissed

That same month, we were tried for the October '88 rescue at Blackwell on the National Day of Rescue in which it was said 5000 people were arrested around the country, and that number less than half of the 11,000 who actually gathered in front of aborturaries that day. Our Philly case was tried in four separate groups. Judge Lydia Kirkland acquitted our group of forty and ours only. (It may have been a coincidence that we were the only group without a lawyer.) In a February '89 letter to friends and family summarizing our rescue involvement thus far, I wrote that Judge Kirkland:

> ...found forty of us "not guilty" after we defended ourselves by expressing our motives and explaining our actions. I referred to my great-grandfather who was crippled in the Civil War fighting over the same issue –

whether a human being could be regarded as property by another. A Supreme Court decision (Dred Scott) made slavery "legal" in that case, too. I cited some of the facts which make it clear abortion is a racial issue. (According to Planned Parenthood's own research in 1987 there are 28 abortions per 1000 white women age 15 through 44, but 53 per 1000 non-whites.

Margaret Sanger, founder of Planned Parenthood[92]

Margaret Sanger, the "free-love" advocate and founder of Planned Parenthood made explicit statements demonstrating her racist "eugenic" intentions. In 1983, for every 1000 live births in the national white community there were about 340 abortions, but for every 1000 live births in the black community there

---

[92] A biography of Margaret Sanger indicates this was one of several PR photographs she posed for in which she deliberately tried to present a more feminine appearance than was her normal – this at the suggestion of her lover Havelock Ellis and other British allies in the eugenics movement. She was usually slovenly in dress and morals.

were 625 abortions.)⁹³ Those of us acquitted were amazed, but thankful. It was the first ray of hope I have seen on the judicial horizon.

In March, a Good Friday Rescue was held at the twin abortuaries in Center City (PP and Blackwell). Fifty U of P students joined about 60 workers from other closed abortuaries to "defend" the clinics. In fact their presence and their noise "contributed" to the rescue, insofar as their loud hostility no doubt drove some of the appointments away! (They did not make the sort of commitments to peaceful and prayerful behavior we did!) The weather was harshly cold, but it did not keep many rescuers home.

Arrested on one of the many "bad weather" rescue days.

On this occasion, 208 of us were arrested in front of Planned Parenthood. Our attorneys, working for no fee as usual, argued eloquently, citing a PA high court decision about the right of a child in the womb to recover damages, and quoting it "pre-born children, while in the womb, are separate individuals from the moment of conception. ." ⁹⁴

---

⁹³ I recently read that more black women had abortions in New York City in 2012, than gave birth to their children.
⁹⁴ Amadio v. Levin

Was That Thunder?

Alone in Jail

In March 1989, back in Chester County Prison, I was the only pro-lifer on a cell block for the first time in my experience. When the main sally port on the block opened up and then the gates clanged shut behind me, I experienced a brief moment of terror, during which I asked what I had gotten myself into. Then I remembered that I hadn't really gotten myself into it, so I didn't have to worry about getting myself out of it.

The amazing thing is that within fifteen seconds of those doors clanging shut behind me, another prisoner came up and welcomed me, asking if everything was going OK. I said things were going all right, except that they hadn't let me bring in my Bible. He immediately went back to his cell and brought back a paperback New Testament for me. At that moment you couldn't have convinced me that angels didn't wear prison uniforms. (I prayed for him for a couple years after that.)

Then I went to my cell, which was empty. However, looking down, I saw an enormous pair of shoes beside the bottom bunk. Again I experienced momentary trepidations, but I went back out to the dayroom, where all the other prisoners were gathered, and I soon met my "cellie" with whom I came to have a great relationship.

We ended up praying together regularly, and he shared some of his burdens with me, taking seriously my counsel. He had a strong gambling addiction, which had led to most of his troubles. His wife had also been arrested, because the two of them had tried to pass a forged check at a store owned by a local judge![95]

---

[95] After we got out, several of us made an effort and later found a job for this fellow, upon his release. We were all heartbroken when the Christian who employed him told us that after several months, he had taken the money from the till and gone to Atlantic City one weekend. The employer did not prosecute, but I lost track of him after that.

STAY IN YOUR CELL

If you stay in your cell
No one will ever get you --
No one can touch or hurt you
Or frighten you by force
(Except the supernumery
Guardians of good or ill).
But if you leave your cell,
Who knows what awful freedom
You may find . . . or give others.

If He had stayed in his cell . . .

  I found a number of things striking inside prison. In one way, it was the most highly ordered life that many of the men there had ever lived – and in many cases this was a good thing. However, the big question was always how many of them could take some of that order back with them in the form of self-discipline in their lives "on the outside". [96]
  I was also struck by how hardened some men seemed. After I'd been there a day or two, I was sitting at the end of a cafeteria-style table in the day room while five or six other prisoners played cards at the other end. One of them reached over and picked up a pack of matches from in front of another.
  WHAM! Without the slightest warning, the second prisoner (whose matches they were) punched the first in the side of the head as hard as he could. The fellow flew off the bench and onto the floor. "Don't ever take my matches without asking again," said the second guy. The first one got up rubbing his head and cursing under his breath, but the card game went forward.

  I had a particular burden to pray for the hard-boiled

---

[96] One daughter recalls I not only thrived under the prison regimen, but brought home the early wake-up, which I continued for a while.

Was That Thunder?

guy that did the punching. Two years later I saw him again in the same prison – just transitioning back from the state penitentiary at Graterford. I was struck with how much softer his demeanor had become -- so much so that I spoke to him about it, and told him I had prayed for him off and on over the last two years. His response was to say that he needed it, which confirmed to me that God is mightily at work in prisons – and in prayer.

WAKE-UP

A volley of electric locks murders sleep,
Executes time's judgment.
Out damned spot -- and Rover and Tray,
Out for master Pavlov's offering :

We will rehabilitate you.
We will box the quick bamboo.
We will bind the erring feet
With fear for a shackle-shoe.

With fear of fines, confines and finitudes
Without mercy, without life, without flexibility.
Open your eyes to morning that has closed --
The king all but dead among his kinsmen.

'Tis only a ghost haunts our feast, bacchanal,
Our screeching and dancing around our kettle.
We have caught lizards' eyes, and adders' tongues,
All under control, soon the spell is done.

And if we cannot clearly predispose,
At least their lives we traumatize --
For when they hate, they worship us :
Gnashing our name engraves it in stone.

Yet -- the spotted hand appears ever spotted . . .
And the unlocked hearts we cannot capture.

National Rescue and Pittsburgh

In April 1989, on another OR sponsored "National Day of Rescue," groups participated in more than sixty cities nationwide. Philly area rescuers held a rally at the end of that month, which featured a showing of the" just released" Operation Rescue video, with footage from five or six rescues around the country.

In May 1989, a group of Philadelphia rescuers set out for Pittsburgh in support of the rescue community there, which had been hammered by both the hardboiled Pittsburgh police and the even more hardboiled prison administration. [97] A rescuer from New Jersey had bought an old luxury-style bus, and obtained a chauffeur's license to drive it. So about forty-six of us loaded up and took the long ride to Pittsburgh. Non-Pennsylvanians don't realize how wide this state is. It takes the better part of a day to cross it. That night after a mini-rally, we slept on the floor of an evangelical church.

The next day thirty-eight locals joined us and we went out to one of the city aborturaries. There were about eight cops there when we arrived. They had set up a small corral of barriers around the doors. If they had just stayed inside the barriers in front of the doors, things might have been a stalemate, but they came out to the outer perimeter, which allowed a few of us to slip through and then as they scrambled to grab us, the rest got through too, so that in the end, we were inside the barriers and they moved to the outside.

That was the first time I had seen unabashed police brutality close up. Several cops deliberately kicked Keith Tucci, the local leader, in the stomach. They brought in small paddy wagons and, again, I watched as several of them deliberately kicked George Krail in the stomach and head.

George told me afterward that one of the lessons of his biker days was how to cover up effectively when being kicked – so the treatment he received from the cops did not

---

[97] I will save longer descriptions of the kinds of atrocity rescuers were subjected to there until a later point in this memoir.

do as much damage on him as it would have on most of us. I was interested to find references to this valuable defensive technique in one of Solzhenitsyn's accounts of Soviet prisons, in either the *Gulag Archipelago* or *In The First Circle*.

Up to this point I had been sitting with two or three others with my back directly against the doors. Inside the doors was a "security man," who worked for the clinic. In fact, he was also an off-duty cop and buddy of the men arresting us. This individual was infamous for investigations underway against him, including one where he had used a gun (apparently not firing it, but possibly pistol-whipping someone) at a professional athletic event. The local rescuers said he was crazy, and that if we let him out, he would be worse than the other cops. So we held the doors shut against him. The cops with reinforcements waded into us, arrested most and tossed the rest of us over the barricades.

As the arrests in Pittsburgh wound up. Holding up baby model.

After we were tossed over the barricades, things got suddenly quiet. Among the officers, I think some, anyway, were embarrassed and troubled about how others had behaved. George had been hauled away, but Keith was lying on the ground groaning. I tried to find out where he was hurt. I thought maybe they had kicked him in the privates, but it was a mixed crowd and I wasn't sure how to word my inquiry. I kept appealing to a female officer who seemed to have some authority, to get an ambulance for Keith. After a while an ambulance did come, and he was taken to the hospital instead of the police station. Apparently the cops in Pittsburgh were "gunning" for Keith, so this was desireable as an alternative destination.

Both Keith and Joe Roach were charged with assaulting an officer, which every witness found grimly ironic. Several counts of assaulting officers' boots with their faces!

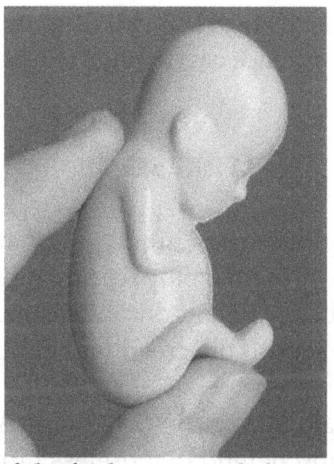

One of the fairly accurate baby models.

Meanwhile, across the street, John Maffei, from Philly, had been filming the whole thing. The cops, realizing this, marched across the street and demanded he surrender his camera. Again, I was shocked. I had not been around long enough to realize that the first amendment was not only the corrupt policeman's enemy, but something he would trample on wherever he could get away with it. John's camera was later returned to him, minus the tape. [98]

---

[98] From what I heard of the trial, I think another cameraman must have been surreptitious and successful in his efforts, because

Was That Thunder?

One mother who had been on her way to an appointment at that clinic consented to talk with our counselors, and decided to keep her baby – which was always the greatest of victories and the ultimate reason for the rescue in the first place. Furthermore, apparently because of rumors of a rescue that weekend, one Philadelphia abortion clinic scheduled no abortions! The sidewalk counselors there were pleasantly surprised to learn they had nothing to do despite the fact that the rescuers were a day's drive away.

The strangest thing to me about this rescue was that I was not arrested. Despite having been directly in front of the doors as long as anyone else, somehow I and maybe five or six others, were never taken into custody. After they threw us outside the barriers, they just ignored us. The photo taken by Charles Gindhardt shows me holding up one of the plastic baby models as the police carry other rescuers away.

ARRESTIVE

The only religious crime in old pragmatic Rome
Was to fail to adore the emperor in minor sacrifice.
Though few believed a god in him dwelt at home,
All agreed to mouth the creed was civilized and nice.

The only religious crime in pragmatic America
Is to hallow and defend defenseless human lives --
Believe God's image linked to the placenta --
Hinder hired unholy knives.

The ancient church was arrested nor treated lightly :
Lions ate unbowed limbs, human flares blazed nightly ;
But now the church rests, grown prematurely festive.
Unbow! None arrests these crimes if none grows restive.

---

apparently the threat of introducing other "footage" considerably modified police threats of charging rescuers with assault.

A Memoir of Pro-life Rescue

Grim Pro-Aborts

In June we held another rescue at Comly Road in Northeast Philadelphia. I believe this was the difficult occasion where the proaborts had our daughter Loren in tears. (We still called her "Toby" in those days.) Her brother Josh wanted to stand with us in front of the doors and Toby wanted to, too. At one point a middle-aged woman came up and did the best imitation of the Wicked Witch of the West you ever saw. She leaned over in Toby's face and lit into a hate-filled diatribe. I think she kept it up for several minutes, but not too far into it, I picked Toby up and moved her back from the front, yet the poor girl was already in tears. Not too long after that I took her over to her mother – along with Josh.[99]

Kimiko and Adriel were arrested along with me. Kim had already been arrested in New York, but I think this was Adriel's first time.

Roseann and I had decided early that we would not both risk arrest at any one rescue, so she took Loren and Josh off to the side with the other prayer supporters.

I have talked to my kids since and shared my retrospective ambivalence over involving them as we did. They don't say much. My regrets are chiefly over the kind of emotional barrages they often experienced in those settings. As far as the issues went, they had no ambivalence about saving babies! Still I'm not sure how much I would allow them to do if we were to do it over again.

There were a number of my children's friends who also got involved. I confess that I look back at this with the same ambivalence I feel about my own children's involvement. On that occasion at the Lewis Tower Building in downtown Philly, Kimiko and a number of friends were in the front lines of our group when a pro-abort took a running charge at them and basically tackled and punched Carolyn, one of the girls. The police, as per usual, paid no attention.

---

[99] Now Loren teaches kids with special learning challenges. Needless to say, she remembers that cruelty.

Carolyn insisted on staying in position, but she was definitely hurting. Not only did they receive physical abuse, but on many occasion terrible verbal abuse.

Many of the young people who were involved seem to have become the special targets of Satan's attacks thereafter. One young man and one young woman come to mind particularly. Would it have better to have discouraged their involvement in the first place?

The answers don't pop to the surface, but on the other side, I keep coming back to the reality that it was these kid's generation that was being put to death.

Young people participating in a rescue
at Northeast Women's Center.

On the other hand our generation was doing the murdering. We were the "liberated" ones who did our own thing, who bought Hugh Hefner's version of paradise on earth, and who bought the "solution" to the results of the sexual revolution and no-fault divorce, in the name of "women's rights". "Adulterer's rights" says it more accurately. Men get a great deal more out of abortion than women. They get the right to be totally irresponsible. The fathers are released from the consequences of their selfishness. The "liberated" moms are still slaves to the father's self-love and immorality.

So the kids are left to take a stand for their own generation. They are the "unwanted" generation, and the trauma is theirs whether they stand in front of abortion clinics or not.

Expectations and Efforts

Around this time there was a level of elation among pro-lifers, thinking that perhaps the Supreme Court was going to reverse Roe v. Wade. (Rumors abounded whenever there were pending cases related to abortion.)

The 135 arrested at Comly Road were found guilty by Judge Rose, but sentences and costs were suspended. [100]

In July many Philly rescuers went up to Binghamton, New York, Randy Terry's home town, and headquarters of Operation Rescue. When more than thirty of these were jailed, a few others followed. Sometime late that month I went to Binghamton with Grace Kuhar, a wonderful character and our nearest rescue neighbor (she lived just a block from our house), together with a young lady, daughter of one of the men in jail there. There were too few rescuers available to be effective that day, so we went over the local abortionist's to picket and do sidewalk counseling.

Grace and the young lady decided to try a tactic prolifers called a "Truth Mission." So by pre-arrangement they came walking along the sidewalk and we sidewalk counselors dramatically and obviously tried to give them literature and talk to them, but they brushed us off and told us (loudly) to leave them alone, as they went on up to the clinic.

There, sitting in the waiting room with other patients, they began to wonder more and more openly about the

---

[100] The judge later decided he should not have suspended the victim's compensation portion of the fine, and attempted to reinstate it. When we stuck with his first ruling – and didn't pay – we ended up going to jail in Philly – but that was the following March.

wisdom of an abortion, citing facts and statistics that your average "client" probably wouldn't know. By the time they had convinced themselves not to go through with the abortion, and got up to leave, the staff was ready to throw them out.

We didn't know if any lives were changed on that occasion, but on many other occasions similar actions did save lives. The fierce opposition with which the abortion industry fought the Pennsylvania Abortion Control Act, which includes stipulations requiring "informed consent," shows how unpopular the truth about abortion is with its advocates.

That evening I was asked to lead a group going over to the Binghamton jail to sing and pray in solidarity with those held there. The OR leadership told me I might be arrested, and with much bravado, I hoped I might be. I was not.

Cherry Hill Rescue

In August we rescued at Cherry Hill, NJ. Several of our kids friends were there, including Kevin McCall. It was this rescue where our good friend Phil, a dynamic young evangelist and beloved brother, recently burdened for the unborn, came along and rescued for the first time. He was not quite prepared for the level of hostility which we encountered. We far outnumbered the "deathscorts," but they were nevertheless incensed when we succeeded in blocking all the doors they were "guarding."

At one point a woman, her face contorted in anger, walked up to our line, and for some reason picked Phil as the punching bag upon which she unloaded her best right hook. It caught him in the stomach, and he reacted as almost any of us might (that is any of us who were not specifically prepared to react otherwise.) He reared back and prepared to return the blow. Since I happened to be next to him, I grabbed his arm and talked him down, which didn't take much really – only ten seconds in which he had time to reflect.

I was completely sympathetic to him, finding the instinct to react that way so strong in my own heart. But it was definitely not what we were about. I never saw any pro-lifer return violence for violence on any occasion – although I saw thousands of rescuers and hundreds of occasions where such a response might have seemed appropriate to someone outside the rescue movement. Repentance was the key.

On the few occasions where someone seemed about to "lose it," leaders would always intervene and ask the person either to leave, or pray with them until their composure was restored. However, I did know one or two fellows who quit rescuing because they said they didn't trust themselves not to retaliate when physically battered.

Jeff White began leading rescues in California summer of 1988, while we were rescuing in Atlanta

Jeff White points out that there were no occasions to his knowledge when a rescuer was convicted of doing anything violent during a rescue.[101]

The most "violent" thing I ever saw rescuers do was one time at a rescue in the Lewis Tower building, a proabort was going around and flashing a cheap camera in the faces of rescuers. She would reach around from behind an unwitting rescuer and flash the thing directly in his or her face. After she had been doing this for a while, someone got fed up enough to knock the camera out of her hand and step on it. Not the spirit we encouraged.

On this occasion I turned out to be a "push-over"

Not long before we were arrested at Cherry Hill, a police officer was trying to move me away from the doors by putting a hand in the middle of my back and pushing just firmly enough that I could not stand up without moving forward. I did not want to resist him, but neither did I want to be moved away so easily, so I made the decision to plant my feet. As he continued to push, I held my hands at my sides and merely toppled forward on my face. He

---

[101] Part Five of five part "The Rescue Movement". . . The Bridgehead Radio, host Jonathon Van Maren of Canada, 2015. See Youtube.

immediately said, "It wasn't me, I didn't do it!" which in a sense was true, but in another sense not. In any case, he dropped that tactic.

We were arrested and three months later fined more than 300 dollars apiece which none of us, but the New Jerseyites paid. Most of them only paid the thirty dollar victim's compensation part of the fee, because under New Jersey law, you lose your driver's license if you don't.

As was usual at Cherry Hill, what followed the arrests seemed to be dictated by the abortion industry. For instance, when we were processed, the police officials actually sat the pro-abort leader down with them and required us, after filling in all our data (name address, etc) to show these documents to her! Am I being hypersensitive to say such a procedure seems completely contrary to justice?

Then the hearings seem to have been deliberately delayed to wear us down. For instance this case was scheduled for 7 Dec 1989. It was rescheduled at the last minute to 9 Oct 1991. It was re-rescheduled to 11 Dec 1991, and finally re-re-rescheduled to 5 Feb 1992. I believe the case was actually tried then! Since all of us had to show up on each of these occasions the inconvenience was considerable and obviously intended.

Another national rescue took place in August in Los Angeles. Not many from our area went out, but a few leaders did. Heavy (felony) charges were brought against Randy Terry, Jeff White, and Mike McMonigal, but the jury found them not guilty. This was one of several times the LAPD proved to be deliberately vicious toward rescuers.

The Philadelphia Rescuers

Our local rescue leaders were a great blessing. These dedicated men and women spent countless hours working on all facets of what we were doing, with no earthly reward at all. Outstanding among them were John Stanton, Jack and Pat O'Brien, Mike McMonigal, Father McFadden, Pastor Bob Lewis, and Joe and Peg Roach. In the early days Owenna

Was That Thunder?

Nagy, Patty McNamara and Susan Odom were also active and indefatigable. But I despair of giving anything like a complete list.

I doubt I could even name two thirds of those who served as marshals at one time or another. Joe Ciepela, Pam Rizzo, Joe O'Hara, Maryann Yorina, Chuck Depoy, Linda Speirs, Joe Wall, Stephanie Claudy, Joe, John and others of the Coffui family, Ted Meehan, Susan Silcox, Gene Epps, Phil and Nancy Beachey, Walt and Laura Gies, Brenda Caley, Linda Beckman, Nancy Kocs-Kennedy, Nancy Major, Bill Devlin, Gene Kreuger, Jo Christoff and sixty or seventy more!

The Philadelphia Rescue movement was primarily Catholic in its early leadership and the majority of its constituents. At its peak, possibly half of those participating were Protestants. But the local leadership remained largely Catholic. There was often a Catholic mass before a rescue. The rallies were often (but by no means always) held in Catholic churches. There were many priests and a number of nuns who participated.

Jack O'Brien, another faithful and gentle servant

On the other hand, men like Bob Lewis, Lou Prontnicki, and Bill Devlin were faithful representatives of the Protestant side, and many of the rallies were held in Baptist or Presbyterian churches: Bob Lewis' or ours', for instance.

The strength which the Catholic leadership had was a consistency, a willingness and sense of responsibility about following up on the nitty-gritty details. Few Protestants seemed capable of sustaining it.

Curiously, on the national scene after 1988, the opposite was true – Operation Rescue was by and large a Protestant organization (both Randy and Keith were Pentecostal) with only one Catholic among its top leaders, our own Mike McMonigal. Of course the earlier PLAN was largely made up of Catholics, and Joan Andrews was the most famous. Other widely respected Catholics included our own John Stanton and Mike McMonigal.

After another rescue at Planned Parenthood at the end of September, several clergymen from our area, including Mike Chastain of Maryland and our own Bill Devlin, helped put together a "Clergy Rescue". A special effort was made to recruit clergymen, with the idea that these "leaders" would thereafter be more likely to mobilize their congregations. A lovely idea, if not a particularly realistic one.

Many of the Protestant pastors bought themselves reverse or "dog" collars, for the occasion, including Bill Devlin! Most wore these with gray shirts rather than black – thus distinguishing themselves from the Catholics. It seemed to us ironical that these men would go "high church" at the prospect of going to jail.

Bill Devlin and I got to know each other well, and our families had fairly close ties – not only through rescue and other pro-life activities, but through church and schools, as well.

A tall, angular man of distinguished appearance, but a puckish demeanor, Bill was a navy veteran, a nurse, and one of the most gregarious human beings I've ever known. He is also one of the most affirmative, to the degree that I once told him that we could not grow closer as friends until he quit agreeing with everything I said. I used to oversimplify our relationship by saying he was the adult son of an alcoholic, while I was the son of an adult son of an alcoholic! So all my defenses went up in reaction to all his defenses![102]

Bill Devlin, Presbyterian elder and activist

But we believed in the same things. We also ministered together at a local nursing home. And we enjoyed each other's jokes. One of Bill's more familiar jokes which he tended to recycle at various speaking engagements went like this. "When I get up in the morning," he said, "I like to read my Bible, and afterward I read *the Inquirer*. {Suitable pause} I try to give equal time to both sides." I owe Bill more credit for encouraging me than I often grudgingly gave him.

The Clergy Rescue

On a weekday in mid-October at Women's Suburban

---

[102] Bill is still taking risks in dangerous places of the world -- mostly for Jesus -- and a little for his adrenaline addiction.

Clinic in Paoli, a group including quite a number of clergymen gathered for a rescue. The weather turned wet, and it was a while before Tredyferin Township decided what to do with us. Eventually 126 rescuers were arrested and taken immediately to Chester County prison, where we were refused to give our names. This was partly as "leverage" for being released on our own recognizance without having to put up the $10,000 bail stipulated! (We had never failed to come to court, and this jurisdiction was aware of the fact.) But in those days Chester County still wanted to "play hardball."

Another among their tactics was to charge two rescuers with felony assault. The basis of this was that the two tried to climb over a retaining wall to get in front of the door before the police. It might not have been the best judgment, but it was in no sense assault, at least not on the rescuer's side. These two had bail set at $25,000.

All of the male rescuers were kept in the "tank," a concrete holding cell which was maybe fifteen by fifteen feet in size, while the women were kept in other holding cells. There were so many of us in the tank that there was no room for most to sit, so we divided into three shifts, taking turns standing, sitting and lying down.

This became another wonderful time of intensive retreat, with much teaching, sharing, praying, and worshipful singing, sometimes antiphonal with the women whose cells were close enough that we could hear each other. The warm sound of quiet conversations and group prayers filled the unstructured times.

The most meaningful time for me came the next morning, when still in the tank. Bill suggested we take an hour for silent meditation and prayer. It was amazing to have that many men packed closely, yet silent together for that long. I started off as I always do in jail, reading my Bible, but I found myself struggling in prayer with a simple idea.

"Lord" I said, "I want my life to be yours. I want you to be in charge of everything. I want more of you." And as I meditated on this, and how little it really seemed to be true of me, it was as if the Lord spoke back to me and said. "I don't want to be <u>more</u> for you, I don't want to be <u>enough</u> – I want to be <u>everything</u>."

Clergy rescue, out of the rain, direct to jail.

No audible voice, but a certain and specific communication and conviction. The awe and joy I felt at that revelation, at that lesson or leading, was profound. I had lost my first love as a Christian, and even the deep sense of meaning and significance of repentance I had experienced in Atlanta, but now the Lord was calling me back to something as important -- shifting the center of the kingdom from me to Him.

The rest of that time was also very rich. I remember talking with a cowled Catholic brother during our last hours there, and listening as he spoke of his vision of a Catholic church which included all the Protestants again – as internal divisions, sort of like "orders". While I doubt that will happen anytime soon or in that form, the overall vision of a unity among Christians is a winsome one to me, nor does it feel so remote, having seen such measures of unity among rescuers.

One thing I gained during my time in the rescue movement, was the ability to participate in worship even where I disagreed. I could worship in a Catholic mass, although I cannot say the last lines of the "Hail Mary" or go along with many other things that seem to me bad theology. The funny thing is that I've gained the ability to worship with other Protestants and even in my own church in a similar way. I can participate up to the point where I think something is wrong, and there I can be silent. It isn't about me, after all.

In early October, Randy Terry was sentenced to two years in prison in Fulton County, Georgia. Randy took a hard line in court, refusing to accept a fine and banishment, but prison proved a very trying time for him, perhaps because retreat and meditation were not the strongest facets of his practice or character. It was complicated for Randy in that he and his wife Cindy were foster parents for several years, and the New York Department of Social Services was threatening to take the foster children away.

There were also issues of finances, and God's direction for them. Roseann and I knew from our own much smaller separations, that rescue could be trying for a marriage. Later, at a national leader's convention in Chicago, Randy said that the Lord had used this time to humble him.

Veteran's Rescue

In November 1989, Art Tomlinson of OR put together a Veteran's Rescue to be held in Washington DC. This was in conjunction with a subsequent series of national rescues called the DC Project.

On the 10th a Memorial Service was held near the Vietnam Memorial Wall. There we veterans renewed our armed services oath to defend the US against all enemies, foreign and domestic.

That evening our rally featured Mike McMonigal, the Philadelphia leader who was also an Annapolis graduate. He asked me to lead in prayer at the end. Recognizing that we were together a peculiar "school of the prophets," I asked all the church leaders there to raise their hands in blessing and supplication as we prayed.

On the 11th, 203 men and women in uniform were arrested at the doors of an abortion clinic in DC. These included a Navy Captain, several Annapolis and West Point graduates, a legless, highly decorated Marine, many career military officers, as well as wide range of other officers and enlisted men and women from all uniformed branches of the service, many of them war vets. I was there in my glorious Army sergeant's uniform.

There was an anarchist group there, too, pretending to be veterans themselves, aggressively threatening bystanders and trying to attack the rescuers. The police intervened, but did not arrest any of them, I'm sorry to say, not even when these men openly and loudly called the legless marine officer a coward and a baby-killer.

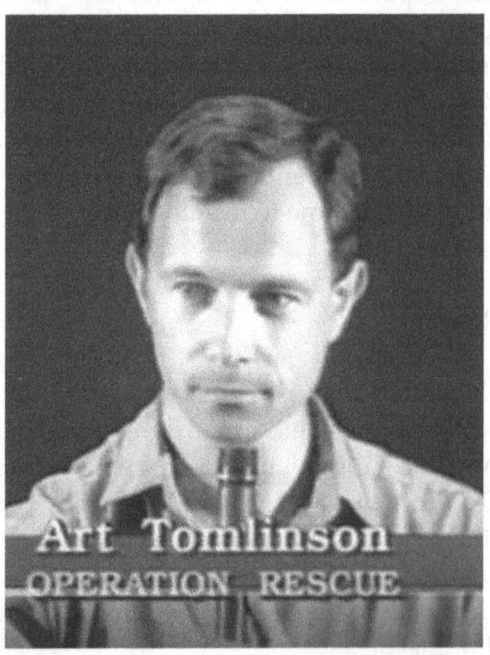

The police themselves had very little evident respect for our uniforms or our purpose. Perhaps they also despised us. Nevertheless, it was humbling to remember the oath we all took to defend our country against its enemies, and yet to be treated like enemies ourselves. It is true, however, that we had another uniform and another and higher allegiance:

The anarchist group surrounding the Vets Rescue issued a fascinating broadside, a copy of which I still have somewhere, which at one and the same time, accused pro-lifers of depriving women of their right to abortion and yet held us responsible for the large-scale sterilization of native American women! Their statistics may have been off a little, and their attributions certainly were off! But in fact "abortion rights" and "birth control" groups have succeeded in sterilizing an astonishingly high percentage of Native American women of child-bearing age. What kind of people know these horrible facts, yet vehemently defend abortion, to the point of deliberately lying and accusing pro-lifers of causing the other results of the eugenicists' agenda?

Roseann and Mike McMonigal at the Vets Rescue in Wash., DC.

Later in November, also in Washington, the "DC Project" series of rescues followed the Vets Rescue. Our family stayed overnight in a motel. There we watched the Berlin Wall coming down via TV. Probably most Berliners never thought they'd see the day. That same night in the Land of the Free, pro-aborts punctured a tire on ours and

Was That Thunder?

several other cars [103] in the motel parking lot.

And they didn't quit there. When we gathered in a shopping center parking lot the next day, they dispatched a team to flatten the tires on the rented buses! They succeeded with several, before we abandoned that approach and loaded everyone in private cars. We drove to an aborutary in Virginia. Large numbers of proaborts soon arrived, but we had hundreds of people in front of the doors already.

State troopers soon came on the scene. They tried several approaches to moving us when warnings didn't work. At one point they even brought attack dogs in, but a more level-headed supervisor told the handlers that was crazy and ordered them to take the dogs away. That may have inspired him, though, for soon they brought in horse cops.

The horses were well trained. Their rider's technique was to whirl as they gradually moved into the crowd. Those big animals were fairly scary when spinning at high speed like that, but they were also pretty amazing in their ability to avoid stepping on anyone. They seemed to have a sixth sense by which they even stepped over a person or two who had fallen down.

The pro-lifers just clung together and let the horses keep pushing them more tightly against the building. Suddenly a big plate glass window exploded from the pressure. The troopers backed off, and that technique was scrapped, too.

This was my son's Joshua's eleventh birthday, and I was proud that he was willing to be doing something so much the opposite of "celebrating." To make matters worse, the pro-aborts there had a diabolical approach. They stood together in front of the younger and more innocent-looking children and talked as loud and explicitly as they could about various sex acts, etcetera.

We were singing "A Mighty Fortress is our God" and other worship songs together. I prayed up a storm that God would protect those children's hearts and minds. Kimiko remembers that Joshua climbed a tree, from which replied to

---

[103] Our bumper stickers made it clear which cars were ours.

the raucous proabort cheer. Theirs, which we heard over and over, went "Pro-life, your name's a lie, you don't care if women die." Joshua replied with the variation, "Pro-choice, your name's a lie, when do babies choose to die!" The pro-lifers who heard him were moved. His was not loud, but heartfelt. Roseann says she remembers tears running down Joshua's cheeks. What a picture of the real battle and the real warriors!

Driving back toward DC and our motel, there was a great parade of pro-life cars, pro-abort cars and law enforcement vehicles. A friend of ours was driving her own car on the highway when the traffic in front of her slowed suddenly. She was able to stop in time to avoid a forward collision, but the guy behind her was not so alert. He smashed into the back of her car. He then got out and, reaching in, pulled a radiophone off his dash, over which he talked for a while. She got out and said, "Are you all right?" He had a big wry grin on his face. "Ya," he said, "Come over here." She walked back to his car which was covered in aerials, and he pointed in at the dashboard – it was a huge array of electronic gadgetry. Obviously this guy was some kind of a plain-clothes cop. She thought he must be FBI. But to him it was kind of a joke. Perhaps he recognized the many ironies involved.

Also in November 1989, the Pennsylvania Abortion Control Act was passed by the legislature and sent over to Governor Casey who soon signed it. True to form, injunctions and appeals were immediately put forward to block it. Again, pro-lifers were somewhat hopeful that this might end up in a Supreme Court case that would put a substantial dent in Roe.

It was during November that Mike McMonigal received a six month sentence for the "siege of Atlanta," charged with obstructing a highway and aiding and abetting others to do the same. He, too, struggled with being away from his pregnant wife, Ceil (the child's birth was imminent), and from the rest of his family, his work, and the pro-life community of Philadelphia. But he used the time well, and had many faithful saints praying for him. At the end of

Was That Thunder?

December he was released on appeal, after a family member paid a reduced fine of $2000.

The judge cited sympathy for his pregnant wife as the reason for his release! As George Krail observed on a similar occasion in Chester County, "Isn't it interesting that an unborn child is the one that gets us off!"

On December 8th, 101 people were arrested at Chester Crozer, but no charges were brought. At least two women indicated they had changed their minds after talking with our counselors. The former Baptist seminary library was normally the scene of about 40 abortions on a Friday, but apparently no more than a few appointments were kept that day. Meanwhile another respected rescuer, Tom Herlihy, was serving a long sentence for rescuing there previously. He thus inspired courage in the rest of us. Probably his perseverance and willingness to serve that long sentence was a major reason most of us who followed never spent any time in jail for rescues there.

Two local rescue friends: Dave Miller and George Krail

In mid-December in hearings for civil contempt against Mike McMonigal and Operation Rescue, the directors of the six aborturies in the area testified that the rescues of 1989 caused approximately 139 mothers not to keep their appointments -- either on the day of the rescue or another day! That was quite a testimony to the effects of our meager efforts. Particularly in light of Planned Parenthood's own statistics that claimed only 20% of women who miss an appointment will fail to reschedule an abortion.

But even in the first few years there were costs to rescuers. Among the thousands who rescued a few times, there were many who decided the cost was too high. I remember two in particular who I don't blame for quitting.

One was a mother with a teenage daughter who the Cherry Hill police deliberately held back in the processing – and through my own fault, since I was her contact person – I missed the fact that these two were not released with the rest of us. The Mom was then threatened with all sorts of dire things: being charged with contributing to the delinquency of a minor, losing custody of her daughter, etcetera. And she was not released for another two or three hours, by which time she was nearly frantic. This would not have happened were it not for my sloppy "leadership," but the effect was obviously to considerably dampen the woman's enthusiasm!

Similarly, a woman from our own congregation was driving in the suburbs with her son, and another woman, when a local policeman pulled her over, and proceeded to do the standard radio check of her license. When he discovered that she had several outstanding bench warrants, due to non-payment of fines, which was our general policy as I've said, he took her into custody, including cuffs and shackles!

Had her friend not been with her, her son would probably have been taken into protective custody, too! Not only did she then pay all her fines, but she quit rescuing in fear of future implications for her family's welfare. Not only that, but others in our church reacted to this event in the same way.

Who can weigh these sorts of things? Especially for others! In the end we had to be thankful that so many pushed the limits and took personal risks so far beyond the rest of the American church.

High school girls at a woman's rescue.

CHAPTER FOUR – THE DECISIVE DECADE (1990)

> God standeth in the congregation of the mighty; he judgeth among the gods. How long will ye judge unjustly, and accept the persons of the wicked? Selah. Defend the poor and fatherless; do justice to the afflicted and needy. Deliver the poor and needy; rid them out of the hand of the wicked.
> Psalm 82:1-4

The last decade of the 20th century turned out to be period of metamorphosis. Hitherto during the battle against legalized execution of babies, the American church had been asleep, but it was beginning to awaken. It was awakening not only to the physical reality of what abortion is and how widespread, but the spiritual implications it held for our country and world. The most measurable result was in the political arena. It seems incontrovertible in retrospect to say that the rescue movement had something to do with this turning, though at the time this was not obvious.

Developments in 1990

During January 1990, our church held pro-life classes for the adult Sunday School. Our first class focused simply on the evidence that abortion was murder. More than a "sound bite," this is the crux and keystone of the prolife position. If abortion were not murder, then prolifers would indeed be foolish. But the evidence of the Bible is incontrovertible along with that of biology. While our Catholic brethren generally believed the scientific arguments might be enough to persuade others, we insisted the Bible was foundational, and that science alone would not persuade an unregenerate mind. [104] So we focused on five or six major passages as foundational for further arguments from biology and traditional ethics.

Psalm 51 is my favorite. In it David tells us he was shaped in iniquity and that his mother conceived him in sin. There aren't a lot of alternative interpretations for this passage. Either we conclude that David was seriously bad-mouthing his own mother, or we agree he is saying something about the point at which he became identified with sin. If he was "in sin" at his conception, then he was a human being – for no other creature (except angels who are not conceived) is sinful. If we were sinners at conception then we were human at conception. Not too complicated.

Mary and Elizabeth, greetings in utero.

My second favorite passage about the humanity of the unborn has profound implications for our understanding of the incarnation and the gospel. It is the hymn Elisabeth sings when she greets Mary.[105] Boiled down to basics, here we have one unborn child recognizing, greeting and praising

---

[104] Of course the Bible isn't going to persuade an unregenerate mind, either! But it, and the preaching of its message, is the primary medium through which hearts and minds are regenerated under the agency of the Holy Spirit.

[105] Luke 1:39-44

another unborn child! Are we to interpret this as merely an externally managed (deus ex machina) miracle – like Baalam's otherwise inarticulate ass speaking?

No, for the passage tells us that the thing which caused John the Baptist to leap in utero was joy! Can one experience joy and not be human?

The passage also drives us to ask the more difficult question – when did the "incarnation" of Christ occur in history?

When was Jesus fully himself? At birth? Are we to imagine that Jesus, the "fetus" was merely a potential person, until he was pushed from his mother's womb, and that suddenly upon emerging he became not only fully man, but fully God! [106] Or do we accept that this incredible miracle, like most of God's work, took place according to the ordinary processes he created – and that Jesus was at the same time fully God and fully man – that is, at the moment when the Holy Spirit "overshadowed" Mary. Although he was a mere "conceptus," like any other child in the womb, he was completely himself -- growing in size but not changing in nature from there on.

This gets into the greatest of mysteries – near the heart of great controversies. The Catholic view of Mary (as sinless) and for this reason contributing only sinless humanity to Jesus' conception is a case in point. But true mysteries are not "solved," thus we are all kept humble by them, regardless of our theological differences. In any case John the Baptist "in utero" rejoiced over the "in utero" Jesus. Two human beings communicating with each other before birth.[107]

---

[106] Fully God and fully man is the formulation of the Chalcedonian Creed, from the Council of Chalcedon, 451AD. It was arrived at on the basis of Scripture – over against false teaching that divided Jesus' humanity and divinity in various ways.

[107] I remember a high school biology teacher rationalizing the virgin birth of Jesus by telling us, his students, that there were records of other cases of human "parthenogenesis," specifically one in the twentieth century in Mexico. In fact that was a complete fabrication.

Was That Thunder?

We also discussed the passage in Exodus 21, verses 22-25, which is so badly translated in the Revised Standard and American Standard Bibles, but is accurate in the King James and several modern translations. It is very germaine to

---

Modern "cloning" has proven that "parthenogenesis" is impossible. None of the "higher mammals" can produce offspring without external cell material – even where a ewe's genes are duplicated by laboratory means. Furthermore, no female creature (with but a few exceptions among the "lower animals") can produce a male offspring without a male progenitor.

Jerome Lejeune, the French geneticist who discovered the cause of Down's syndrome (trisomy), testified at length in a couple of US court cases. He spoke of some remarkable facts about human life at its beginnings. But the underlying theme of all his testimony is that God has made us unique from conception – that we are "fearfully and wonderfully made" from that point on.

Geneticists say the amount of information contained in human genetic material, were each element of the code translated into a single letter, would amount to a hundred volumes of a good-sized encyclopedia. Note that this is only the "blueprint." In addition to this, the "conceptus" also contains the timetable and the step-by-step procedural information for "building" each and every part and system of the individual in the proper order, beginning with the first division from one to two cells! How many more libraries would that information take to record!

Science shows us the "fetus" (Latin for "baby" pure and simple) has a detectable heartbeat two and a half weeks after conception, and detectable "brain waves" five and a half weeks after conception. The fetus has its own DNA, its own fingerprints, and its own gender. All the science accrues on the side of the humanity of the unborn. Is it any wonder you never hear a proabort citing the facts of embryology?

The closest you get to embryology from a proabort, is the slogan "ontogeny recapitulates phylogeny," a thoroughly debunked motto of nineteenth century "science," which essentially means that we (and all creatures) actually repeat our "evolution" as we progress through the stages of embryological growth. Next to the bogus diagram of horse evolution in our biology books, we were often given a diagram showing a human embryo developing from fish to salamander to rodent to ape, etcetera. Modern intra-uterine photography and embryology have shown this is baloney.

abortion since it talks about the proper legal penalties for someone negligently striking a pregnant woman. The difference in the translations is exactly along the lines of the proabort vs. prolife argument – whether harm to the unborn child is to be treated as equivalent to harm to any other person. The accurate translations say it is. The inaccurate ones add two words that are not present or implied in the Hebrew.[108]

We further discussed Psalm 139 (verses 13-16) which speaks of how each of us is "fearfully and wonderfully made" and designed by God from the very beginning, each in his "mother's womb".

Civil Disobedience – Biblical?

The second week of Sunday classes we looked at "civil disobedience" from a biblical perspective. On this subject as well, a Bible survey gives the Christian a solid foundation.[109]

Since this had been a very difficult issue for me to work through, I was very sympathetic with the questions and doubts of others. Most of us had been raised with a high respect for law and law officers. Even those of us who had less respect for government and its machinations knew that

---

[108] Several decades ago, *Christianity Today* carried two articles advocating the alternative "positions" on this passage – and the humanity of the unborn. The opposing author subsequently submitted to the more accurate reading of the passage which requires the unborn child be defended with the full weight of the law (eye for eye, life for life), thus as "human" in God's eyes.

[109] This issue was the one opponents of rescue spoke about most. Unfortunately a number of generally respected evangelical teachers had not done their New Testament homework, including John MacArthur, James Boice, and Charles Stanley. Their opposition appeared connected with other loyalties, as of that of MacArthur toward Assistant LA Police Chief, Bob Vernon. Vernon was in authority over LA officers who used nunchuks on rescuers there – see later chapters. Other respected Protestant leaders like D. James Kennedy, Jerry Falwell, and James Dobson were early and openly supportive of rescue.

honesty and submission to elected and appointed officials was part of the Christian life. Almost all of us equated lawbreaking with criminality and knew there was no place for criminal behavior among Christ's followers. We were puzzled by the Bible passages which show the apostles more or less defying constituted authority, but had always justified this by saying the Roman and Palestinian governments were pagan, and the elders of Israel legalistic and unbelieving.

Closer study of the Bible had brought us to a different perspective, which we shared in our Sunday classes, in the form of several biblical principles.

First, the Bible tells us God ordained the civil authorities to punish evildoers and care for or protect the righteous. [110]

We are commanded to submit to them for a number of reasons. The Reformers saw this as an extension of the command to honor thy Father and thy Mother. If it's important enough to be included in the Ten Commandments, it is the rule, and any acceptable departure from it is an exception. But the three leading apostles show us situations under which the exception is legitimate.

First, Peter and John responded to the high priest's and the elders' command that they "speak henceforth to no man in this [Jesus'] name," with the famous words, "Whether it be right in the sight of God to hearken unto you more than unto God, judge ye. For we cannot but speak the things which we have seen and heard." [111] Some argue this passage shows only one exception to civil submission --when if it has to do with preaching the gospel – that we can only disobey the civil authorities when they tell us to quit speaking of Jesus. But notice the apostles didn't get into trouble on this occasion for preaching, but for <u>doing</u> something in Jesus name, namely healing someone.

And the Apostle Paul gives us further evidence. In the wonderfully ironic passage where he "brags"of his

---

[110] See Romans 13, I Peter 2, Titus 3.
[111] See Acts 4.

credentials,[112] he winds up the long list with an account of his escape from Damascus, where:

> ...the governor under Aretas the king kept the city of the Damascenes with a garrison, desirous to apprehend me; And through a window in a basket was I let down by the wall, and escaped his hands. (verses 32-33)

Paul, the leading apostle to the Gentiles, he who gave us two of the three passages about submission to civil authority, enlisted accomplices and deliberately evaded legally constituted law enforcement officers seeking his arrest. This was to act in direct contravention of civil law and order, no doubt compounding a felony or two!

The *Westminster Confession* formulates it thus:

> To assert that civil authority is of divine origin is not to say that it is unlimited... As long as civil government is content to punish crime and violence, protecting the good and punishing the evil, the Christian must support, pray for, and honor that government. But when that government punishes the righteous and rewards the evil... it is the duty of Christians to resist that power because it subverts the ordinance of God." [113]

The exception to civil obedience is very simply divine obedience. Where the commands or prohibitions of the civil authority directly oppose the biblical prohibitions or commands of God, the man of God must obey the latter. This is not to say that we should not obey evil rulers in neutral things, nor even that we should not bend over backward to be submissive wherever possible despite some injustice to ourselves, but only that absolute obedience is to be given to

---

[112] II Corinthians 11

[113] Westminster Confession of Faith, Chapter XXIII. Those who find this topic of great interest may want to go back to the Calvin quote in the early pages of Chapter Two.

Was That Thunder?

only one Ruler: He before whom all scepters must bow.
    I wrote this meditation on the danger of absolute obedience to human authority:

THE CENTURIONS

We the dead salute you. So they say centurions said:
An admirable vow, though morbid. Indeed we all are dead
Before long, and why not join mortality to some scheme :
An empire, a cause, a fraternal effort or dream?
But if Caesar dreams a roaring pyre fueled with the wood
Of soldier limbs, soldier vows and fool-hardihood --
As often he did: if Caesar be Genghis Khan, Nero, or Stalin,
Is blind loyalty admirable among the files or the fallen?

It is said there was no captive of faith in all Israel,
Like that centurion who carried his mantle well,
Knowing how to obey orders and how to issue commands --
Under authority, yet with power in his hands
To send, enforce, call back -- seeing with other eyes,
Which earned death-bound praise, a backward Caesar's prize.
Rome could not hold his allegiance against one higher.
He submitted to a leader pledged to perish on a pyre.

Not as diplomatic perhaps as Capernaum's soldier saint,
Peter claimed his prerogative, a higher law's restraint,
'Whether it's right to obey man or God, you must decide,
But as for us we'll obey God,' for which salute some died.
Two armies, then, we may descry, centurions heading each:
One bows before "the law," in no case brooks its breach;
The other saluting one dead who lives, sure of no law but his.
Lest we think this impractical, we should remember this:

At Nuremburg soldier files saluted another Reich,
Testifying to absolute faith in a Caesar not unlike
Old Rome's, saying "we obeyed our legal orders,"
Raising consternation among both their judges and warders,
Who, though relativists, like so many in judgment's hall,

Could not excuse the enormity of the infamy withal.
Indicted under some higher law, those brought before the bar,
Got death's salute for obeying a law that was but of their Czar.

As I have said, I was a "civil legalist,"[114] myself, before becoming involved in rescue. Many American evangelicals are unquestioning "law and order" people. Justice and mercy under God are the higher principles upon which all good law and good order are based. The transition had been painful for me, but I believe it is one most Christians in the rest of the world have already gone through.

The third week of January our Sunday class discussed the spiritual significance of the unborn. We looked at the scriptures, particularly the prophetic books, which speak of the weakest and least powerful members of a community: the orphan, the outcast, the stranger and the poor. We looked through the lenses of James 1:27 [115] and Matthew 25.[116] The conclusion we came to was twofold: first, that how a people treats their children or orphans shows who they worship. The worshipper of Baal and Moloch sacrifices his firstborn to those gods. But our second conclusion was that those who worship the true God, recognize <u>themselves</u> as orphans, widows, helpless, naked, blind, prisoners, strangers and outcasts. Ezekiel 16 gives us this picture in Technicolor.[117]

God found and rescued us in the discarded, unwanted, and helpless condition of bondage to sin. He saved us from death and destruction, therefore it ought to be second nature for us to want to see others in analogous

---

[114] Aka: Erastian, a term somewhat inaccurately coined by Richard Hooker to describe someone who believed the civil authority ought to be superior to that of the church. He took the term from Thomas Erastus, a Zwinglian Swiss theologian who opposed church excommunication as unscriptural, advocating instead punishment by civil authorities. He said the state had both the right and the duty to punish all offenses, ecclesiastical as well as civil.

[115] See epigraph, beginning of next chapter.
[116] See epigraph, beginning of previous chapter.
[117] See epigraph, beginning of Chapter Two.

condition saved, and to have a special compassion for them.

More Rescues, More Lessons

During our last week of pro-life classes we emphasized the great importance of repentance as the keynote of our opposition to abortion – that it was "our sin," intimately linked to our idolatries, sensuality, lusts, and greed. We spoke of the need to repent of our cowardice (fear of man) as well. Ironically, in the midst of these classes, on January 13, we had a rescue at Cherry Hill, which sobered me up a good deal. I came face to face again with the reality of the spiritual warfare we were involved in. I had gradually lost track of what I first learned in Atlanta, that rescue was as much an act of repentance as an act of confronting evil. I had lost track of my conviction in the "tank" at Chester County during the Clergy Rescue – so that Jesus as not "my all" on this occasion. Indeed I went out to Cherry Hill with entirely the wrong attitude.

There were two women associated with the abortion industry in Philadelphia who seemed to show up at almost every rescue – working for NARAL[118] and/or for a consortium of Philly area abortionists. One of them was there on this occasion, and since I was one of the marshals before the doors, she made me a particular object of her harassment.

I stepped away from the group at one point to see what was going on around the corner. When I came back, she had moved a line of her people in front of our group, so that I could not get back to them. Instead of patiently bearing this, I became angry, and on the spur of the moment made up a stupid stratagem. I pretended I was looking down around the corner, where neither she nor the police could see, and began to shout as though there was some kind of altercation taking place there.

Instead of luring the pro-aborts away, as I had intended, I only incensed the cops, who grabbed me, threw

---

[118] National Abortion Rights Action League.

me down and cuffed me. It was the best thing that could have happened. It didn't take me much reflection to see that I could not possibly lead others well if I was not in proper spiritual condition myself.

Kimiko, Adriel, and one of their friends were also arrested there. We parents had to show up in Camden at Family Court and sign some paperwork. They were given juvenile releases without much ado. [119]

Annual March for Life in Washington, D.C.

Many prolifers from Philadelphia once more attended the National March for Life in Washington DC. Although crowd estimations are notoriously unreliable, I well recall looking down the wide Constitution Avenue from the hill near the Capitol to see it solid with people for its entire length. Year after year hundreds of thousands of people, totaling millions, come from all over the country. There has never been any other movement in American history that could consistently mobilize these numbers of people – and no

---

[119] Kim remembers Roseann taking her to Village Thrift to buy a "court outfit". They found themselves 25 cents short, when in the door walked Linda Sauerwald, who when Roseann asked for financial help, reached down and pulled quarter out of her sock! Jehovah Jireh.

movement that ever gathered such a crowd with so few motives of "self-interest".

Those on the platform have included many moving speakers. Sad to say, the earlier marches also included some who later sold out and became public proponents of abortion – like Dick Gephardt and Jesse Jackson. [120]

Jesse Jackson's stand against abortion was strong in the 70's. He called abortion "genocide" in a *Jet* magazine article in March 1973. Jesse and Dick Gregory spoke vigorously against abortion in 1975, and Jesse was scheduled to speak on the platform at the March for Life in 1978, but was too ill to attend. In January 1977, in an article for the *Right to Life News*, he opened with these observations:

> The question of "life" is *The Question* of the 20th century. Race and poverty are dimensions of the life question, but discussions about abortion have brought the issue into focus in a much sharper way. How we will respect and understand the nature of life itself is the over-riding moral issue, not of the Black race, but of the human race.
>
> The question of abortion confronts me in several different ways. First, although I do not profess to be a biologist, I have studied biology and know something about life from the point of view of the natural sciences. Second, I am a minister of the Gospel and therefore, feel that abortion has a religious and moral dimension that I must consider.
>
> Third, I was born out of wedlock (and against the advice that my mother received from her doctor) and therefore abortion is a personal issue for me. From my perspective, human life is the highest good, the *summum bonum* . Human life itself is the highest human good and

---

[120] Al Gore, too, was "pro-life" early in his political career. During his first term in the House he voted on 17 abortion measures and had taken the pro-life position 13 times. It was not until his 1985 Senate bid that he began to flip-flop, but even in 1987 he still said negative things about abortion and spoke against federal funding thereof.

God is the supreme good because He is the giver of life. That is my philosophy. Everything I do proceeds from that religious and philosophical premise.

Life is the highest good and therefore you fight for life, using means consistent with that end. Ufe is the highest human good not on its own naturalistic merits, but because life is supernatural, a gift from God. Therefore, life is the highest human good because life is sacred. . . . only once in a while do the egg and sperm bring about fertilization. Some call that connection accidental, but I choose to call it providential. It takes three to make a baby: a man, a woman and the Holy Spirit.

Former fervent pro-lifer Jesse Jackson

Jesse went on to confront the "population control" agenda of the pro-aborts:

> . . . I raise two issues at this point: (1) It is strange that they choose to start talking about population control at the same time that Black people in America and people of color around the world are demanding their rightful place as human citizens and their rightful share of the material wealth in the world. (2) People of color are for the most part powerless with regard to decisions made about population control. Given the history of people of

color in the modern world we have no reason to assume that whites are going to look out for our best interests.

Politicians argue for abortion largely because they do not want to spend the necessary money to feed, clothe and educate more people. Here arguments for inconvenience and economic savings take precedence over arguments for human value and human life. I read recently where a politician from New York was justifying abortion because they had prevented 10,000 welfare babies from being born and saved the state $15 million. In my mind serious moral questions arise when politicians are willing to pay welfare mothers between $300 to $1000 to have an abortion, but will not pay $30 for a hot school lunch program to the already born children of these same mothers. [121]

We got to the gathering place for the March for Life early, There was a guy near the speaker's platform with a strange sign. We talked to him and found out his schtick -- that he thought we ought to change the name of abortion to something else, since "abortion" classically referred to natural miscarriage, not to deliberate ending of a baby's life. Kimiko told me afterward that stood out in her mind as a paradigm of majoring in the minors. Here we were with a million and a

---

[121] Jesse Jackson was pushed out of Ralph Abernathy's SCLC, in 1971 and founded Operation PUSH the membership of which Jackson referred to as a "Rainbow Coalition" from the beginning. The name "Rainbow Coalition" was first used in 1968 by Chicago Black Panther, Fred Hampton to describe the multi-ethnic federation he founded. Though not a member and often at odds with the Panthers, Jackson copyrighted the name, preventing others from using it. In 1984, as part of his presidential campaign, Jackson called for Arab-Americans, Native-Americans, Asian-Americans, young people, disabled veterans, poor farmers, gays and lesbians to join African and Jewish-Americans in a political movement. It is extremely ironic to see what a symbol, which once stood for a pro-life agenda, has now become. If I recall, God gave the rainbow to Noah as a sign the world would never again be destroyed by flood – but by fire next time!

half babies dying from legal, elective abortion, and this guy's campaign was to change the name of the procedure! The futility of academic precision! [122]

One of the most memorable March for Lifes was when our family rode down to DC on a bus from St. Ambrose, the Catholic church next to ours. We had a good time getting to know many on the bus. The rally and march were great, but Joshua, my thirteen year old, feeling comfortable among the national pro-life family, and perhaps testing his wings of independence a little, got separated from us during the march. When he asked a policeman how to get to the intersection where he accurately remembered the bus was supposed to pick us up, the cop followed official protocol and detained him as a lost child.

Our whole busload from St. Ambrose went through an anxious hour and a half before the proper police procedure resulted in him being delivered back to us. A large cheer, followed by a prayer of thanksgiving was offered up by all. Needless to say, we Protestants were once more humbled before the Catholic brethren!

Also in January 1990, Randy Terry got out of jail in Atlanta through agreeing to the Georgia court's requirements. He had spent part of his time on a chain gang.

On the 3rd of February, a "Women's Rescue" took place at Planned Parenthood and Blackwell Center in Philadelphia, while another rescue went on at Northeast Women's Center. The "rally" or "information night" for this rescue was divided between two churches – one in the western suburbs, and our own building on Roosevelt Boulevard in Philadelphia. The double rescue in Center City (the two abortuaries are only a block or so apart) was led by women and the majority of the rescuers were women.

Most of the male rescuers went to a third site, the abortuary in the Northeast. It was the first time in

---

[122] One sign I remember more distinctly was one carried by a proabort woman at PP during one rescue in Philly. It read, "My mother didn't have a choice." There was endless speculation about that one!

Was That Thunder?

Philadelphia we had a completely silent rescue. Usually we had singing and prayer and even speakers during rescues, but the women decided they wanted reverent silence the whole time they remained before the doors.

A Women's Rescue included our daughters
and some of their friends

It was quite moving. Someone brought roses and every woman held a single rose. 151 women were arrested, with 25 or so left before the doors when Blackwell closed. Meanwhile, 36 men and one woman were arrested at the Northeast, for a total of 188 arrested – 48 of them first-timers. Roseann "shared her testimony" before the other women in custody at the Police Academy. She actually preached, but we never admit that. Over the ensuing years I heard myself quoted from her testimony on the proper perspective when being carried away from the clinic doors, "Just relax and think of yourself being carried to heaven by angels."

A number of rescuers from our area, including Joe Roach, went to Burlington, Vermont, early that year. This hardcore jurisdiction had been giving long sentences to rescue stalwarts there. Ninety five rescuers were arrested there and spent 77 days in custody, at a cost of about $500,000 to the state. The vocally pro-abortion governor lost the next election, partly through her waste of public funds on this occasion.

On 28 February there was another Philly rescue at Planned Parenthood. Judge Morton Krase, for whom pro-lifers came to feel a certain affection[123], found four "sacrificial lambs" guilty, since he said there were probably about that many actually blocking the entrance. The rest of us were found "not guilty" of "blocking a highway". (This was the standard charge in Philadelphia, although many variations and additional charges were brought at different times. It was also the charge commonly brought against prostitutes.)

In March a number of us went to jail in Philadelphia for refusing to pay the 25 dollar court cost from Judge Roses' sentence of June 1989. This was a memorable occasion of me. Philadelphia does not run your fancy suburban jail! There were many holding cells in the induction area and they were full of as motley a crew as you could wish to find. I was held for a while in one cell of about twenty-five men, including yet another fellow I knew from his family's church connections! He tried to find a hole to crawl into when he saw me, but I felt called to suggest to him that the Lord loved him and was pursuing him. "Those whom the Lord loves he disciplines, and he chastises every son whom he receives."

After we'd been processed and put in uniforms, we were kept in an area by ourselves, where we grew hungrier and hungrier. I'm not sure, but I think we finally got a baloney or cheese sandwich about 11:00 that night. The next day, however, all of us marched down to the prison mess hall.[124] The mess hall seemed to hold about three or four hundred inmates, 95% of them black. The place absolutely erupted when we came in. Men at the tables, in line, and

---

[123] One of the ironies of the rescue movement was that prolifers, in Philly, at least, came to prefer liberal judges to conservatives. One Catholic veteran put it like this, "I'd far rather have a liberal Jewish judge than one of those Jesuit-trained Catholics! The Jewish judge might actually listen to what we have to say!"

[124] Joe Roach writes there were about seventy men, but it seems to me we were fewer.

walking between clapped and cheered. Some stood up and raised their arms as they applauded.

My first reaction was shock. Then I had the fleeting thought that they were getting a kick out of these mostly middle-aged, white guys tasting prison life, but then I realized the prison grape-vine had worked as it always did, and these guys really knew who we were.

The hair stood up on the back of my neck as the wonder of it hit me. These men, most of whom would consider us aliens and even enemies out on the street, were honoring us for what we stood for and what we had done. I still can't quite imagine or understand it. I was also struck with the fact that the guards did not squelch this outburst. Normally in prisons large scale celebrations are regarded as dangerous and thus repressed. But these guys welcomed us with perhaps three minutes of unrestrained ovation. It was overwhelming. It also established for me what I continue to find – that the African-American community is at it heart, pro-life.

Randy Terry, not the first rescuer,
but the founder of Operation Rescue.

Operation Rescue as such shut down its Binghamton office in March 1990. As of 1988, OR included fifteen staff members. But under great legal pressure it now disbanded. Local groups and occasional national events continued. "Operation Rescue National" and a few other permutations were to emerge, but not directly derived from OR. I think "Operation Rescue" continued to be a DBA ("doing business as") of Randy Terry for a time, but I may be wrong.

At the end of March, Philadelphia rescuers were back at Comly Road, statistical "recidivists," and further failures of the criminal justice system. We often rescued on holy days – Ash Wednesday, good Friday, etcetera. After being released from custody following an Ash Wednesday arrest I wrote this meditation on the cloud-streaked sunset:

ASH WEDNESDAY AT DUSK

Ashes to ashes, dust to dusk,
Our days pass away like our flesh.
Tonight the dying forehead of day
Is streaked with cloudy wisps of ash.
I come from a brief stay in a cell
And yet the sky itself is barred
With purple and blue --
No escaping this prison.
There is suffering and death
Yet to see, to bear, to be locked in
This cell of flesh
We have been lent
To pass this hastening Lenten time.

See the message scrawled by another prisoner?

Regular Rescues

The pattern for my participation had become a rescue per month on average, which was about the average for rescues occuring in the Philly area .

In keeping with a growing tradition of Holy Week rescues, we gathered again in front of the former seminary library at Chester Crozer on Maunday Thursday. Good Friday, found us again before the doors at Blackwell Center.

At Blackwell, the pro-aborts had mobilized large numbers of very vulgar and blasphemous demonstrators, many of them from the New York and Philadelphia homosexual communities. [125] The pro-lifers, both rescuers and prayer-supporters, behaved themselves admirably in light of the provocation directed at them. There were some ticklish situations where the rescue leadership showed great wisdom and restraint, preventing physical confrontations where less-wise men might have allowed them.

Huge crowd at Blackwell rescue, largest to date, giving us hope that numbers would continue to increase.

Kimiko recalls we arrived en masse, coming round the corner from the northeast, where we were met by a large crowd of pro-abort chanting "Shame! Shame!" She said it felt like the mobs yelling at Jesus on Good Friday. Bob Heppe good friend and kinsman, rescued with us that time. Among

---

[125] Their representatives told reporters they outnumbered pro-lifers two to one, but given our count that is unlikely.

their noxious behaviors, some of the homosexuals were deliberately "making out" in front of Loren and our neice, Gillian. In Kim's words, "Evil was so present."

This was the largest local rescue to date (over against the "national rescues" of 1988), with 360 arrests including 30 juveniles.

The court date for the January rescue in Cherry Hill was the 3rd of April. We were fined 250 dollars plus 30 dollars victim's compensation, plus 25 dollars costs, plus 6 months probation. The poor judge. It was like trying to squeeze blood from a turnip.

I believe it was that April in which James Dobson of Focus on the Family held a onetime Rally for Life in Washington. It was an amazing gathering -- perhaps the largest rally in history of the United States. My niece, Annie, from Montana attended with us. We saw many people we knew there. I remember having a conversation near the end of the day with Jim Kopp, whom I knew from Atlanta, as my kids knelt among four thousand plus white crosses someone had put out to symbolize the number of aborted children who died each day in the US. Perhaps inspired by my lovely, but definitely-too-young niece and daughters, Jim asked playfully if I couldn't find a nice evangelical girl for him to marry!

Joshua praying among the crosses

In May, a Mother's Day rescue was once more led by women. That same month another Veteran's Rescue was planned for DC on Memorial Day. Whether it came off or not, I don't know. I wasn't there at any rate.

Under Summer Sun

The weather was a tremendous factor in rescue, in that we always had to think about it, and very often suffered from it – from freezing to frying.

Possibly in June again, but definitely once more in July we rescued at Stanton, Delaware. It was a hundred degree day, and Brenda Caley, the stalwart who had rescued with me at that same clinic in 1989, fainted from the heat and fell upon a sharp metal stake, cutting her face so badly she needed 51 stitches. Ninety-two others remained faithfully at their posts despite the heat.

July 6th 1990 was the date of the "Survivor's Rescue," at Comly Road, which resulted in the arrest of 41 juveniles and 83 adults. This was particularly exciting in that two fifteen year old women from our rescue community, one of them closely related to us, led their fellow "Survivors of Abortion," as people of the generation born since Roe v. Wade.

Roseann and I helped prepare the literature which included a signed statement from the parents that went like this:

Parent's Grant to Freedom of Conscience

I understand that my child desires to act on behalf of pre-born children.

I grant my child the liberty of his/her own conscience in this matter.

I am aware that there is a risk that my child may be arrested. I have made sure my child is aware of this risk as well.

The killing of pre-born children is a crime which courts and police ought to prevent and prosecute, however the Supreme Court's immoral Roe v. Wade decision has made the immoral "legal".

My generation has failed my children's generation in allowing this atrocity, therefore I humbly and prayerfully leave the decision of my son or daughter to his/her personal beliefs and good judgment. I have neither forced or prohibited my child's participation in the "Survivor's Rescue" on July 6, 1990.

Abortion Survivors, rescuers under 17

After the arrests the juveniles were taken to the National Guard Armory for processing. They were released to their parents and guardians there. Our own kids were among them. Roseann and I also signed for several other high schoolers, including a girl from Pittsburgh whose sisters were among the rescuers there abused by prison guards.

The *Daily News* article was title "40 Kids Busted In Pro-life Strife" and included this summary:

> Forty juveniles were among 124 anti-abortion activists arrested yesterday in a "Survivor's Rescue"

demonstration at the Northeast Women's Center. Terry McNitt, a spokeswoman for Pro-Life Non-Violent Direct Action, organizers of the protest, said some children under 10 years old were among those carried onto buses by police. . . .

McNitt said her group considers the children "survivors" because they were born during the 17 years that abortion has been legalized. She said there also were a number of teen-agers 17 and under in the group. (Scott Heimer, *Daily News* Staff Writer)

Our logo for Survivor's Rescue

    Yet another unusual part of the "Survivor's Rescue" occurred late that afternoon. After we returned home, we received a phone call from Robin Macintosh, a respected reporter from Channel 10 News. He called asking if he could come out and interview us. Full of paranoia and suspicion in re the media, I told him I had two stipulations: first, that he interview the kids, not Roseann and me [126] and second, that

---

[126] I felt like an interview with us might turn out to be about us "manipulating" them.

he not reveal our address. He said the first was his intention and the second was standard policy. He asked that we just go about our normal evening and they would sort of butt in on it.

So, we went ahead and ordered pizza from Dea's on the corner as usual on Friday night. Soon after that Robin showed up with his cameraman. First they filmed us around the table stuffing down pizza.[127] Then he interviewed the older four (Loren, the fourth, was only ten) and they were wonderfully straight-forward and simple in their answers.

"It was an ordinary Friday evening in the Trott household..."

We were amazed when we saw the whole thing on the news later. They had treated us very respectfully. I guess our kids got their fifteen seconds of fame early. Josh said: "I'd do it a 1000 times to save the babies. It's worth it to delay someone's death." Loren, too, spoke clearly.

The Survivor's Rescue was also memorable to me in that those adults who were arrested went to court on my

---

[127] Eight year old Jed, the youngest, had his shirtfront liberally anointed with "gravy" by then.

birthday, July 24th. There Judge Lydia Kirkland found us all "not guilty" after the Women's Center failed to produce persuasive evidence. She had delayed the beginning of the trial until someone drove over to NEWC to get a prosecution witness. Then upon examining the witness the judge discovered the witness could not testify to the no trespassing order. She then gave the prosecution one more opportunity to come up with a case – at which they failed — out on the third strike!. She found us all not guilty. It was quite a birthday present.

The day after the Survivor's Rescue another 134 rescuers went back to the doors of Northeast Women's Center, Kimiko, Adriel and Joshua among them! It had been a grueling, but bountiful three days.

On 21 August we had a rescue at Chester in which several handicapped rescuers led us, three of them in wheelchairs. Ninety-two were arrested. I think this was the rescue in which I let my youngest, Jed, accompany me. When we were processed at the government offices in Media, the head deputy, who was something of a dandy, looked down his nose as Jed and I filed by, and sneered, "They're even getting their kids arrested!" But of course, kids were what it was all about.

On the 24th of August, District Judge Huyett, another judicial activist with a political agenda, ruled against several key elements of the Pennsylvania Abortion Control Act; namely, the 24 hour waiting period, spousal consent and parental consent.

On the 25th of August, local prolifers did two rescues: one in the morning at Killer Kaji's Bordentown clinic; and one in the afternoon at his Yardley abortuary. There were 44 arrested in the latter. I don't think I was in on either of these.

On the 27th of August 1990, Federal Judge Lowell Reed, also an activist, issued a new injunction for the "protection" of NEWC at Comly Road.

In contrast, after another rescue on 8 September at Planned Parenthood , where we stood 3 ½ hours in front of the doors, Judge Retacco's court found all but 10 of us "not guilty." He ruled the rest of us were in exercise of our First

Amendment rights. (The leadership asked for volunteers, so I became one of the guilty "highway blockers".) Kimiko, Adriel, and Josh "risked arrest" on this occasion, too, and in keeping with Philly policy were given juvenile releases.

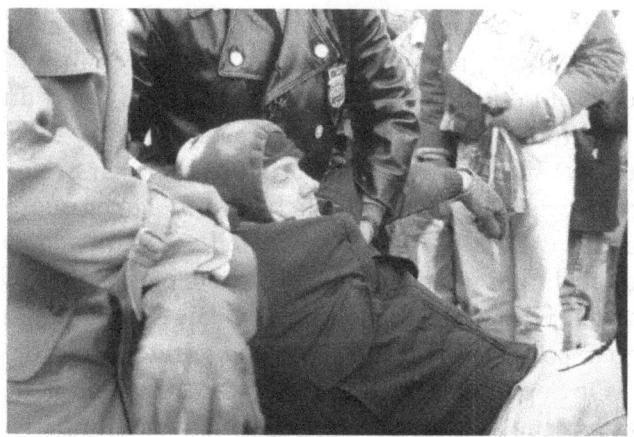
Dave Miller carried by police from a Center City abortuary

Dave Miller, a close friend from church, began to participate, and was in on several Center City rescues. Dave went on to become a pastor and missionary. The Philly rescuers enjoyed having him lead in prayer and encouragement.

Also in September, the pro-aborts brought a new tool to bear against us. In March 1989 the Third Court of Appeals had upheld the use of civil RICO (Racketeer Influenced and Corrupt Organization Act), against twenty-six rescuers. This was a case brought by the Northeast Women's Center alleging that each of the six rescues held there between 1984 and 1986 had been acts of extortion, despite the fact that the law requires criminal intent to prove extortion. This case was further appealed to the US Supreme Court.

Also in September 1990, NOW (National Organization of What?) added a long list of Delaware Valley rescuers to the defendants in the RICO case they were pursuing against Joe Scheidler and other national leaders. It seemed quite an honor considering what small fish we felt ourselves to be. Nonetheless it was incredible that this law passed to make it easier to prosecute organized crime figures would be used against us. We certainly weren't organized! But by that time there were 100 local branches of Operation Rescue around the country, and the abortion industry was working hard to find weapons to use against us.

Although most of us were soon dropped from this case again, others in our area were to be "successfully" prosecuted under RICO. And in other parts of the country some prolifers were successfully prosecuted to the tune to hundreds of thousands or even millions of dollars. Not that the pro-aborts ever collected much. (I only heard of one case where they collected big – it was in a Florida suit against an Episcopal church which had been the site of some rescue rallies. The church decided to pay the large settlement rather than go to court, for fear they would lose their buildings.)

On September 8th, the Krails were involved in a separate rescue at Morristown, NJ, which ended up in a case rescuers hoped might go to the Supreme Court. A Christian fellow named Alexander Loce had met a girl at a Bible study. They became engaged and then had gotten sexually involved. He was willing to do whatever it took to bring the child into the world and care for him, but the girl went to an abortion clinic on the 7th and had laminaria inserted, as the prelude to an abortion scheduled on the 8th.

Through a series of contacts on the 7th, George and Tina Krail received a phone call from the distraught young father asking them if they could help him. Tina said they would be glad to go and talk to her with him, but he said he had already tried that and she would not listen anymore.

They got hold of a lawyer and went with him to a judge to get a restraining order, but the judge refused to issue one. They appealed this ruling but another judge also denied an order. They then went to a justice of the State Supreme Court, who required the attendance of the woman, too. She came accompanied by a proabortion escort. This judge, too, refused to grant a restraining order. So the legal channels were exhausted.

At that point the Krails told Loce they would be willing to go to the clinic and block the doors, but only if he would rescue with them. He said he would do anything to save this child. So they gathered a total of fourteen people at late notice and went to the clinic the next morning, where most of them actually went inside and shackled themselves together using bicycle locks. They were there from 9 in the morning until 4:30 in the afternoon, but the abortionist had brought the girl in through a back entrance. Not sure if she were there or not, the father called out repeatedly trying to talk to the mother. Nonetheless, apparently about three in the afternoon, the child was killed.

Steve Osborn and I near the door at Paoli watch and pray as Kathy Sobicinski talks to a woman about her health and her baby.

Ultimately they were all arrested. They were found guilty of trespass, but their lawyer argued the father had some rights in the case and it was appealed up the line. It wasn't until 1994 that the US Supreme Court would decide whether or not to hear the case.

On 27 September, we rescued again at Paoli. No problems with police, no mothers being taken through our midst into clinic, no bails, no being held in jail. My good friend, Steve Osborn, living at the time in Chicago, was visiting me and joined us. From before the doors, he and I watched in awe and prayer, as Kathy Sobicinski talked with a woman for perhaps an hour, eventually persuading her to re-evaluate her decision and protect her baby's life.

Winding Up the Year

A "Life Chain" was held in our area on Oct 6th. This high profile, but low cost pro-life tactic was to become an annual thing in many places around the country. Pro-lifers would stand along major public highways holding signs with various simple statements: "It's a Child not a Choice," "Abortion Stops a Beating Heart," "Pray for Life," "Life What a Beautiful Choice," etcetera. These included many people from local churches who were not able or willing to participate in rescues.

On 12 October, Brenda Caley and I held a recruiter's seminar at Newtown Square Baptist Church, where Bob Lewis was pastor. This turned out to be one of my more embarrassing moments – since I showed up forty minutes late – leaving Brenda to forge ahead as best she could without knowing what had become of me. In fact, I had driven back from an elder's retreat in the Poconos with a fellow elder, and we had taken a very bad turn that took us way out of our route.

I was embarrassed and fuming and probably not a great deal of help. Once more, so much for leading from a position of weakness! The inspiration for this seminar was that Brenda and I had begun to realize the very things that made for good rescuers, made for bad recruiters. So we hoped to give some concrete suggestions about how to use more subtle and gentle approaches than were natural for many of us.

It is sad that, as two Protestants, we had very little to show for all our great ideas. Participation from churches I was connected with had been hopeful in the previous year, but was now beginning to slacken significantly, and would soon run into opposition from influential men in church leadership. Brenda, on the other hand was an independent from Anabaptist background, I believe, and there, too, recruiting was not going well. I suppose all of us, Catholic and Protestant, couldn't help thinking bigger was better.

We still envisioned a day when hundreds of Christians would turn out in front of every abortion facility every day it was open, but such a day was not coming soon. In some sense perhaps ours was a special calling at that time. Nonetheless, we thought about and tried to implement ways to appeal to other Christians and enlist their involvement.

This same thing seemed to be true for other areas of pro-life work . For instance in politics, Mike McMonigal was trying to enlist help with the Joe Rocks v. Alison Schwartz campaign but found fewer rescuers willing to help than he wished. The active people in any church often feel there is great untapped pool of Christians who aren't doing anything about anything. Such things are difficult to assess. Maybe a lot of people are called to faithfully watch football!

A "Clergy Rescue" took place on the 17th of October at Chester Crozer. There were 113 rescuers, including 19 clergymen. Kathy Sobicinski took one woman to a pregnancy center. The previous night, Kimiko got a phone call from a woman she didn't know, saying a friend of a friend was scheduled to kill her child at Paoli on the 17th. We scrambled around a little, but since none of us knew what she looked like, we could only tell the regular sidewalk counselors there to be as zealous as they usually were. This foreshadowed another crisis event in our own pro-life lives a few years later.

Also in October I went over to Bordentown, NJ, to join friends in front of the abortion clinic of the infamous Vikram Kaji, an abortionist who had offices in Yardley, PA, as well, and who was eventually prosecuted for sexual abuse of patients among other things. There were only a few of us and we did not "hold the doors" long before we were arrested. Part of the reason we rescued there was that sidewalk counselors were often harassed by police and even arrested there in their efforts to offer alternatives to women going in.[128]

---

[128] This arrest led to my most direct experience of brutality committed by a law officer. More later.

Was That Thunder?

On the 2nd of November 1990, Michael McMonigal, Patricia McNamara and Howard Walton began sentences of 45 days in jail for refusing to pay money to NEWC after Judge Lowell Reed found them in violation of his injunction. They were released six days "early" on 10 December, none of them giving in on anything.

On the 3rd of November, George Grant came to Philadelphia to speak at Chestnut Hill College about the origins and agenda of Planned Parenthood. George, a Presbyterian minister, whom I got to know over the next few years, was a great inspiration then and on several other occasions when he spoke to us. He had written extensively about Planned Parenthood, the ACLU, and on many other subjects. [129]

On the 10th, I was part of another rescue at Cherry Hill – this time with my full spiritual armor on. It was very bad weather and the cops were having a bad hair day. They not only threw us down and cuffed us with "bag ties," but they dragged us through mud puddles into the middle of the parking lot and left us on the cold, wet pavement in the rain- some of us for hours. They treated some of us pretty roughly, lifting by arms bound behind the back, etc. --- particularly a few older rescuers. When some crawled back, despite bag-ties, we were once more dragged into the parking lot, where they linked our leg-cuffs or hand-cuffs to others.

My two oldest daughter were "cuffed" together, but they not only discovered they could slip in and out of the "bagties," but they were pretty cavalier about it, so that the cops caught on, and tightened the cuffs up much more tightly (and painfully) behind their backs.

Perhaps the officers were particularly incensed over the fact that the recent township "ordinance" which threatened pro-lifers with additional legal penalties, did not do a better job of keeping us away. It was our expectation

---

[129] In 1999, George was the chief human agent in bringing about the publication of the poetry anthology Roseann and I edited, *A Sacrifice of Praise*. Nevertheless he would never accept any reward for that service.

that ordinance would be found invalid. [130] In the typical Cherry Hill manner, the court date was initially scheduled for 1 Apr 1990, then 21 Aug 1991, then 20 May 1992!

On the 16th and 17th of November, OR staged rescues in the DC area. I was arrested at an abortuary there, but released with the standard DC protester's fine of $50.00. At this rescue a Maryland woman brought the body of a late-term baby which had been pulled from an abortionist's dumpster. She had carefully washed it and wrapped it in a baby blanket. She carried it in her arms, not risking arrest, but showing it to the spectators at the rescue. She had even named it. Needless to say, this caused a certain amount of perplexity and consternation among the police officers present. Finally they confiscated the body -- without admitting it was a body, of course.

Local rescuers were back at Yardley on 23 Nov 1990. A handful of us were arrested and tried. My court date for this rescue was scheduled for 22 Apr 1991. However, a Yardley rescuer, who also did a lot of sidewalk counseling there, called me and said the court had granted me an extension, rescheduling my case on the 6th of March. She also hinted my case was likely to go well. I still don't know what she knew, but when I arrived at the town office for court, I went before the judge who declared me not guilty, due to no prosecution. I guess the arresting officer was on vacation.

My carpentry business was more and more irregular during the first year of my involvement. Rescue dates, court dates, and jail sentences tended to make planning and completing jobs difficult. Roseann and I talked about buying a house to renovate, since that would allow for more flexibility of schedule. In 1989, while working for some friends in the church, I learned that the elderly lady next door to them might be interested in selling, so I spoke with her, and then with her children. They were indeed very

---

[130] However an injunction of similar import had held sway over pro-life activities in Englewood NJ for many years. More later about our part in the rescue series which brought that down in the late 90s.

interested.

The upshot was that we bought a house on Morris Street before the first of the year, and began renovations in 1990, hoping to sell it within the next six months. However, the housing market continued to slump, and despite having fixed the place up with lots of little extras, it sat on the market for quite some time. I had borrowed money from my parents and a local businessman, and needed to sell that house!

Finally in November 1990, it sold. My tremendous relief was somewhat tempered by my final calculations which showed I had worked a thousand hours on the place and made a net profit of $9000! Nine dollars an hour was not real good money! But the Lord had provided for us. That Christmas I made a lot of the presents I gave my kids, and looking back, they were pretty lousy presents – but the kids didn't complain. They were part of a team that could go through tough times together. Roseann had long kept a "Jehovah Jireh" scrapbook in which the kids drew pictures of special ways the Lord had provided for us over the years. Looking back through it we can see his mercies were truly abundant.

Phil Beachey, dragged on his face at Cherry Hill

That month there was another rescue at Cherry Hill.

There Pastor Phil Beachey from central PA and a number of others were treated pretty roughly.

On 7 Dec 1990, seventy-four of us wound up the rescue year at Comly Road clinic. This rescue was held partly as a show of solidarity with the three in jail for non-payment of Judge Reed's injunction fines. We were processed downtown at the Roundhouse, where the singing in the cells was downright catacombical. I was cited as "Jim Troot."

Men taking responsibility – patriarchy in prayer.

Was That Thunder?

Tina Krail leading us in worship in Pittsburgh

CHAPTER FIVE -- MOVING ONWARD (1991)

But be ye doers of the word, and not hearers only, deceiving your own selves. For if any be a hearer of the word, and not a doer, he is like unto a man beholding his natural face in a glass; For he beholdeth himself, and goeth his way, and straightway forgetteth what manner of man he was. But whoso looketh into the perfect law of liberty, and continueth therein, he being not a forgetful hearer, but a doer of the work , this man shall be blessed in his deed. If any man among you seem to be religious, and bridleth not his tongue, but deceiveth his own heart, this man's religion is vain. Pure religion and undefiled before God and the Father is this, To visit the fatherless and the widows in their affliction, and to keep himself unspotted from the world. -- James 1:22-27

There are certain struggles common to any individual, be he prophet, priest or king. There are similar struggles common to any group of people: communities, churches or organizations. One such struggle is over what to do with success. Another struggle is how to keep from being entangled in lesser and secondary matters – how to keep focused and motivated toward the primary goals.

By 1991, the rescue movement had both of these struggles. Of course the chief goal of the proaborts in relation to rescuers was to entangle them in legal obstructions. Through local, state and federal courts they had succeeded in throwing heavy fines, long jail sentences, and ominous-sounding injunctions at us, particularly at our leaders. They had brought racketeering and extortion suits through RICO. By then, through the liberal press, they were continually trying to move popular opinion to regard rescuers as fanatics and violent people. In Philly, rescues were increasingly likely to get no press coverage whatever.

While some local governments became more

reasonable in the way they dealt with rescuers, politicians with proabort commitments (like our Mayor, then Governor, Ed Rendell and District Attorney Lynn Abraham) eventually raised the level of charges. The prejudice here was transparent. For instance, a group of minority students protested against Temple University policy by blocking Broad Street for three hours with no charges, while in 1993 we were charged and tried for blocking streets in Center City for a much shorter time. These things were not the focus for us – we knew there was no justice as long as they were tearing four thousand little babies to pieces everyday.

Nevertheless at times we were concerned about the small-in-comparison injustices we experienced. Some argued that since our own mistreatment was a product of identifying with the babies, to oppose it was one way of pursuing greater justice for them. Maybe so. In any case, the more serious brutalities and atrocities against rescuers did become important to other rescuers around the country. Some of these cases ended up as "causes" in themselves.

Nonetheless, the outward opposition was not the chief struggle. The rescue movement was born in conflict. Rescuers came aboard ready to face adversaries. Many rescuers had already proved they could and would endure severe mistreatment peacefully, just as they could and would go to jail for as long as it took.[131] The chief struggles were what to do with "success," what to do with something that had now been proven to work, but didn't seem to be making much progress toward the ultimate goal. Particularly on the national level, these struggles centered about what that goal should be, who should lead, and what principles should guide us.

Our 1991 Church Classes

In January 1991, our church had a series of adult

---

[131] The Allentown Seven were about to show us they would stay for a year rather than compromise.

Sunday classes beginning with the theme "Abortion as Spiritual Battle". We showed the film *Massacre of Innocence*. We talked about the Old Testament contrast between pagan idol worship and true worship of God. We highlighted the extremes – child sacrifice on the one hand and self-sacrifice on the other, as they tie into the radically different messages of idolatry and gospel. A central theme: Christ laid down his life for us, and calls us to lay down our lives for others. Our attitude toward the weak and helpless is to be like his toward us when he rescued us, unwanted children left on the ashheap to die (Ezekiel 16). Whatsoever you do unto "the least of these my brethren" you do (or do not do) unto Christ (Matthew 25).

The next week our class was led by of a representative from Bethanna (other years we had representatives from Alpha Pregnancy Services, Bethany, Family Policy Council, etc.) who discussed adoption –"the necessary substitute". These organizations were among many that labored to minister to moms and children. In our own church, as within the rescue community at large, there were quite a number of adoptive families, as well as many foster parents. [132]

The third week we discussed the "belief system" of the pro-abortion person, going into the historical, philosophical and religious bases which lie beneath his or her arguments. We talked about how many different levels of involvement and commitment existed among abortion supporters, and discussed some of the ways our members could speak with their "pro-choice" friends.

The 4th week, (on Saturday – because Mike had his own church to attend to on Sunday) Pastor Mike Chastain and his wife Joanna came up from Maryland to teach us about "Talking to the War-torn Mother." These two, who had been out at abortion clinics offering counsel and alternatives to abortion for years, shared many insights about approaching and winning the moms and dads going into abortion clinics.

---

[132] Curiously, the first two families in our church to rescue, Lauritos and Fesis, were both involved in foster care and adoption.

Was That Thunder?

Mike had one anecdote which sticks with me, although I'm sure he did not tell in it the public setting of the class. He spoke of two sidewalk counselors who were present in front of one Maryland abortion clinic where the law enforcement people would not let the counselors get within sixty feet of the door. Thus the people coming for abortions could only hear them if they called out loudly – not usually an effective way to persuade someone. [133]

That morning the police had been nasty, and none of the moms and dads going in had responded to the counselors. As a young black couple walked toward the doors, the two white counselors (husband and wife) called out asking them to take a minute to talk about alternatives. The wife seemed to hesitate, but the tall athletic-looking husband hurried her in through the doors. A few minutes later he came out again and went back to the car to get something.

As he came back, the male counselor with a sort of desperation, but a desperation focused on the desperate act about to take place, called out, "Do you know what you're going to find when you go back in there?" The young man hurried on toward the doors. The counselor continued, "One wounded woman . . . and one dead 'Nigger'." The immediate effect of this statement on the young man was what you might expect. He turned from the door, his eyes wide in anger and strode over to the much shorter counselor. He grabbed him by the lapels and pulled his face up to his own. "What did you say!" he hissed through clenched teeth."

Somewhat frightened himself by the enormity of what he had said, the counselor nonetheless went on to reply. "Hey, I'm not the one that's treating your child like a 'Nigger'. I'm not the one who's about to lynch him."

The young man pushed him back abruptly, releasing his grip. He turned on his heel and marched back into the clinic. But five minutes later, he and the young woman emerged, went to their car and drove away.

---

[133] This same situation existed at NEWC on Comly Road in Philadelphia.

Not a tactic to be repeated, but a powerful picture of the incredible ironies of what legalized abortion has done to us. Of all ethnic divisions in our society, the urban African-American population has been hit hardest by abortion. The social engineering of the liberals in the sixties and seventies, mainly through "dependent child welfare" radically decreased the number of male-headed households in that community.

Now abortion removes even more male responsibility for children by offering a legal way for men to "pay and play". Two black children are aborted for every three born, compared to one aborted for every three born in the white population. In Philly the proportion is even higher.[134]

The Chastains are just two individuals among many private volunteers who go out to offer compassionate help to moms and dads in difficult circumstances. There are many of these in the Delaware Valley, too. For instance the Pat Stantons, at the same time as they were involved in rescue, worked to facilitate a mothers' home in the northern 'burbs. Another family whom I admire are the Denny Greens of Petersburg, Virginia. They were not only regularly at the clinics in their area, but invited pregnant moms to stay with them while they found financial and medical help. Many go out weekly or even daily to deal with the rejection and abuse that go with sidewalk counseling at abortion clinics. Some operate crisis pregnancy centers. Some work for foster and adoption agencies. Some coordinate medical and legal help. Some do all of the above.

One of my favorite moments during a rescue was when eighty or ninety of us were gathered in front of the doors at Northeast Women's Center while one of our best-

---

[134] As many have observed from Margaret Sanger to Jesse Jackson, the population control movement and abortion industry have been oriented toward the poor and ethnic minorities from the beginning. It has reached the point, according to the Pennsylvania Pro-life Federation, that nearly half of the African-American babies in Philadelphia are aborted each year. In 2002, 10,880 were born, while 9,259 were reported as aborted.

loved pro-aborts was standing in front haranguing us about what hypocrites and losers we all were. Her rhetoric picked up steam until she was veritably preaching at us. Then she came to a climactic rhetorical question, "How many of you have taken in foster children or adopted babies yourselves!" About forty hands went up. Even she was silent for a few seconds. "Well, it's not enough!" she finally responded in a more subdued tone, and walked away. I suppose she was right.

Denny Green, another friend who poured out his life for Moms and babies from rescues to providing housing and food.

Early 1991 Rescues

We started the rescue year early in 1991. On January 2nd we were tried for the Dec 7th rescue at NEWC. Our motion for demurrer was granted, and Judge Cosgrove found us not guilty. This was unusual enough to produce considerable celebration.

On the 5th, 128 people were back at Planned Parenthood. Kimiko and two of her friends joined us, and were released as juveniles. (Only Joe Roach and George Krail were found guilty -- of obstructing a highway – when the court date came around.)

On the 10th of January the State of New Jersey informed me that my driving privileges had been suspended there for failure to pay the compensation board penalty assessment (victim's compensation) portion of my fines. I was nervous whenever I drove there over the next decade.

That year we went to the Washington March for Life on a Christian Action Council bus, leaving from Glenside. Bill Devlin had enlisted quite a few participants from the northern suburbs, which was encouraging. Montgomery County has some staunch prolifers, despite the strange politics there. [135]

On the evening of January 26th Randy Terry spoke at a rally at the George Washington Motor Lodge in Norristown/Plymouth Meeting. The OR movie "The Brutal Truth" was premiered. Along with various pamphlets that had been in use for a few years, and Bernard Nathanson's movie "The Silent Scream," this movie reminded us a picture is worth a thousand words – in this case pictures of aborted babies, combined with others of healthy babies in the womb.

At the end of January some rescuers from our area went to Dobbs Ferry, NY, in support of "Operation Goliath," one of many rescue efforts that didn't quite live up to its name (although in this case the point of the name was that David beat Goliath, despite his size and strength). Rescuers had been held there for several months, but the authorities seemed to be waking up and smelling the coffee, for there were no arrests despite 140 rescuers sitting in front of a clinic When they went to another clinic, they were arrested but quickly released. I was not on that trip.

---

[135]Pennsylvania has been one of the most pro-life states, but the Republicans in the southeast counties include many sell-outs, while PA Democrats have produced a few high-profile pro-life leaders, like Governor Casey.

Was That Thunder?

National Leaders Meeting

My involvement reached its greatest pitch in 1990 and 1991, during which on the average I rescued once every three or four weeks. Although I was informed about most of the rescues in our area, I tried to keep my participation at a sustainable level, that is as frequently as possible without completely compromising my work and income, and my family's needs. Obviously those in leadership were doing a very great deal more than I was, and their incomes and families suffered more, particularly when they served longer jail sentences.

On the other hand, there were many people who only rescued once or twice during a year, and quite a few others who only rescued once or twice altogether. No one grudged another rescuer his intensity or his lack of involvement. It was pretty universally recognized that we were there out of conscience and that conscience, while it can be informed by others, is ultimately directed by God. [136]

In February or March 1991 the Philadelphia leaders kindly invited me to come along to a national conference in Chicago. I believe there were seven or eight of us who went. Roseann came with me and we stayed with my brother Jon at Jesus People USA (JPUSA). We rode out to the meetings with Denny Cadieux, an elder there. Randy Terry, Keith Tucci and Mike McMonigal spoke along with several others. But most inspiring to us was George Grant, again.

I don't think this was just my Presbyterian prejudice. He shared with us a biblical and long range vision of how we must fight the battle, while avoiding the prevalent paradigms for "social change" which were most likely to pull us off-track.

George gave us several mini-history lessons. One of his regular themes was "righteousness cannot be known in a

---

[136] For a few years I held a grudge toward those who never rescued at all. I thought every Christian should be involved. But as someone recently said, "Holding a grudge is letting someone else live rent free in your head!"

land of forgetfulness." (Psalm 88:12) He illustrated this most particularly with the story of Israel's unwillingness to enter into their promised place because "there were giants in the land." The tribes of the giants are named very particularly, and George took us through the Old Testament scriptures to show that Israel should have recognized these names. They were the same tribes Abraham had previously defeated despite the giants among them. But Israel had forgotten God's faithfulness.

George Grant, pastor, author and valuable teacher

He concluded that the people of God are always up against giants – but they are always giants that God has enabled them to defeat in the past. It is only when we forget God's mighty deliverances, and God's word, and his particular faithfulness to us that we become afraid and try to avoid the battles he calls us to.

George outlined six theories of social change. Not all these are his labels, rather my summaries: 1/ that secret knowledge of mystical principles is the key to social change (Gnostic); 2/ that learning, right analysis and right formulations are the keys (academic); 3/ that mechanical principles and legal systems are the keys (legalistic); 4/ that feelings are the key (existentialist); and 5/ that tyrannous (or revolutionary) power is the key (Machiavellian/Marxist). He said this fifth one was the most tempting to Christian activists, but self-defeating because it short-circuited God's plan. The revolutionary will always neglect the eternal things, either the word of God or his relationships with people. Finally, he said, there is: 6/ the theory that eternal things are the key (covenantal). Those who work for social change according to God's will have two anchors in the eternal things: their relationships to people and the word of God.

In his second talk, George focused on a biblical strategy for spiritual warfare. He pointed out that God's worship is always central and the beginning point, while God's plan always involves moving out in radiating circles from there. He said there are five levels of covenant: Worship, acknowledging God's sovereignty; Family, acknowledging God's order; Community, acknowledging God's ethics and obedience; the World, where we bring God's judgment and sanctions to bear; and posterity (the next generation and the unreached nations) where God's promises are perpetuated and extended. He warned that we must always come back to the refreshment and rest of worshipping God, or we will spin off and become cause-centered rather than Christ-centered.

George was very encouraging. He reminded us that the 19th century pro-life movement had not only mobilized thousands of people, but it had brought about laws prohibiting abortion in all 50 states.

Roseann and I enjoyed meeting people from other parts of the country. I remember in particular the Uchtmans, a couple from North Dakota who had been jailed for home-schooling their children before they got involved in rescue! We also got to know the other Philadelphians a little better in a less "active" setting.

At one point Randy spoke about the things he had gone through in the last year, and followed up with a time for questions. He asked that people write their questions out and send them up. I felt like he had approached something at one point in his talk that didn't come through clearly, so I wrote a message to this effect, "Are you saying that God used the time in Georgia jails to humble you?" What I didn't know was Randy asked that we sign our questions. So I sent it up without my name on it, and when he got to it, his first reaction was frustration that someone had ignored his request – particularly when it was a sensitive question.

Alan Keyes, a courageous voice.

However, he read it and answered it pretty much with a "yes." From my perspective this was encouraging, for my own experience is that leaders who will publicly confess weakness are better leaders. But after the meeting broke up, I went up and told him I had written the question, not realizing we were supposed to sign them. He responded warmly.

I also shared with him the melancholy news that a mutual friend, an early Protestant leader in Philly rescue, had left his wife and moved in with a younger woman. We prayed together that God would intervene.

In March, back in Philly, Dr. Alan Keyes spoke at the annual Celebrate Life Dinner. He was famous in our circles as being one of the most outspoken moral conservatives to run for president. His stand against abortion was loud, clear, and consistent, where so many nationally respected politicians waffled.

Brutality Against Rescuers

I was involved in four more rescues during the first half of the year, and in quite a number of courtroom appearances. The tales are too many to tell, but there was one series of events in mid-March I cannot skip.

There had already been four or five infamous cases of law-enforcement atrocities against pro-lifers. The *Wall Street Journal* (18 August 1989) printed a long article by William B. Allen, chairman of the U. S. Commission on Civil Rights, referring to the three cases most widely known among rescuers.

The first was a case in which Pittsburgh police and jailers, including the warden there, had harassed and physically abused several female pro-life inmates. Mr. Allen wrote:

> Women – from college age to grandmothers – are dragged by the bottom of their blouses, their breasts exposed to hooting male prisoners. . . . Complaints are filed with an assistant district attorney, who does not process them, allegedly on orders from her superiors.
>
> These female rescuers also testified to being verbally threatened with being stripped and raped. Jailers deliberately blew smoke in the face of one who had serious respiratory problems, in the presence of a nurse who was supposedly there to care for her, to the point that the prisoner could hardly breathe. After 15 minutes of this, the nurse said she couldn't stand anymore and put an oxygen mask over the rescuer's face.

Efforts had been made to pursue legal action, but without avail, largely due to "stonewalling" at every level.

Mr. Allen's *Wall Street Journal* article reported that Hosea Williams, a civil rights leader and companion of Martin Luther King Jr. in Selma, participated in a news conference in Pittsburgh decrying the brutality against rescuers there, but again to no avail. Jim Kopp, whom I knew from Atlanta and had seen again in D.C., took time out from other rescue activities to spend many months doggedly pursuing legal channels in Pittsburgh trying to get some sort of action against the perpetrators of these outrages, to no avail.

Another well-known incident involved Father Weslin and his crew, the Lambs of God, who rescued in East Hartford, Connecticut in June 1989. There officers removed badges and name tags and locked them in the trunk of a police car, before severely abusing the rescuers in the course of "arrests" and "processing". This, as in a number of other cases, was deliberate brutality, designed not only to hurt, but to injur. *US News and World Report* published an article (6 August 1990) by John Leo, in which he interviewed many of those rescuers. One mistake police made in this case was arresting two reporters and confiscating their film and notes. Journalists often have the last word. Yet again, no prosecutions followed.

In Los Angeles yet another famous day of abuse had occurred in June 1989, under a deputy police chief, Robert Vernon, "A Christian leader" who had appeared on James Dobson's TV show, and whose testimony was published in 1977 as *Peacemaker in Blue*.[137] The LA police officers arrived equipped with "nunchakus," the oriental weapon which consists essentially of two nightsticks connected with a chain. Using these as "nutcrackers," the officers wrapped them around rescuers arms and legs and twisted. The nominal goal of this tactic was to get rescuers to "comply" to their orders.

However, in many cases no orders were being given to the rescuers. Those present reported it looked and felt more like open sadism. Many rescuers were seriously injured. One woman was reported to have miscarried following the treatment, and a film taken at the time captured two officers snapping a man's arm. Although the cameraman was a considerable distance from the officers and their victim, the "crack" can be heard distinctly in the sound track of the film.

Again no penalties or prosecutions were sustained against these Gestapo tactics. Robert Vernon was quoted in *Christianity Today* , 29 Apr 1991, in full defense of LAPDs behavior. His statements were a hotch-potch of deceit or self-deceit and civil legalism. When the Rodney King video hit the networks, with all the chaos that followed, many rescuers felt this was God's discipline of LAPD and Robert Vernon. George Wills wrote an article on LAPDs violence in 1991 (*Inquirer*, 14 March) in which he said $8 million had been awarded LAPDs victims in brutality suits during the last year. So far as I know none of that went to rescuers. Vernon resigned in 1992.

---

[137] Robert Vernon's early book about his conversion was a factor in at least one friend's conversion – that friend, by the way, participated in rescues with me! In 1993 Vernon wrote *LA Justice* about the Rodney King incident, which resulted in his own firing.

A Memoir of Pro-life Rescue

LAPD's Bob Vernon, "armbreaker in blue"

William Allen's *Wall Street Journal* article ended:

> Nonviolent protestors should all be accorded the same treatment no matter what the subject of protest. To do less is to destroy the most prized achievement of the civil rights movement – the recognition of the rights of everyone. And we will have destroyed that achievement, not just for Operation Rescue, but for all.

Ignoring their *Wall Street Journal* subscriptions, the attorneys of the ACLU didn't pick up on that one.

Nonetheless, pro-lifers were of two minds about pursuing the prosecution of such flagrant abuses of US law. As I have said, we wanted justice, but most of all we wanted it for the babies. We even felt that a certain amount of suffering on our part was inevitable. Where was the balance?

My own personal experience had involved only one injury worse than the wounds received in Atlanta. During one arrest at Chester County the deputies were really out of control in a kind of reckless festive mood. We had remained limp as they loaded us on the bus, and in protest against their recklessness, we remained limp. When we reached the detention area in Media, they unloaded us as though we were sacks of potatoes. I think I was the last one taken off the bus. One deputy carried my legs, and the other had hold of my nylon jacket by the sleeves.

As they exited the bus, going at reckless speed, I slipped out of my jacket and the back of my head came crashing down full force on the concrete, a drop of about three feet. I saw the proverbial stars. I was completely limp when this happened, and I decided to stay that way for a few minutes when they took me into the building. I waited until I could hear just a little anxiety in their voices, before I opened my eyes. I had a goose-egg on the back of my head the size of a goose egg, and I haven't been able to do differential calculus problems since that day. [138]

But in March 1991, I saw deliberate violence toward rescuers first hand. Ten of us had been tried in early March for an October rescue at Killer Kaji's Bordentown place. This case had been rescheduled. [139]

We were found guilty and offered the options of a $250 fine or spending eleven Saturdays doing weekend "community service," i.e,. picking up trash along New Jersey highways. This was a program run from the Burlington County Jail in Mount Holly. Most of us chose the "community service".

We prolifers arrived the first day, and stood around with a few others there for the same purpose. When a bus pulled up driven by a prison guard, we all filed on. Gradually a variety of others showed up, until the bus was fairly full. Another young guard got on. I sat with two other prolifers up near the front, but most of our guys, another five or six of them, were sitting farther back.

A couple of the pro-lifers were already "evangelizing" the other inmates. A few listened, but others told them to

---

[138] Nor before that day!
[139] During the first hearing, the corner of my trial notice was chewed by a baby named Melody, whose mother Mandy, sat next to me. She chose life for her daughter during an earlier picket at Bordentown.

shut up. One of the "evangelists," who shall go unnamed here, had a talent for irritating people. In fact at times he seemed to think this was part of his calling. Apparently an inmate wearing a red cap told one of the pro-lifers to get out of the seat he was in, because it was his seat. When the prolifer refused, this guy, "red cap," went inside and got a sergeant.

Sgt. Booker Harris, a veteran prison guard, came out and got on the bus, going toward the back where most of the pro-lifers were sitting. He told those in "red cap's" seat to move. George Krail said they would be glad to give up their seats, because "we love Jesus and want to show his love." The sergeant responded by saying, "I don't want to hear any more of this Jesus B___ S___." Chuck Matson responded, "You're a public officer, you're not supposed to talk like that." Sgt. Harris told Chuck to get off the bus. George Krail spoke up in gentle agreement with Chuck. Sgt. Harris responded by punching him in the jaw, which knocked him back in his seat. Harris said if anyone else agreed with Krail, they should get off the bus, too.

Karl Slove, Tony Sulpizio and I were sitting further up close to the door, and although we knew some sort of craziness was going on, we didn't hear exactly what it was. The first concrete thing I saw was Sgt. Harris, who was black, dragging Tyrone Malone, the only black rescuer there, up the center aisle of the bus. The others told me later that Tyrone had told Harris he had no right to hit George. The sergeant then hit him, and perhaps Dan Lichteig, too.

As he was being dragged by, Tyrone was protesting, "You can't do that." When the sergeant got Tyrone to the top of the bus steps, he whipped out a can of mace and began to spray it in Tyrone's face, making a point of spraying under Tyrone's glasses directly into his eyes. He then pushed Tyrone out of the bus. Tyrone fell to the ground and staggered away, crying out, "What kind of person would do this?" Harris chased after him and unloaded another dose of Mace into his mouth and nose, saying, "I'll show you what kind of a person I am."

All the others from the back had stumbled off the bus

Was That Thunder?

by then and the sergeant sprayed an arc of Mace across them. They ran away in different directions, the worst hit falling down at a mud puddle and trying to wash the stuff out of their eyes. After a few minutes, Dan Lichteig came back to the bus, thinking the sergeant had gone inside the building. "Who was that officer that sprayed us?" he asked, not realizing the sergeant was there with his back turned talking to the driver. The sergeant turned around and charged him again, thoroughly dousing Dan with mace again. Dan fell down and was crying out and crawling around on the pavement on his hands and knees.

The others who had gotten off the bus moved away and congregated on the other side of the street away from the prison. Some others of us, rescuers and non-rescuers, had gotten off the bus, and when the driver got off and asked, "Are you with them," I answered, "We're with you." In addition to instinctive cowardice, my rapid rationale was that the others were likely to be charged with something serious, since that seemed to be what happened to people officers assaulted.

To the extent I was thinking at all, I thought it would be better if some of us stayed along for the ride, and could testify as "objective" witnesses. But I was also as shook-up as I could remember being. I have to admit I wondered for a moment if I was like Peter denying Christ. Frankly, this incident terrified me as much as the first couple hours of my basic training in the army when a whole cadre of Airborne Rangers, Vietnam vets, had us convinced they were going to kill us.

Back on the bus we listened to the driver and the other guard, who with great hilarity, referring to Sgt. Harris as "the Mad Macer". They recounted three or four episodes inside the prison where he had deliberately sprayed Mace on incarcerated prisoners. I made careful mental notes, including the names of some of his other victims. The guards took great delight in recounting the morning's jollities, punctuating each re-telling with the sound "Psh-sh-t" for every shot of Mace. The bus was driven to the gas pumps and the guards ended up talking on the phone with the prison administration or the sergeant for quite a while. I remember the one saying to the other, "we got to come back this afternoon and write the whole thing up."

Tony and Karl and I spent the rest of the day along the highways picking up trash with about twenty other inmates. We got a chance to talk quietly a few times and agreed to pay close attention. We agreed on the goal of being ready to write up accounts of what we had seen and heard.

I was rocked by this series of events. I don't think anything else happened to me in the years I did rescue to compare with how this hit me emotionally. It was the flip side of that deep respect for law enforcement that had made the first arrest so hard. I genuinely thought of the cops as forces for good. In general I had seen cops and prison guards act responsibly, and even in a godly manner. When I was confronted with them acting like this, it almost unmanned me. I sent in the balance of my fine the next day.

That night several of the other guys were there to meet us when we got back. They wanted us to come to a lawyer's office and make a deposition. It turned out we got there too late in the day, but I suggested it would be best if each of us went home and wrote up our own impressions of the day. I stayed up late doing that. How naïve I was. If it were to happen again tomorrow, I would get together immediately with everyone involved and compare notes until I knew exactly all the "pieces" that I had not personally experienced. Why? Read on.

That night I got phone calls from AP wire services and some Los Angeles new bureau, who took short interviews about the events. Apparently the subject resonated with these people, because it was along the lines of the Rodney King story. I was surprised to see one or two pieces where I was quoted. These were sent to me by friends around the country.

Charges were brought against Sgt. Harris. Burlington County eventually mounted "an internal investigation," which most of us recognize may mean "investigation lite". I remember being called to come over and tell the investigators what I had seen. I made the mistake of taking along my write-up. It was a mistake, because by writing it down I had unconsciously produced a fixed version of my own which included "filling in the blanks". The experience had been traumatic enough that my mind refused to accept "blanks". I had come to think I knew a number of things which I didn't in fact know – such as some of the events leading up to Tyrone being dragged down the bus corridor.

One old and one young "detective" questioned me, read my account, and went off to consult. They came back and asked if I would be willing to take a polygraph. I said I would.

I had taken polygraph tests in Military Intelligence and been trained in the general practice of how they're given, what the operator looks for, etcetera. The overall effect of that training was to make me wary of the utility of the polygraph. I knew that it worked best on those who thought it was infallible, more or less like magic. I thought neither.

The polygraph operator was an old guy, who should have known what he was doing. But apparently he didn't. He ran a few test questions in a short time, then went back for the actual test. He told me to sit absolutely still, which is nonsense --- I've never sat absolutely still for more than a minute in my life. The questions were spaced out over six or seven minutes. I moved several times in my chair – I guess those were the lies. After it was over, the young guy came in and told me I had failed the test. I told him resignedly that I was sorry to hear it. However it seemed to me by then that the investigation was not about finding out if Sgt. Harris was guilty of crimes. Nevertheless, had I been a better witness, perhaps it would have helped.

Furthermore, those naive (?saintly) pro-lifers let him off the hook at court! Those assaulted obtained the services of a lawyer and brought criminal charges against Sgt. Harris. They all went to court, where the preliminary procedures were being taken care of. Just before the trial proper was to begin and in order that the lawyers might discuss a few last points, the judge sent the pro-lifers and Sgt. Harris out. They were sent to wait in the same room. There Sgt. Harris broke down and begged the pro-lifers to forgive him, claiming to be a penitent Christian and deeply sorry for what he had done. Those beloved idiots not only forgave him, they went back in and told their lawyer to drop all the charges! The saints can be imbeciles sometimes. I'm told that Sgt. Harris's subsequent interviews with reporters were quite the opposite of repentant.

I have wrestled with this apparently superlative obedience to the Lord's command to love your enemies. Since the chief thing I wrestle with is my own anger and sense of sharing in the wrong that was done Tyrone and George and Dan, I have had to "give it up" over and over. "Taking up an offense" is Bible language for exactly that – getting angry, and ultimately bitter, over a wrong done to someone else – when the someone else has the "grace sufficient" to deal with it -- and you don't! We are commanded NOT to take up an offense.

But by now the reader may have begun to see the parallel that has occurred to me. While it is wrong to take up an offense, it is also required of us to do justice. It is required of us that, as a rule, we submit to those who "bear the sword," that is the civil authorities charged with punishing wrong-doing. And slightly more complex, we ourselves have responsibility to participate to the fullest in that process. Not only as voters (electing "Caesar"), and not only as jury-members and soldiers and policemen (participating in "bearing the sword"), but as witnesses and complainants and supporters of the legal process. I have come to the conclusion those three saints were wrong – not in forgiving Sgt. Harris -- but in letting him off the legal hook.

Where wrong-doers are both sinners and criminals, the Christian can only forgive the sinner – not his criminal behavior. Thus the dramatic repentances of several notorious convicted criminals during the last decade have not kept them from the punishments their crimes deserved, and rightly so. Not even God "pardons" serious crime. Rather he commands its punishment, to such a degree that he says he will discipline the people who refuse to punish it.[140]

---

[140]. Deut 21:1-9.

Was That Thunder?

In fact, that is what the Christian's attitude toward abortion must be. We must forgive the repentant mothers, nurses, and abortion doctors—but what they do is still a crime, and needs to be called a crime in law – as it was before Roe v. Wade. Nor ought we "pardon" assault and battery against ourselves. To do so makes a mockery of civil law. As far as I know, Sgt. Harris may still work in a prison, and may still be abusing prisoners.

Yet there is also the issue of our hearts. When our efforts to seek justice seem to fail – whether in relation to a particular act of crime or crime on a large scale or even the legalization of a crime – we are prone to "taking up an offence," with the concomitant anger and bitterness. The symptoms are thoughts of personal vengeance, and an oppressive obsession with the wrong-doers. Despite the Psalmist's injunction we "fret ourselves because of evildoers" and we thus become further victims of it. I wrote these lyrics as a self-exhortation on that score:

Fret Not Yourself Because of Evildoers (Psalm 31)

> Fret not yourself because of evildoers
> That prosper in the way.
> Fret not yourself because of evildoers.
> Hear what the Lord has to say
> They will soon be mowed like grass.
> They will wither like weeds.
> Trust in the Lord and do His will
> And he will provide all your needs.
> And he will provide all your needs.
>
> I have been young and now am old.
> Put away your dread.
> I have not seen the righteous forsaken
> Nor his children begging bread.
> Delight yourself in the Lord alone,
> He'll grant your hearts' desires.
> Commit your way unto the Lord --

And see what transpires.
And see what transpires.

See that perfect man, Lord Christ.
Behold, his end is peace.
The wicked all shall be cut off
But the righteous never cease.
Rest in the Lord, wait patiently.
Cease from anger and wrath.
Do no evil in return –
Soon the Lord will laugh.
Soon the Lord will laugh.

Evildoer's days shall end,
Gone without a trace.
You will not find any sign of them
Though you diligently search their place.
The little of the righteous is better by far
Than bank accounts of the bad.
The righteous will never be ashamed
And in hard times they'll be glad.
In hard times they'll be glad.

I mentioned that Jim Kopp was one of those pursuing the legal efforts against the "Pittsburgh Nightmare," as the abuse of rescuers there was dubbed. According to those who knew, Jim spent many months pursuing every legal channel and every civil official he could. He was trying to bring those who had abused our women at the prison to justice, or at least into court. When federal, state, and local authorities continually turned deaf ears to him, Jim became depressed and weighed down by it. No charges were pursued, no investigation carried forth (except by pro-lifers themselves), and no penalties were ever meted out to the vicious warden there and his cronies.

Some who knew him spoke of Jim's heroic efforts in Alleghany County on that occasion, but also of the toll it seemed to be taking on him. Where those whom God charges with justice refuse to pursue it, those under them are oppressed. Jim's reversion to violence several years later was serious sin, and not to be excused. But when the news finally broke that Jim had indeed pulled the trigger in the death of Dr. Slepian, it was the general conclusion among those who knew him, that Jim's turn to vengeance was connected with his experience of civil injustice – particularly that of the Pittsburgh cases. To use Bible language perhaps he had "taken up the offense" of the women abused in Pittsburgh.

Jim Kopp, weighed down by "the Pittsburgh Nightmare"

Miscellaneous Developments

At our April 1991 court date for the Clergy Rescue at Paoli,[141] Patty McNamara came up to me and told me I was in charge of keeping Pat Carroll in order. Now this was one of the most difficult assignments I ever received as a rescuer. Pat was an 80-something former post master with the disposition of a drill sergeant and no desire to pretend he liked something he didn't. Pat had been incarcerated in Vermont, and his health had gotten so bad the officials

---

[141] The rescue had been clear back in 1989.

released him. Joe Roach said at the time he did not think he would see Pat alive again. But Pat recovered, and was as feisty as ever.

It was Pat's intention to make a clear statement to Judge Melody about what he thought of the court, of abortion, and of stupid people in general. So my only tactic was to continually misinform Pat about what stage the trial had reached. In this way we were able to keep his tirade bottled up until the trial was actually over and the judge had returned to his chambers. Patty-Mac was no longer my best friend, however, and I was no longer Pat Carroll's.

In April we bought a new (hundred year old) home. We did it not only because of our large family, but because two women from our church who spent a lot of time at our house had become good friends, and after praying about it, said they would consider moving in with us if we had room. Then a realtor friend called us to say he had a house he wanted us to see. It turned out to be a huge Victorian pile of stone that needed an infinite amount of work.

It was an eight bedroom house in the East Oak Lane section of Philly and it still needs a tremendous amount of work. But due to the circumstance of cash in hand after the relatively unprofitable Morris Street renovation, we were able to buy it. So within a year, that is, after Victoria was born, we had ten people in nine bedrooms and quite a happening place. I slowed down a little in my rescue involvement, taking two months to get the house in passable shape.

In April, Jerome Lejeune testified at a court case in Morristown, New Jersey, concerning the legal status of several living, frozen human fetuses. He stated "Human life begins at the moment of conception." Dr. Lejeune was internationally famous, a French genetic pioneer who discovered the genetic cause of Down's syndrome, and had opened up the field to many other new discoveries.

The case was a contest between the father and the mother of the babies over the "disposal" of one of the babies, and whether to "dispose" of the rest of them or preserve their lives.

Was That Thunder?

Jerome Lejeune, Father of Modern Genetics

Lejeune's testimony was compelling enough that in the conclusion of that case Judge Michael Noonan said:

> I find based upon the undisputed medical and scientific testimony presented before this court, that the eight-week-old fetus in this case was a living person, a human being... I find that the eight-week-old fetus in this case, a living human being, was legally executed pursuant to Roe v. Wade ....

In May, however, we were back in Chester County prison for the Clergy Rescue at Paoli in 89. During that stint in Chester County, I got pretty close to a prisoner from Coatesville, named Jimmy, whom the Lord had already been working on. The chaplain, Pastor Christmas, had been ministering very effectively to this man. The last I heard Jimmy had gone from Chester County to Keswick Bible School in New Jersey and from there to Word of Life Bible School in Schroon Lake, New York.

I had a couple of interesting interactions with other inmates that time, too. The block I was on had no day-room, but it had a television out in the bay upon which all the cells opened. One evening when we were out of our cells, the guys got the guard to turn to a program that had way too much female flesh in it for me. Having struggled with lust a great deal in my life, I had come to the place where I knew not looking was the only option I could handle, so I deliberately wandered off to the corner of the bay where you couldn't see the set. A couple prisoners came over and asked me what I was doing When I told them, they seemed to respect me for it.

I also had a chance to talk to a homosexual prisoner there about a ministry I'd been involved in, called Harvest, which helped people with sexual issues. I had seen and heard his cellmate when I was in Chester County before. He was a very large and very loud homosexual who talked as obscenely and outrageously as he could a good deal of the time. The first night I was there, this guy talked and carried on for several hours as though the two of them were engaged in an orgy. It was pretty obviously theatre, born out of a desperate need for attention.

Prison offers one thing to some guys beside Christians -- you always have a captive audience! I think it was that same hitch during which a young white guy sat up singing broken-hearted love songs the first night he came in.

One of the times I was in Chester County, my friend, Bob Demoss, came to visit me with two younger friends, Annette and Bill. Their visit was unexpected. Unconsciously I had been learning the instinct Solzhenitsyn writes about, of abandoning everything in my life as I went behind bars. Therefore friends seemed strange in that setting! As always with prison visitors, the time went way too fast. Nonetheless I was deeply appreciative of it. Afterward I wrote this poem:

THE VISIT

Who are these people not wearing green?
The room belongs to the prison --
It is guarded and watched,
Yet here they are, people I have seen,
It seems a dream.

Was That Thunder?

And they take my hand,
They embrace me,
Speak words of courage.
Are they my own race,
Free to come and go?
They tell me so,
And promise love and a hope
That I have deliberately
Left out of my calculations.

They ask me and I talk
Far too much, for time cataracts
Away though I want them to say
So much more.
But another voice says "time's up".

And when I leave I must submit
To stripping and being searched
For contraband, dangerous substances or tools
They might have passed me.
FOOLS! They gave me love!

    I'm pretty sure it was that jail stint where the judge released us "early," after six or seven days, then told us if we did not pay the costs of prosecution, we would have to go back and "finish" the sentence. There was quite a bit of malarkey in all this, but the upshot was that we ignored it while our attorneys arbitrated, and it was quite a while before anything came of it.

    One could write several books about the sacrifices of pro-life attorneys. I remember six or seven who put in constant long hours with little or no remuneration. God bless 'em! They sure blessed us. Jim Owens, in particular, became a personal friend.

    We almost never paid fines. Part of the solidarity of the Philadelphia rescue movement consisted in this. We would not help compensate the local governments while they protected child-killing. If they were going to prosecute and imprison us, they would have to pay for it. True, it cost us more than it cost them (in income lost, etc.), but by making it cost them something, we at least gave them something to think about personally and politically.

Jim Owens, Christian gentleman and lawyer

    May also brought the sobering news that Joe Ciepela, a former neighbor and fellow rescuer, who had done a great deal of sidewalk counseling at the Northeast Women's Center, got up Sunday morning and fell back on his bed with a massive heart attack. It was sobering, particularly since he had a number of children still at home. Joe, a retired police photographer, was the first of many rescuers I knew who went to be with the Lord.
    The May dismissal of a RICO suit by NOW against Joe Scheidler, Joan Andrews and John Ryan was good news, particularly since there had been at least one other dismissal of RICO suits against pro-lifers in the previous year.
    I heard from Philly rescuers that Randy Terry had been treated to a three day deposition in this case, toward the end of which the NOW lawyers asked how the rescuers had gotten from the hotel to the abortion clinic at a NY rescue.

Randy answered, no doubt with the wry face he used on such occasions, "by spaceship". A NOW attorney put into the record her opinion that Mr. Terry was on drugs. [142]

But the proaborts were not to be deterred on the legal front. In early 1991, they began a move to use the "civil rights laws," specifically the 1871 "Ku Klux Klan Act" against rescuers. The heart of this law involved "class animus". The question the courts considered was whether rescuers feel a class animus against women seeking abortions! The appeals in the test case had not yet been settled.

In early June a "Father's Rescue" was held at Planned Parenthood and Blackwell, with 75 arrested, including seven first-timers. One of these was a doctor on the staff of Bryn Mawr Hospital. In our trial a clinic worker testified that twelve out of thirty-two appointments failed to appear. Another testimony to our success. We were found guilty and offered the choice of a small fine or three days in jail.

Summer Again!

On June 29th, with temperatures soaring to 97 degrees, a relatively small group of rescuers blocked doors at NEWC, PP and Blackwell. (Bob Brothers noted the sign on Blackwell's door – "Reproductive Immunology") Sixty-six people were arrested

In early July 1991, a nationally known journalist fastened on the "human interest" story of some young rescuers from Milwaukee, minors Kimiko's age. The Milwaukee rescue community was small but dedicated and they were severely opposed by various abortion interests, as

---

[142] Randy's sense of humor could be a controversial thing. I've already mentioned his nationally televised answer to his innovative new cell phone in Atlanta, "Maxwell Smart," in the manner of that early TV spy. Some thought his levity unseemly – many of the same people who thought rescue was unseemly, no doubt. As President Lincoln answered when rebuked by a woman for laughing while thousand of men were dying in the Civil War. "If I didn't laugh, I'd have to cry."

well as political, judicial and law officers. Their sacrifices had been high, and they were willing that their children be instruments of raising public awareness about what was going on.

This "anchor" and his camera crew followed the "Milwaukee kids" around for several weeks, then Roseann and I got a phone call from their parents asking if they could come out for a weekend of rescues they had heard were planned for Philly. Not thinking through all the implications, we said, sure, the more rescuers the better! We let some of the Philly leaders know they were coming, and housing was arranged for them.

But when the kids arrived with their journalistic entourage not far behind, we immediately ran into difficulties. First several of the kids were staying in the homes of hospitable pro-lifers who were used to a little more formal respect than some of the kids exercised. I must admit, I found it slightly silly when someone complained that someone used the toothpaste without asking, but perspectives vary widely on such things. Certainly it's better to err on the side of being too courteous.

Much worse, the journalist and crew called up Roseann and asked, "where are the kids from Milwaukee staying?" which question she naïvely answered. She told them the name of one of the kind Catholic ladies who was hosting them and even furnished the phone number! They then called the lady, citing Roseann as their contact, and asked when and where the prayerful preparation meeting or rally was going to be held. She, as naively, told them.

The next evening, I was supposed to speak at the rally. When we arrived the kids were already there and right behind them, cameras already running, the film crew. I went over and talked to the anchor. I don't recall all of the conversation, but I asked him not to reveal the site of the meeting and I think I asked them not to bring his cameras into the meeting. That first conversation was fairly congenial.

However when the meeting was about to start a number of the leaders got together and told me, in no uncertain terms, that the advent of network TV there was a major problem. They were particularly concerned about getting the clergy of the church in trouble – due to some tension over our meetings there. (Perhaps the church's lawyers were predicting dire consequences.) When it became known that these kids were connected to my friends, and that my wife had told the TV honcho where they were staying, the other leaders of the meeting let it be known it was not only a problem, but it was _my_ problem.

I had planned a sort of biblical/theological talk that evening. It was a fairly big crowd that had turned out. Putting that aside for the moment, I went over to the entrance of the hall and waited for a few minutes as the meeting was about to start. Sure enough, in through the door came the network talking head with his cameraman not far behind.

I met him about ten paces in. I was frustrated and keyed up and I looked him in the eye and said, "You are not welcome here. This is a private meeting and you have not been invited."

He answered mildly enough, but I was not about to give him any slack, "We know you," I said, "We grew up with you. We've watched you lie, cheat, and steal to push your own agenda. If you really want to report the truth about abortion – then show what abortion really is and what it does. You haven't done that have you. Why? "

I went on, and I suppose I was preaching indeed, "The tapes are available. Bernard Nathanson's "Silent Scream" has been out for several years. Go back to your network and get them to run the killing of an unborn baby on TV. That's what this is all about."

I repeated that this was a private meeting and that he was not welcome.

Meanwhile he had waved away his cameraman, whose instinct was to close in and get this diatribe on film. When I finished, the correspondent hesitated, then turned on his heel and himself left the building.

Bernard Nathanson's video "Silent Scream"

I went back to the front and sat down as the meeting started. Our format for these meetings was basically that of a worship service. We prayed, sang songs and hymns, had a couple of homilies, gave out the news of upcoming events, and made any special announcements that were needed.

When my turn to speak came, instead of my prepared stuff, I basically gave my own testimony. I had come to see my personal contribution to abortion in the "woman-as-object" mentality that went with pornography and sexual fantasy. These were the things that had driven me to Christ in my late teens. Pornography and fantasy had continued to crop up as one of my chief forms of self-indulgence.

As I got involved in rescue, I realized part of our need for national repentance tied into our sexual indulgence. Writing a paper "Abortion – A Man's Sin" had helped me formulate the things I shared. I talked about how "woman as object" (the Playboy philosophy) leads so naturally to "baby as object" (abortion) since the "freedom" of the man could only be matched for the woman when she could eliminate the responsibility of the child.

Just as the man used and discarded the woman, so the woman discards the child, the fruit of that temporary "use". I suggested America as a nation needed to repent of "people as objects" and that rescue for me was "bringing forth works in keeping with my repentance" in the words of John the Baptist's exhortation.

Afterward I remember two men who spoke to me. One came up right after the meeting and asked me, "Do you know where I was planning to go after this meeting?" "No," I answered. "To a porno store," he replied. "You spoke directly to me, and I know God was in it." I prayed for him briefly, surprised but encouraged to see someone touched in that particular way.

While I hadn't known this man, the other man was someone I had come to know and deeply respect. We were two of the last to leave and he asked me, with genuine bewilderment in his voice, "How can you share openly like that, especially in front of your daughters?" I don't know if is the love of honesty my father and mother instilled in me, or the church traditions I have been a part of, but I have always found that when leaders publicly confess sin, people begin to take Christ more seriously. Then again, perhaps the emotionally trying evening had something to do with the extent to which I had "let down my hair" that evening. I've never believed my children have many illusions about their father's sinfulness.

The leadership decided against risking arrest the next day. We were determined to make it more or less a non-event for the film crew that dogged us. So we had a "Jericho March" around several abortion clinics in center city. The Milwaukee kids were bored and disappointed. Frankly, I was, too, but maybe we all needed to "cool our jets" a little. The emphasis on prayer that day helped restore a proper perspective on the small part our actions played in God's will. Over the next three days further "non-rescue" prayer marches took place in Philly, Paoli and Bala-Cynwyd.

That five day "Freedom Week" campaign ended on July 4th with a rescue at Yardley, where the clinic closed for the day with no babies killed, and no arrests. Two hundred people participated. Police asked us to leave the abortuary steps, and we agreed to do so as long as no one was going in.

No one did, so we weren't arrested.

Kids from Milwaukee join us in Center City prayer march

Late that summer, Kimiko went to Witchita with a few young people and quite a number of adults from our area. There the notorious late-term abortionist, George Tiller, "Tiller the Killer," operated his awful business complete with incinerator in the backyard sending up its column of black smoke very much like its predecessors at Dachau and Auschwitz.

Rescuers had begun an active campaign against his horrible trade on June 20th. By July 30, 13 rescues had taken place, and Tiller had been closed for an eight day period (apparently trying to encourage rescuers to go home by his inactivity.) One rescue took place for 32 hours continuously from early the 23rd to the afternoon of the 24th, despite a thunderstorm during the night.

Tiller's was nationally known as the place to get a late-term abortion. Late-term abortions were generally not popular with abortionists. Therefore they had become incredibly lucrative. They resulted in more injuries and deaths to mothers. They nauseated and depressed clinic staffs. They even turned doctors' stomach, which is saying something.

Yardley demonstration after rescue closes clinic.

In fact a whole series of "techniques" had been employed to try and overcome the several very unpleasant aspects of late term abortions– which were to culminate in the very efficient "partial birth abortion" that, in the late '90s, helped publicly reveal the abortion industry for what it really is.

Tiller's own technique involved injecting the children of his patients with killing chemicals, inserting swelling "laminaria" (seaweed) plugs in the mothers' cervixes, then depositing his "patients" in a nearby motel where, after some hours, the women's bodies began to react to the dying babies within them. He then gave them pitocin to induce contractions, after which extreme discomfort, physical and emotional, they "gave birth" to the poisoned remains of their children.

The rescuers gathered there for a "Summer of Mercy" campaign, which involved ongoing rescues and other pro-life rallies and activities. Kimiko and a number of other minors endeared themselves to the police by going back to block the gates every chance they got, to the point where even the leadership, including our own Joe Roach, was asking them to cool it! It's a terrible thing when our children take our principles seriously!

Those present in Witchita, including Mike McMonigal, who was not generally noted for sanguine analysis, saw the "Summer of Mercy" as one of the most blessed events rescuers had ever participated in. It seemed that a very large number of local people were supportive, which made a big difference. Most of the local officials were at least restrained if not supportive. It was only Federal Judge Kelly who put a dent in the event, coming down with an injunction and beginning to jail leaders. But the US Justice Department came in on the side of the rescuers against Judge Kelly's injunction!

Pro-life activities continued into August in Witchita, by the end of which 31 babies lives were known to have been saved. More than a thousand people had rescued for the first time and 130 pro-life doctors had joined "The Bernard Nathanson of Witchita," a Dr. Davis, in offering free care to any mother in crisis pregnancy. Chapters of "Lawyers for Life" and "Nurses for Life" had sprung up, and 35,000 people had turned out for a rally on August 25th. Various legal initiatives were being pursued against "Tiller the Killer."

Father's Rescue at Blackwell Killing Center, administrated by Alison Schwartz[143]

---

[143] Alison Schwartz was soon to be a Senator.

Was That Thunder?

In Philly there was another "Father's Rescue" at Planned Parenthood and Blackwell in Center City during August. Despite the name, there were just as many women as men, at least at Blackwell. Fifty-eight were arrested, the last being "the Kissing Bandit," Joe O'Hara.

In court, we were joyfully surprised to find Judge Meier Rose allowing us to present the justification defense – denying the prosecution's motion *in limine* (to prevent the use of this defense). He deferred the verdict, but came back with a twenty-five dollar fine per each. [144]

At Washington, confirmation hearings for Judge Clarence Thomas began in September. I can't remember ever being more ashamed of my country than when Anita Hill's psychotic accusations were aired during those hearings. It was clear that Harvard law professors and the liberal machine would do anything to stop a prolife justice from being appointed to the Supreme Court.

One striking moment in that hearing, which many of us watched on C-Span when we could, was when PA's Arlen Specter, himself an open pro-abort, but still party loyal, was cross-examining Anita Hill about her allegations of Judge Thomas's misconduct toward her, and Edward Kennedy interrupted with some shrill disagreement. At that point Spector turned to Kennedy, noted expert on the abuse of women, and said, "we'll cross that bridge when we come to it, senator." Kennedy didn't say another word for the rest of the hearing. I'd love to know if Spector knew what he was saying. It sounded as though he intended it as a reference to a place and event in Massachusetts. [145]

---

[144] This was the second fine that ended up in a "judgment" against my home. This despite the fact that technically, because my wife and I owned it together, it was illegal under Pennsylvania law to collect a judgment against it for a "crime" that was solely mine.

[145] However older Philadelphia pro-lifers remember Arlen Specter as the District Attorney who refused to prosecute illegal abortionists operating on Walnut Street back before Roe v. Wade. And later, a consummate politician, i.e. pragmatist, Senator Specter, nevertheless told state prolife leaders he supported abortion on

Other Battlefronts in the "Cultural War"

One of the things that kept happening to us during our rescue years was that we found ourselves involved in related issues. Abortion seemed to tie into every branch of evil. It became obvious that abortion was a sinful attempt for the chief purpose of facilitating sinful behavior. In my mind it always remained a "man's sin," since it was an open door to male sexual license. What about dealing with the sinful behavior, too? Roseann, with many other friends, became involved in the fight to bring abstinence education to the schools. But first they had to fight a whole concatenation of ungodly alternatives to abstinence education.

There was a strong cabal firmly ensconced in the Philadelphia Education Administration, with an agenda of promoting, not only "birth control," but homosexual "tolerance," and active promiscuity among students. For instance, at the select public school some of my children attended, homosexual advocates were allowed not only to promote tolerance, but to hand out sexually explicit materials promoting homosexuality. A "LGBT et al" club was officially recognized by the school.

The parents who opposed this sort of thing were strictly a grass-roots movement, but after appearing in large numbers at several school board meetings, where various speakers eloquently cited studies and statistics as well as moral principles, the policies began to change.

Lines of coordination were built with parents in New York who had fought similar battles, and various local organizations added their expertise.

Spokespersons were invited on TV talk shows. Press conferences featuring parents, students and pastors set up a wide resonance among Philadelphians. This effort was eventually to lead to a large coup and general overhaul of the Education Administration, and four or five years after that, with the incorporation of abstinence education in our public

---

demand "on principle". In the end of course, he switched parties. Another strange product of strange times.

schools!

In September a few rescuers from our area went down to Atlantic City to join rescuers from New Jersey and New York during the Miss America Pageant being held there. Bicycle ("Kryptonite") locks were used in this rescue, because there were only about 80 people and the police there tended to expedite arrests. Bob Pawson was quoted in the Atlantic City Press, "Aborted babies will miss America. The aborted baby girls will never have an opportunity to be Miss America. And these aborted babies are citizens you will miss, America."

In November we rescued at Tabor Road off North Broad Street, at the offices of Berger, Benjamin and Kline.

Allen Kline was a Philadelphia native.[146] He, like many abortionists, went to medical school, but didn't exactly shine there. Oh that universal human tendency to develop a pecking order! In prison the swindlers are at the top and the sex offenders at the bottom. The medical community also has an order of precedence, and while the brain surgeons are near the top, the OB/GYN guys are often looked down upon by the others. But abortionists are undoubtedly the rock bottom.

Kline was the abortionist responsible for the death of a thirteen year old girl, Dawn Ravenell, in 1985 in New York, which in 1990, resulted in one of the largest damage awards up to that time. After that he worked in Pensacola, Florida and then returned to Philly. He worked for years at the Northeast Women's Center where staff close to him [147] recalled he and the other abortionists would gather in the clinic after a long day of killing babies to unwind together smoking marijuana.

His victim, Dawn Ravenell, was a honor student and church soloist. Kline and his nurse left her in a coma after a secret abortion, and she died three weeks later. Her parents were Pentecostal ministers. The first they knew about the

---

[146] By coincidence, I later learned that in high school he dated the sister of a friend who rescued with us!

[147] Yes, there were former abortion staff people in our church community. I learned these details firsthand from one.

abortion was when they got a call from the hospital. She never gained consciousness to speak to them, though she lingered for weeks in a coma before she died.

Mike McMonigal talks with rescuers after we were released

Berger, Benjamin and Kline appear to have been partners for a number of years. Benjamin was reputed a high-strung and erratic physician. Berger was associated with Temple University Hospital. The three of them still maintained offices across the street from Einstein hospital [148] along with another couple of abortionists. However the first two seemed to have dissolved any official connection with Kline. Nonetheless, pro-lifers had known them as Berger, Benjamin and Kline (B., B. and K.), and thus we continued to speak of them.

A medical student who attended our church told me he was doing one rotation in Einstein Hospital's emergency room when a woman came in with "complications" after an abortion. The physician on duty in the emergency room referred to B, B and K, across the street, as "those butchers,"

---

[148] Einstein is the Philadelphia hospital where the most babies are aborted every year. One wonders how Albert would feel about that!

divulging that she and the emergency room had seen a lot of women suffering their botched work. These never got into the press because malpractice insurance agents negotiated monetary settlements with the injured women which included "non-disclosure" agreements – they didn't get the money unless they promised never to tell what had happened to them.

This rescue was particularly close to our hearts, because these abortionists operated more or less in our back yard -- soliciting customers from Olney, Logan, and North Philadelphia – our "hood". Roseann and I had followed in the footsteps of others, going out on Saturday mornings to do sidewalk counseling there. This was without doubt the hardest thing I ever did.

Rescue involves various hard things, including discomfort, pain, and a high degree of insecurity, but sidewalk counseling involves continual rejection. Nonetheless, the effective counselor must be gentle, winsome, and cheerful. Sweetness under fire is not only unnatural for me, but the furthest thing from all my inclinations. It was a definite crucifixion for me every time I went out there.

Our presence there was certainly effective, directly and indirectly. It was the spark plug for a whole series of things every day we were there. First the clinic staff would often come by us on their way in and we might greet them with a reminder, "God loves you. You don't have to kill any babies today."

Abortionist Berger was particularly interesting in his reaction to our presence and our greetings. For the first years we went there, he invariably answered us, "If what I am doing is wrong, may God strike me dead." After the first couple of abortionist-shootings he didn't say that anymore, which is one of the few good things I can think of connected with the abortionist shootings.

There was also one woman on staff there, whom Roseann and I had only little influence on, so far as I know, but others in our circles and in other parts of her life, brought the gospel to her. She left the staff there, eventually telling us about her conviction and repentance. We became good friends. That was tremendously encouraging.

But on the discouraging side, after we had been there a few months a pro-abort "deathscort" began to show up regularly.[149] He was one of the meanest old sons of a bitch I've ever met, and I was as naturally capable of loving him as I was of jumping to the moon. The first day he was there he went off on me. I then went off on him, and the tone of our exchanges varied little thereafter. I was too small a person to see him with any perspective – it was much easier to enter into an adversarial relationship than a Christ-like one. I took the easy way.

At most abortuaries in Philadelphia the pattern had been long established that Civil Affairs officers would come out whenever the abortuaries were open and pro-lifers were present. The cost of this over the years must have run into the millions. Very soon, police officers began to show up whenever we were there. The clinic found it easy enough to get the cops out. All they had to do was make up a report we had threatened or harassed a client -- or that we were trespassing inside the building -- and the special protection machine began to roll.

In any case, the pattern was set and soon it was applied to our clinic. Curiously for a long time it was always the same two officers who came out while we were there, and at the end of the day as we were leaving, they would always go into the building and take the elevator up to the abortionists' offices. I wondered what sort of transaction took place during these regular meetings.

One day I asked to the two officers what might be going on there. They in turn challenged me to say what I thought was going on, so I just held my hand behind my back, palm upward. At that point they seemed to take a great deal more offense than they would have at a false accusation, getting huffy and pretending shock, but in another sense they took a great deal less offense than I would have expected --

---

[149] We were by no means the first to sidewalk counselors there, but at the time we started going no one had done it for a while.

Was That Thunder?

were I wrong.

Each Saturday ten to fifteen women would come to the clinic. There were also other medical offices open during the period we went there. One general practitioner started off very hostile to us, but warmed up and became a friend. The dentists with offices across the hall from the abortuary, had put up big signs in their windows making sure people knew what they were – and weren't. There was more than once that windows were broken in that building – and certainly the denizens had no way of knowing we weren't handing out literature by day and bricks by night. [150]

With all the moms and dads going in and out of the clinic, we must have handed out thousands of pieces of literature and spoken briefly to hundreds. On several occasions we had the great privilege of seeing people come out and leave. On one occasion a young woman had given evidence of a change of heart and had gone back in to get her deposit money, but when she didn't come out for quite a while, I went across to the civil affairs officer on duty (not the usual one) and asked him if he would do me the favor of going in to check on her. He did, and a little later he came and said he was going to escort her out, but that she did not want to talk to us further, which was fine with me. I did however ask him to give her the pamphlet with phone numbers for crisis pregnancy centers, in case she wanted it. She waved to us as she left.

After we'd been involved there a while, we began to hand out literature to passers-by. Included in this literature was a long printout we'd made up and read at one of our Center City rescues, enumerating the women killed by "legal " abortion with dates, places, and the names of abortionists involved. This list included Dawn Ravenell the young girl Kline had killed in New York. Many passersby were shocked

---

[150] Although it isn't hard to fantasize shortcuts like throwing bricks at buildings, somehow I can't see throwing bricks as an act of repentance. If ever I found myself fantasizing in that direction, I would know it was a sign I was getting burnt out and drifting from Christ as my center.

to hear that there were abortionists operating in the building. There were quite a few customers of the pharmacy that fronted on the clinic entrance, so we were able to disseminate the news pretty widely.

One day I gave the list to a passerby who turned out to be a new abortionist! I only figured that out when he got loudly incensed, and claimed harassment. He tried to get the police to arrest me.

Winter 1991

Our November rescue at "Berger, Benjamin and Kline's" on Tabor Road was particularly satisfying. We went back there several times over the years. This was the first time I was ever in a rescue where we went inside the building. In this case we did it because we felt ambivalent about blocking the other offices. Therefore we went up to the second floor and actually gathered in the hall in front of the doors of the various abortionists' offices.

In the hallway at Berger, Benjamin and Kline abortion offices

Although there were only 56 of us, the sidewalk counselors that day got to have much longer conversations with the women coming there than Roseann and I normally did. The office manager for Berger and Benjamin testified at our trial that none of the 24 appointments for that day showed up. Allen Kline testified he could do no business that day, either, so it seems many lives were saved.

Also that month in the national news the proaborts' split personality showed up sharply with the prosecution (and persecution) of the "Butcher of Avenue A" in New York. Dr. Abu Hayat's failure was not in doing too much harm, but in not doing too little. He did an abortion on a 20 year old women about 32 weeks pregnant. All he succeeded in doing to the baby was cutting off her right arm, after which, the baby was born alive and rushed into emergency care.

Somehow this made Dr. Hayat a "butcher" and all the proaborts with one voice denounced him. The headlines said he "cut the arm off a fetus"! He ended up sentenced to 29 years in prison! Cut off a life – we honor and pay you! Cut off an arm – we jail you for life!

Abu Hayat, "The Butcher of Avenue A"

However, Ralph Traphagen, a soft-spoken rescuer and fervent Christian, went to Hayat's trial. After several sessions, Ralph had the opportunity to invite Dr. Hayat to have lunch with him. Seated at a café, Ralph told Dr. Hayat who he was, and how opposed to abortion he was, but he also told him the gospel – that there was real forgiveness for sin, and real love for everyone who would receive it. Ralph told him Jesus was the one Person in the universe who afterward never holds a grudge against the repentant sinner.

Apparently Dr. Hayat was deeply moved that someone, and especially a pro-lifer would show care for him in the midst of total rejection from all other quarters. He said he wanted to think about what Ralph had shared. Ralph sent him literature and began a correspondence with him

Abu Hayat had his license permanently revoked and went to prison. Ralph had spent considerable time behind bars himself, as one of those most adamant in refusing to knuckle under to injunctions, stay-away orders, and "parole agreements". It was Ralph's stated belief that Dr. Hayat was coming to understand the gospel.

There was another rescue in Philly in early December, where Adriel risked arrest, followed by the last rescue of 1991, on December 28th. This was the first time I was involved in a rescue at the Lewis Tower Building in Center city where another abortuary had opened up, and again we went inside the building in order not to block legitimate businesses in the same building.

Toward the end of 1991 there was some hope that the US Supreme Court would take the appeals[151] concerning the Pennsylvania Abortion Control Act as an opportunity to overturn Roe.

There were also some ambitious aspirations to make pro-life inroads in local and national politics. Rescuers, while not the best of politicians, contributed considerable energy to distributing literature and other tasks during these and other campaigns.

A few from our family went to a rally near the Windham-Franklin Hotel where President Bush was speaking when a bunch of anti-Bush proaborts were rallying against him. We were across the streets from them with a lot of pro-

---

[151] These appeals were made in 1988 and 1989 by the abortionists, and in 1991 by the PA Attorney General.

lifers, and Kimiko saw Nora a friend from school. Kimiko went across the street to talk to her. When they talked again the next Monday in school, Nora asked Kim about her rescue involvement and expressed envy of Kim for getting arrested! We hoped for converts, but perhaps with better motives than this!

Our own Mike McMonigal announced his campaign in the Republican primary for State House in the 194th district [152] and many of us worked the phone lines and the polls for him. Steve Friend, an important pro-life voice in the State House, announced his candidacy against US Senator Arlen Specter. It was the man of principle against the consummate politician, so again many pro-lifers signed on to work for Steve.

That winter of 1991, Roseann, along with friends from church, Nancy Devlin, Esther Miller, Kendra Holden and Robin Ingalls, all had children at James Russell Lowell School in Olney. They met once a week to pray for the children and the school. Esther Miller was the president of the Lowell Home and School organization and thus kept informed of the Philly school board meetings and decisions. She heard that the school board would be receiving the report from the Task Force on Adolescent Sexuality at its March 4 meeting and that the Task Force would be recommending that condoms be distributed in Philadelphia junior and senior high schools.

These moms decided they couldn't let this go by without challenge and made plans to give speeches at the board meeting. Bill Devlin put them in contact with parents in New York who had already faced this sort of battle. They helped coach Roseann et al on points to argue and where to go do research. Jack Hartigan, a retired lawyer and grandfather, was especially generous with time and information. Terri Taylor (a good friend of Esther Miller's), and soon to become a good friend of Roseann's, spent hours fleshing out that facts and statistics that showed condom distribution failed to lower teen pregnancy rates.

They showed up at the March 4 meeting as the only

---

[152] Roxborough / Wynnefield

parents speaking about the sexuality policy. "Speaking about it" is euphemistic. They blasted it. A *Daily News* reporter and photographer captured Esther (the Home and School president) in an impassioned pose and wrote an article about the parent protest. *AM Philadelphia* saw the picture and called the ProLife Union of SE PA asking if they had a parent who would appear on the show. All this interest was surprising to Roseann, but apparently it's true that sex sells… everyone wants to talk about it.

Roseann appeared on the show and our friends from Christian Stronghold Baptist Church found Sherry Neal, a school nurse and parent, to appear with her. Mike McMonigal coached Roseann, "No matter what question they ask, say what you've planned to say." What she planned to say came from the picture that Jack Hartigan had drawn for them, as well as research by Terri. Roseann nearly memorized a fact sheet on condoms that Terri had researched and written. Roseann put in her own two cents wherever possible.

Sherry Neal (with Roseann) told it like God says it.

However Sherry stole the show simply by being straightforward. She said what we were talking about was fornication and adultery and since God said it was wrong, we ought not to do anything to facilitate it to our kids destruction. . This was an engaging and effective approach: the Presbyterians would haul out the statistics which gave the ambivalent administrators something to chew on, while the Baptists came out with the Word of God, which was our bottom line. The direct statement of Christian morality was quite effective with many parents.

By phone calls and letters parents were able to shake up the board to the point that they decided to hold a day of hearings. By this time Roseann and Terri were seeing the facts from their "Now for a Little Condom Sense" sheet quoted by Focus on the Family and others in national papers.

They decided to hold a press conference in front of the Board of Education on the day of the hearings, besides getting everyone they could possibly recruit to speak. They had the benefit of others' experience on how to hold a press conference. A variety of people spoke beside mothers: a teen-age girl, and, a health official from New Jersey, Richard Smith, who explained legal liability particularly well.

This was all strange new territory to Roseann and when a reporter asked her what she objected to about the Task Force, she hedged on pointing out that two of the three subcommittees where headed by gays or lesbians, who clearly had a personal agenda. The reporter coaxed her to go ahead and say that, but Roseann demurred. After second thoughts, she went back and offered to make a statement, but the reporter said, you had your chance. Roseann says is probably better that way, "Your 'best shot' isn't always best to shoot." Over time they went to so many board meetings that they got to know the administration power brokers – and vice versa.

The hearings were crowded and got good coverage. Pastors Bruce Becker and John Julien spoke from the point of view of ministers; Heather Ramsey spoke; Kimiko spoke; as did Richard Smith. Health officials said this was a matter of life and death. Two separate rooms were set up for the hearings. Roseann et al not only spoke against contraceptive distribution to teen-agers, they also (at Terri Taylor's insistence) presented information about abstinence programs.

Terri had sent for a number of abstinence programs and had reviewed them and made up a comparison sheet. So they continued on the course of creating controversy, presenting the scientific case against condoms, and presenting an alternative that had been shown effective in reducing teen pregnancy rates. It was a policy that you could support with your mind and your conscience.

Kimiko wrote an opinion piece that was published by the *Daily News* and that led to *AM Philadelphia* inviting her to come on the show with Roseann. They also had Molly Kelly appear together with the Girls' High student who had spoken in their own press conference. Slowly they gained ground, using every opportunity to talk about abstinence programs.

Linda Ronning and daughter

In June another rescue took place at Northeast Women's Center, despite all the attempts of judges to banish any pro-life presence from that vicinity. Charles Gindhart snapped a wonderful photo of Linda Ronning and her daughter during that rescue.[153]

The School Board voted June 24th to accept the task force recommendations. Our family was at the Jersey shore

---

[153] Linda was she who met her husband John in he exercise yard in Atlanta jail back in 1988.

for the week-end, where Roseann saw the headlines. They had voted to put condoms in the school. We were sick at heart. It was sad to see some of those cave in, whom we had thought of as stalwarts on behalf of children. But the labors of the moms had modified the agenda enough that condoms were available only in 10 high schools and no junior highs. Furthermore, they had made abstinence programs a viable option, to be respected and not derided, if not yet used.

Roseann's involvement faded for a few months. We bought the big house that needed lots of work. She got pregnant. Terri got pregnant. But the controversy continued. Seven months pregnant, Roseann debated the head of Act-Up in Philadelphia on TV.

But the Catholics held candlelight vigils for abstinence at board meetings, and Veronica Joyner of Parents United for Better Schools aided by lawyer Dennis Abrams of Beth Yeshua brought a lawsuit against the district demanding an abstinence program. It was finally adopted in 1992. Roseann went to the board and thanked them. She also asked talk host Wally Kennedy if she could come on his show and thank the board. It wasn't the best abstinence program in the world, but it was a fresh wind. The moms wanted to be partners.

During this time the moms also lobbied to have someone on the committee that made decisions about the curriculum. Nancy Devlin, a nurse as well as mother of public school children, attended many meetings. Roseann's friends often prayer together to support Nancy in her heroic participation. She got no respect. It wasn't much fun.

Our good friend Art Bucci went to one of the Department of Ed committee meetings, but when he turned on a tape recorder they had him escorted out of the building.

John Stanton went to the Board to inform them of some dirty details we had learned about the curriculum. He got an appointment for a meeting with Jacob Jacovino and Cathy Ballesley and invited Roseann to go.[154]

---

[154] An old friend, Frank Speyers called the night before and told her he'd had a bad dream about her and wanted to make sure that she was OK. We told him to keep on praying for us!

In that meeting Roseann pressed about whether or not the curriculum was based on the work of Alfred Kinsey. The coincidence level was too high for any other explanation. Cathy Ballesly hemmed and hawed and ultimately hedged. Afterwards, Roseann wished she had pushed harder.

Then the board came out with Policy #102, defined as "multi-cultural, multi-racial, multi-gender" education. But this time, the moms had their list of parents. They'd been doing a newsletter. The highlight of this campaign was a board meeting at Lincoln H.S. They managed to make it such an event that someone got nervous and hired extra security!

Bonnie Brooks, a parent, became the poster girl for the parent protest ...appearing on *AM Philadelphia*. She also spoke at their press conference and then in an *Inquirer* article. But Linda, the president of the Lincoln High School PTA stole the show by getting up and blasting the board that had just given her an honorary award. She rebuked their Policy 102.

Following that fiasco, David Hornbeck [155] came to Philadelphia with more "Outcome Based Education". But what happened then was amazing. The school district went broke, the state took over, dissolving the school board, (who had been appointed by the mayor) and hiring Paul Vallas as CEO in July 2002. Vallas had made quite an impact on the Chicago Schools. He opened the doors of the school district, at least for a while, to abstinence educators.

In early December rescuers went back to "Comly Road" and Joshua was among those taken into custody. The two officers who carried him found it was light work. Ought a child advocate for children? Our working answer was yes. Call it education for justice.

---

[155] Philadelphia Head of Schools from 1996 -Aug 2002.

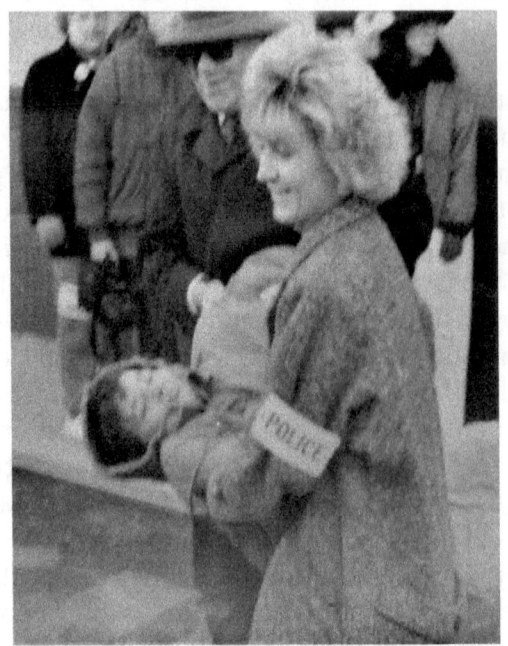
Josh taken into custody at Comly Road in Philly.

CHAPTER SIX – DEVELOPMENTS (1992)

A wise man is strong; yea, a man of knowledge increaseth strength. For by wise counsel thou shalt make thy war; and in multitude of counselors there is safety. Wisdom is too high for a fool; he openeth not his mouth in the gate. He that deviseth to do evil shall be called a mischievous person. The thought of foolishness is sin and the scorner is an abomination to men. If thou faint in the day of adversity, thy strength is small. If thou forebear to deliver them that are drawn unto death, and those that are ready to be slain; If thou sayest, Behold, we knew it not; doth not he that pondereth the heart consider it? And he that keepeth thy soul, doth not he know it? And shall not he render to every man according to his works? Proverbs 24:5-12

    The rescue year began at Chester Crozer on January 2. Thirty-five people were arrested. It was a sad occasion in that after we were arrested, a woman still went in for an abortion, although sidewalk counselors had talked with her for nearly two hours. Such failures always caused sorrow, but also reflection and resolve. We reminded ourselves we were there for long-term results as well as short term life-saving – and that doing what was right was not ultimately results-based. But our sadness was real – as was our happiness whenever we knew of immediate saves of mothers and babies.
    Our church's "Pro-life Month" Sunday classes started off that year with a survey. We were taking more seriously the fact that different people had different gifts and different callings. We had come to accept the fact that our church wasn't going out to rescue en masse. We also were growing in respect for other important pro-life activities. So the survey was set up to help people see their own strengths and weaknesses, and inform them about pro-life functions they might perform.
    We designed the survey to direct people along one of

four tracks the rest of the month: Alternatives to Abortion (adoption and foster care – Sue Laurito); Sidewalk Counseling (Stan and Eunice Kalbach); Christian Political Responsibility/Informing Others (Mark Hoyle); and What I've Learned Through Rescue (Trott).

OR National Capital Project

Toward the end of January OR National undertook the "Capital Project" in DC. I remember the pro-aborts there were doggéd, assigning teams to follow the leaders around and harass them. It was wonderful to see the leaders use this opportunity to share the gospel graciously with these women.[156] We rescued on 21 January. There were 384 arrested at two clinics.

My three oldest kids were with me at the back door of one abortuary, where we had about thirty people. We sent representatives around the front every now and then to report on the progress of arrests there. When they came back and said there were only about fifteen people left in front of the doors, we whispered the message around that we would hurry out there en masse after the second verse of the song we were singing. It was pretty obvious that a couple of the people with us were not "with us" so the message wasn't communicated to them.

Everyone moved out right on cue. We all ran around the corner and out to the front. When we got to the front, the police had already formed corridors to bring women into the clinic. Some of our people tried to dive between the officers, and I ended up having to exhort them not to push or resist the police. We saw no evidence we had stopped any abortions, but we had done our best. I later ran into Joe Foreman, and he said he knew there had to be a Presbyterian

---

[156] Jeff White has a wonderful story of leading his "shadow" to Christ. He says that this became so common that the pro-aborts started telling the "shadows" not to engage in conversation with the rescue leaders! Listen to Jeff's Bridgehead Radio interview on Youtube.

or two in that bunch when he saw them come charging around the corner.

Joshua was arrested again, and someone snapped a photo of him that showed up in a New Jersey pro-life newsletter. It is a poignant photo – a big cop leading off a young boy with tears in his eyes. It still puts a lump in my throat.

I was processed out late that night. Roseann and the kids had been waiting for many hours. They spent part of the time trying to get some sleep in our old camper-van and part of the time in the court where a long line of rescuers was gradually brought before a judge.

Roseann recalled listening as one woman came before the judge and was asked if she had any legal representation there. She answered with the boldness typical of many rescuers, saying her lawyer was Jesus Christ. The judge asked the clerk , "Beside the fact that Miss So-and-so has a good attorney, what else do we know about her?" I don't think we stayed for the second day of rescues, but another 140 risked arrest then.

Philadelphia Area Rescues

Early in 1992 Philly leadership decided not to have rallies the night before each rescue. I think one reason was the proaborts had gotten pretty good at keeping track of what we were up to this way.

I remember several occasions when proaborts were "discovered" at rallies, mainly through the fact that none of the rest of us knew them. Nor could they give believable answers as to how they found out about the meetings. However, in the end it was usually basic questions about Christian faith that exposed them most clearly.

A couple years earlier, at a rally held in our own church building in Philadelphia, three pro-abort women once showed up. Prolifers are friendly people, so those around them greeted them and asked a few questions. Their answers raised other questions. So Mike McMonigal and

Patty McNamara took them aside and asked who had invited them to the meeting. They gave an unknown name. So Mike asked how they knew that person. The answers were nebulous. But the three ladies really started getting nervous when he began to ask about their church connections and what they believed. Since these were not public meetings and they were uninvited, we escorted them out.

Instead of holding rallies just prior to rescues, we began to have pro-life meetings interspersed between rescues, principally for purposes of encouragement and information.

On Feb 15th Kimiko and Adriel joined us in a rescue in front of Blackwell, and in the first week of March we were back in front of Planned Parenthood. I think this was the one where Kimiko and a number of her friends were led around the corner and released by the police. They took off and ran all the way around the block, arriving in front of the doors again, much to the chagrin of the supervising officer, who did not make the same mistake twice.

Tony Sulpizio, who lived pretty close to us in Olney, was sent to jail indefinitely for refusing to pay fees to the NE Womens Center (Comly Road). Judge Reed ordered the fines and jailing despite the fact that Tony was not named in the injunction. Now "raw judicial power" was being expanded through injunction. And it was much worse elsewhere in the country. Tony was finally released after 51 days in jail.

In Boston OR leader Bill Cotter was serving a 2 ½ year sentence (the maximum penalty) for violating an injunction of Superior Court Judge Robert Bohn. [157]

Nor did they need injunctions as a basis for the exercise of judicial tyranny. Michael Schmiedicke was serving a two to four year sentence in Mercer State Prison, PA, for having been involved with Kevin Cleary in a "lock" rescue in August 1990. They had locked themselves to a car. The parole board was about to release him on minimum time

---

[157] Judge Bohn sentenced a first time rapist to six months probation a week after sentencing Cotter.

(two years), but Mike's refusal to sign the parole papers [158] made them unwilling to release him. Bob Roethlisberger had gone into prison in April 1991 to begin a four year sentence for rescuing a total of four times in the city of Atlanta. At that rate, many of us in Philly would soon be serving three life sentences!

But instead we rescued at Planned Parenthood both on March 4th (Ash Wednesday) [159] and again on March 8th (Good Friday).

Rev. Johnny Hunter of Buffalo

Black Leadership

In April, Rev. Johnny Hunter came down from Buffalo to speak at a rally. It was a rich blessing and a novelty for

---

[158] Signing these kinds of papers seemed to rescuers not only to be promising not to rescue again, but also "admitting" to a crime.

[159] On Ash Wednesday there were 36 arrested.

many of us to hear a Black Baptist preacher get going! He was inspiring as well as solidly biblical.

I think the rally was held in a Catholic Vets Club in Conshohocken. Johnny started up not one, not two, but at least three biblical threads, which seemed at first to diverge in all directions. But as things wound on amidst wonderful illustrations, and disarming humor, Rev. Hunter pulled it together in a powerful gospel call.

After this rally, on April 18 (Holy Saturday) 77 rescuers were arrested outside Comly Road (NEWC) and Blackwell killing centers.

Dr. Alveda King, niece of Rev. MLK, Jr.

I was blessed to hear Rev. Hunter speak on several other occasions. He was able to keep his eyes on the eternal purpose, and thus to always communicate hope. He continues to this day, to be active in a growing circle of African-American church leaders organized as Life Education and Resource Network, LEARN. LEARN includes pastor and former Eagles tailback, Herb Lusk, and Rev. Martin Luther King Jr.'s niece, Dr. Alveda King, among many others.

A Memoir of Pro-life Rescue

Later that month many Philadelphians returned Rev. Hunter's compliment and went to Buffalo where courts had been increasingly repressive of rescuers through injunctions. Five rescues took place, involving 597 persons arrested. At least 9 women decided not to kill their babies. Judge Arcara who issued the injunction, ordered the arrests of a number of leaders, including Rev. Robert Schenck who had been physically attacked by pro-aborts several times earlier in the month.

Rev. Paul Schenk

Battles on the Legal Front

That same month the US Supreme Court began its review of the constitutionality of certain provisions of Pennsylvania's 1988 and 1989 Abortion Control Acts – *Planned Parenthood of Southeast Pennsylvania v. Casey.*[160] Somewhere in there the Arthur DeMoss Foundation began to run its wonderful pro-life television ads with the theme "Life.

---

[160] This case came the closest to overturning Roe v.Wade of any case the Supreme Court has heard thus far. It is said that on the first round of votes, the majority voted to overturn , but that Justice Kennedy was subsequently talked out of it.

What a beautiful choice." Many of us were encouraged to see such a message broadcast over national networks. Arthur and Nancy Demoss were well known in the Philadelphia area for their commitment to the gospel.

In May, Judge Reed sent John Stanton, Mike McMonigal, Pat McNamara and Joe Roach to federal jails under RICO [161] charges. They were to spend as much as 88 days behind bars, but the rest of the local movement pitched in to fill the gap. We were all encouraged by their stalwart faithfulness.

Also notable was *Time Magazine's* cover story in early May, a tirade against pro-lifers for setting back the "abortion rights" cause over the last decade. You take your encouragements wherever you can find them.

In May, Kimiko and Adriel spoke before a gathering of rescuers. They shared perspectives from their own involvement. Young voices were increasingly heard, and they encouraged the old-timers. Another local rescue followed.

Then on the 19th of May, up in Allentown, "The Allentown Seven" were sentenced to a year in jail. They were given the option of probation if they would sign a pledge to stay away from the Allentown killing center. Judge Gardner told them "the key is in your hands".

The "Allentown Seven" included a pair of newlyweds, Mark and Gretchen Nelson! What a way to spend your honeymoon! These seven hardy Christians were to stay the full year in Lehigh County jail rather than compromise. Their example together with that of the four "RICOS" from Philly put steel in the backbone of many of us lesser souls.

Among them was also a rescuer much-loved in the Delaware Valley, Joe O'Hara, from Wilkes-Barre. Joe was known as "the Kissing Bandit" among Philly rescuers. A retired Navy petty officer and submariner, Joe invariably embraced and kissed everyone he knew, of either gender,

---

[161] Racketeering and Corrupt Organization Act, special legislation designed to make organized crime more susceptible to law enforcement efforts.

every time we got together. Few people successfully avoided this, and after becoming accustomed to it through the first time or two, most found his holy kiss a blessing.

Joe O'Hara, the "Kissing Bandit"

Judge Retacco of Philadelphia Common Pleas Court, made an effort to clean-up all the rescue fines and sentences outstanding. We were all gathered into a courtroom in City Hall and basically given the opportunity to do three days community service to purge each of our warrants, etc. from the system. This was effective for seven or eight cases I had outstanding, but two others had been turned into liens against our house.

On the 1st of June 1992, due to the back-breaking imposition of fines against the organization by Federal Judge Reed, the Southeast Pennsylvania Pro-Life Coalition was officially disbanded. Among other things, the judge had ordered the organization to pay out large deposits each month, which would be forfeited should the judge find anyone connected with it in violation of his ever-expanding injunction.

Was That Thunder?

Mixed Message Among Evangelicals

In mid-June Bill Devlin actively gathering foodstuffs for the Billy Graham Organization to distribute to the needy during a crusade here. Afterward Bill had a chance to speak with Billy himself, and asked him why he did not take a stronger stand against abortion.

Graham's answer was "You know, we could talk for about an hour on abortion... You and a lot of other people want me to be more outspoken on this issue. But I'm just going to take the middle ground and keep preaching the Cross." As Bill pointed out, reflecting on this afterward, it's kind of hard to figure out what the middle ground is on life – "either we have a dead child or an alive child."

Since Billy Graham had something to do with my own conversion, I would not like to speak disrespectfully of him. Nevertheless on the basis of several obvious examples, I cannot avoid the conclusion that Dr. Graham tended to waffle on abortion. On a national talk show he was asked when life begins. He said, "I don't know when life begins." Not too long after this his organization sent out a prayer/support letter stating that overpopulation was among the biggest problems the human race had to face.

Some say these mixed messages originated with Dr. Graham's father-in-law, L. Nelson Bell, co-founder of *Christianity Today* magazine. It is said Dr. Bell, while in the China mission field, was personally involved with abortions, and was exceedingly ambivalent about the subject. Yet, strangely enough, it was at the home of Dr. Graham, with the leadership of his wife, Ruth Bell Graham, that evangelical leaders were called together to begin the Christian Action Council.[162] The CAC had been one of the first Protestant organizations active on the national level in opposition to abortion.

The scripture is clear that an army cannot follow an indistinct trumpet call into battle – and on a number of occasions Billy Graham failed the evangelical church -- and

---

[162] Jesse Jackson was also involved with the CAC at its founding.

the babies, by such a call.

However, when Billy Graham's book *Storm Warning* came out, wonderful to say, it contained much firmer statements against abortion than had previously come from the famous evangelist -- perhaps partly the fruit of challenges from Bill Devlin and others.

Rev. Franklin Graham, Billy's son, and new leader of Dr. Graham's ministry has sounded a much clearer note in publicly opposing abortion and affirming efforts to reestablish the legal protection of the unborn.

Franklin Graham

Mike Schmedicke was released 14 June, without paying the restitution fee that had thitherto been required of him. Here was yet another reward for perseverance and long-suffering.

Our Own New Babies

Our own biggest pro-life event of the year occurred on

Was That Thunder?

29 June, when Victoria Ann Trott was born. When we found out Roseann was pregnant, we looked hard for a non-aborting birth center that was also affordable, and we ended up at Fitzgerald-Mercy where a talented nurse-midwife team oversaw the delivery of our daughter. We named her Victoria in reference to Christ's work, but also in anticipation of a Supreme Court decision on the PA Abortion Control Act, in hope it might be a "victory," significantly limiting or even overthrowing Roe.

Mike and Ceil McMonigal

We were surprised to run into Ceil McMonigal at Fitzgerald-Mercy. She, too, was planning to deliver there. Mike was still in jail as her due date approached. As I anticipated the birth of my own child, I was struck with how hard that sacrifice must be. It weighed on my meditations until I felt moved to write a poem from their child's viewpoint, expressing some of what that child would one day feel. Ceil delivered Brigid on the 19th, ten days before our own daughter was born. Mike was not released until the 2nd of July, thirteen days later, after 59 days in jail.

Meanwhile, of course, Mike was still running for office! Randy Terry put it nicely when he said Mike should be elected because "unlike many Philadelphia politicians, Mike got his jail time out of the way before he is to take office." Unfortunately, many conservative voters in his district didn't see it that way and were put off by his jail record.

The final Casey decision by the Supreme Court, despite upholding the Pennsylvania Abortion Control Act, was very disappointing in its language, and in largely affirming Roe. Written by three Reagan appointees, Souter, Kennedy and OConner, it was nonetheless New Age in its relativist and mystical pronouncements. Justice Kennedy wrote the "mystery clause" which was later quoted as precedent in rulings as perverse as that on Oregon's euthanasia legislation.

Our bench trials for the 1988 Atlanta rescues came up. I rode down to Atlanta with Art Tomlinson of OR Binghamton, during which trip he got sick and tired of my "wisdom" on nearly every subject. [163]

The day our bench trials took place there were eight or nine defendants, each tried separately. The first was from New York City, and he had a lawyer with him. He testified this was not the first time he had been in this kind of trouble, since he had come down in the 60's and been arrested for participating in the Civil Rights marches. The judge, a sober black woman, was obviously moved. I can't remember his sentence, but it was no doubt "guilty," with a small fine or community service of his choice. Most of us got that sentence.

I was perhaps the third one tried. I told about the peaceful way we had conducted ourselves, and contrasted that with the fact that the police were so rough I was bleeding in eleven places at the end of the day. The judge asked me if I knew what police officer had used the pain-compliance

---

[163] At one point he asked me if there was anything he could say I wouldn't disagree with! Many of my acquaintance would agree with him.

pressure holds on me. I honestly did not until that day, so I said, "No but he had blond hair – and a red neck." It was only when I got back to my seat among the other defendants that one of them pointed out Major Burnett. He had come in and was sitting right behind where I had stood as I testified. He was the man.

When we broke at lunch, a woman from Atlanta cautioned me, "Be careful what you say, you're playing with fire." It reminded me of Bob Dylan's song, "Slow Train Coming" and the lines, "Boy without a doubt, you got to quit your messin', straighten out. You could die down here and be just another accident statistic." But we sighted no mysterious cruiser following us. I think we stayed the night out at Bob Jewitt's off of one of the enumerable Peach Tree Roads.

Bob, whom I met in jail there in 1988, was later active with the Christian Defense Coalition, and was much quoted in the media during the 2003 debate over removing the Ten Commandments from Judge Moore's courtroom. He instructed me on the proper preparation of grits. We also had a chance to hang out with Joe Foreman again, who was active with OR Atlanta at that time.

My sentence was community service. I asked the judge if I could fulfill it in the activities I was already involved in. I told her I went regularly to a nursing home to hold Sunday services and I worked with an organization ministering to people coming out of homosexuality called Harvest. She said that was fine. Watching her up close it was obvious she found herself in a very uncomfortable position personally – between a measure of sympathy on the one hand, and the political machine on the other. I finished my "community service" at Harvest and the nursing home in August 1992.

To Save A Life

1992 was the year of the most wonderful experience Roseann and I had while sidewalk counseling outside Berger,

Benjamin and Kline. It was a fairly slow morning – few appointments and few passersby. We had handed out a lot of alternatives-to-abortion literature that gave addresses and phone numbers of organizations set up to help pregnant women. We had also handed out pamphlets containing some basic facts about abortion. A young woman came up the street toward the clinic, I began to give her the five second riff, "We are here to help women understand alternatives to abortion. Would you be willing to talk to us for a moment?"

Roseann's version was usually, "Lots of people coming in here don't know what their baby looks like, so we just want to make sure you do."

The young woman responded by holding out her hand, in which she held one of our pamphlets! She told us later she had picked it up in a phone booth up the street!

Roseann said she should know about the physical risks associated with abortion as well as the alternatives that were available to her.

She stopped and stood with us, remarkably relaxed and quite willing to speak, which was not usually the case. She told us she had two children already, and the father was in the picture and supportive of her. But she'd had miscarriages, and when she found she was pregnant and went for a check-up, the doctors had told her she couldn't have another baby right away. "They told me this baby wouldn't have a chance, and if I had another baby it would injur me." They had recommended an abortion and referred her to B., B., and K.

We went to the heart of the matter. "Maybe it doesn't have a great chance, but wouldn't you want to give this baby every chance it can get?"

We talked about the child being made in God's image. "If God decides to take this baby, that's one thing. But do you want to be the one that ends its life?"

After five minute's conversation, the young lady told us she was going to cancel her appointment. She went in, and sure enough, ten minutes later, came back out. She thanked us and we prayed together with her, exchanging phone numbers, including that of Alpha Pregnancy Center. She said she didn't need any other help. She wouldn't even take a ride from us.

Our daughter Tory at a prayer vigil, downtown, Philly

Part of our joy over this event had to do with the fact that three month old Victoria was part of that save. Roseann was holding her in her arms while we talked to this young woman. Our own joy at Victoria's birth in June was barely greater than what we felt four or five months later upon receiving a letter with this woman's baby's photograph. I carried that photo in my wallet for twelve years after that – both as a reminder of God's grace and as a reminder to pray for that child and her family.

In July the Democrats held their convention at Madison Square Garden, where PA' pro-life Democratic Governor Bob Casey was denied any opportunity to speak due to his pro-life commitments.[164]

---

[164] Even the liberal pundits acknowledged that the party and Bill Clinton feared he would speak against abortion. I find it amusing that a few of my friends still talk about "pro-life Democrats," as though that party will ever allow a pro-lifer to gain

A Memoir of Pro-life Rescue

In mid-November we had a rescue at Planned Parenthood in Philly, where 82 were arrested. Judge Lydia Kirkland found us guilty and gave us the option of a small fine or 48 hours in jail.

Governor Bob Casey, last of the pro-life Democrats

In the November elections, Mike McMonigal lost, although he put up a very respectable showing. I worked for his campaign – manning phones one night in his headquarters, and the polls in the Belmont section of Philly, an upper middle class and largely black community.

At that particular polling place, I was the only pro-life and pro-Bush worker. At one point a retired school teacher lit into me, "How can any sane person be for George Bush?"

I explained that he had consistently stood for the unborn child, and that I thought legal abortion was the most destructive thing going in America today. She fussed and

---

anything beyond local office! Casey's son, for example, is a Democrat but not pro-life.

fumed, but by the end of the day, not only were we friends, but I had good conversations with her and many other poll workers, several of them college students.

Mike McMonigal, pro-life candidate

My standard five second line to voters on Mike's behalf was something like, "His opponent has no community experience, she's a center city lawyer." I remember one attractive woman sliding icily past me, saying, "I'm a center city lawyer myself!"

Of course the worst of the November elections was Clinton's victory. This pro-abortion nobody who local police told us had worn them out the previous summer [165] was now the most powerful man in the world!

At an unguarded moment during the campaign – in Florida, I think -- Randy Terry had managed to present Governor Clinton with a dead, aborted baby in a small box.

---

[165] We spent a lot of time with Philly police, and thus had a lot of conversations. On this subject, they told us they had grown weary of following the candidate around listening to his endless bickering with his feisty wife.

Governor Clinton's response was disgust. Randy was prosecuted for this awful crime – work out the logic of that for me somebody.

Another Allentown Rescue

In early December, a number of rescuers went up to Allentown, where the faithful seven were still in jail for their rescue back in May. Those of us risking arrest went knowing there was a possibility we might receive similar sentences – but also intending to add our testimonies to that of the Allentown stalwarts –our testimony that stiff sentences weren't going to stop our active opposition to child-killing.

The abortion clinic at Allentown shared a building with a methodone treatment program, which made for interesting dynamics. Two sleazy businesses whose clients placed a high priority on secrecy. Furthermore it was in no local jurisdiction, so the State Police were in charge of "protecting" it. About ten of our number had no intention of risking arrest. These had jobs or other responsibilities which they could not afford to miss. So they stood off to the side and prayed, or held signs.

Five or six of us went inside the building and up the stairs where we sat in front of the abortuary doors. The rest gathered in front of the main doors of the building, while a few others went around back. The police showed up fairly soon, and first sent an officer in to ask those of us inside to leave the building. He said that we could receive higher charges if we stayed inside. After asking him if he knew what went on inside that place, we agreed to leave. We went out and joined the others at the front door.

More police arrived and then together they sort of "pounced" on us. They herded everyone, even those far from the doors into one group. Those of us intending to risk arrest, dropped to our knees, then all fours. The police rush was to herd us together and force us away from the doors – dragging and pushing. Since we were on our hands and knees it was not too effective. At one point in this rather tense imbroglio, an officer dropped his name tag, and I picked it up, handing it back to him. It seemed to me the whole atmosphere of the thing changed at that moment. Not only was I completely calm, but it seemed to me the police were more relaxed, too.

State police and rescuers before arrests at Allentown rescue. These were the first law officers I heard lie under oath.

But eventually they arrested all of us, a total of 28, including all the "supporters" who had been nowhere near the doors when the arrests began. We were processed using a xeroxed copy of the charge sheet for one of the "Allentown Seven" – four felony charges per each. I'd hate to think what they would have charged us with if we'd stayed inside!

Prolifer rescuers had been charged under a lot of statutes! As I have mentioned, the Philadelphia charges were often "Blocking a Highway," highway being defined as a public sidewalk. We were charged sometimes with "Trespass," and sometimes with misdemeanor level "Criminal Trespass," which required that we be given proper warning by the property owner. We were charged with "Disturbing the Peace," with "Refusal to Disburse," and sometimes, when a jurisdiction wished to raise the ante, with "Conspiracy..." to do various things.

Though much less common, rescuers were charged

with "Reckless Endangerment," with "Assault," and with "Assaulting An Officer," although I never heard of any case when a prolifer actually did do that. Occasionally going limp earned us charges of "Resisting Arrest".

I have already spoken about charges under various local ordinances, usually designed directly against us (which made them "Bills of Attainder" one of the things our founding fathers prohibited under the Constitution). We were also charged with breaking various injunctions which were put in place by judges sympathetic to the abortion industry. As I have mentioned, particularly in connection to Judge Reed, these injunctions were used quite contrary to what an injunction is supposed to do, to prosecute people who weren't named in them, and for activities not specified.

Then the proabort lawyers dug deep and brought charges under RICO. They also attempted to prosecute rescuers for "Hate Crimes" and under the Civil Rights or Ku Klux Klan Act, but were stymied by the higher courts. Then they really got to work and succeeded in getting the FACE (Freedom of Access to Clinic Entrances) Bill through the US Congress, a pure bill of attainder. But I'm getting ahead of myself there.

John and Linda Ronning and daughter

Was That Thunder?

Walt Gies, with his wife Laura,
among many dedicated young leaders.

CHAPTER SEVEN - COUNTER-ATTACK (1993)

Psalm 51:1-5 Have mercy upon me, O God, according to thy lovingkindness; according unto the multitude of thy tender mercies blot out my transgressions. Wash me thoroughly from mine iniquity, and cleanse me from my sin. For I acknowledge my transgressions; and my sin is ever before me. Against thee, thee only, have I sinned, and done this evil in thy sight; that thou mightest be justified when thou speakest, and be clear when thou judgest. Behold, I was shapen in iniquity; and in sin did my mother conceive me.

A person lost in a dark cavern may not get out. But if he is to have a chance of getting out, there are certain things he must do, common I suppose to all people in states of lostness. He must recognize he's lost. He must admit that his is not a minor problem, but a very dangerous one. He must make his best calculations as to how he got there and then begin moving in the opposite direction. It will remain dark at first. Although he does not yet see the light, his goal is to see the light and to move toward it and into it. In some situations of lostness, the lost ones only hope is help from outside.

The prolife movement, and that part of it known as the rescue movement, as the prophetic vanguard of the Christian church in America, began with a realization of how far wrong we Americans had gone. Repentance was the constant theme in many, many speeches I heard at rallies and other gatherings of rescuers. We needed to repent, we needed to call others to repent, we needed to accept the consequences of our actions as we made that call – in repentance.

Discouragement

But we needed, and repeatedly got, a further lesson: that we could not change our condition by ourselves. We were more profoundly lost than we had thought, and while it was right to struggle forward, doing the best we could, it was only going to be the Grace of God that delivered us from legal abortion.

Elijah huddling under his juniper bush.

Yet that goal seemed far away and it continued to feel like we were groping in the dark. In fact, from certain standards of measure, we seemed to be gradually less effective at what we were doing. The darkness seemed to be getting more organized and more adept at throwing more obstacles in our way. We were increasingly inclined to the attitude of Elijah as he hid beneath the juniper bush (I Kings 19:1-10). 1993 was a year of many small victories in the face of apparently insuperable obstacles to rescue.

In January at our church we ran a modified version of our previous year's Sunday School classes. We also distributed a handout which was a summary of the full range of pro-life activities in which various of our members had been involved in the previous year.

Very early in January the Supreme Court announced its decision in re the Virginia "Bray" case. The Court said the civil rights or Ku Klux Klan law could not be used against prolifers, because they did not have a "class animus" against mothers in crisis pregnancy. We had grown so dubious of the courts that we were surprised by the decision, though certainly agreeing with its logic.

In mid-January twenty-three rescuers began prison stretches at Chester County[166], as the settlement of a long-running wrangle over sentences from Paoli rescues. On 20 January, 82 of us reported to Judge Lydia Kirkland at Philadelphia City Hall, from which we were dispatched for two days to the Detention Center (men) or Laurel Hall (women) for the mid-November rescue at PB and Blackwell. This was the largest-ever local jailing for rescue. We were released on the 22nd of January, the sad anniversary of Roe, while thousands of others from Philadelphia were in Washington DC for the annual March for Life.

In Washington, President Clinton used this occasion to make clear what he intended to do about the small steps the first Bush administration had taken to curtail abortion – that is reverse them. Clinton on 22 January celebrated by issuing executive orders to end restrictions on fetal-tissue research; to refund abortion counseling at federally assisted clinics; and to open up RU-486 and the "morning after" abortifacients for "study" toward licensure for legal distribution in the US.

The next day we rescued at the Lewis Tower Building with several juveniles, including Adriel. Fifty-seven were arrested there and at Planned Parenthood. During this rescue a clinic worker came running full speed and tackled the front line of rescuers gathered on the sidewalk. One of the juveniles who had come with us was apparently the deliberate victim of that violent attack. The high school girl whom she struck was very stoic about it, but it was obvious she really had been hurt. However, she would not leave, and stayed in her position. It gave me very mixed feelings – of

---

[166] Prolifers and prisoners – even when they were not the same, found humor in strange places. I found it amusing that Chester County Prison shirts said "CCP" across the back, which struck me as close enough to the Cyrillac "CCCP" meaning "Union of Soviet Socialist Republics"!

deep admiration on one hand, but also of anger and some guilt. Police standing by did nothing about it.

In mid-February we again rescued at Northern Medical Offices at Tabor Road, the office of Berger, Benjamin and Kline. Berger and Benjamin were still doing second trimester abortions. Although there were only 36 people risking arrest, sidewalk counselors encouraged one mother to a decision to keep her child that day, and two weeks later we found out about another save as a result of that rescue.

On that same day, 17 Feb, Mayor Ed Rendell signed an ordinance which City Council had passed on the 4th, creating a new crime, "blocking access to a reproductive health care facility". This ordinance required judges to impose a mandatory sentence of 100 dollars or ten days for the first offense; 200 or 20 days, for the second; and 300 or 30-90 days for a third or more. It was clear that along with Clinton, Rendall was committed to paying back the lucrative abortion industry for its political and financial support.[167]

Parallel to this, on the 9th of February, Philadelphia, Bucks and Montgomery County legislators sponsored a bill including mandatory heavy sentencing for rescuers under state law. This bill, at least, had little chance of passing in the PA State House.

But up at the federal level the dominant proaborts introduced the "Freedom of Access Act," a federal version of the same thing, in Congress.

Then in early March, Michael Frederick Griffin shot an abortionist, David Gunn, in Pensacola, Florida. Gunn, who commuted from Alabama, got out of his car to find a number of pro-lifers carrying signs and others sidewalk counseling.

But when Michael Griffin came running out of the crowd, Gunn turned and ran back toward his car. Griffin shot him three times in the back with a 38 pistol.

---

[167] One of the big unanswered questions following the arrest and conviction of the diabolical abortionist Kermit Gosnell, was about who his political protectors had been. It was no coincidence he got away with so much evil and squalor for so long. Wouldn't it be informative to see a record of his campaign contributions!

A Memoir of Pro-life Rescue

Michael Griffin, first abortionist shooter, later repented

Police arrived expecting another routine day of keeping a protest in order. They were shocked when Griffin walked up and surrendered the pistol, saying he had shot Gunn. Despite being rushed to a hospital, Gunn died a few hours later. Griffin, a thirty-something factory hand, was a Navy veteran, with two children. He had some history of abnormal behavior, but definite connections with rescuers.

According to a published interview with him, Griffin had warned Gunn to stop doing abortions only five days earlier, citing Bible passages about God's judgment.

A week later, Phil Donahue had Paul Hill, another Florida pro-lifer, on his national program, along with two abortionists and David Gunn's son. Paul Hill spoke highly of Griffin's actions and said the death of Dr. Gunn was as good as the death of Dr. Mengele.

NARAL's Kate Michelman, on the other hand, called for immediate passage of the FACE bill.

The pro-life community, and particularly the rescue community was thrown into confusion and consternation.

Was That Thunder?

Phil Donahue gave Paul Hill national air time

The issue of violence was not new: a number of people had spoken out suggesting either that "lethal force" might be a legitimate option or that it would inevitably arise from continued repression of pro-life dissent. But thus far it had all been talk and distant theory. Now it had happened.

Paul Hill publically supported Griffin's actions

Michael Griffin's trial took place in February 1994. His lawyer asked to pursue an insanity defense, but the judge denied it, at least in part because Michael refused a psychiatric evaluation.

Before the trial, thirty-four rescuers from around the country signed a "defensive action statement" as follows:

> We, the undersigned, declare the justice of taking all godly action necessary to defend innocent human life including the use of force. We proclaim that whatever force is legitimate to defend the life of a born child is legitimate to defend the life of an unborn child. We assert that if Michael Griffin did in fact kill David Gunn, his use of lethal force was justifiable provided it was carried out for the purpose of defending the lives of unborn children. Therefore, he ought to be acquitted of the charges against him.

Fifteen of those signing were familiar to me in person or by reputation. Among them were the Brays, Paul Hill, the *Life Advocate* folks, and our own "Kissing Bandit," Joe O'Hara. Joe Foreman had helped write the early drafts of the statement, but did not feel he could sign the final version.[168] The motive of most of these people was simply to make a strong statement. The heart of their intention was to say "Babies are babies. All babies should be protected with the full force of the law." But one of the signators was soon prepared simply and literally to shoot an abortionist himself. Nor were the others helping the rescue movement or the cause of the unborn, contrary to what they thought.

In his trial the next year, Michael Griffin was found guilty and sentenced to life in prison. At the earliest he might be released after 25 years. Within less than a year in jail he had recanted his theoretical position and repented his sin as murder. In an interview to be published in March 1995 he would say:

---

[168] Monica Migliorino Miller, *Abandoned*, p.282

Was That Thunder?

I used to think it was justifiable homicide. I don't anymore... My change of mind has come from reading the Bible and praying. I've had two years to think about it and look at everybody's viewpoint....You have to read the Bible in its full context. You can't just take one chapter or two and use it the way you want it... I'm trying to keep some harm from other people. I'm trying to prevent violence around the abortion industry.

On the 10th of April 1993 (Good Friday) 75 rescuers were arrested at Blackwell in Philadelphia. Joe Roach was quite concerned when he found he had received only 74 registration/communication cards of those participating, although 75 had been arrested. He sent out notice of this, afraid someone would get lost in the judicial process -- until he realized the 75th rescuer was himself!

Joe Roach gave countless hours to bless rescuers

There was one known save on the spot at the Good Friday Rescue – sidewalk counselors took one mom to Alpha Pregnancy Services, an alternative pregnancy center nearby. I knew several of the dedicated women who worked at that place, and again, I felt their job was much harder than mine. They, too, experienced rejection or manipulation, and dealt regularly with unjust criticism and false propaganda. On the positive side, however, they often got to see the babies who were born as a result of their compassionate labors.

Not content to expand Title X funding to distribute tax dollars for both contraception and abortion, the Clinton Administration began to push forward the FOCA (Freedom of Choice Act).[169] Our own senator Arlen Spector was a co-sponsor of the bill and for it in committee was PA's Harris Wofford. This legislation was intended to knock down all state restrictions, that is, do what Roe did initially, until after Webster, the Supreme Court slowly began to recognize state restrictions again.

At the time this and like legislative efforts felt like major defeats. We could not see that it was in fact an all-out testimony to our long term success. The proaborts were rattled enough that they were unmasking all their guns and calling in all their markers – the aim was to reverse the inertia, but it was the opposite of a grassroots effort. We were the ordinary people, the man on the street. They were the big bucks and powerful political machines. In that sense it felt crushing. It felt as though we had made no political progress – or were losing whatever ground we had gained.

From the 10th through the 12th of May a bunch of us went to prison in Philly again rather than pay Judge Kirkland's fine. 22 men and 12 women from the 17th February rescue at Berger, Benjamin and Kline's, got to see the inside of Philly's finest public accommodations.

Another blow to the pro-life cause came with Oregon's passage of a Euthanasia bill. We learned all the grassroots groups had opposed this, versus the HMOs with big bucks and extensive advertising. After all, this was going to save money, right? Somebody said 90 percent of an

---

[169] The 2007 version of the bill included Sen. Barack Obama as a co-sponsor. Obama made a campaign speech to the Planned Parenthood Action Fund on July 17, 2007, saying, "The first thing I'd do as president is sign the Freedom of Choice Act. That's the first thing that I'd do."

average person's lifetime medical expenses occur in the last six months of life. Getting rid of granny is just good business. Another bitter pill (gallows humor intended) came when "Casey" was quoted in precedent – the infamous mystery clause from the pagan philosophy of Justice Kennedy:

> At the heart of liberty is the right to define one's own concept of existence, of meaning, of the universe, and of the mystery of human life.

Curiously, rescuers took this more in stride than many other Christians. Back in the late 80's, Randy Terry and others had said we were far down the slope on the slide to destruction. Randy asked how we would have felt twenty years earlier had we been told abortion would become legal throughout the United States in 1973.   Well, he said, what will it be like twenty years further on? Legal euthanasia had been one of the things he and others prophesied.
It wasn't much of a reach to predict more getting rid of more "unwanted' people. But many others among evangelicals at least, seemed to hear something closer to a personal deathknell ringing from the legalization of euthanasia where so many had been deaf to that of abortion.

During Cities of Refuge, with fellow marshall, Gene Epps,

Summer Rescues – Cities of Refuge

In late May we had a rescue at Chester with 50 arrested. About the same time, six of the "Allentown Seven" were released after a full year in jail. Judge Gardner kept the one remaining in jail, rather than give her concurrent credit for time she had spent behind bars in Pittsburgh.

At mid-year Mayor Rendell and pro-abort legislators launched a drive for state funding of "family planning services". State funding had been removed by pro-life legislation back in 1981, through the efforts of such pro-life stalwarts as Steve Friend and Joe Rocks.

Steve Freind, Pro-life Legislator

In June we received a little encouraging news from Washington where the Hyde Amendment was upheld by the House. Under fierce attack by the administration and its running dogs in Congress, the Hyde amendment restricted federal Medicaid funds from being used for abortion.

July 1993 was to prove the last big series of rescues in

Was That Thunder?

Philadelphia. It was organized under the rubric "Cities of Refuge," and was carried out despite a very large "wet blanket" of adverse legislation, judicial and executive administration – exacerbated by abortionist-shooter rhetoric. The abortionist shootings were being successfully parleyed into a whitewash or should I say red-wash of the whole pro-life movement by the media, which claimed the "dark side" of the movement was now dominant.

Joe Rocks, Pro-life Senator

Nonetheless, we were successful in Philly at gathering a good number of people to a whole series of peaceful rescues, while six or seven other cities in the country had similar events during the period July 8 through 18. (My old "cellie" from Atlanta, Chet Gallagher and his wife Joann helped lead the San Francisco/San Jose rescues.)

During the week, many nationally respected speakers addressed large crowds at the Valley Forge Hilton. Keith Tucci, head of Operation Rescue National, was arrested here on the 14th by Merion Police. The arrest was purportedly based on a Broward County, FL "non-appearance" bond, but in fact, Keith had told the Florida court where he was slated to appear as a witness that he would be away that week. He also told them where he would be. What's more, our law in Pennsylvania does not allow for extradition for crimes bearing less than a year's penalty, and "non-appearance" in Florida bore only a six month sentence. In any case no doubt it gave certain pro-abort authorities a sense that they were still more clever than we.

Before the "Cities of Refuge" campaign began, our leadership decided they would not talk to the media at all. They publicly urged rescuers and supporters not to talk with the media, either. The intensity of the negative propaganda since the Griffin/Gunn shooting so betrayed the media prejudice, that our leadership felt there was nothing to gain from granting interviews to the networks and newspapers.

On the 9th, 117 people, including 5 juveniles, were arrested at Chester Crozer clinic. I think those five juveniles may have been mine – that this was the Chester rescue where Jed, the youngest, was arrested with me. [170]

The rescue the next day was one of my favorites to

---

[170] See previous year where I thought same of another at Chester!!! At one or the other I was part of a diversionary group pretending to go to Paoli and thus misleading proaborts.

remember. It took place at an abortuary I had never seen before, the Brandywine Valley Women's Health Center, on the outskirts of Wilmington. We arrived early and parked a few blocks away. Approaching the building I could see some women approaching, so I went ahead with only a handful of people, including Joy Fesi, if I remember right. We got in front of the door, and politely told the women there would be no abortions there that day. It was actually a house, makeshiftedly turned into an abortuary, so it had a wooden framed porch, which was to prove a key architectural feature.

Gradually the rest of the rescuers arrived, and soon we had the medium-size front porch pretty much filled up. [171]

As we stood packed rather tightly together before the doors and around the porch, we could look down the sidewalk to the street, and suddenly we saw a fairly large man come lunging up from the street toward us. He broke into a run. Reaching the porch steps, he thundered up and Eric Harrah, a pro-tackle-sized abortion administrator, charged into the middle of the crowded porch, shoving people before him and packing them even more tightly.

At that instant, the center of the porch collapsed. Apparently a joist broke in the middle and the others quickly followed suit. It seems Mr. Harrah was the straw that broke the camel's back. The effects were interesting. We were all too tightly packed to fall down, so we merely slid even closer together in middle of this great wooden funnel. We dropped together about three and a half feet, and even Mr. Harrah was momentarily nonplussed.

The clinic door flew open and three or four workers stood gasping as they surveyed the ruin of their former porch. Then Mr. Harrah waded through us toward the door and the three or four workers tugged and gasped until they hauled him in. The rescuers were extraordinarily quiet, musing over the turn of events that had taken place. It was amazing the kinds of things we had learned to take in stride.

Meanwhile other rescuers kept arriving as sidewalk

---

[171] Of 130 eventually arrested, I'd guess about 90 of us were on the porch when the next great event transpired.

counselors kept their eyes sharply pealed for women approaching for appointments. I remember a brief hurly-burly as a policeman told a bunch of prolifers they couldn't park next door at a drycleaner's. The drycleaner himself came out and said he was happy to have them part there, and that he would love to get rid of the neighboring "business".

The media coverage was unusually active, perhaps as a result of our leaders decision not to talk with them, so that when a woman drove up with Maryland plates, got out and began to talk to counselor Christine Elliot, the reporters were all ears. Soon we rescuers were alerted to the conversation that was taking place. Those of us perched amidst the former glory of the porch became fervent and pointed in our prayers. I can't remember how long the conversation went on, but it was quite a while.

In any case, Andrea, the woman from Maryland, decided to keep her baby instead of going through with the "discount abortion" for which she had already given a deposit to Mr. Harrah. So when she came up the sidewalk, we moved to the side and helped her as best we could to clamber up to the door and knock. The door was answered with some hesitancy, but when she told them her name, the helped her up and in. Five minutes later she emerged with her refund in her hand.

Needless to say, we were deeply joyful as she returned to her car. A reporter was waiting for her, and articles appeared in the *Inquirer* the next morning giving wide witness to the life-saving effect of that rescue. One other woman definitely made the decision to spare her child's life after talking with Bob Lewis's wife, Jean, and other compassionate counselors. The way we felt reminded me of a song we sometimes sang together at rescues and in jail:

> We are standing on Holy ground,
> And I know that there are angels all around.
> Let us praise Jesus now.
> We are standing in His presence on Holy ground.

The police eventually began to take us away, but the

clinic was pretty much closed all day. Toward the very end, a young man from Europe who had been visiting pro-lifers here, knelt down on the sidewalk near the street to give

Arrested toward the end of rescue
at Brandywine Valley abortuary, Delaware.

praise to God. Eric Harrah,[172] who had emerged again, came

---

[172] Eric Harrah was one of many unusual people associated with the abortion industry. For a time he became one of the many unusual people associated with the Christian church! His two abortuaries in Delaware were just coming under investigation at the time, although we didn't know it. A few months later the papers carried courtroom testimony, including that of his staff, about illegal disposal of "fetal material" and other violations. He soon showed up in Pennsylvania trying to start a new clinic, and perhaps another one in NJ.

But imagine the surprise among us in November 1997 when we heard he was officially resigning as administrative director of an abortuary in State College, PA, owned by the notorious Stephen running down the sidewalk and kicked this young fellow in the back.

The police standing by declined to arrest or charge him, although I think they did discourage him from doing it too many more times. The young fellow was taken to a hospital where he was found to have broken ribs.

And this was only the third day of ten! Speakers, vigils, and other activities went forward. On the 13th, 250 people showed up ready to risk arrest at Paoli, but the clinic operator cancelled all appointments and closed for the day, so no arrests took place. On the 14th, 250 showed up again, this time at Cherry Hill, where it was decided to "demonstrate" and not rescue, despite the fact that at least some

---

Brigham. Harrah said, "my focus at the present times is to learn to be a follower of Jesus Christ and to thank Him for sending me the love that I had always been looking for." He also wrote in a news release, "it is my desire to be given the opportunity to explore what God may have for me in privacy, apart from the public spotlight".

By October 1998, he was speaking for pro-life groups in New Jersey, as a "former homosexual, former abortion kingpin, now a born-again believer." By July 1999, he had spoken in a number of national Christian media venues. That month in an interview by Dr. Wilke of National Right to Life he described details of the dirty business of abortion.

But by early 2000, people were becoming suspicious of some of the things he said. He appeared to embroider for his audiences. There were claims that evidence of other improprieties was emerging. Harrah said later he had come to feel exploited, that his claims about "feeling loved" were false. In fact, he said, he came to feel like no one cared about him in most of the settings where he was lionized. That year he announced he had "left the church".

Christian publications carried various allegations about his conduct. It wasn't a very pretty picture of the church or even the pro-life movement. Some pointed out that those around Norma McCorvey, the woman famous as "Roe," had been much more circumspect in keeping her out of the public limelight and giving her a grounding in her new faith before she became "national news". Apparently Harrah's earliest Christian friends tried to do the same, but much less successfully.

appointments seem to have been kept and some babies died there.

But on the 15th, my second favorite rescue took place. The proaborts had been gearing up against us for several weeks. They had been importing "deathscorts" from as far away as California, with quite a contingent from New York, as well as students from nearby Penn and Bryn Mawr and other local nurseries of the pro-abortion "movement". Most of these had concentrated in Center City, around Banned Parenthood, Blackwell, and at Lewis Tower, etcetera. They were itching for us to come there, where police barricades had been erected, and where the proaborts were lined up six deep to prevent us getting near the doors.

A few days earlier, Roseann and I were surprised to find police barricades erected even at Berger, Benjamin, and Kline, when we went to sidewalk counsel! It's certain more women were turned away by those barricades than reassured by them! But Rendell's purposes were political, not altruistic. He cared about the women the same way Hugh Hefner did. Hefner it will be remembered, contributed a hefty part of the funding for Roe v. Wade and companion cases. I suppose one could say butchers care a lot about meat.

About 8:30 all the rescuers gathered at a parking lot in the western suburbs. There they line up in a long column, after which I had the distinct honor of numbering them off – "1, 2, 3, 4, 5, 6, 7, 1, 2, 3, …" After they gathered into teams by numbers they were assigned to cars and minivans, and departed on their way to the sites planned. The proabort and police infiltrators called in dutifully and began to tail the rescuers. Imagine their glee when it became apparent all the cars were headed for Center City.

About twenty minutes later I remember pulling up into a public parking lot in downtown Philly, as a carload of proaborts behind us sped ahead. They appeared nearly beside themselves with excitement as they hurried to tell their friends at Planned Parenthood of our advent.

But we weren't going to the clinics. Within another fifteen minutes, small groups of us, none larger than sixteen, had assembled at designated intersections, none of them

A Memoir of Pro-life Rescue

closer than two blocks to the clinics themselves. Exactly at 9:30, all of us stepped into the streets, where we sat, knelt, or stood, silently praying and holding signs indicating our purposes and God's perspective on abortion. Meanwhile one or two of us stood in front diverting the traffic that would have gone down each particular street.

It was the middle of a busy morning in the center of a good-sized city. Yet all at once all the streets approaching Planned Parenthood, Blackwell, and Lewis Towers were empty and silent. There was no traffic at all within two blocks of these places of killing. The police were at the clinics, congregated in large numbers. The proaborts were there in even larger numbers. But no pro-lifers were evident except a few faithful sidewalk counselors.

The "Streets" Rescue, downtown Philly

Some extremely artful dodger among our leaders had figured out how to cut all traffic within that deadly section of

Was That Thunder?

Philadelphia by blocking the streets in seven strategic places. Due to the preponderance of one-way streets, it was not only possible but extremely practical! They say the silence around the abortuaries was eerie. The police immediately sensed something strange had happened.

A few minutes later the pro-aborts knew it, too, and many of them came running down the streets to where the blockades were. In retrospect it seems as though the proaborts must have deliberately recruited some anarchists for this occasion. Two of them waded into prolifers at another intersection, punching and kicking. Police standing by actually arrested these two – the first time pro-aborts were ever arrested in Philadelphia, to the best of my knowledge. These uniformed policemen must not have done their politically-correct homework!

Bob Lewis, Baptist pastor, pro-life leader

In our case, Bob Lewis and I were leading a group sitting in the street in front of University Hospital. I was directing traffic with as much appearance of authority as I could muster, diverting it to the right and left, as several drivers came straight forward threatening to run us over. One actually pushed her bumper up against Bob. We hoped she would realize her insurance probably didn't cover that, and sure enough she finally backed off.

Four proaborts who came running down the street were less restrained. They began shouting in our faces, as one snatched signs out of the hands of our people, tearing them in half and throwing the pieces back at them.

One of our guys, a fellow from upstate, lost his composure for a moment, and got up ready for combat. Grabbing him and pushed him back down, face to face, in my best sergeant's manner, I said, "Either start praying, or else leave!" He started praying. The proaborts continued to rampage around.

I took up my stance again standing in front of our people next to Bob. A proabort woman, no more than twenty-three or four came up and stood in front of me with her face about twelve inches from mine. (I think she chose me instead of Bob, because he's about three inches taller!) She began to rebuke me for my oppressive and superstitious tyranny against womankind. She was not particularly profane nor blasphemous to my recollection, but her hatred was written large in her intense features and her tone.

Suddenly I began to pray for her. Looking into those hate-filled eyes, which nonetheless reflected the image of God, I prayed and asked God to give me love for this anonymous but no doubt hurting young lady. I prayed hard and gradually I began to feel what I prayed for, though I never said a word. This went on for perhaps ten minutes.

Then it was as though she began to get it. Gradually her words slowed, then ceased, her intensity faded and softened into some sort of bewilderment. She backed away, looked once more at me, and left. I'm usually not much for this sort of thing, and I really have no right to do it, but I've always claimed her for Jesus. If I'm right, when I get to heaven she is one of the first people I want to talk to.

The police were slow to show up where we were. First a young traffic cop appeared, who frankly got a kick out of the whole thing. But then the big bosses got on the horn, and things livened up. It was kind of hilarious, really. When the order went out to arrest us, the first thing the cops at our blockade did was to handcuff or shackle us together in improbable ways – hand to ankle, ankle to ankle, etcetera. We were still in the street, mind you – so traffic was still blocked.

Arrest at end of "Streets Rescue"

Then when the paddy wagons came, the policemen had to carry us in pairs – twice the load, twice the awkwardness. And when one of them suggested they should uncuff us first, the other one said the guy with the key had left.

We were taken to the roundhouse where we were kept in holding cells all night. Once again the singing in the catacombs was worthy of the early Christians.

We were released the next morning through hearings in the police court at the roundhouse. Toward the end several of us heard that the pro-aborts who had assaulted some of our number were about to be arraigned, so after we were released, we slipped into the little visitor's gallery overlooking the police court. There were heard the details of the arraignment. I jotted them down in a small notebook. I had not realized this was not kosher, until the guard in the court said something and pointed up at me.

It took me two seconds to realize the court was focusing on me, and I said something to the other two guys and booked out of there. We hid on the far side of the roundhouse parking lot behind a retaining wall, while I feverishly copied down the details and gave the copies to one of the other guys, in case I was re-arrested.

Stupid! I so often went from the sublime to the foolish. Who cared when those two were going to be tried! It's so easy to go from doing something important to believing that one's whims are important.

Later on the same day of our release (the 16th) there was a rescue at Yardley, where Killer Kaji agreed to close his clinic, so no arrests took place.

So the "Cities of Refuge" were richly blessed, and even felt successful, especially considering that there were only ninety-some people involved in the "streets rescue".

Other Ministries

Nevertheless, the reality was that the numbers of people involved were steadily declining. The good side of this was that all kinds of small and unspectacular pro-life ministries had been springing up all over our area and all over the country.

For instance, that July, Wayne Brauning, a wise and godly man with a lifetime of experience as a city pastor and a parole officer, officially announced the launching of MARC (Men in Abortion Recovery) ministries under the oversight of the CAC. Wayne had been an active pro-lifersince the early '80's. A fellow rescuer, Tad Mahan, also got involved in MARC, having been active in rescue. This ministry had a very positive impact on our own church, where three or four men had met together with Tad and worked through the devastating effects of their own involvements in abortions.

A number of similar ministries to women, the co-victims of abortion had been operating effectively, and many women in our own circles had been blessed through these.

At one point some women from our church asked my

input on the issues raised in an abortion recovery pamphlet they were using with a group of women they were leading. The question was about the eternal state of the unborn. This obviously was a touchy point – both theologically and emotionally.

After long study and research, during which I found a considerable range of opinions among godly teachers, I wrote up a series of biblical conclusions. The bottom line that all theologians agreed upon was: 1/that coming to God in repentance is also coming to him in faith, and faith means trusting him with the unknown, and 2/the Bible indicates we cannot demand what we desire [173] but we are supposed to ask for the desires of our hearts, and furthermore we are supposed to believe God for good – which means having a positive expectation that he will give us good things beyond all we ask or think. When all is said and done, however, it is in his hands, and our peace of mind will be based on trusting Him with things we don't know and can't see.

I confess, I continue to find the idea that the unborn child killed in the womb is automatically taken into heaven simplistic and doubtful, though a few respected theologians from many branches of the church, including our own, have expressed it. Perhaps I am influenced by the fear it could serve as a great apologetic for abortion! If your child who lives may go to hell, but your child aborted is sure to go to heaven, then every good Christian should be aborting all his or her children – even if he or she is going to hell for it! That's frighteningly twisted logic.

Not that anyone was actually saying so to my knowledge. But there are always people in the church ready to run with bad theology. And there are currents of "folk theology" out there which have a lot of effect. What other explanation is there for the not uncommon phenomenon of women who say they would rather abort their babies than put them through the potential hardships of adoption!

Another sort of encouragement came in July, when

---

[173] Such as the salvation of a child we aborted or for that matter the salvation of any loved one.

Judge Retacco struck down Mayor Rendell's Philadelphia Ordinance 298, which mandated tough sentences for rescuers. Judge Retacco's arguments were: a/City Council has no authority to rule on obstructing access to abortuaries since the situation is not unique to Philadelphia and her citizens; b/mandatory sentencing power rests exclusively with the General Assembly of the State; c/mandatory sentencing should be reserved for conduct inherently much more evil than this; d/mandatory sentencing weakens an independent judiciary; and e/all parts of the ordinance are stricken because they are not severable due to the apparent intent of Council to duplicate present state law except for sentencing.

While the federal legislators seemed to be gearing up to put through a "bill of attainder" in the form of the FACE bill, Judge Retacco gave cogent reasons why Philadelphia City Council at least could not do so.

Also encouraging was the 18 July commentary in the *Inquirer* by David Boldt[174] on the "Dirty Business of Abortion". Although pro-lifers regularly sent letters to the editor which were occasionally published, it was very unusual to see this "party-line" newspaper be forthcoming about the ugliness of abortion in an editorial.

As a result of the "Cities of Refuge" campaign in July, a consortium of "abortion providers" filed charges claiming that the local leaders had acted in concert with OR and Randall Terry [175] specifically by rescuing at Chester. However, in December, Judge Newcomer was to completely reject this case.

At a pro-life gathering that fall, Father Pigeon, a young and much-respected priest, spoke on "Is this My Hour?" In many ways with FACE looming ever larger, it looked as though this might be the message for the rescue movement. He reminded us of Jesus' reply to Mary at the wedding in Galilee, which might be paraphrased "It isn't my time yet." He reminded us how the authorities were not able

---

[174] Boldt was generally "pro-choice" in his commitments.

[175] Terry was named in a much earlier injunction signed by Judge Newcomer.

to stop Jesus in John 7, because "it was not his hour". But he also reminded us how at the end, Jesus prayed "Father the hour has come." If we are called to an extreme hour, an hour when crucifixion seems imminent, then we need to pray as he did "Nevertheless not my will but thine be done."

Fr. Pigeon and Fr. McFadden at a vigil, Chester County Prison

    He went on to enumerate four other responses, those of spiritual immaturity: 1/ pride (it's about me) 2/ self-righteousness (I am the most effective and perhaps indispensable instrument); 3/ looking for a political messiah – purely or primarily political solutions; and 4/ earning love (trying to save ourselves by our good deeds). This stood out to me as another among many wonderful sermons and talks heard over the years from rescuers.

    Less spectacular was my own sharing at a meeting in November. Fortunately Father McFadden also spoke. Our theme was "Tell it to the Next Generation," with the appropriate note of passing the baton.

    Part of passing the baton was encouraging those we knew who fought the same battle on different fronts. Roseann and her cronies continued to fight against the perverted sex education agendas that were coming out of the

School Administration building in Philly, along with condom distribution in a number of inner city schools.

In December we had another meeting with Bob Lewis and Gene Kreuger speaking. Bob, who increasingly had to fight battles within his church, was growing weary. That summer Bob had written, in a Cities of Refuge memo to marshalls, "You have been selected to serve on the basis of your experience, demonstrated maturity, spirituality, and the bare fact there are so few of us left!" Gene, though he had been involved for a while, was in a sense picking up the baton – organizing a lay order called Guardians of Life.

Gene Kreuger became a servant-leader to Philly pro-lifers

Allentown Trial

In December our Allentown trial finally went forward. Twenty-eight of us spent the 6th through the 14th sitting through what was a pitiful charade calculated to entirely destroy ones faith in our judicial system. The trial did have it's moments of humor and even a few of glory, in the midst of a great deal of pathos.

Was That Thunder?

Still trying to support my family by carpentry, I had been working on a basement renovation project in the western suburbs. Jack O'Brien very graciously consented to finish the project for me while I went to trial.[176] Thus a fellow pro-lifer contributed significantly to my peace of mind in that important area of my life. Many others were praying for those of us on trial.

There were 28 defendants. Judge James Knoll Gardner presided. The same judge had put seven rescuers in jail for a year five years earlier. Everything we had seen indicated Lehigh County did not intend to compromise, that they were committed to being "tough" on us, too. Quite frankly, I was constantly dealing with anger throughout this trial. It was chock full of injustice. Toleration of injustice, particularly that directed toward myself, is not my strong suit. But retrospect allows for more forgiveness, and I recollect quite a number of wonderful stories.

Three of my favorites have to do with "tainting the jury." From the outset, the judge exhorted us not to communicate or have contact with the jury candidates, nor were we or our attorney or any of our witnesses allowed to mention the "justification defense" or anything related to it.

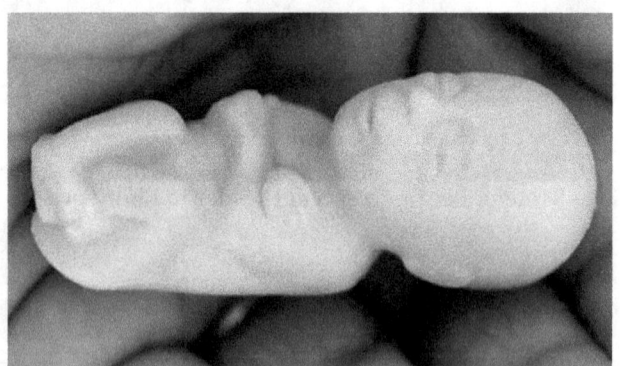

The forbidden baby model!

Nevertheless on the first day of jury selection,

---

[176] Not only that, but the blessed guy sent the balance of the money due on the project to my wife! In other words, he did the work for nothing!

someone, possibly Walt Gies, dropped a little plastic fetal model in the aisle between the defendants and the jury candidates. It must have been done pretty subtly, but one of the hawk-eyed bailiffs either saw it fall or saw it lying there soon after.

The first I knew about it was the sudden furor: a rushing about of guards, a hasty consultation with the judge, culminating in a rushing out of jury candidates. When the judge had cleared the court, he read us the riot act! I mean if one of those jury candidates had actually seen a plastic representation of a 12 week baby in the womb, American justice would have crumbled around our ears!

The second "jury tampering" incident happened the second or third day. Joe "the Kissing Bandit" O'Hara, one of the "Allentown Seven," brought in a pile of *Voices of the Unborn* newspapers. Joe was not a defendant in this case, but he knew everybody in the Allentown courthouse and jail – and many of them were his friends. So he left his pile of *Voices* in the office of one of the secretaries down the hall from the courtroom. His intention was to pick them up after the trial and distribute them around to cars outside the courthouse – 1st amendment-protected activity, even in Allentown.

However, unbeknownst to Joe, Howard Walton had also brought in a few copies of that edition of *Voices*. Howard, a defendant, may have had a more specific audience in mind. Someone was said to have traveled around the courthouse, depositing Howard's copies in strategic places like phone booths near the jury room and so on. Some guard apparently found one, and once more we were on the hot seat.

When Judge Gardner cleared the courtroom this time, keeping us for another tongue-lashing, he had a very particular person in mind to lash – and that was Joe! It was absolutely hilarious for those of us who thought we knew who done what to see Joe, retired career submarine NCO, standing head-bowed contritely before the bench as the Judge tore a strip off him and inquired why he shouldn't lock Joe up again for contempt of court. Joe answered softly and in

Was That Thunder?

penitential tones! I think he had a private discussion with Howard later concerning the importance of cooperative communication among news-distributors.

The third piece of jury-tampering illustrates the greatest dangers to our system of justice – namely judges and lawyers. During "voir dire," the questioning of the jury which is part of jury selection, the prosecution was allowed to stand before the panel of candidates and ask, first, "Without telling me which side you're on or what your specific feelings are on the issue, do any of you feel so strongly about the issue of abortion that you could not be impartial in a case which involves people who were arrested outside an abortion clinic? If so raise your hand." Six or seven hands went up, and these people were dismissed.

I suspect most of them were pro-aborts who didn't want to waste their time on a jury, but the next question was different. It was only aimed at one "side". "Now, it's important you be completely honest in searching your hearts as you answer this. Would any of you find it difficult to send a pastor to jail?" He asked this because Bob Lewis, a Baptist pastor was one of the defendants.

At that, one sweet twenty-something woman raised her hand, and when the DA's assistant repeated the question, said, "Oh, I could never send a pastor to jail!" She was then dismissed. And so, of course, she did send the pastor to jail! With that and a number of similar questions, our jury was pared down to a panel of young, white pro-aborts.

As I recounted earlier, we all were intially charged with four felonies, and eventually all stood charged with four misdemeanors, although a number of us had not actually been anywhere near the doors until the state police herded us together. Those people had definitely planned NOT to risk arrest nor did they do anything illegal. They were there ONLY as prayer supporters, holding signs, etc. So in order to "prove" the charges against these, the police had to openly lie under oath. And they did. Nor was it a mild oath. It included something to the effect of ". . .so help me Almighty God, before whom I shall stand in eternal judgment."

It was quite interesting development for a

"conservative" like me to think about continuing to trust his safety and the enforcement of law to men who had no qualms about lying under this oath. Had they admitted the actual location of those who were far from the doors, their case against them would have been sunk. If they showed doubt about identifying some of us or describing exactly what we were doing, even the "selected" jury might have developed a doubter or two.

So it was "by the numbers". They all agreed, it had happened exactly like this . . . and in addition they could identify all of us by name (having done their homework using the arrest file photos). But, hey, in a country that kills a million and half babies per year, do you expect extra justice for "trespassers"?

I wrote a number of poems during the trial. It helped me keep sane amidst the inanities and outrages of an institution gone wrong. By the end of the week I was getting tired of looking at the floors in the halls of courthouse:

Marble Floors

The intolerable squares in these courthouse halls
March in perfect order without variation or question.

The one upon which I now stand
Is the only one with any bearing to my eyes.

The others leap away in quick diminishing
Into complete insignificance.

But my heart's eyes see the lines parallel –
Not converging – and extending into eternity.

Conspiracy Charges

According to the judge one is a criminal conspirator
If he or she enters an agreement, not necessarily explicit

Was That Thunder?

To commit a crime and any one party thus agreed
Goes ahead to perform an overt act that is a crime indeed.
The essence, says the judge, is a common understanding.
An accomplice acts to promote or facilitate a crime.
Which standards if Christ should apply to his Bride,
Makes us conspirators and accomplices in infanticide.

The Burden of the Proof

For the purposes of a criminal court the prosecution
Bears the burden of proof, in theory if not practice:
Must demonstrate beyond reasonable doubt;
Guilt in terms of what law and what fact is.
But the burden of proof in another court
And penalty each will pay
Will rest strictly with the defense –
All will lose who are pro se.

My poetry received its highest earthly accolade during the Allentown trial. I had put together a chapbook a few years earlier, called *Prisoner's Pardons*. It is a "cycle" of poems built around eight or nine themes surrounding legalized abortion. I had printed far too many of these, and ended up giving them away at a national rally or two. I even gave a boxful to the Prisoners of Christ organization. But I had brought ten or twelve copies with me in a cigar box to distribute to my fellow rescuers or anyone else interested.

On the fourth or fifth day of trials, as we came in the courthouse and through the metal detectors, a deputy opened the box and told me he was confiscating them as "contraband"![177] But how wonderful! Censorship!!! The greatest compliment a poet can be paid. I was elated. It was particularly interesting, because I had taken them into the courtroom with me on previous days. At the end of the trial, I autographed copies for the judge and all the bailiffs.

---

[177] This was no doubt a closing of the barn door behind the earlier distribution of the *Voice* newspapers.

Jim Owens our lawyer was a great saint during this trial. I could not well describe his patience and godly demeanor during all the baloney that we endured. He took the few opportunities afforded him to glorify God, and no one could have done better. For the rest, he patiently did what he could. He and his wife Cathy and daughter Mary Sue became friends of our family, and blessed our family on many occasions.

Our sentencing was put off, pending appeals.
On the 21st of December, for an early Christmas present, 127 of us were tried in Delaware for the Brandywine clinic rescue. We were sentenced to one day in jail, the largest mass jailing in Delaware history, with 102 of us going straight from court to Gander Hill Prison. We were kept together more or less barracks style, and had a wonderful pre-Christmas retreat together.

To prepare for the New Year, there was another rescue at Paoli on the 28th of December. 56 of us were arrested and each given one summary level charge.

Next to Joe O'Hara, at a Paoli Rescue

Was That Thunder?

The dynamic duo – Jack Klotz and Brian Woznicki

A Memoir of Pro-life Rescue

CHAPTER EIGHT - CHOKE HOLDS (1994)

And Mary arose in those days and went into the hill country with haste, into a city of Juda; And entered into the house of Zacharias, and saluted Elisabeth. And it came to pass, that, when Elisabeth heard the salutation of Mary, the babe leaped in her womb; and Elisabeth was filled with the Holy Ghost; And she spake out with a loud voice, and said, Blessed art thou among women, and blessed is the fruit of thy womb. And whence is this to me, that the mother of my Lord should come to me? For lo, as soon as the voice of thy salutation sounded in mine ears, the babe leaped in my womb for joy.   Luke 1:39-44

January Pro-life Classes

Since our church had grown to the point where we were holding two worship services on Sunday mornings, our January Pro-life Sunday School classes were in a new schedule in 1994, being held between services. Our initial adult class opened with Bill Devlin describing the past year in terms of pro-life developments. Bill's CAC [178] chapter had expanded to a going concern with three or four full-timers and lots of volunteers. They were fighting the media battle better than any other Protestant group in the area, making statements on the crazy political developments that marched regularly down the pike. But they were also involved in promoting alternatives to abortion, and abstinence education. Bill was often quoted in *The Inquirer* and on the radio.

The second week of classes, a doctor from our church ran a class suggesting how medical people could influence

---

[178] The Philadelphia branch of the Christian Action Council, founded in 1977 by Lou Prontnicki and Tom Seelinger, became the Philadelphia Family Policy Council somewhere in the early 90's, and later became the Urban Family Council with Betty Jean Wolfe, director.

the establishment from the inside. We had quite a few medical people in our church, and most of them did a good job of taking their faith into the workplace. I ran a parallel class, still on rescue.

The third week I talked about the Christian in the courtroom, and some specifics about submission to civil authority considered over against the Deist democratic ideal. I pointed out that the Bible appears to place great responsibility on those who have authority to make public decisions: to reward good and punish evil. I suggested that the American citizen through offices of voter, juror, and impeachment, had that authority. The bottom line was that under our form of government we <u>are</u> "Caesar," the authority of whom the New Testament speaks.[179] Therefore we will be held responsible for how we have "ruled".

The fourth week we had two women lead and teach us about crisis pregnancy ministry and sidewalk counseling. These two had been active for a number of years in these important ministries. And I think that was the year we did a fifth class on "separation of church and state," seen historically and biblically.

We also held Senior High Sunday School classes during January. Kimiko led the 1st week, then Roseann taught on the myth of overpopulation, and Kim Bennett from Alpha Pregnancy Services led the third week, describing her ministry. Kim was one of several women who sacrificed a great deal to offer a wide range of services to women in crisis pregnancy at Alpha, a ministry largely supported through Tenth Presbyterian church. The fourth week we showed a film made by A.C. Green, the pro basketball player, who ran crisis pregnancy centers on the west coast.

Early in 1994 I spoke to a Messiah College Social Ethics class about the questions I had to deal with as a Christian involved in rescue. It was good for me to be

---

[179] This important application of a Bible theme is one evangelicals seem never to have considered – as I heard a seminary prof say once – all Americans are anabaptist in their view of government – even the Catholics!

reminded how theoretical the academic life is, and how strange it was to these students to talk with someone whose ethical conclusions were regularly putting him in jail. Nevertheless, the students and professor gave me an opportunity to engage in some good dialogue, and I found it a blessing. I hope they did.

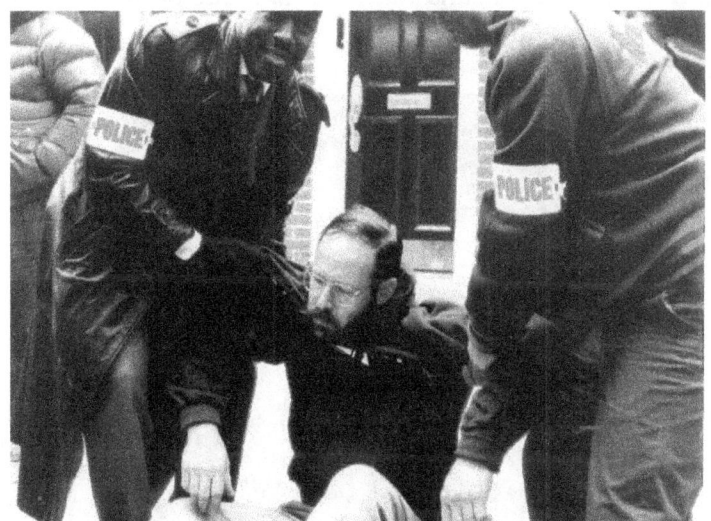

Arrest at one of the Center City Philadelphia abortuaries

Area Rescues

Owenna Nagy and Father McFadden spoke to a local meeting in mid-January. Then, just before the March for Life in January, rescuers from Virginia and Maryland sponsored a rescue in the Washington DC area, calling it the "Joshua Project". The veteran rescuer, saintly Dave Lytle, in his 80's, was one of the coordinators.

About this time we were praying that the US Supreme Court would agree to hear the rescue-related Loce case, originating in 1990 from New Jersey.[180] We thought this case had a good chance of pushing back Roe. Several of the women arrested with Loce had had abortions and deeply

---

[180] See details of the Loce case back in Chapter Five.

regretted them.

The original trial included some of the Jerome Lejeune testimony, scientific evidence for the humanity of the unborn.[181] Judge Michael J. Noonan ruled "...based upon the undisputed medical testimony by arguably the foremost authority in genetics in the world, I found that human life begins as conception; and that Roe vs. Wade permits a legal execution of that human being." [182]

Fr. John McFadden

Before the year was out, however, the court was to announce it would not hear the case. The Supreme Court did announce a decision allowing the use of the Racketeering and Corrupt Influences law (RICO) against pro-lifers. RICO was originally designed to eliminate a few obstacles to law officers pursuing organized crime. The court allowed it to be used against prolifers despite the fact that there was no conceivable "economic motive" involved. Practically speaking, however, this decision had little effect.

Although RICO suits had been used against

---

[181] Dr. Lejeune died that spring.

[182] Municipal Court of New Jersey -- Law division, Morris County criminal action docket no. C1771, et seq. State of New Jersey v. Alexander Loce, et als., Defendants, April 29, 1991, Honorable Michael J. Noonan.

A Memoir of Pro-life Rescue

Philadelphia rescuers since the mid-80s, they had not yet produced profit for the proaborts or much hindrance to prolifers. My guess is these suits were ineffective in Philadelphia because there were so many co-leaders. There were many in the ranks willing to fill in when someone was in jail or otherwise unable to lead. However, in other places a few cases against one or two leaders could do a lot to slow down or halt rescue activity.

On 28 January there was a trial for the Paoli rescue of 28th December, where 56 had been arrested.

Bob Lewis speaks to rescuers in front of a clinic

Two weeks later[183] we rescued at Blackwell and PP, where 41 were arrested, including ten juveniles. The juvies were not charged. Adults were initially charged with two misdemeanors, in accordance with Mayor Rendell's "get tough on prolifers" policy. When we were processed through

---

[183] on February 12th.

the roundhouse, the records, notoriously out of date, showed Bob Lewis with nine and me with eight outstanding bench warrants.

This was after Judge Retacco had dealt with all of the outstanding warrants the previous year! The people running the system were so aware of the ongoing inability of City Hall to keep its records up to date, that they readily accepted our own documents showing Bob with none and me with one outstanding warrant. In court the charges were reduced to one summary charge. Three guys eventually went to jail for three days, with no consequences for the rest of us.

I believe it was on that occasion, as the last of us were being released, that I pulled our van into the Roundhouse parking lot in order to pick up a few rescuers and take them to their vehicles. When I moved away from my car as I was gathering people, a sneaky uniformed cop put a ticket on it for illegal parking! I had run into this particular individual before – he was one of the few Philly cops I'd encountered who was vehemently pro-abort and did all he could to make our lives difficult. I fumed some at the injustice of it, but others pointed out inevitably that it was a lot better than they were treating the babies.

After an exciting rally and rescue in Ft. Wayne Indiana, a fellow named J. L. Horton claimed to have received a vision of what the Pro-life movement would soon become. Copies of this made their way into our hands. "I saw an abortion clinic but instead of being surrounded by demonstrators or rescuers, I saw musicians, singers, dancers and praisers. When they lifted up their voices singing, "The Kingdom of heaven is here! . . . pro-aborts, police, clinic employees began falling under their power . . . no abortions could be performed under those circumstances." Good idea, but maybe a heavenly rather than an earthly vision. Our experience was that prayer worked, but it didn't work magic.

Other Labors

There was a prayer vigil at Berger, Benjamin and Kline

on Tabor Road, on Ash Wednesday. The Catholics had been holding prayer vigils in conjunction with sidewalk counseling at clinics around the region for years. There is no way to calculate how many mothers turned away after seeing these faithful folks praying out front of the clinics, or after God moved in their hearts through other means. Prayer was more than merely effective.

Prayer is acknowledging God's sovereignty, opening our empty hands and asking him to work his will in the midst of things to great and difficult for us. It is thanking him for his mercy to us and asking that he extend it to others. It is praising his name because he alone is worthy. Frankly Protestants weren't very good at this. Oh, we were great pray-ers! Often the Catholics would ask us to lead extemporaneous prayer in public rallies, rescues, meetings, and in custody together.

Reading the Bible to fellow rescuers at NEWC

Was That Thunder?

But we Protestants were not much good at sustained prayer – at coming out regularly and keeping at it. The formula prayers of the Catholics always seemed to us fairly thin on content, but often a little of something is better than a lot of nothing. I sometimes toyed with the idea of concocting a Protestant rosary – a series of Bible prayers we could memorize and say in good conscience without feeling we were compromising our theology. But I never did. And the Catholics were the ones who kept (and keep) these prayer vigils going regularly at many aborturaries around our area. They also organized vigils on a larger scale on the high holidays like this one.

Mr. Horton of Indiana was substantially wrong in his vision, but there was something true in it, too. And when Roseann and I prayed outside Berger, Benjamin and Kline's, spiritual changes were taking place, although we could only see the ones in us.

On the 3rd of March, several from our church went to Westminster Seminary to hear C. Everett Koop speak on the issue of euthanasia before the Eastern Conference of the Evangelical Theological Society. His presentation was very biblical and contained some valuable insights. Especially powerful was his statement that there was a very great danger for an individual or a nation in making decisions on the basis of "compassion which is not filtered through morality."

I and other pro-life people had been troubled by some of the things Dr. Koop had written and said. I had been struck by these things both because of my prolife commitment and my involvement for a number of years with Harvest Ministries, a ministry to those struggling with homosexual issues and other issues of sexual brokenness. After considerable research I had written a paper called "Koop versus Koop," highlighting his inconsistencies, particularly in regard to some of his actions and statements while serving as Surgeon General (1981-1989).

My paper more or less set various of his statements side by side and suggested they were irreconcilable. After he stepped down as Surgeon General, I sent a copy to him and asked if we might talk about it sometime. I never received a reply.

Surgeon-General Koop, sounded indistinct trumpet

He and Francis Schaeffer[184] had been at the forefront of evangelical opposition to legalized abortion with their book *Whatever Happened to the Human Race* [185]and their film series under the same title.[186] Generally speaking evangelicals had been slow to realize what Roe v. Wade really did. Perhaps for the first time the 1980 elections showed the issue was not at all settled by the Supreme Court's decision. Koop and Schaeffer's book acted as sort of a battlecry. The book opened with a chapter discussing the danger that infanticide,

---

[184] Francis Schaeffer originated Randy Terry's oft-repeated observation that every clinic ought to have a sign saying "open by permission of the church".

[185] Published by Good News/Crossways, 1983.

[186] This film was produced/directed by Frankie Schaeffer, Francis' son – who first converted to the Eastern Orthodox church for a number of years, but sadly now has renounced his Christian faith, out of who knows what personal pain and self-indulgence.

that is killing of children after birth, was likely to follow. It worked up to a strong case again any legalization of "choosing death" for a human being.

But the next year the "Baby Doe" case came up, and Koop's pronouncements and reticence to act seemed pusillanimous. Then in 1988, Surgeon General Koop issued the infamous AIDS letter, a copy of which was sent to every American home, and which, while it contained fairly strong language about intravenous drug use, made homosexual practice sound like just another "choice".[187] Since Koop stated clearly in that letter that he had written it himself, we were left to conclude he did not believe it was his business to speak against sexual morality in connection with the plague of HIV/AIDS going on among homosexuals and, soon, adulterers. A further disappointment came when he refused to issue any official statement about the link between breast cancer and abortion, saying it would take a decade before the studies and data were conclusive enough.

In writing my paper "Koop versus Koop," I came to the conclusion the medical and scientific mindset profoundly hindered the leadership of a Christian man like Koop in public office. On the one hand he considered himself the final word, but on the other, he thought he could remain neutral on moral issues, as indeed a doctor often has to do when it comes to treating particular patients. But civic leaders are called to moral leadership and a didactic role in submission to God's rulings. That precludes neutrality on the moral issues.

As one of the world's foremost neonatal surgeons I have no doubt Koop's judgment on a great many medical matters was the best to be had. But as a civic leader he had been one more indistinct trumpeter. After finishing the paper, I wanted to arrange an opportunity to talk directly to Dr. Koop and have some genuine dialogue about these matters.

---

[187] We see here how "small failures" on the part of those whom God calls accumulate toward major victories for the devil, as for instance Koop's shilly-shallying helped prepare the way for the incredible Supreme Court decision in favor of "Gay marriage"!

So when the question and answer time came at the end of his talk at Westminster, I raised my hand and asked how he thought his AIDS letter tied into the things he was saying about euthanasia. He responded by asking me what I thought about the AIDS letter. I responded by using his own words about euthanasia, that I thought it represented "compassion that was not filtered through morality."

He replied curtly that he had been Surgeon General of all the people, not just of the Christians. And after another sentence or two, he went on to the next question.

Following the meeting, he came around front to get his coat and when I saw him in the lobby I asked him if we might meet sometime and talk about the issue. He said what issue. I said I had sent him a letter and copy of my paper. He said he didn't get it, because he always replied to every letter he got. I told him the title was "Koop versus Koop" and he grew indignant, replying, "Oh you're _that_ guy!"

I said I was a PCA elder as was he, and felt we had an obligation to follow Matthew 18 on such matters. He seemed to thoroughly incensed and replied, "Or what? Are you going to have my head cut off!" I was astounded, and retreated in considerable disarray.

Both because of our denominational tie and since we had several mutual friends, it seems to me ironic that Dr. Koop somehow classified me as an enemy and dismissed me so cavalierly. I suppose over the years he ran into various degrees of enmity, and was not always careful to distinguish.

Troops Growing Thinner

Our rescue numbers were continuing to decrease. A March 10th Guardians of Life meeting was sparsely attended. Also in March, a number of national rescue leaders planned to meet in Birmingham, Alabama, for an update on RICO and FACE. They also planned to discuss "violence and non-violence and how to work with disagreement," among other things. This topic of discussion was of great importance to the future of rescue – but this meeting did not come off, due to Holy week scheduling conflicts. Another meeting was planned for late April in Chicago.

On Ash Wednesday, 30 March, there was a rescue at Chester, in which fifty-one were arrested, but no charges brought.

Then on Good Friday, (1 April) 120 rescuers gathered at Hamilton Township in New Jersey. At the start police handcuffed and hauled away ten people, but the abortionist decided not to open, so police made no more arrests, and eventually decided not to charge anyone.

I was sent over to the police station to check about the release of those who had been taken into custody. The officer in charge told me he could only release them to someone who could confirm their identities. I didn't know three of them, but I was the only one at the police station at the time. When I hesitated over these three, he began to give me broader and broader hints, until he basically asked things like, "If I was to ask you if this was Joe Baker of Collegeville, Pennsylvania, what would you say?" I was just bright enough to say 'yes,' and departed with all ten accounted for.

A number of the Philadelphia leaders at a rescue in New Jersey

I remember reading something Sartre said after his experience in the French underground. He spoke of the unanticipated impact he felt from being plunged into the world of action and real consequences. There was a new sense of being three-dimensional and alive in contrast to the safe world of academia, of being swept into a realm where nothing was merely theory and where ideas always led to deeds. I don't recall his exact words, but the gist was that going from academia to the underground and back again (at the close of the war) was a qualitative shift of the highest order. And the active seemed to trump the academic life.

Rescue was perhaps less of a leap for many or most of us who became involved. Few of us were chiefly "thinkers" or 'ivory tower intellectuals' before the leap. Most of us were already inclined "to do" things in our churches and communities. It was not quite the same as WWII being suddenly thrust upon us. Rather we came to recognize our position in the midst of a subversive conflict which was destroying the unborn and would destroy us and ours unless we deliberately set out to fight back.

Nonetheless, once we were involved, we shared something of Sartre's sense of contrast between, and prejudice for, the world of the active versus that of the theoretical and passive.

Often prayer vigils at clinics were the alternative to rescues.

Was That Thunder?

To be sure a few among us were visionaries as well as pioneers: that is some considered, planned, and then went into uncharted territories first -- often alone. I think of Joan Andrews whenever I think of the first rescue pioneers.

Monica Migliorino Miller wrote of her:

> By the time Joan was convicted [to a five year prison term] she was already a seasoned veteran of the pro-life rescue movement, having been arrested over one hundred times. In the early 1970s Joan attended St. Louis University and was very active in protests against the war in Vietnam. But in the end she left the movement, disillusioned with the anger, hostility and violence that too often attended anti-war demonstrations. In 1973, when Roe v. Wade struck down state laws protecting the unborn, Joan turned her activist energy to defending the unborn at abortion clinics. Joan's steadfast convictions were wedded to a very warm, gracious and compassionate personality. Many people in the pro-life movement were inspired by her spiritual and philosophical vision of the rescue of the unborn as an act of intense self-immolation.

As we have mentioned this women spent 2 ½ years of a five year senetence in jail in Tallahassee, Florida for disabling a suction abortion machine. She refused to sign any probation document that included a promise not to do the same thing again.

Joan popularized the concept of "solidarity with the unborn" at least in the fuller application of remaining "helpless" (ie. non-cooperative) not only in front of the clinics, but in custody and /or prison afterward. I was involved with Joan in five or six rescues. She was gentle, compassionate, and above all firm. I would sooner try to shake Gibraltar than change Joan's mind.

The subsequent "wave" of rescuers were more "reasonable" and to a greater degree submissive to direction. Nonetheless most were still pioneers, insofar as that what they were doing was not popular or profitable, nor did it accrue rewards of the sort most "followers" seek. Furthermore, they had minds of their own and would speak up quickly where they did not agree with the plans or direction leaders proposed. How well I remember some of the "policy" debates where a few hard-headed rescuers prolonged discussion as we tried to make decisions about how to respond to some civil authority or situation.

Wanted: Heavy Thinkers

But rescuers weren't philosophers – not idea people – not theoreticians. There were only a few of them who, like Sartre, were going back to academic pursuits if and when this war came to a conclusion. Action was at the center of their unity, and a willingness to act was high on the list of virtues for which they respected each other. [188]

For that reason, I suppose, when careful and precise thinking was needed, the rescue movement was not always at its best. In particular, the difficult and complex issues which arose around the question of "use of force" in connection to the first abortionist shootings, put the rescue movement in a complex position. Most of us had felt a heart response to the statement "if you think abortion is murder, then act like it." Everyone involved in rescue [189] felt the logic of that dictum.

But using force, which most of us would do in a simple case of defense against attempted murder, raised the question to a more sophisticated level of ethics and doctrine. Few rescuers could articulate the specific ways in which abortion was NOT a case of simple attempted murder. [190]

---

[188] I must add, however, that I was once in Chester County prison with two others who had graduated from some branch of Harvard. A number of the early pro-life activists were definitely intellectuals. And many rescuers were better thinkers than their peers.

[189] Rescue was always defined and practiced as "peaceful and prayerful".

[190] Eg., because of the number of parties involved, and their physical and ethical relationships to one another.

"Rightly dividing the truth" became a much higher priority than most rescuers, including most leaders, had hitherto made it.

In short, at this juncture, we needed thinkers and carefully concerted thinking – to a greater degree than most of us were willing or able to admit. Even realizing the need for serious thinking required more serious thinking than most were giving the problem! Some years earlier, after reading some of the things I'd written as I worked through issues rescue raised for me, Joe Foreman told me I was answering a whole lot of questions that no one was asking.[191] He would have been nearly right, except that I was asking them. But now we had come to a place where a lot of new questions needed first to be accurately formulated, and then carefully answered.[192]

In late April there was a meeting of national rescue leaders in Chicago, which several men from our area attended. Representatives were present from many of the local rescue groups around the country. The stated purpose of the meeting was to reorganize and reunite the rescue movement on a national level. The subtext of the meeting was the need for some measure of agreement about the use of force.

This issue had been simmering, and occasionally boiling over on the back burner. To start with, from the very

---

[191] Joe had written quite a few things himself, at that point, and I suppose many rescuers would have said the same about his writing.

[192] In defense of rescuers here, I must add that everyone knew about the most salient violence, murderously directed toward the babies. In most minds this eclipsed any deep concern about a few abortionists being killed.

Furthermore, as we have discussed, there was violence directed against prolifers on many occasions and continued to be. Pro-lifer James Pouillon was shot to death by Harlan Drake, a resident of Owosso, Michigan, because Drake objected to the graphic sign of an aborted baby Pouillon held during a one man abortion protest there on Sept 11, 2009. (M.M. Miller, 134) This didn't even make the national news!

beginning of the rescue movement, there had been the question about how we should regard those who used destructive force against property.

A convicted arsonist was serving a 42 year sentence for a fire in a Tennessee clinic in 1982. A Texas man had been sentenced to 20 years for arson in 1984. When I first got involved in rescue, Michael Bray, a Lutheran minister from Maryland, was spending two years in jail for trying to destroy an abortion clinic. His wife was a respected leader in the early days of Operation Rescue. In those days there was a latent question among rescuers and those considering rescue about how one ought to regard Michael's alleged actions.

Michael Bray

Others were serving time or would soon be serving time for going into clinics and overturning furniture -- or like Joan Andrews, for disabling abortion equipment.

Joe Foreman had an old line that always resonated with irony-prone rescuers. "I believe we should use dynamite," Joe would say, -- and then after a dramatic pause

– "I think we should put it under the pews." But since Michael Griffin shot Dr. Gunn, the issues no longer inspired much humor.

Related to this was a question about the point where prophetic utterances of threatened judgment against abortionists became legally-actionable threats. A Montana man went to prison for writing a letter to an abortionist and asking her how she would like to torn apart like the children she was aborting. Apparently he also suggested that what happened to Dr. Gunn could happen to her. For a while some pro-lifers were putting up "wanted posters," referring to abortionists as criminals. Was this some sort of threat? Particularly in a nation that was in the throes of inventing a legal category of "hate speech," one never knew. [193]

In the early 90s, respected pro-lifers began putting out a list called "Prisoners of Christ," which listed people in jail – mostly for rescues, but also those accused or convicted of attempts to destroy property or using threatening speech. By 1993/4 there were another four or five people serving time for arson on these lists, alongside rescuers or even sidewalk counselors serving long sentences (up to 2 ½ years) particularly in Wisconsin and Massachusetts.

The compilers of the lists insisted we need not make judgments as to the morality of the actions of the people in order to "visit them in prison" with our letters, etcetera. Then, of course, the shooters hit the headlines. What were we to say about them? They, too, were soon included on the lists of Prisoners of Christ, which rather begged the question.

The relatively isolated incidents of "violence" against abortionists resonated with the political efforts of the abortion lobby which by mid-1993 made the FACE (Freedom of Access to Clinic Entrances) Bill appear certain to become law. It was obviously a "bill of attainder," that is a piece of legislation designed to target one group and one group only, exactly the

---

[193] After 2000, federal courts granted huge settlements against a number of old rescue leaders for exactly these sorts of "charges," although none of the proofs indicated any specific intention to do harm to any of the "victims".

sort of legislation which our founders specifically prohibited.

The effect of the various judicial and legislative efforts to suppress the rescue movement was indeed to discourage the involvement of some rescuers, while stirring up frustration and anger in others. At the beginning of 1994, an obviously weary Joe Foreman bemoaned the apparent failure of the fading rescue movement:

> Over the last few years, we passed up our opportunity to dismantle these high places ourselves in a decent orderly fashion. I'm sure that 1994 and following will reveal a handful of people who will take it upon themselves to do so alone and in the dark. They will feel compelled to use matches and guns but only because we failed to use sufficient spiritual and social pressure to bring change from within. I would love to condemn them. It would make great public relations for me, but how can we condemn people who are doing what we failed to do – what we had the opportunity to do – what we had the spiritual tools to do – what our pastors could have led in – what so many believers were begging for their leadership to do? The shame of a burning clinic is that we permitted it to function as a death camp up until the day an anonymous individual loomed out of the night to grind its bloody wheels to a stop. The shame of seeing a dead or wounded abortionist is that he was still going into his death camp unhindered by us. . . .

But the issue of "the use of force" had been raised to the fore by actions of Michael Griffin and then Rachelle Shannon and by the published statement supporting their actions as ethical. In March 1993 Michael Griffin was convicted of homicide for shooting abortionist Gunn, and then in the August 1993 Rachelle Shannon was convicted of attempted murder for shooting the notorious Witchita abortionist,

Was That Thunder?

George Tiller, in the hands. [194]

Those in the rescue movement did not know how to respond. There was some emotional sympathy with these "shooters," mixed up with a shared sense of frustration over the kinds of legal trumpery the pro-aborts were pulling off in collusion with the Clinton regime and local pro-abortion administrations. But for most rescuers there was also a strong sense this was the opposite of "pro-life" activism.

Rachelle "Shelley" Shannon

Trying to maintain what they seemed to have thought of as a "middle road," a few respected rescuers from around the country had signed the document which stated that they could not condemn the "shooters" because there might be a biblical argument for the use of force in defense of the unborn child. This then became the shibboleth which was already

---

[194] She was apparently trying to incapacitate rather than kill him, shooting him in the hands. But his wounds were so slight that he was back at his bloody work within a week or so.

polarizing the national pro-life activist community and would lead to an open division at the 1994 Chicago meeting.

The diversity of the rescue movement was very great. Most of those at the Chicago meeting were people who had been leading rescues since the late 1980s, but a few were there who had actively opposed abortion back into the 70s. There were men like Terry Sullivan of Denver, who had been a peace activist during the Vietnam era, and who was deeply committed to peaceful means to peaceful ends.

There were also several members of the *Life Advocate* staff from Portland, Oregon, who had recently been known for making the theoretical arguments in defense of use of force "by some". It was generally recognized that Rachelle "Shelley" Shannon, who shot and injured "Tiller the Killer," was influenced by *Life Advocate's* arguments. Randy Terry and Keith Tucci, former leaders of Operation Rescue and Operations Rescue National were absent. Randy had not been active in rescue for a while. Keith had publicly refused to participate in events with those who did not condemn the use of force.

Flip Benham and Norma McCorvey

Was That Thunder?

In place of these men, and saying he had come under the "anointing" and was "wearing the mantle" of national rescue leadership was Flip Benham. Flip's credibility was significantly strengthened by the fact that he had reached out to Norma Jane McCorvey, "Roe" of Roe v. Wade, as a principle agent in her conversion to Christ and her affirmation of opposition to abortion. [195]

Joe Foreman, who initially helped draft, but did not sign the document which publicly refused to condemn use of force, was in Chicago, and acted as moderator of some of the meetings over the next two days.

Flip Benham reiterated a strong statement that Operation Rescue National, which he now headed, would not participate in any official activities or events with organizations or individuals who advocated the use of force.

---

[195] McCorvey testified she had not had or even originally sought an abortion herself. But as one who had "a crisis pregnancy" she had been sought out and used by those who wanted the federal court to strike down existing state abortion laws.

Co-counsels in Roe v. Wade, Sarah and Ron Weddington, had aborted their own only child, as Sarah described in, *A Question of Choice*, published in 1992. Ron had a vasectomy and they divorced. He wrote a letter to President Clinton, accessible online, which elucidates the pitiful philosophy that drives the proaborts, sometimes described as "a war on population," and summarized in Ron Weddington's letter thusly: ". . .I don't think you are going to get very far in reforming the country until we have a better educated, healthier, wealthier population."

Mr. Weddington's formula for achieving this was to prevent the stupid people from having children. This was part of the agenda which motivated the fanatics that created Roe v. Wade pretty much out of whole cloth. An added horror is that he classified his own child among those not worthy of life!

Of course Roe not only took down Texas's abortion laws, but those of all the fifty states. McCorvey later began her own organization "Roe No More," and published a couple of books, including *Roe v. Roe*, telling her story. Sandra Cano, "Doe" of Doe v. Bolton, also turned out to be opposed to abortion, and became a pro-life speaker!

Terry Sullivan, in 2012, still going strong

A couple of speakers, including Paul Hill, stated they could not in good conscience deny or ignore what they thought were biblical arguments for the use of force. But Terry Sullivan spoke emotionally of how he had seen the Vietnam-era peace movement shanghaied by violent factions, and how much it grieved him to think the same thing might be happening to the pro-life movement. At one point he retired from the meeting in tears.

On the other hand, members of the *Life Advocate* staff spoke with some emotion of their feelings at being excluded from the movement they had sacrificed so much to strengthen. Others asked if we could not come to some manner of compromise, an agreement to disagree, while pursuing the main business of the rescue movement. But this late in the game, "agreeing to disagree" wasn't treated as an option.

It was clear many in leadership were weary. There did not appear to be much hope of any quick resolution. Joe Foreman proposed that Joe Scheidler, respected and long-suffering activist leader since the 1970s, be asked to act as a national moderator over regionally defined activist organizations. The proposal was that these in turn would each be headed by a respected regional director.

When one man stood and formally proposed that those gathered appoint or commission a study group to forge a unified and biblical statement on the use of force, Foreman dismissed his motion as impracticable. His exact words were, "this isn't a Presbyterian meeting." The meeting thus failed to achieve any reconciliation or amelioration. The polarization was merely formalized there.

Several of those attending discussed this failure via phone and mail in the ensuing weeks. A group of about ten coalesced around a commitment to some kind of discussion toward a common biblical understanding, believing such a thing could still be achieved. I had the privilege to be part of this discussion.

In the following six months, essays, position papers, and summaries were exchanged through the mail, in an informal debate and response format. The actual arguments of the "use of force" advocates were examined, and brought under closer scrutiny than they had henceforth received. Pacifist arguments were set aside: not so much invalidated, as recognized as obtuse to the heart of the disagreement. [196]

A few members of this "colloquium" dropped out due to other responsibilities. But ultimately most of the participants agreed there was no conceivable situation in which traditional or biblical arguments for the ethical use of force could be applied to the situation of legalized abortion. At the simplest level this agreement was based on the fact that the life of the unborn child could not be preserved apart from the agreement of its mother, whose murderous intent, if you will, could not be averted by the use of force. Beyond this preserving the life of the unborn required the imperative of civil law exercising both the didactic and protective functions for which God ordained it.

The abortionist, heinous as his trade and acts are, is a hired assassin. The mother is almost always his chief

---

[196] This is not to say there were no members of the colloquium sympathetic to pacifist or use of force arguments.

accessory and co-conspirator, albeit often deluded. She may even be his conscious and relatively knowledgable employer. All ethical models allowing for the use of force to prevent the killing of an innocent third party involved three relatively independent people, while this one obviously involved at least one highly dependant person, the potential victim. No forceful intervention was possible between the mother and the child, apart from restoring the criminal status of abortion. No intervention, that is, more strenuous than that self-sacrificing and passive force which rescue represented.

The members of this colloquium planned a meeting at which formal conclusions might be written up and signed, in order that they could be published. The goal was to urged that the rescue community to adopt these conclusions and thus regain a greater unity. Unfortunately due to various misadventures, including pusillanimity on the part of a few participants, the meeting did not come off, and no conclusions were published. Legislative developments were soon to lead most rescuers to suppose the movement was not likely to revive in any case.

Like Sartre and the other intellectuals of the French resistance movement at the end of the war, most pro-life rescuers were precipitated out of that active life and back into more humdrum rounds. Yet I would now say it was specifically the lack of a unified and respected intellectual leadership which hastened the halt of the movement.

But I've run ahead of myself. Out of one side of the Chicago meeting a new organization, American Coalition of Life Activists (ACLA) formed. According to Joe Foreman, discussing this in June 1994, the reason for the new organization was that Operation Rescue National (ORN) headed by Flip Benham, refused to participate with anyone who didn't agree that violence against abortionists was inherently sinful. While opposed to violence in practice as most of them were, the ACLA guys were not willing to agree it was inherently sinful.

On the 9th of May, a Harris County, Texas, jury awarded Planned Parenthood of Southeast Texas 1.02 million dollars in punitive damages against Operation Rescue and

Was That Thunder?

Keith Tucci, and also against Rescue America and Don Treshman, for protests made during the Republican National Convention there in 1992. Although the case was appealed, it was discouraging.

Slightly encouraging was the news that another Pennsylvania abortion clinic shut down, this one in York. However, while its operators said PA's new abortion laws were one of the reasons they went out of business, pro-lifers pointed out Planned Parenthood had recently opened a competing abortuary. This was the new strategy of Planned Parenthood – to expand out into the smaller cities of the hinterland.

In May 1994, the FACE Bill was signed by President Clinton. This was the most serious blow the rescue community had sustained on the legal front. Simply speaking it threatened in concrete terms to extract significant judgments, and legally mandated multiple payments from pro-life rescuers and even active sidewalk counselors.[197]

In the spring or early summer, Roseann and I were privileged to host Fr. Frank Pavone and several of his staff in our home. Father Pavone had been recently commissioned by Cardinal O'Connor of New York to fulltime pro-life work. Father Pavone picked up the baton of Priests for Life, which was founded in 1991. We met him and invited him to stay with us if he needed a base while making himself acquainted with the Philadelphia area pro-life community. It is a joy to read now that he has a staff of sixty fulltime workers!

One memory of that time is an embarrassing one. I had repaired and painted a wooden picnic table a week before Frank and staff arrived. We kept it in our back yard, and offered it to them as a pleasant place to confer during the day. But alas, for some reason, one small spot on one of the benches had not dried – and Fr. Pavone ended up with blue oil-based paint on his black clerical trousers! I think someone was able to remove it with solvents, but I felt pretty silly

---

[197] In fact it was to be used against sidewalk counselors on a number of occasions, and even against pro-lifers picketting abortionist houses.

about it. Soft-spoken and cheerful Frank was hardly bothered by it at all.

Fr. Frank Pavone of Priests for Life

Some rescuer leaders had anticipated the increasing financial pressure of the legal assaults against us. Some had taken appropriate measures to render ourselves less vulnerable to such judgments. However, most rescuers were ordinary people with ordinary jobs and financial situations which left us far from "judgment proof". The "chilling" effect of the FACE law upon most folks cannot be denied.

Yet even at the time, some of us had a glimmer of consolation: that with so much of the proaborts' money and political capital being spent in opposition to rescue, those resources were not available to use elsewhere. We might be cannon fodder, but at least they were using up their ammunition against us, rather than on other fronts where other efforts were gaining ground.

In June 1994 Philadelphia wrote me it was bringing liens against my house for rescues in 1991 and 1992. The amounts were small and uncollectible under PA law on joint property, but represented a further hassle. We knew of some Philadelphia rescuers who indeed eventually lost their homes through refusing to pay fines or judgments against them.

Rescue Approaching Standstill

A "Summer of Justice" campaign was planned for Little Rock, Arkansas, and a Jul 6-9 planning meeting announced, but the meeting was sunk over discord: ORN vs ACLA. Don Treshman reissued a modified invitation asking only those committed to nonviolence to attend. The ACLA guys planned an alternative activity in Jackson, Mississippi, with the focus on exposing the abortionists there.

Paul Hill in prison garb

Then on 29 Jul 1994, Paul Hill, committed the double murder at Pensacola Ladies Center, in Florida, shotgunning an abortionist and his bodyguard, while wounding a female assistant who rode with them. Paul had been an Orthodox Presbyterian minister, until his statements on the need for "direct action" or the use of force brought him up before his presbytery for discipline. He refused to back down and was defrocked.

Paul, whom I met briefly in Chicago, was a man of quiet and calm demeanor, whom most people found pleasant and affable. He had been interviewed on national TV and his simple arguments sounded persuasive. One man in our church, whose own life had been devastated through his participation in abortion, told me he found Paul's arguments during an interview on national TV very reasonable.

Paul had adopted his ethical/theological arguments under the influence of some of the wildly theoretical teachers of the theonomist school of reformed theology, who were subsequently quick to deny any connection with him. Not being as intelligent as they, nor as confined to theory, he fastened on one set of syllogisms which were to carry him all the way to his execution as a double murderer. As I think I have already indicated, on top of the FACE bill, these abortionist shootings were likely the biggest factor slowing, then halting the rescue movement.

Peg Luksik, an ardent pro-lifer and fairly successful political aspirant, announced her candidacy for Governor of Pennsylvania. At the same time pro-life U.S. Representative, Rick Santorum, announced he was running for Senate against pro-abortion candidate, Harris Wofford, in the summer of 1994. During that campaign season many rescuers poured considerable energy into these and other pro-life races.

On the 22 August, the Philadelphia *Inquirer* printed a typical "puff piece," a prejudicial article about the wonderful "services" offered by Planned Parenthood, and specifically about a mother of five having an abortion there. The article was supposed to be "human interest" but its ultimate agenda was simply to promote the abortion industry.

The walls of the rescue movement were being stormed repeatedly and each "wave" of attack did damage. But it was more significant that the unity of the movement was being shaken within. Nor were these the only sorts of attacks. In late 1994, my family was "blind-sided" by something much more personal. As in so many other cases, I was not spiritually prepared for it.

Rick Santorum has always been openly pro-life.
My wife and daughters worked on his behalf in Philadelphia.

A friend came to us deeply burdened with news of the pregnancy of another close acquaintance. Since we knew the pregnant woman, we shared the emotional burden with our informant, but for several reasons we felt we could only act through her. Nonetheless we offered her the resources at our disposal. Not too much later, our informant came back and said the young lady had scheduled an appointment at Paoli abortuary. Suddenly this monster we had began fighting at that clinic seven years earlier was spitting fire back in our personal faces.

It would not be unfair to say I fell completely to pieces. If the case had been put to me as hypothetical, I'd like to think I would have mobilized a crew of friends to do a last minute rescue. If the relationship between the young lady and our informant hadn't been a factor, I might have acted with better determination. But instead I turned inward. Instead of thinking about that woman and her baby, I felt

God had treated us unfairly. I was feeling sorry for myself to such a degree that I was essentially paralyzed and did next to nothing. I might as well have curled up in a fetal position and rocked back in forth in a corner. Lord forgive me.

I had one opportunity to talk with the pregnant woman several days before the appointment. Not knowing we knew what was going on, she was outwardly cheerful, while I was smothered in melancholy. I essentially said nothing. We half-heartedly told some sidewalk counselors we knew about the appointment and asked them to talk to the young lady if they could, but we didn't go to the clinic ourselves. We let someone we cared about kill her own child – and did next to nothing.

I continued to be filled with pure self-pity. That God would let such a thing happen after we had sacrificed so much! This time he had gone too far! His response was more or less – "Now we know how omnipotent you are on your own." I was a worm and no man. We still feel a kind of sorrow nothing in this world can assuage – both a deep disappointment in ourselves, and the sense of losing someone precious.

At the other extreme, there was a strange and wonderful event soon after this. My wife was able to lead a friend dying of cancer to Christ. Among this woman's burdens was an abortion she had many years earlier. We prayed with her and rejoiced in the forgiveness which she found in the Lord. Not long after that she went to be with him.

The transposition of these two events left us deeply humbled, but grateful for God's mercy and grace toward sinners. We were repenting as accomplices to an abortion, but rejoicing in leading others to a forgiving Savior.

By November, cigar-smoking Attorney General Janet Reno had mobilized the FBI and a grand jury to investigate VAAPCON -- another unwieldy acronym meaning something like "Ve Are After People Conspiring, Oh No!" only that wasn't it. I think it was "Violence Against Abortion Providers Conspiracy" or something close.

It was an FBI and grand jury investigation set up by

Was That Thunder?

AG Reno and her companions to search out the roots of the national pro-life conspiracy. This investigation and the grand jury hearings ran until February 1996. But meanwhile they hauled in quite a few prolife leaders for questioning. One or two brave souls refused to give them all the information they wanted, and some were cited for contempt and locked up. It would take the grand jury 16 months to decide there was no nationally organized conspiracy to do violence to abortionists.

Meanwhile FACE violations were being actively prosecuted by a bevy of Justice Department attorneys.

A rescue of committed people was planned for mid-December in our area, but too few indicated interest. It was re-scheduled to the end of January.

Some local leaders signed a statement requesting Paul Hill's sentence be commuted. Reasons given for opposing it included: 1/Paul killed a serial killer and his accomplice; 2/he was denied an attorney of his own choosing; and 3/he was prevented from presenting his reason for his actions in court.

My correspondence in the colloquium on this issue led me to conclude Paul had indeed committed first degree murder. Therefore I could not sign on. My own correspondence with Paul on death row eventually strengthened that perspective, although I wished for him to repent and imagined, as a consequence, that he might receive a lesser penalty.

And I wrote an article for *Life Advocate*, regretting all the "scourging" Paul was receiving in the Christian press. I argued there for a lesser penalty – just as I would for a mother who was accessory to the death of her own child – on the basis of mitigating circumstances.

On the 30th of December 1994, John Salvi added to the sad list of murders outside abortion clinics. He also wounded three others, in Brookline, Massachusetts. He then drove down to Virginia, where he did some further shooting, apparently threatening some pro-life sidewalk counselors as well.

That same day Bill Devlin issued a statement on behalf of the Philadelphia Family Policy Council (PFPC) which was very much on point. I quote it in full here:

> As we have always since the beginning of our organization in 1981, we condemn any form of violence toward any person or persons such as the events earlier today in Brookline. No social movement of any kind will win the hearts and mind of the nation by practicing violence against their opposition. The pro-abortion folk should be cautious to characterize this as "anti-choice" violence and then go on to condemn the entire pro-life movement. To allege that today's events in Brookline represent the pro-life movement is to say that Jack Kevorkian represents every medical doctor in America. The two previous perpetrators of violence at abortion facilities are now convicted felons. They do not represent pro-life. Michael Griffin had a long history of mental illness and Paul Hill is a twice-defrocked minister from two different denominations.
>
> Every great movement of justice has had its detractors. John Brown and his sons did not represent the anti-slavery movement. H. Rap Brown and Bobby Seale did not represent the civil rights movement. Today's violence does not represent the pro-life movement which has been faithfully caring for the unwanted women and children, born and unborn, for over two decades.

John Salvi committed suicide in his jail cell. Few people thought him sane, except the pro-aborts propagandists who tried to portray him as a typical pro-lifer. As Bill Devlin said, real pro-lifers continued to promote life, rather than taking it. But there was one thing the active members of the pro-life movement had been doing for more than a decade that they were not going to do much more – namely rescue.

Was That Thunder?

John Salvi, said to be deeply disturbed.

CHAPTER NINE – DISPERSED, DISBANDED (1995-6)

> I will praise thee; for I am fearfully and wonderfully made: marvelous are thy works; and that my soul knoweth right well. My substance was not hid from thee, when I was made in secret, and curiously wrought in the lowest parts of the earth. Thine eyes did see my substance yet being unperfect; and in thy book all my members were written, which in continuance were fashioned, when as yet there was none of them.
> -- Psalm 139:14-16

Our church opened 1995 with another series of pro-life Sunday School classes. Visiting pastor Bob Lewis led the first week with a summary of the year's events and an assessment of where things seemed to be going. Bob sounded down-in-the mouth and gave a somewhat pessimistic presentation. The other Sundays of the month we offered various options along the lines of previous years' classes. These were oriented toward specific kinds of pro-life ministry, including again post-abortion counseling.

The ACLA ran a campaign in DC, from January 21st to 23rd, calling it "Capital Spotlight." It consisted not of rescues, but demonstrations specifically aimed at exposing the NIH Fetal Research programs, which utilized aborted fetuses.

A milestone was reached that month when the Paoli clinic closed. The owner of the building asked the abortion clinic to leave and when they refused, took legal action resulting in their removal. This was not only the site of my first rescue and arrest back in 1988, but the place where, very recently the child of a close acquaintance was aborted – the one to whom I had been absolutely no help in her crisis.

On the 27th of January, one of the last rescues in the Philadelphia area took place at Planned Parenthood with 28 rescuers arrested. We spent two days in custody, were charged with four misdemeanors each (in line with Mayor Rendell's new policy) and were released on our own recognizance. A few received extra charges like resisting arrest.

Twenty-eight of the best and bravest blocked PP doors in 1995

    For reasons we never knew, but probably tied to the Mayor's "beefed up security" at abortion clinics, a squadcar full of uniformed officers[198] pulled up beside Roseann and me one morning as we sidewalk-counselled at B. B. and K. An officer called me over, and asked what we were doing there. Since this news was a couple years old, I found it somewhat ironic to tell him. But when I described our purposes there he asked, "Sir, are you armed?"

    I was incredulous at this question. He was serious! I stared at him for a moment trying to figure out which of us was on the wrong planet. Then I answered, "No, I'm not, but my wife has long fingernails and sharp teeth. She's pretty

---

[198] There were four officers in the car – a very rare thing in Philly!

dangerous." I walked away. [199]

A little later Joe Roach was interviewed by a reporter from *The Inquirer*, and written up in that rag. The article was about as fair as could be expected. He seemed almost human.

In March there was a tempest in a teapot when a Chester County Judge granted "amnesty" to the 169 rescuers who did not appear in court for the July 88 rescue at Paoli. Needless to say the pro-aborts, who had been seeking pro-life blood wherever they turned, found this outrageous.

About then the Partial Birth Abortion issue was rising to the fore. A ban passed the House and passed by Senate on the 7 December 1995. Pennsylvania's own Senator Specter led the fight against bill. It was ultimately sent back to the house with a "life of the mother" exception – as though that had anything to do with it. This issue was a principle influence toward my participation in my next two rescues.

In October, Physicians for Life, ran an ad in the *Inquirer*. Physicians for Life was originally formed back in the 70s by the late Dr. Jim Kelly, husband of the indefatigable Molly. This ad was a strong statement of pro-life principles, signed by hundreds of doctors and medical professionals, including several from our own church.

Toward the end of November, a preliminary injunction was issued by the Federal court for the Eastern PA District, naming 35 defendants in a FACE case, including "James. M. Trott," no doubt my distant cousin. The list of defendants was based on recent rescues at Chester-Crozer.

In January 1996, having spent a lot of time cleaning up my essays and articles (mostly on pro-life subjects), I published a list of these and distributed it in my own circles.

Included on this list was the book-length typescript for "Shattering the Image: A Pursuit of Biblical Ethics in Relation to the Issues Raised by the Shooting of Abortionists." The third chapter, in particular, was an exposition of Bible passages dealing with the death of human beings. This was

---

[199] In defense of the police, perhaps they had received a bogus call from the clinic or some other "alert" suggesting we had diabolical intentions that morning.

my personal summary of the conclusions of the colloquium on violence. It brought me even more firmly to conclude the shooters had committed the sin of murder and that there was no biblical defense for their actions. But beyond that I saw with new clarity how precious human beings were to God and how seriously he took the death of each and every one.

Chester-Crozer – flanked by two faithful wheelchair rescuers

With the help of two of my students, [200] I set up a website "oakandyewpress.com" where many of my pro-life papers and poems were posted. [201]

---

[200] I was teaching home school classes part-time including literature, composition, history and biology.

[201] This site was attacked a few years later by some fairly powerful virus/trojan horse/whatever that took over the website and substituted pornographic thumbnails in its place, so that anyone going to the website was invited to feast his/her eyes on porn. This was quite a disabling blow to me . Of course, any invasion of what one considers one own space is a violation, but it was also a blow because as I mentioned early in this memoir, I had been attracted to pornography at many points in my life. I made a few half-hearted attempts to recover the site from this attack -- which even bewildered my "provider" — and then gave up on it. How naive I was – now under similar circumstances I would immediately contact the FBI.

A Memoir of Pro-life Rescue

Our 1996 Sunday School classes kicked off with the video, *The Hard Truth*,[202] chiefly a photographic presentation of the bodies of aborted babies, thousands of which had been recovered over the years from dumpsters and incinerators at abortuaries.

Attending this class was one friend, a Christian doctor and cancer specialist, who was completely devastated by the film. He sat after the class with his head in his hands, barely able to speak. Later we talked and he said that his shock was double – first at the awful facts of what he had seen, and second the dawning of the realization that this had been so successfully hidden from him. He said it had been so covered over with euphemisms and technical language during his medical training that he had never an inkling of that horror until this day. Multiply that story times how many medical professionals?

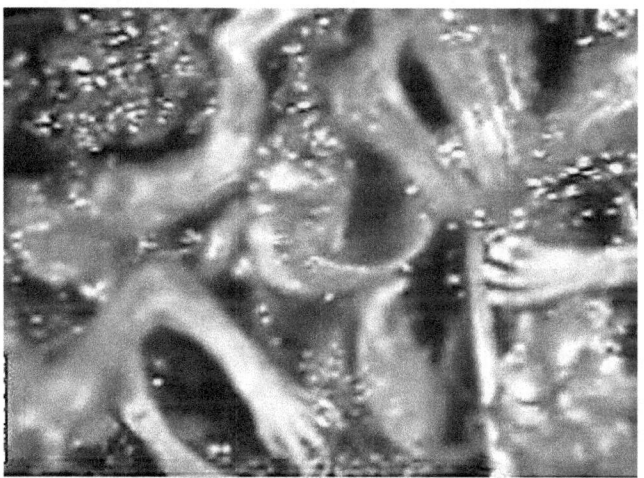

A frame from the video "The Hard Truth"

We went on to the second week of Sunday School with a class on ministry to aborted women run by two women in our church who had been there. The third week, we once more encouraged people to become involved in

---

[202] Made by American Portrait Films, with Greg Cunningham. Available on Youtube.

sidewalk counseling through the example and the teaching of another couple from the church, together with Roseann. And on the fourth week, I led a class on barriers to involvement, beginning to emphasize the idolatry of the American church, which I was coming to see as the root cause for the nation's and church's compromises at other key points in history, such as the Dred Scot decision.

On January 16th we rescued at Chester Crozer, peacefully and prayerfully as per usual. We spent four cold hours at the doors, but one rescuer was heard, to utter a description out of a rescuer's dream, "It's getting boring!" Kimiko and I were at the back door when arrests eventually went forward. We were passive, but orderly, as officers from several jurisdictions carried us onto buses. When we arrived in Media, we negotiated for fifteen minutes of time in which to pray together, after which we agreed to voluntarily walk off the buses rather than make officers carry us. In this way we were able to keep the buses from being returned so fast that they expedited arrests. Thirty four people risked arrest, 21 of them local rescuers, and the rest from six other states.

Although we had not been prosecuted there for quite a few years, the FBI contacted attorney Jim Owens twice after this rescue. The agents responded to Jim's incredulity by confessing they had been detailed to investigate this rescue by their DC chiefs!

A soft-spoken and respected New Hampshire rescuer, Steve Mears, of Missionaries to the Preborn, was jailed for three months there. Steve was the second Northeast director for ACLA.

Also in January 1996, an organization based out of state, Christ's Bride Ministry, bought poster space in the buses and subways of SEPTA to advertise the link between breast cancer and abortion. Although they had legally agreed to these and approved them, SEPTA nonetheless tore them down within the first month. Lyn Yeakel, well-known pro-abort, now a Clinton appointee and local head of the US Health and Human Services (HHS) apparently convinced SEPTA to do this. In response, a suit was filed against SEPTA, which case went to court in late June.

Also in January the so called "VAAPCON" federal grand jury finally disbanded. They had failed to find a national conspiracy of violence against abortion clinics. Cheryl Richardson of Maryland, who had refused to testify, was released from jail near the end of the month. A *Washington Post* article quoted a Justice Department official, "The national conspiracy only exists in the minds of people who have a political interest in keeping this thing going." [203]

In February, my wife's parents, Jack and Rosemarie Miller spoke at the Arche Church in Hamburg, Germany. The previous fall, the pastor, Wolfgang Wegert had asked Joni Eareckson Tada to recommend an American pastor to speak at his church. She mentioned Jack Miller, and thus the invitation. While my in-laws were there, Pastor Wegert told them a remarkable story.

In mid-November 1995, a photograph had been printed in the Hamburg paper with an accompanying article. The photo had been taken in June 1936 and showed about sixty workers in a crowd gathered at the Hamburg shipyards during a visit by Adolf Hitler. Almost everyone in the crowd has his right arm raised in the familiar "Heil Hitler" salute. The caption to the photo indicates it was taken as the Nazi song, "Horst Wessel," was being played. But in the center of the crowd in the photograph stands a man with his arms folded. He is most definitely not saluting. The newspaper indicated the photo had been found in old Nazi files. Apparently the SS had the same question back then. In the November 95 article, the photo was printed with a large circle around the man and the caption "Who was this man?"

Pastor Wegert was both astounded and deeply moved as he saw the paper that morning – for the man was his father! When Rosemarie brought this story home to us, we were also greatly moved.

---

[203] Despite this decision by that grand jury, various organizations have continued to promote the image of the violent or even "terrorist" pro-life movement. Sadly, one of these has been the Southern Poverty Law Project, which once upon a time gave itself to regaining and protecting American's civil rights rather than seeking to have them taken away.

Was That Thunder?

Seite 16 | Hamburg | 15. 11. 1995

1936 – Nur einer ließ den Arm unten

Am 13. Juni 1936 bei Blohm + Voss in Hamburg: Alle recken bei den Feierlichkeiten zum Stapellauf des Segelschulschiffes „Horst Wessel" den rechten Arm zum Hitler-Gruß, nur einer verweigert sich (im Kreis).

Schriftsteller sucht Zeitzeugen: Wer war der Mann?

A Memoir of Pro-life Rescue

As Solzhenitsyn pointed out in *From Under the Rubble*, totalitarian regimes topple only when ordinary "good people" do something – perhaps as small as refusing to clap for an evil speech or laugh at an evil story. In a similar way, every rescuer feels it is an honor to be listed in police files as one willing to take a small stand for the unborn. May our children have some such small memorial to our resistance to this evil.

In February, Randy Terry joined a number of ministers who flew to Hawaii to lobby and demonstrate against legislation which was an attempt to redefine marriage under that state's laws. Randy had become a radio-talk-show host, and a political activist, although he had not been involved in rescues for several years. In a vote on March 3 the Hawaiian Lower House voted 44 to 6 to amend the state Constitution to define marriage as existing only between a man and a woman.

Dr. Beverly McMillan was one of the many former abortion providers who became a strong pro-life voice

In April Joe Scheidler and the Pro-Life Action League

hosted a conference near Chicago called "Meet the Abortion Providers" which featured Norma McCorvey (Roe), Sandra Cano (Doe), and four former abortionists, speaking against legalized abortion and telling in detail about the wave of destruction they had been part of and had seen abortion cause.

Over the years in our own area we had come to know several people who worked at abortion clinics until they were finally sickened and brought to repentance over their involvement. A couple of these were in our own church circles.

At one point, George and Tina Krail called us from New Jersey, inviting us to a Baptist Church where a former abortion assistant was going to give her testimony. I suppose there were about ten pro-lifers who came, and we were deeply blessed to hear this lady, who had formerly been on the staff of NEWC. She testified to Christ's redeeming work in her life and family. We eagerly went up to talk to here afterward, and told her who we were. We were further moved to find she was actively involved in a church where we had many friends and pro-life connections.

We urged her to speak more in public, since her testimony could be widely used to inform others toward a heightened awareness of what abortion really was. However she said that she needed the privacy to strengthen her own faith and her family. Knowing what too much public ministry too early could do [204] we commended her decision.

The highest profile abortionist to make a turnaround was Dr. Bernard Nathanson, whose wife, Adele, spoke at Valley Forge in July 1988. He had been foundational to NARAL and the abortion industry in New York. His courage in turning against the tide he had helped to release was remarkable.

It was the supposed "safety" and "success" of New York's legalized abortion which, in turn had been foundational to the "medical" arguments considered by

---

[204] See for instance the account of Eric Harrah in Chapter Seven.

Justice Blackmun in Roe v. Wade. One of the ironies of this was that the "safety" of New York's abortions was due to extensive regulation and inspection under state law, which Roe abolished, as it did in all states!

But beyond that the statistics were false, according to Dr. Nathanson. He knew – because he helped to fake them!

> We persuaded the media that the cause of permissive abortion was a liberal, enlightened, sophisticated one," recalls the movement's co-founder. "Knowing that if a true poll were taken, we would be soundly defeated, we simply fabricated the results of fictional polls. We announced to the media that we had taken polls and that 60 percent of Americans were in favor of permissive abortion. This is the tactic of the self-fulfilling lie. Few people care to be in the minority. We aroused enough sympathy to sell our program of permissive abortion by fabricating the number of illegal abortions done annually in the U.S. The actual figure was approaching 100,000, but the figure we gave to the

media repeatedly was 1,000,000.[205]

Many people do not realize that approximately thirty women per year died from legal abortions in the first few years after Roe – about the same numbers that died from illegal abortions during the years just previous to legalization.

Nathanson had become a vigorous opponent of abortion as soon as he saw ultrasound movies which revealed the unborn child in agony during an abortion. His film "The Silent Scream" became one of the most powerful visual tools to awaken people to what abortion was and what it did.[206] Around the country forty or fifty voices of former abortionists sounded from time to time in various efforts to educate the public over against the general propaganda blitz for "women's rights" and "choice". [207]

These repentant abortionists, in tandem with reports about the many sorts of skullduggery for which various other abortionists were being prosecuted, contributed to increasing public disdain for these "doctors" and what they did for money.[208]

In April, only weeks after speaking at the Arche Church in Germany, my wife's father died following emergency heart surgery in Spain. It was a difficult time for us all. Many of the family had no opportunity to spend any time with him during his last days on earth. However Paul,

---

[205] And we now know that most of these illegal abortions were being carried out by medical doctors. We know this partly because as soon as Roe came down, they began to brag about it!

[206] Ultrasound imaging has become so sophisticated now that any objective person can now see with his or her own eyes that the myth of a baby in the womb being merely a "mass of tissue" is pure bunk. Ultrasounds can show not only "snapshots" but "movies/videos" of the unborn child active inside his or her mother's womb.

[207] Many of these testimonies are now available on Youtube

[208] Philadelphia's own Kermit Gosnell was deeply allied with the rest of the abortion industry until he ws at last prosecuted, since when the other pro-abort agencies have tried to distance themselves from him and his shop of horrors.

Barbara and Keren did get to Spain before he died. Rosemarie was brave but hurting. The outpouring of honor and consolation was amazing. The memorial service took place in a large, but crowded sanctuary.

The fact that Jack had teetered on the verge of death twice before, and that we had all worked through some important things then meant a lot to us. One blessed thing he said to me came as we walked arm and arm up and down a hospital corridor back when he had been battling lymphoma. "Thank you for being my Barnabus".

I'm not sure I can process that properly this side of heaven, but since Barnabus stands out as the guy that on the one hand encouraged Paul but on the other, parted ways with him over which way the Lord was leading them, I take it he meant something like, "thanks for disagreeing with me." Although that was not the keynote of our relationship, it had been its tenor at a few important points. But death, as familiar an enemy as it had become, left us shaken and deeply aware of our own mortality – as well as crystallizing our appreciation for Jack.

Another very meaningful conversation during Jack's earlier medical battles took place with John Yenchko in Germantown Hospital, where I was visiting Jack. John read the story of Abraham's going out from Ur of the Chaldees at the Lord's behest. Afterward he said, "many people say faith is the opposite of works, but so far as I can see the real opposite of faith is security." Abraham believed God and therefore he was willing to enter wholeheartedly into the great insecurity of going he-knew-not-where. There's an antinomy there. John's conclusion, which was intended to encourage Jack's faith, was parallel to that rescue saying of Susan Odom's, "the safest place in the world to be is in the center of God's will."

After any number of delays, a Partial Birth Abortion Act was passed by both houses of Congress. President Clinton vetoed it. He was surrounded by women whose lives had been saved by the procedure – so it was claimed! Republican Governor Christine Todd Whitman of New Jersey said in her opinion he had done the right thing.

Was That Thunder?

Former Surgeon General C. Everett Koop told AM News:

> I believe that Mr. Clinton was misled by his medical advisors on what is fact and what is fiction in reference to late-term abortions. Because in no way can I twist my mind to see that the late term-abortion as described – you know, partial birth, and then destruction of the unborn child before the head is born – is a medical necessity for the mother.

On May 14, in Akron, Ohio, a national rescue was held at the abortuary run by Martin Haskell, who was becoming notorious as a pioneer of the Partial Birth Abortion. For the first time, through courageous debate in Congress, abortion had been shown for what it was. Legislators, including Pennsylvania's own Rick Santorum, had set up diagrams that showed the baby being fully delivered, except for the head, while the "physican" inserted the dagger blades of scissors into the base of the child's head, killing it, so that the brains could then be sucked out and the head collapsed.

One of the first public exposures of this diabolical procedure had been in *Life Advocate* magazine, and the diagrams used thereafter were essentially those they had published.

Toward the end of June, federal judge Harvey Bartle heard the suit over SEPTA's removal of the posters advertising the link between breast cancer and abortion. Christ's Bride ministries charged SEPTA with violating civil rights, specifically First Amendment rights. Dr. Joel Brind gave strong testimony about the "science" behind the posters. A strong counter-attack was mounted in the court.[209] However, in July the judge came down with his verdict against SEPTA, requiring them to fulfill their contract.

---

[209] Dr. Polly Newcomb, among the opposing witnesses, refused to use the Bible in her swearing in. As per Bill Devlin's old joke, perhaps she should have used a copy of *The Inquirer*.

A Memoir of Pro-life Rescue

On 30 July, the Justice Department filed a "Complaint for Injunctive Relief and Statutory Damages, Summons and Motion for Preliminary Injunction" against me (still as "James M. Trott") along with 34 others under the civil side of FACE, citing the Chester Crozer rescue of 16 January. [210]

Rescuers tended to develop weird sense of humors. Someone -- I think it was Bill Devlin -- sent me a March 24th article from *The Inquirer* quoting recently accused Metrobank principal and city controller, Jonathan Saidel, "I live in a difficult world where anybody can make unbelievable charges against me". Bill wanted us to sympathize with this poor persecuted man! - except that, unlike us, he seems to have made money out of his difficulties!

Over the years, various pro-life leaders, including many active in rescue had participated in visual demonstrations of the results of abortion. Photographs drawing parallels between racist lynchings, the Nazi holocaust and abortion were effective in not only informing the public, but getting people to think. Since the major media continually stonewalled the truth about what abortion really did and who to, most people still believed the "blob of tissue" myth. This tactic was one way of changing that.

"Show the Truth" campaign poster.

In late June, Operation Rescue West (Jeff White, Gary McCullough, et al) organized a "Show the Truth" Tour which

---

[210] Among other things, the suit said Chester Crozer has been "blockaded" 19 times in the last six years.

traveled through the Southwest and along the west coast. It consisted in displaying large posters containing un-retouched photographs of aborted children. The "Show the Truth" tour continued on into October and November mostly through the Midwest and up into the eastern US. On October 23rd they came to Center City Philly, and displayed the posters around City Hall.

In August, Steve Mears, recently released from jail in New Hampshire, invited activists to participate in a picket in our area to expose Joel Stein, a circuit-riding abortionist, who traveled from Virginia to New Hampshire killing babies. [211]

Kimiko went out to Chicago with other Philadelphia rescuers. The occasion was the Democratic convention. The pro-life demonstrations were kept at quite a distance from the convention and the media "blackout" pretty much masked pro-life events there.

In August 1996 a rescue was held in Englewood, New Jersey. The following month, the partial birth abortion (PBA) clinic which was the site of this rescue was exposed in the *Bergen County Record*. The article by reporter Ruth Padawer quoted abortionists there as saying they were doing thousands of PBAs per year, contrary to nationally aired claims that only a few PBAs were done in the US per year.

In late September, Joe Roach suggested we disband the core leadership group in the Philadelphia area. He cited seven points 1/ limited interest of former participants, 2/ general lack of interest in promoting rescues, 3/ limited availability of time from former leaders, 4/ decreased need to work out the tactics of legal cases, 5/ the fact that political and ministry organizations were taking over our functions, 6/ diverse political priorities and perspectives among those in the group, 7/ the redundancy of pro-life groups, and availability of other groups for any activity we were likely to be engaged in. The demurrers were few and feeble. While all

---

[211] A similar expose had occurred in January, when local traveling abortionist George Danoff was introduced to his fellow passengers in the airport gate waiting area by an obliging pro-lifer. He was flying to Milwaukee, where snow delayed his return flight.

of us hoped an era of rescue might somehow revive, we recognized it was, for the time being, pretty much over.

In a sense we felt superseded. Active pro-life organizations in our areas included many crisis pregnancy centers, the Pro-Life Union Inc of Southeastern Pennsylvania, The Philadelphia Family Policy Council, the Pro-Life Legal Fund, the Pennsylvania Pro-Life Federation, as well as local manifestations of the National Right to Life group, in addition to many mothers' homes and church-specific groups, particularly on the Catholic side of the sanctuary.

In mid-November 1996, a news item dominated the local headlines. It told of the arrest of Amy Grossberg and Brian Peterson, former high school sweethearts, attending colleges in Delaware and Pennsylvania, who were charged with first degree murder in connection to the birth and death of their son. A police dog found the body of the newborn wrapped in a gray plastic bag in a dumpster behind the motel where his eighteen year old parents had delivered him.

Delaware medical examiners found the cause of death "... to be multiple fractures with injury to the brain due to blunt force trauma and shaking," but authorities added that asphyxiation and hypothermia might also be involved in the child's death. Under Delaware law the death penalty could be sought where the victim was under 14 years.

Curiously, the young parents were from Bergen County, New Jersey, site of the partial birth abortion facility which had gained considerable notoriety after the article two months earlier in the *Bergen County Record*. That clinic, in Englewood, was to be the scene of my last two rescues.

During the fall of 1996, I was invited to speak to grade school students at Valley Christian school class where we had many connections, including Kerith Finegan[212], fifth grade daughter of close friends who were active in foster care and later adoption. It was a good challenge for me to speak clearly and yet appropriately to these younger students. Both teachers and students were very attentive and encouraging.

A few years earlier Kimiko and Roseann and I spoke

---

[212] Now a pediatric nurse at Children's Hospital.

Was That Thunder?

at Spruce Hill Christian school in West Philadelphia. Roseann's brother had been founding headmaster. He was no longer there, but our children had attended and we knew many other parents and teachers.

We had separate assemblies for the younger and older kids. Roseann and Kimiko noted how the younger children were astounded by the idea of abortion, while the 8th graders seemed quite blasé, many of them apparently already indoctrinated with "right to choose" rhetoric.

There was a sad sequel to this. Roseann got a letter a week later in which a parent from that school declared in no uncertain terms that we had no business telling her child that abortion was wrong. We learned this parent actually worked for Planned Parenthood. Roseann tried to dialogue with her, but she was completely hostile and threatened legal action if we contacted her again. The school administration was firmly committed to right to life principles, however. I'm afraid the parent withdrew the child from the school.

Pat Carroll

On 7 Dec the venerable and much-loved Pat Carroll, died, he whose speech I forestalled before Judge Melody.

CHAPTER TEN - ENGLEWOOD AND ALLENTOWN (1997)

It is our duty as Christians to pity those in prison. It is our duty to pity those who are just now out of prison. But how much more is it the duty of a Christian to pity those rich and complacent who cannot ever get into prison. What! Never even to have felt the grip of a policeman? To have watched his bold and suspicious eye; to have tried to make a good show under examination; never to heard the bolt grinding in the lock? And never to have looked round at the simplicity of the cell? What then emotions have you had you unimprisonable rich and complacent! Oh what do you know of active living? Or what do you know of the faith? And what of adventure? -- *The Path to Rome*, Hillaire Belloc (quoted by George Grant 1991 Chicago)

Birth Control and Abortion

Despite being snowed out the first week, our church started off the pro-life Sunday School in January 1997 with classes on ministering to post-abortion America which we divided into separate men's and women's groups. The next week we went on to talk more about sidewalk counseling and adoption. Then, in addition to an update of political and legal events of the last year, we finished up by going into the new (to our classes) but related territory of birth control.

Our Catholic brethren and a number of Protestants, including many of the early rescue leaders, felt these two issues were inseparable. Insofar as "birth control" means use of abortifacient drugs or devices, every pro-lifer is compelled to agree. Abortion by any human agency is taking a human life, regardless whether it is chemical or physical abortion. It is always wrong. But when it came to non-abortifacient birth control between married people, the issues are different. In contradistinction to some of our evangelical and nearly all of our Catholic brethren,[213] we had come to the conclusion that the debate about non-abortifacient birth control was merely an argument over language and means, not really about ethics. In fact the Catholics were gung-ho in promoting "natural family planning" methods, although they preferred not to call it birth control. [214]

In our class we emphasized the biblical parameters – no abortion, no self-indulgence, no money-grubbing, no lust. We emphasized the necessity of taking God seriously when he says children are a gift from him and "blessed is the man whose quiver is full of them." But beyond those principles, we stated what I believe is solid biblical doctrine and a keystone to reformed theology that what God commands we must command, what he prohibits we must prohibit, but what he neither commands or prohibits, we can neither command or prohibit. [215]

We encouraged Christ-centered decision making in this area of family stewardship within God's guidelines.

My own observation is that individual calling on <u>any</u> specific issue seems to have a lot to do with where any one of us is led on the faith-stewardship continuum. For instance, I

---

[213] Monica Migliorino Miller, however, gives this bit of dialogue, between a proabort and herself, in *Abandoned*, p. 61:

"Isn't it true that you so-called pro-life people are trying to enact legislation to restrict contraception?"

"No, " I said, "that's not true at all. The pro-life movement is not trying to make contraception illegal except those methods which are actually abortifacients – that abort life already conceived."

But her distinction here may be about legislation rather than morality.

[214] In re "natural family planning" I can't shake the rather jolly memory of a pro-life priest I once heard talking enthusiastically to a group of rescuers about such things as the cyclical variations in women's temperatures and cervical mucus!

[215] There is definitely disagreement on this issue among Protestants, however, and even among conservative Pesbyterians. An issue of the Orthodox Presbyterian magazine *New Horizons* presented several alternate perspectives. This same series of articles was re-published in the *Life Advocate*.

personally have grave doubts about the compatibility of insurance and the life of faith, yet I know and am related to several Christian insurance salesmen, who obviously feel differently. My lifestyle in relation to insurance looks quite different than theirs.

Each of us will find some areas where it is agonizing to seek and follow God's will. Some of us will end up strong "stewards" in areas where others are committed to "pure faith". Things each of us feels strongly about may be matters of gifts and calling rather than God's universal will.[216] Again our views of what's normative must be a matter of what the Bible says, what it prohibits or commands – or doesn't.

Early on, the knowledge that I had lost a sibling through a natural miscarriage gave an existential reinforcement to biblical and biological data which made me oppose abortion. Through learning of that miscarriage, I had a sense of the humanity of the unborn long before I could lay out an argument for it, and perhaps this had something to do with my sense of calling to rescue. I only learned about this event when I was in college, as I recorded in this poem:

INFANT MORTALITY

> I went to quintessential college
> Full of the sense of my own potential,
> Robust with the prospect of things to come,
> Full of fervor for my own importance.
> Not long after I hopped the continent
> And landed in a place of brick and dust,
> I sought respite, a freshening of my zeal

---

[216] This seems to me a very important explanation for many conflicts which Christians are prone to. The Bible speaks clearly, but it is applied by the Holy Spirit where it is spiritually "profitable" – not for our general (or independent) knowledge. We know God's will best as it applies to us. We do not necessarily know much about things that are not part of our callings. In other words, the Presbyterian tendency toward trying to be a Renaissance man may have more flesh in it than sanctity.

Was That Thunder?

>With kindred in a greener town.
>Little did I know before -- nothing --
>Until my uncle opened eternity's broad door :
>Telling me my mother miscarried there,
>A thing I only dimly dredged
>From images of a childhood mystery.
>My brother, my sister, I know not,
>Passed into the limitless unseen
>Without so much as greeting me.
>Returning to Cambridge I heard
>Pompery but peep, saw circumstance cower,
>And my own importance run off into the distance.

If I was haunted by the knowledge of a sibling lost through miscarriage, how many forms of potential devastation must there be for those who learn their siblings and other relatives have been deliberately aborted.

A further impetus for my rescue involvement came in learning more about "the pill." Roseann and I had used "the pill" in the early years of our marriage without a clue that its third mechanism was as an abortifacient. After we learned what we had done, we I looked back with confusion, and deep regret. We prayed together for forgiveness and God's glory despite us – not knowing how many of our own children we may have rushed from conception to eternity.

We felt definite contrition and an act of repentance was necessary for what we had done. Now, like so many repentant moms and dads, one of the expectations we have as we look forward to heaven, is the hope that we may meet those children there.

One of our church members had found "the pill" to serve as an apparent blessing for her peculiar medical condition. Herself a medical professional, she was unhappy with our strong statements against it. Nevertheless, having learned what we had from respectable doctors and researchers, as well as from the fine print which the manufacturers themselves publish, we felt obligated to tell people the pill was indeed an abortifacient, even if only 3-6 percent of the time. Thus it is not an option for any woman who might become pregnant.

Specifically, as its "third mechanism," the pill prevents the conceptus (the conceived child) from implanting itself in the uterine wall, by rendering the uterine wall "hostile" to implantation. Thus it aborts the baby at a very early stage.

Even as we were teaching the class, one of our doctor-members brought in an article from a medical journal illustrating how the "experts" muddy the waters. It seems some would like to deny a woman is even "pregnant," or a "fetus" even formed, until implantation has occurred. In fact they were trying to call <u>this</u> event "conception," contrary to the meaning of the word itself. So in their scheme, there can be no "pregnancy" and therefore no "abortion" before this event.

This is pure modification of rhetoric concocted for political and commercial agendas. David dates his existence to his conception (Psalm 51); Christ became a man when God caused Mary to be "with child" (at this point the ovum in Mary's fallopian tube must have been "fertilized") as the Holy Spirit came upon her. Is there an alternative explanation? I have never met any Christian who wanted to argue the Incarnation took place half way through Mary's pregnancy, or at Jesus birth, rather than his conception!

The non-abortifacient birth-control issue remained one on which there were opposing positions within the rescue movement. There were also some who felt strongly that no human being could ever kill another human being in any circumstances – pacifists, in other words, who also opposed the death penalty and even lethal force in self-defense. Since we were all one hundred percent in agreement that abortion was murder, we felt we could work together to make it illegal again, despite these disagreements.

The last Sunday of the month I led a class on "The Myth of Pro-Life Violence," not knowing I would soon be involved in a long correspondence with one abortionist-shooter on death row, or that another man I knew would shoot another abortionist. But the class was meant to "arm" the average pro-lifer with the facts. The facts included these, that less than one out of ten thousand pro-life activists had engaged in violence [217] and that contrariwise, ongoing violence continued to take place on a huge scale inside the abortuaries.

Englewood – Partial Birth Abortion

On the 18th of January, Kimiko and I went over to Englewood, New Jersey where an event originally advertised for Inauguration Day (the 20th) was sponsored by a coalition of respected activists. There we were arrested for the first time in a year. The events leading up to the series of rescues at Englewood make a sad tale of deceit and hypocrisy.

The previous November (1996) the US House passed the Partial-Birth Abortion (PBA) Ban, 288 to 139. A week later Kate Michelman of NARAL told a press conference that opponents lied in saying PBAs were done as elective surgery rather than out of medical need. She also averred:

> ...experts have made it clear that the fetus undergoes demise before the procedure begins. And because of the anesthesia, which is, you know, something like 50 to 100 times what a fetus can withstand, because it's given according to the weight of the woman.

But ten days later the president of the American Society of Anesthesiologists told the Senate judiciary committee any reference to anesthesia killing fetuses was "medical misinformation" and patently false.

Through early December national news repeated falsehoods about PBAs. NBC's "Dateline" and ABC's Sam Donaldson said PBAs were only done for serious health reasons. AP reporter Diane Duston said,

> Late second or third-trimester abortions are performed

---

[217] This is a substantially lower rate than that of the general population.

A Memoir of Pro-life Rescue

to remove a severely deformed or already dead fetus that could cause the mother to die, become infertile or otherwise desperately ill.

The fight in the Senate got nasty – or silly – depending on what you expect of legislators. Senator Barbara Boxer attempted to add "health" or "serious health" exceptions to the ban, a la President Clinton's expressed desire. However her colleagues defeated the effort, having learned the bitter lesson that "mother's health" as in Doe v Bolton, is transformed by the courts into "any reason whatsoever."

Senator Lautenberg attempted to put a "gag ruling" in effect over part of the debate, and Boxer tried to get a ruling that pictures illustrating PBAs could not be displayed on the floor of the Senate (and thus not appear on C-Span where all America might see them.)

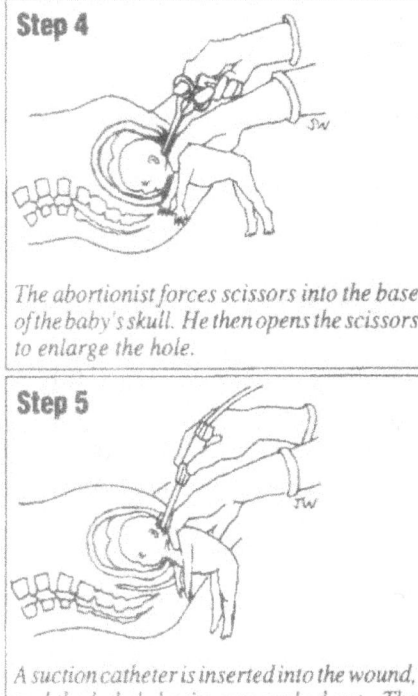

Partial Birth Abortion illustrated.

Was That Thunder?

Finally despite an 11th hour "killer" amendment, the Senate passed the bill on December 7th, 1996. Then, in April, President Clinton, newly elected for his second term, made a song-and-dance production out of his unconscionable veto, claiming that he could not sign it because it provided no exceptions for cases where the life of the mother was in danger.

But the effort to stop PBAs had begun much earlier. Back in February 1993, reporter Jenny Westberg wrote a cover story for Life Advocate describing the "D and X abortion" after Abortionist Martin Haskell had cheerfully presented this technique to a Dallas conference of the National Abortion Federation in September 1992.

In March 1993, *National Right to Life News* carried an article on PBAs using Westberg's illustrations. A pro-life ad in the *Minnesota Star-Tribune* headed "Do these drawings shock you?" appeared the same month.

In July 1993 the *AMA Newsletter* published an article about "shock-tactic ads," which nonetheless quoted Dr. Haskell and another doctor doing PBAs "that the majority of fetuses aborted this way are alive until the end of the procedure." Haskell was also quoted as saying Westberg's illustrations were "accurate from a technical point of view."

In a 1995 "Nightline" program, Ron Fitzsimmons, executive director of the National Coalition of Abortion Providers announced that partial birth abortions were rare, with only about 500 per year in the US. He also said PBAs were performed only in cases where the child was severely deformed or the mother's life and health threatened.

The horror with which the average citizen regardless of political commitment reacts to descriptions and illustrations of PBA makes it amazing the abortion industry would ever use this technique or allow its use to be revealed. But it was developed as a result of several serious problems abortion doctors had been dealing with since their back-alley days. PBAs seem to them like the solution to these problems – and therefore were something that made them cheerful. Thus they were inclined to be chatty about the subject.

The question of "technique" was important to those

doing second and third trimester abortions. First they were afraid of the "dreaded complication," a "failed abortion," that is, a live birth. A 1984 *New York Times* article, "When Abortion Becomes Birth," said, "The number of children surviving abortion is still tiny, and their chances of leading a healthy life is still small, but they are posing extraordinary problems for doctors and hospital administrators." The most widely known example of this "complication" was the one-armed Rodriguez baby, born after a "failed abortion" performed by the "The Butcher of Avenue A," Dr. Abu Hayat in 1991.

Gianna Jessen, literally a survivor of abortion

There were also a few notorious cases where doctors had delivered a live child and then done what New Jerseyites Amy Grossberg and Brian Peterson[218] were being prosecuted for, that is for killing and disposing of their baby in a dumpster. The logic was good: a child unwanted is "fair game" two minutes before birth, so why isn't it still "fair game" two minutes after birth?

---

[218] see previous chapter. Strangely these two were also from Bergen County, NJ!

Was That Thunder?

A few other cases, famous among pro-lifers, involved caring nurses who had "fetus-knapped" live children. Some of these "failed abortions" had thus survived. At least one such child, Gianna Jesson, "born" in 1977, had become a scarred but articulate speaker on the pro-life circuit as early as 1991.

From 1973 to the early '90s the three favored late term techniques (other than hysterectomy/abortion) were: saline, prostaglandin, and D&E (Dilation & Evacuation.) Saline abortions sometimes resulted in live births with the living babies disfigured by the burns which resulted from the salt solution. Abortions utilizing Prostaglandin, a drug that causes severe labor, resulted even more frequently in live births.

The D& E, on the other hand, that technique which Abu Hayat had employed, was generally reckoned the "safest," since most certainly fatal to the child, technique. The 1984 *Times* article said, "Some hospitals are switching to an abortion procedure that eliminates any possibility that a fetus might live." D & E involved cutting the child up in the womb, crushing the less wieldy parts (particularly the head) and pulling the resulting dis-members out of the woman by means of forceps. An assistant usually stood by and re-assembled the parts to make sure they were all accounted for.

Unfortunately (for the abortionist) this technique too had major complications, for which reason the *Times* article called it "the most controversial" of the three techniques. Permanent injuries to the woman were sometimes caused by the surgeon's knife or by jagged baby parts as they were removed by forceps. Statistics showed a significantly higher risk of injury to the woman from second and third trimester abortions.

The second complication of the D & E was psychological wear and tear on the abortion staff. Said the *Times* "It is . . . generally considered the most traumatic for doctors and staff."

When PBA or "D & X" (Dilation and Extraction) was introduced by McMahon and Haskell, it seemed the answer to whatever abortionists do instead of pray. It had the natural

A Memoir of Pro-life Rescue

ease and speed of childbirth for the abortionist, and felt much less like slaughter, at least to rest of the staff, yet like D & E, it never resulted in a live birth.

Although Charles Krauthammer wrote: "There is only one 'advantage' to the partial-birth procedure: guaranteeing a dead baby," [219] there were those several related advantages from the abortionists' point of view.

As the House version of the PBA ban was first proposed by Charles T. Canady, the *LA Times* accurately described the procedure. It took a full year before CBS did a "60 Minutes" segment on PBA. Even then, they were still repeating the falsehoods which abortion advocates had been throwing around for several years.

In September 1996, New Jersey reporter Ruth Padawer wrote an article in the *Bergen County Record* entitled "The facts on partial-birth abortion: Both sides have misled the public". The particular details of the article which caused the most ruckus derived from two interviews Padawer conducted with an administrator and an abortionist from Metropolitan Medical Associates, Inc. of the *Record*'s hometown, Englewood.

The two men told Padawer that the clinic did about 1500 PBAs per year, and that "most are Medicaid patients, black and white, and most are for elective, not medical reasons: people didn't realize, or didn't care, how far along they were. Most were teenagers."

Attempting to sound balanced, Padawer also criticized opponents of abortion for saying the PBAs were being done in the third trimester. But the hue and cry of abortion advocates in response to her article did not include any thanks for her balance!

Governor Christine Whitman (R) had just been quoted in the *Trenton Times* (Sep 11) "I researched this issue . . . and there were no abortions like that performed in New Jersey last year." Congressman Robert Torricelli (D), whose district includes Englewood, spoke on the soon notorious *Imus Show*, Sep 16, "no partial birth abortions were performed in New

---

[219] *Philadelphia Inquirer* opinion, March 1997.

Was That Thunder?

Jersey."

After the *Bergen County Record* article was published Senator Frank Lautenberg denounced it in the *Congressional Record*! NOW waited until November to issue a statement that articles like Padawer's and similar ones in the *Washington Post* were "planted by abortion opponents".

Then in February, 1997, in the kind of vindication which is a dream for investigative reporters like Ruth Padawer, Ron Fitzsimmons [220] experienced a change of heart. He went public confessing "I lied through my teeth" in the 1995 "Nightline" statements in which he claimed there were only 500 PBAs per year in the US and those only where the fetus was deformed or the life and health of mother at stake.

Interviewed by the *AMA newsletter* (March 3), he said he lied because he was afraid the truth about PBAs would damage those who support abortion, but that he had come to be convinced that debate on the issue must be based on truth:

> When you're a doctor who does these abortions and the leaders of your movement appear before Congress and says these procedures are done only in the most tragic circumstances... it makes you feel like a dirty little abortionist with a dirty little secret.

Briefly, immediately thereafter, for the first time in many years, national news took on an anti-abortion tone! Major newspapers as pro-abortion as the *NY Times* and the *Washington Post*, with such network notables as Tom Brokau and Ted Koppel spoke in indignant terms about the deceit practiced by pro-abortion leaders and – even in outraged terms – about the partial birth abortion technique itself. They also directly linked Fitzsimmon's misinformation with President Clinton's claims at the time of his veto.

Thus the abortuary in Englewood was a good place to rescue. Even the Congress of the United States agreed what went on there should be illegal!

There were other good reasons to rescue there having

---

[220] Director, National Coalition of Abortion Providers.

to do with an unconstitutional injunction that imposed unbelievable restrictions on pro-lifers in Englewood. This injunction allowed only one hour of picketing per week, in only one place – across the street from the clinic. Anyone picketing or doing anything else "pro-life" any other time or in any other place in town was liable to penalties. On the basis of this injunction many prolifers had been kicked out of town or prosecuted!

Bill Calvin, faithful leader in NJ from the early days, with John Hegerty, another steadfast rescuer from Jersey.

Another good reason to rescue there was dedicated legal support for pro-lifers in the form of the nearby Legal Center for Defense of Life in Morristown, run by Richard Traynor, Esq. In addition, Bill Calvin, a former local Police Commissioner, whose wife was an early pro-lifer, was committed to assisting rescuers as they dealt with legal institutions in his state. [221]

Nonetheless, there were not many other rescuers

---

[221] In a Bridgehead radio interview, Bill spoke of his wife who was herself adopted. Together they started a crisis pregnancy, and were always available to help out young mothers who courgeously chose life. See: Youtube.

either of the occasions I was arrested there [222] and even fewer in the other two Englewood rescues [223] nor were the rescues terribly effective in immediate or measurable results.

On January 18th, we had started the day with a service at a nearby Catholic church, from which we walked down to the clinic, carrying signs and such. Only a handful of the pro-lifers intended to risk arrest.

However, somehow Kimiko and the others had gone across to the doors before I knew it. When I Irealized this, I hurried across the street to join them, forgetting to leave my wallet with someone else. [224] An elderly clergyman and I were about the last two taken away. My wrists had been "bag-tied" together by the police already, but I was still sitting next to the doors, where I kept appealing to the women going in, saying that if I was going to jail for their children, at least they should consider letting them to live.

It turned out the elderly clergyman with me was Bishop Lynch, who I later learned had been the first Catholic bishop in US history ever to be arrested. Also with us was Ralph Traphagen, who had ministered to Dr. Hayat at his trial, and Joan Andrews Bell, who with her husband was running a crisis pregnancy center in New York. There were a total of fifteen arrested. We agreed beforehand that we would not go "non-co-op" after our arrests.

Because I had my wallet with me, the police were able to identify me right away, but the others withheld their identities for the time being. We were taken to Bergen County jail, where the men were all placed on one block.

Being processed into the jail had one new wrinkle for me. They insisted on taking my wedding band from me. I told them I hadn't had it off for years, but they said they'd cut it off if they had to, so using some soap they provided, I did indeed get it off. I had been locked up many times before – even in Philly, but never before had I removed my ring.

---

[222] 18 January and 15 March 1997

[223] August 1996 and 23 January 1997

[224] We had been asked not to bring ID on this occasion, in order that our anonymity could be used as one basis for negotiation.

A woman and a man being arrested at Metropolitan Medical Associates, Englewood, which performs partial birth abortions.

Photo in local paper of my first arrest in Englewood.

There on the cell block I met "Tugboat Louie," Louis Menchaka, an affable rescuer with a nautical bent and the general slightly-kempt appearance of a street person. Louie had been arrested on a number of occasions with "The Lambs" and Father Weslin. He had the interesting habit, which I can relate to, of saving everything that might be useful. Thus by the end of our time in Bergen County, he had about sixty paper cups stashed under his bunk.

We met together regularly, talking, praying or worshipping. Ralph Traphagen became inside leader more or less by consensus. I'll never forget his account of meeting the warden, which I witnessed from across the cell block. The warden, unbeknownst to many of us, was a pious Catholic, and he apparently came down to the block to make sure we were doing OK. Ralph, a Protestant, was introduced to him and Ralph described a few things on our minds, in the course of which Ralph said "the bishop... this" or "the bishop... that" merely mentioning Bishop Lynch in passing.

The warden suddenly stopped Ralph. "You have a bishop here with you!" he asked, "a Roman Catholic bishop!"

"Yes," said Ralph, "Bishop Lynch was arrested with the rest of us in front of the clinic." The warden didn't seem to want to talk much more. He turned on his heel and went out of the block. Not much later, a priest showed up, one of the chaplains there. His first order of business was meeting the bishop.

If I remember right the bishop was released a few days later. The rest of us spent a week or so. But we were treated very well, being taken down to the chapel on several occasions for group worship (with the women) and consultations with our legal advisor.

While I was in jail, my family participated in the pro-life assembly in downtown Philly on January 22 in commemoration of Roe v. Wade.

Kimiko was the last rescuer released, and I stayed overnight with some Catholic brehtren. The Krails kindly drove up to pick up Kimiko and me.

Allentown Sentencing – Lehigh County Jail

In February 1997, those of us arrested in the Allentown rescue of December 1992 were at last sentenced. The jury had found us guilty in December 1994. Now we reported to the courtroom where we got an opportunity to be grilled by the same frat-boy ADA concerning our intentions to be law-abiding in the future. Specifically he asked, "Do you intend to obey the laws of this county, this commonwealth, and of the United States in the future?"

To this I answered, "To the degree that the laws of this county, this commonwealth and the United States are in conformity with the law of God, I intend to obey them." However, this was too long a sentence, and I ran out of breath two-thirds of the way through, somewhat spoiling the dramatic effect. I suppose it sounded like an exasperated rather than a solemn affirmation – and I admit it was both.

Given the opportunity to make a short statement before sentencing I told the judge I knew most of the people sitting there, and they were the salt of the earth, the very foundation of a good America. I told him treating such as criminals was wrong and dangerous. According to a report in the April edition of *Voices for the Unborn*, I also said that should "peaceful, prayerful people" and "their non-violent protests be suppressed, the violent people would come out of the woodwork." The next day, the *Morning Call* of Allentown, mentioned my reference to being arrested on nearly sixty occasions for similar activities in other places.

This was the occasion when Jim Owens gave his powerful testimony about Barry Howell's conversion to Christ in response to the DA's presenting Barry's "rap-sheet" for consideration in sentencing.

The judge gave us sentences ranging from twenty to forty days. I was ashamed to be one of the short-timers.

When all the paper work and other ceremonies had been completed, we were marched through a tunnel directly to Lehigh County jail.

Barry Howell, trophy of Christ's mercy

Most of the men spent three or four days in the induction block of the prison. We had many opportunities to minister to other inmates, most of whom were young, and many Hispanic.

My "Cellie" was Ed Gerlach and we became good friends there. Ed, a retired union carpenter, and a Catholic Eucharistic lay minister, was a good hymn-singer. Each morning we would look out our small window high up in the prison and give each other weather reports. "Clear and sunny, temperatures climbing to 45 degrees, wind out of the southwest at 5 miles per hour, barometer 29.6 and rising; Pocono and shore weather in half an hour. " One night Ed reported the weather as "dark" and one morning "mushy and freezy".

The first or second night we were there, I had been talking to a young man of Puerto Rican descent, and he asked if I knew any good lawyers. I did know a godly lawyer from Bucks County, so I said I would get his phone number, which I did when I talked to Roseann that same evening. I wrote it on a scrap of paper and went over to give it to the young man where he sat with his buddies. Suddenly a guard came rushing out of his glass booth and into the block. He strode up and grabbed the piece of paper off the table, then abruptly told me to follow him and marched out into a vestibule beside the guardroom.

"What were you doing?" he demanded. From his demeanor and his tone I would normally have thought I must have done something really wrong, but I had been warned by another prisoner that this guard was a snap case. [225] So I replied softly, "I was giving him a phone number."

"C'mon! " He said, "tell the truth. What were you really doing?"

"I'm sorry if I did something wrong," I said, "If you'll tell me what it is I will be sure and not do it again." Meanwhile I was noticing out of the corner of my eye that the other guard (there were always two in the guardroom) was quietly smirking as though the whole thing was kind of amusing. "What did you think I was doing?" I asked.

"What do you think I thought?" he demanded.

---

[225] I had noticed that he was the only guard that wore a bullet-proof vest all the time.

Remembering the prison rules, which I had read the day before, I answered, "Maybe you thought I was soliciting."

"And were you soliciting?" he asked. "No," I said, "I was giving Willie a phone number for a lawyer." The other guard seemed to be having difficulty controlling his face by then.

After that the "snap-case" seemed to suddenly switch gears. "Stay away from those guys in there," he said, "they're dangerous. You could get hurt."

I thanked him for his advice, but did not remind him I was one of "those guys in there." He gave me back my scrap with the phone number and when he opened the door, I went back in and directly gave it to Willie. As I went back up the stairs to the second tier where my cell was, somebody called out and asked what happened. I answered forthrightly, "I'll talk to whoever I want to talk to!"

After that my status seemed to rise in the place. Perhaps it contributed to the many opportunities I had to speak of spiritual things with other prisoners, especially in the first few days. Frequently I would end up praying with a group of guys around a table in the evening. I was feeling pretty elated about this, and no doubt overestimating the impact we were having when Barry Howell gave me some needed reality therapy. He kind of took me aside and said:

"It's really good you're talking and praying with these guys. If we can preach the gospel to them, when they reach the end of their rope maybe they'll come to Jesus. But I was just like them at that age – and God had to do a lot more things in my life before I was ready to receive it. So I'm just saying don't get your heart set on anything. They haven't reached the end of their ropes yet."

Barry recounted how he had spent a lot of time in jails, including the old Eastern State Penitentiary in Philadelphia, where he said the guards were constantly on your back. But even the harshest regime didn't soften his heart in those days. According to Barry your world has to fall apart so that you recognize the Bad News before you're ready to hear the Good News.

As always, everything in the cell quickly became

Was That Thunder?

familiar and even an object for study. For instance, I particularly enjoyed the "emergency button" in the Allentown cells. Every day or so, one of the Corrections Officers would read a stern warning, "that button in your cell is for emergency purposes only -- it's for <u>medical</u> emergencies." I kept wondering what the other kind of emergencies (which it was NOT for) were?

I wrote a poem after the first morning when the sun shining in on my bunk seemed like God's kiss.

Sun in my Cell

The Sun baptizes me
Every morning after breakfast –
Coming through the high muzzled window.
The first morning it was a blessed sunrise.
Now it is daily bread –
Bread to my soul
Broken by the bars
But to me communicating . . .
Can it be
That He with whom the Father
Is well-pleased
Is also pleased with me!

My cellie, Ed, was quite a joker. Several times he told me he was doing something or other to "save time," with a wry grin at the irony of "saving time" in jail. He inspired this poem:

Saving Time (for Ed)

My cellmate jokes at our common crime –
That is we both try to save time
Here, where there is no congruing
Of time-saving and time-accruing.
We do time well by doing all
We're given to do this side of the wall.

> This situation may also be
> That of those who think they're free.

Ed and I could look out almost every day and see below us pro-life picketers walking up and down along the street in front of the prison. One day there was quite a crowd there, and I could make out a number of our friends.

Most of the other pro-lifers were transferred down to a regular cellblock a couple days before I was. At first this seemed depressing, and on top of it, many of the other inmates I had met and prayed with were gone. But the new guys coming in found out who I was from somebody or other, and before long, I had another prayer crew! In fact, that first night after that, just before lock-up, I had eight guys, including a long-timer just in from Graterford, all holding hands around a table and praying for Christ's mercy and His leading of us. I also was getting more time meditating on and memorizing Bible passages than I ever take at home.

One fellow who prayed with me several nights turned out to be another of those "coincidental" connections. He had worked for a Christian carpenter and been involved in his church. Even though we lived more than an hour apart, I had worked for the very same carpenter on a few occasions and regarded him as a friend! Strangely, that carpenter was probably the only resident I knew in all Lehigh County! I was able to check on that prisoner's progress over the next few years through the carpenter friend.

After seven days I followed the other guys down to the "general population" blocks. Contrary to my hopes, I got a cellie there who had a TV. Furthermore he had it running 24 hours a day. I talked to him about it and he said he couldn't go to sleep unless it was on, so I asked if he minded me turning the volume down after he went to sleep. He said that was OK, so that's how it went. I dozed until about 1 in the morning, then looked down to see if he was asleep, which he always was. I then climbed down off my bunk and turned the volume down, back to bed and to sleep myself. It worked out pretty good. He was an easy guy to be around and we talked some about spiritual things, but I never did get too close to him.

For the rest of my sentence, I tended to hang out with the pro-lifers and spent less time with other prisoners. We had outside ministries come in several times while I was there, and we were allowed to have our own little Bible studies (usually with a few other inmates) in rooms off the day area. There was one really godly guard who ministered to us and encouraged us. Once or twice he dropped in on our Bible studies and contributed some wisdom.

One sad note for me was that in our Bible studies and conversations I found out that one of the older rescuers had been getting weirder and weirder in his religious perspectives and life. When I first met him six or seven years earlier he had been quite an evangelist, who loved to share the gospel. But according to another fellow who was close to him, he had recently gotten involved with a younger woman with a drug habit, who was "playing " him.[226]

My family wrote me many letters, and I still treasure them. The kingdom continued to come in Philly and elsewhere. During this time Roseann and Bill Devlin responded to a one of our pastor friends in Boston who was raising money to help a single Mom with her medical bills. All of the money was raised one way or another. One of my favorite anecdotes from home had to do with Tory's friend, a neighbor girl. Tory had told her about my whereabouts and when they had a fight, she said, "Well, <u>my</u> dad's never been in jail!"

Later, it seems the same girl's mother had just returned from the Carribean and was explaining to her about the poor people there and their trials. Suddenly Tory's friend chimed in, "Mr. Twott is in jail!" The parents called Roseann to find out what was up.

Roseann and Joshua appeared on the *Voice of the Unborn* TV program during my stay in Allentown. Josh was invited particularly because of his part in the 22 January pro-

---

[226] His situation and condition weighed on me for months, but all I could do was pray. Within a year his physical condition deteriorated, too, and he passed out of this world. God rest his soul.

life event in front of City Hall. Roseann was interviewed in her role as prison-widow.

As usual most of us who were Allentown defendants chose to serve our full sentence rather than pay fines and sign probation papers. Nonetheless, Lehigh County Prison tried to extract ten dollars per day from us for our time there. This is a vicious cycle. The prison charges ten bucks a day, which obviously comes to quite a bill before very long. Then when the prisoner gets out, they bill him, and if he doesn't pay, cite him for contempt of court and put him back behind bars – which costs ten dollars per day – ad infinitum. It's just the same as "debtor's prison," one of those things from the bad old British days we're so proud to have gotten rid of! This should be illegal. Prison shouldn't pay – for anybody – not even county governments.

In talking with other prisoners, I found another thing hard to stomach about the probation system there. Under certain conditions prisoners were released to stay in a sort of trailer-park minimum security facility. From there they could go out to work regular jobs during the day. But the rules there were so stringent, including a complete prohibition against cigarettes and other tobacco products, that a couple of cigarettes in ones possession was all it took to get locked up in the jail again. There's something way out of balance there!

On the day I was released, Bill Devlin kindly drove up to take me home. While I was waiting for him in front of the courthouse, the whipper-snapper DA's assistant walked by. Somehow I found it amusing to see his shining face that morning. I don't think Bill found me much of a conversationalist. Going to jail for me is something like spending time in the wilderness – you come back with a clearer, slower perspective – and don't feel very well synchronized with the speeding world. But as it happened, it wasn't very long before I was behind bars again. One effect of that stretch in Lehigh County Prison was that it rejuvenated up my sense of calling to rescue.

Was That Thunder?

My Second Englewood Rescue – Bergen County Jail

Therefore, along with Bob Brothers from Philly, I went back to Englewood for the rescue in April. We stayed the night before at Krails in New Jersey. They drove us up in the morning.

The police had really geared up for this one, inviting officers from I don't know how many other jurisdictions – but the total number of officers can't have been fewer than fifty or sixty. They had police vehicles parked all along the street in front of the abortuary and barricades on the sidewalk immediately in front. They themselves were packed into the space behind the vehicles and inside the barricades. I'm amazed anyone went there for an appointment that day! But whether "plants" or genuine appointments, a number of women did go in.

My second arrest at Englewood, with Bob Brothers
AP photograph in *New York Times*

In addition to a dozen or more rescuers, there were about a hundred supporters there. These prayed and sang. Someone addressed the group through a bullhorn. Those of us risking arrest decided to go in small groups to see if we could get in a few counseling opportunities before we were arrested, so we crossed over up the street and waited for anyone walking that way.

After a while a couple came along, and then another couple right behind them, so Bob and I walked along with them and tried to talk to them, offering them literature with the phone number of Joan and Chris Bell's pregnancy center. They took the literature but did not slow down. We followed them and pleaded with them to consider the alternatives.

When we got to the barricades, the police let the couples through, as we made last minute pleas for an opportunity to talk to them. We were technically outside the police lines, but remember this place had this incredible injunction covering the whole town, which the police were still enforcing. The police decided to arrest us on the spot. I remember one sharply dressed young officer saying, "I'm making a judgment call here. Arrest them!"

Three or four cops grabbed me and I collapsed. Bob went down on his knees. A press photographer was apparently shooting pictures from across the street, and captured the scene. They cuffed us and took us to the Englewood Police Station, where the officers remembered my ID, although this time I had remembered to leave my wallet behind!

But there I found the other rescuers were planning to go "non-co-op". I had not expected this, and frankly, having thought about it over the years, didn't like it.

While I agreed with Joan and many others that there was support for abortion up and down the line in our public offices, I did not believe the problem was with "the system," because frankly I thought "the system" was a Marxist category, not a Christian one.

Therefore after wrestling with this over against a desire not to "break ranks" with my fellow rescuers, I announced to the three or four who had not yet been dragged out to the prison transport, that I could not go along with it, and they encouraged me to follow my own conscience. When the young and adrenalin-flushed cops came to drag me out

Was That Thunder?

(they had been very rough with some of the others, and frankly that made it all the harder for me to cooperate) I said I would walk, and they were even more elated, thinking at first, I suppose, that fear inspired by their machismo was my motive.

However, after they took me to the prison van, one of them came back and asked me why it was I was cooperating when the others weren't. I explained to him that we all thought abortion was a terrible evil and a crime, and that it was wrong for law enforcement to be used to protect it. "However," I said, "they think you guys and the rest of people in the system are more guilty than the average citizen, and I don't. We agree on the main issue, but we have a variety of opinions on smaller things."

But I've left one important event out of my narrative!. Before they took me to the prison van, one of the deputies took me into the adjacent police court, where I was seated off to the side while his honor dealt with some other miscreant.

Suddenly there loomed up before me a galoot in a suit who said, "Mr. Trott?" I looked at him benignly, but had little to say, as he laid a ream of papers across my cuffed hands. He had his script, however, "I'm US Marshall Slumgullion. You are being charged under FACE," and then, with a level of portentiousness seldom achieved in the worst television drama, he leaned down and grimaced inside my personal space, at the same time growling out, "Now this is a FED'RUL matter!"

I could think of no response adequate to the moment, except to raise my cuffed hands from my lap, which caused the papers to slide to the floor, and then quake all over, letting out a low moan, "Oo-oo-oo!" The Bergen County Deputy with me tried to keep a straight face. When I got back to the cell, it was festooned with copies of the FACE case, as it still was when we left.

Another event worthy of a chuckle or two occurred about then. John Broderick, a dedicated pro-life lawyer who had done much for New York rescuers over the years, came in while we were being held at Englewood. He had another lawyer with him, and the moment the deputy brought them back to our cells, the US Marshall came busting in and angrily demanded that the two lawyers produce credentials. The intensity of his demands was quite out of proportion to anything going on.

One received the definite impression he had been specifically detailed to keep an eye out for persons posing as lawyers. I did know one pro-life person who had functioned as an assistant to a lawyer, while not an attorney himself. Nonetheless, somehow it was funny seeing real lawyers being treated this way! Our two lawyers were able to convince the marshall they were the genuine article.

At Bergen County Jail, although the prison officials were able to identify most of us, none of the others were processed into the prison population, since they were "non-co-op." Rather they were put in solitary confinement, which was what they had expected. Bob Brothers told me later, he was planning to cooperate with the Bergen County officials, but they never asked him! They just treated him like the others.

The officer who processed me into the jail, an Englewood native, chatted with me and said he recalled the old days before Roe, when the abortion clinic, though illegal, carried on the same trade in the same place. This was also a matter of record, since the founder, Robert M. Livingstone had challenged New Jersey to prosecute him for illegal abortions in 1972. But the guard claimed abortions were done there -- by doctors -- back into the mid-60s.

For the first few days I was placed in the induction block, which was a wild and crazy place. Eight or ten guys were in there wearing only a sort of paper hospital gown. I learned most of these were "deadbeat dads," men who were behind on child support payments. They told me they were always hauled in at Christmas and around Mother's Day. They were in the strange clothes because they were on special "suicide watch" for having made some sort of scene when arrested. In fact the weird garb was functionally a way of "teaching them a lesson".

A few prisoners gravitated to me when they saw my Bible, including one guy, Tommy, who had his own KJV and turned out to be a voluble character. Other prisoners told me he had been arrested with his dog, and laughed about it. He said they were making fun of him, because when they arrested him his dog had been in heat and had gotten blood on his bed, about which the cops made rude suggestions. He wasn't terribly forthcoming about the real nature of his charges.

The next day the Catholic chaplain came to see me, but we were in the middle of chow, and like most prisoners, that was important to me, so I told him I was a Protestant and went back to my chow. Afterwards I felt genuinely sorry for not being more cordial and informative with him. In fact I was convicted of being rude.

My new buddy, Tommy, told me he wanted me to talk to his sister and mother on the phone that night. I asked why and he said he wanted them to bail him out. I had gotten to know him well enough by then that I told him straight up that I wasn't going to tell them that, because I figured he probably needed to be in there for a while longer. But nothing would do but he had to put me on the phone when he called them that evening. I told his sister what I told him. "Don't baby this guy. He needs to take responsibility for his own actions." They were quite appreciative of my counsel – but Tommy acted as though I had betrayed him.

The Catholic chaplain sent down the Protestant chaplain the next day, who turned out to know of me through another one of those funny overlaps. During our previous incarceration in that establishment, someone had given me a used Bible with the name of a local Baptist church inside the cover, and I had ended up taking it home. So back at home, I sent twenty dollars to the church, thanking them for their ministry to me and others at the jail. It turned out that was this chaplain's church.

Apparently, the event was unusual enough he remembered it. He and I spent five minutes in wonderful union in prayer, our hands clasped, sitting there just outside the induction block.

I got into a discussion with three Rastifarians one morning. One of them was really more of a "five percenter," vehemently anti-white. I gently suggested that it was hard to distinguish his perspective from racism. But another of them said not all Rastifarians felt the same about this. The guards seemed to be a little anxious when they saw this discussion going forward, but I think it went well, and there wasn't really much hostility in it.

There was one guy in the induction block, Italian or Hispanic, whom I didn't talk to. He was a cold, tough-acting, self-confident guy. He carried himself like one bad dude. I decided he was definitely not among the elect.

Tommy and a couple of others joined me for a Bible study up in one of the 2nd tier cells one evening. We had just finished praying when another head poked in the door. "Can I join you guys?" It was the bad dude! And when we began to talk about the scripture, he not only knew his stuff, but he knew "reformed" (Presbyterian) theology!

Looking back, I must admit it was fishy – especially because a day later I was transferred into the bad dude's cell! We had some good prayer together after I listened to him loudly berating his wife on the wall phone right outside our cell. She allegedly had just got herself busted in New York driving his Cadillac with a couple of black guys riding shotgun. They had supposedly been trying to cop heroin in a bad neighborhood. It was really a little too much. All things considered, it seems to me certain now he was a "nark" – I guess undercover cops can have good theology!

In every jail certain things are especially precious. In Bergen County jail I learned there are twice as many "lights" in a pack of matches as I thought. The prisoners would carefully tear a match in half – between the flat layers of the cardboard "stick". In addition to this they would save the striker panels from exhausted matchbooks. Half cigarettes completed the frugal nicotine habit. Cigarettes are universally a precious trade commodity, except (or especially) where they are "contraband" as they are at Allentown.

Back at Atlanta's Key Road in 1988, a rescuer who had been there before told me packets of salt were a valued commodity. Prisoners there hoarded them. Perhaps this went back to the chain gangs where a packet of salt might really be a factor in survival.

In prison as in war other basic things are highly valued: food, and drink (coffee, water, juice) for instance. But uniquely in prison certain other things are also much appreciated. I, like many prisoners, had my favorite spots from which I could look out through a barred or grated window and across the barbed wire, to see green grass or hills, or trees and blue sky.

An experienced prisoner takes every opportunity seriously – whether it be for a shower, laundry, exercise, rest, quiet, a breath of fresh air, a few minutes in the sunshine or a bathroom break.

One time at Philly's Detention Center, I remember Mike McMonigal ducked into an open induction cell in order to take advantage of a chance to relieve himself. We were just being processed in, and when the guard realized where Mike had gone, he yelled at him, made him strip down, and put him through the whole search routine again. I suppose the amount of contraband being smuggled in and out and back and forth in Philly jails is tremendous, so that keeping prisoners separate during processing is part of the regulations, but on the other hand, those guards knew who we were. That guy knew he didn't need to re-search Mike. Another "lesson" was being taught.

Some prisoners were entrepreneurs, their businesses flourishing most in the few hours after "commissary" or "store" hours each week, when prisoners received the commodities they had ordered against their accounts. At this time they paid back or made loans to each other against future pay backs.

Elaborate bookkeeping sometimes was carried on, with a single entrepreneur wandering from cell to cell catching up on his collections and accounts. The completely broke prisoners could "work" for the entrepreneurs to earn a few smokes.

At Bergen County I watched across the corridor as a surprise inspection went on in an adjacent block. The team of seven or eight inspection guards all came in together and ran elaborate checks over, under, and through each prisoner's belonging, bunks and persons. At the end of this "raid," the guard team took away a cart loaded with contraband, including a huge ¾ wheel of cheddar cheese! No doubt that had originated in the prison kitchen.

Although a similar inspection of our ward was not so fruitful, it was an education watching the guards test every metal part of the bunks to make sure none had been loosened for possible use as a weapon. Even cups of juice were confiscated. [227]

After a few days as the only prolifer in the transition "pod" at Bergen County, I was transferred to a regular smaller block, and the minute I came in the doors, several guys came up to me and said, "Hey, you're the one that was in the *Times*". I said I didn't think so. They said, "Weren't you arrested over at that clinic in Englewood a few days ago?" "Well, yes." "Hey, man, it was you."

They hauled a newspaper out from under somebody's bunk and sure enough, there I was with a couple of cops kneeling on my back as handcuffs were being applied. Bob Brothers was right behind me, down in a kneeling position! So I was known before I got there!

There were a number of sincere believers in that block, and I got to pray with them a number of times. Apparently a guy who used to lead prayer had just gotten out. So the others were glad to have someone else suggest it. But I was surprised when we gathered together around a bunk in the middle of the block, because all the guys reached out and took each others hands when we went to prayer. It was not at all a "macho" thing to do, but it demonstrated unashamed unity in Christ, and I felt privileged to be part of it.

This kind of thing, which I saw in many of the jails I briefly visited, was one of the most hopeful things I garnered from my rescue experience. It meant to me that the gospel was going forward, often with little or no outside direction, in dark places. Like the nursing home ministry, it showed me Christ has power to reach and comfort those in extremity –

---

[227] I was told prison "hootch" was made from fermented koolaid, etc. Alas, that was a pleasure I never experienced.

and that he is doing it.

A bunch of the younger guys on that block would sleep-in during the morning and really perk up about eleven at night. These guys would be making noise until two or three A.M., but I found I could kind of blank them out, even though my bunk was right next to some of them.

After I'd been on that block for a few days, one of our prayer buddies got real sick, and I tried to minister to him a little – cold towels and such, but when the nurse brought his medicine to the gate of the block, they would not let me take it to him, even though he said he could not get up, so reluctantly I went back and told him he would have to come get it, which he eventually did.

We were allowed out once into a small yard where there were several basketball hoops. Some guys just walked the perimeter while others got up basketball scrimmages. After we'd been out there ten minutes or so, I realized that a couple of the guards and several prisoners were standing over to the side, watching one of the windows on another wing of the prison. It didn't take much observation of these guys to realize they were watching a female prisoner put on some kind of illicit performance. It was pretty sad to see them, especially since it stripped the guards of the dignity they were supposed to represent.

One advantage of being in jail as a representative of Christ was that whatever temptation I felt to take a peep, too, was counterbalanced by the knowledge that his honor was directly involved.

The next morning I woke up early and heard a young guy who was the "trusty" for our block talking with a couple buddies about the stinking prison and the "effing" system and so on. This surprised me because he had been unusually cheerful during my first days there, as he brought in our chow cart, etc. I realized he was not just blowing off steam, but was really despairing, so I got up and went over and sat with them, and asked him if I could pray for him.

The four of us held hands and the Lord gave me a prayer for him and for the rest of us that we would trust him more and learn what he had for us. It seemed to be a blessing to this guy and the others. As we finished up, another guy came up and angrily berated the others, "Don't be holding hands with the man!" he said. But the others said I wasn't the man, I was a brother.

I got to go to Protestant chapel a couple of times. A lady with a Central European accent was ministering there. When she found out who I was, she was unabashed in praising me, and told the other inmates that just showed that sometimes people went to jail for doing good. I got a chance to share a testimony there about Christ meeting me in the midst of my sin.

There was a big construction project going on in the middle of the prison, right next to our block. Because of it, they had nailed plywood over our windows on that side, and had set up big fans to compensate for the terrible ventilation. Bigger and bigger prisons. Another symptom of the national slide. It isn't bigger prisons we need, it's real revival.

The episode of our release is another paranoid passage for me. But they say even paranoids have enemies. All the rescuers were pulled out of solitary, and I was brought down from my block. We were dressed in our own clothes and given our property back minus any cash up to $40, which in my case meant all $28 I had with me.[228] We were then put together in a small holding cell.

Curiously there were two other prisoners in there with us – and these guys were interesting for a couple of reasons. For one thing, they were as nervous or hyped up as if they had been on speed. [229] For another thing, when I passed around my pocket spiral notebook in order to get the addresses of several of the rescuers I didn't know well, one of these guys grabbed it and put his name in it, staring avidly at the other names.

Then, of the fourteen or so of us in the holding cell, the first three guys processed out were me and then these two guys! And although there were two women with cars outside

---

[228] Bergen county is another of those "paying" prisons.
[229] I once worked with a speed freak for a few months on a roofing crew, and they reminded me of him.

waiting for them, the guys, who I didn't know from Adam, came over and gave me a hug before departing! Candid shot -- Anonymous released prisoners affectionately hugging outside Bergen County Jail!

An hour later, when all the rescuers had been released and had gathered with our attorneys at a nearby restaurant, I reached into my pocket for the notebook – and it was gone! Never seen it since. The addresses bugged me, but beside that I had written a couple poems in there that I really regret losing. So if some FBI file clerk somewhere reads this and has compassion, I hope he will at least copy the poetry pages out of that notebook and send them to me!

One of the effects of rescue was that we grew increasingly shock-proof. There was so much horror and ugliness surrounding the evil of the child-killing. Yet there was one new shock for me in the Bergen County experience which came as I did some research into the history of the Englewood abortionists. I was spurred in this research by the prison guard's mention of the pre-Roe abortionists in Englewood. I spoke to a Christian magazine editor who said they would be interested in publishing an article if I could come up with the facts of that history.[230]

It seems the owner of the clinic now doing the Partial Birth Abortions was originally Stephen Jaffe, an abortionist who had sold it and had his own "practice" a couple blocks away. But I also came across the name, Frederick S. Jaffe, in a book about the Eugenics Movement[231] aka: Population

---

[230] I was disappointed, when after sixty hours of searching library and newspaper records and seven drafts I presented a finished article only to be told the editors were no longer interested.

[231] A few years earlier, I discovered an interesting phenomenon. If you look in old encyclopedias, published before 1945, the end of WWII, you will find glowing descriptions of many organizations in Europe and the US, discussed under the heading "Eugenics". In other words the Nazi program of racial purification was popular in the rest of Europe and the US until Hitler's genocidal policies made it a bad name. Did the goals change after that? No, it appears only the name changed. Thus in looking through a section of an old *Philadelphia Inquirer*, I found a full page

Control Movement, which was the philosophical foundation to the whole abortion enterprise. I could not determine if these two Jaffes were father and son, but the shock came in reading a 1969 memorandum[232] which Frederick, founder of the Alan Guttmacher institute and Planned Parenthood vice president wrote. It is an outline for a multi-facetted agenda suppressing human reproduction. He opened thus:

> This memorandum is responsive to your letter of January 24, seeking ideas on necessary and useful activities relevant to formation of population policy, defined as "legislative measures, administrative programs, and other governmental actions (a) that are designed to alter population trends... or (b) that actually do alter them."

Then come eight pages of proposals and outlines for proposals requiring further research. The ninth page, an incredible display of hellish hubris reads thus:

Proposed Measures To Reduce Fertility By Universality or Selectivity of Impact In The U.S.

UNIVERSAL IMPACT
<u>Social Constraints</u>
Restructure family:
     a) Postpone or avoid marriage
     b) Alter image of ideal family size
     c) Compulsory education of children
     d) Encourage increased homosexuality

---

article on "One hundred percenters," which incredible as it sounds, extolled the highest form of human being, the blond, blue-eyed Caucasian!

[232] This "Jaffe Memo," far from being denied by Planned Parenthood, is recognized and even called "a source of controversy" by its defenders! *Wikipedia*, for instance, seems to think it becomes more acceptable when viewed as "merely a listing of current proposals."

e) Educate for family limitation
f) Fertility control agents in the water supply
g) Encourage women to work

SELECTIVE IMPACT DEPENDING ON SOCIO-ECONOMIC STATUS

Economic Deterrents/Incentives -

Modify tax policies:
    a) Substantial marriage tax
    b) Child tax
    c) Tax married more than single
    d) Remove parents' tax exemption
    e) Additional taxes on parents with more than 1 or 2 children in school

--Reduce/eliminate paid maternity leave or benefits
--Bonuses for delayed marriage and greater child-spacing
--Pensions for women of 45 with less than N children
--Eliminate Welfare payments after first 2 children
--Chronic Depression
--Require women to work and provide few child care facilities
--Limit/eliminate publicly financed medical care, scholarships, housing, loans and subsidies to families with more than N children

Social Controls -
--Compulsory abortion of out-of-wedlock pregnancies
--Compulsory sterilization of all who have two children except for a few who would be allowed three
--Confine childbearing to only a limited number of adults
--Stock certification permits for children
--Housing Policies:

> a) Discouragement of private home ownership
> b) Stop awarding public housing based on family size
>
> Measures Predicated on Existing Motivation to Prevent Unwanted Pregnancy
> --Payments to encourage sterilization
> --Payments to encourage contraception
> --Abortion and sterilization on demand
> --Allow harmless contraceptives to be distributed nonmedically
> --Improve contraceptive technology
> --Make contraception truly available and accessible
> --Improve maternal health care with family planning as a core element.[233]

There is so much here to shock any sane and sensitive person that it almost leaves you speechless, but I am shocked by two additional things now – first, that so much of this agenda has been successfully implemented despite whatever resistance the American public has made. And second, that I could still be shocked by anything said or done by those promoting this Satanic program with no holds barred.

As I mentioned in an earlier chapter, unlike many of our brethren, we did not think non-abortifacient birth control was intrinsically evil, but when you see how it has been used as the tip of a wedge – and now is being used as the excuse for all the other evils perpetrated by those of this dark religion called eugenics/ population control – we can understand how our Catholic brethren feel so strongly opposed to it.

What next – compulsory abortion as has long been practiced in China? Licenses to have babies! Euthanasia – oops we've got that. Homosexual marriage – oops, we just

---

[233] This section and the whole memo are available online. I first learned of it in Jacqueline Kasun's book *The War Against Population*. Ignatius Press, 1988.

Was That Thunder?

got that, too, didn't we! So remind me again who the extremists are. How strange to find these things linking together in our opponents' agenda – and finding these things out because we took the risk of sitting in front of the door of a partial birth abortion clinic!

Bob Lewis carried away from the doors

CHAPTER ELEVEN – WRITING PAUL HILL
(NOV 1997 – DEC 1998)

> (2) If a thief be found breaking up, and be smitten that he die, there shall no blood be shed for him. (3) If the sun be risen upon him, there shall be blood shed for him; ...   --Exodus 22:2-3a

In November 1997, a rescuer from New Jersey wrote me a note. Priscilla Taylor, a tall independent Protestant could always be found at rescues and demonstrations with a diminutive Catholic, Patricia Dugan.

Both of them were grandmotherly with white hair. These "Siamese-twins" were pleasant to be around, but quite different in personality. Patricia was nearly silent, whereas Priscilla was quite outspoken. They were such close "buddies," that when Patricia died, Priscilla suddenly seemed an orphan. Curiously, she became a Catholic herself a year or two later.

My family's favorite story about Priscilla took place when she was in jail. A letter she sent mentioned how the women there missed having makeup. My kids therefore sent some "crayon" pictures with resplendent reds reinforced by layers of lipstick, etc. Priscilla wrote back that these gave visual pleasure in more ways than one. She was always straightforward to the point of being blunt, and could be relentless, so that at times I felt a certain compassion for her son, a small town New Jersey police chief .

But on this occasion, Priscilla was writing me to suggest that it would be nice if I sent a letter to Paul Hill on death row in Florida. Apparently she had been writing to him for a while. I'm not sure why she thought I would be a good correspondent.

My first reaction to Priscilla's letter was that I wasn't sure it was a good idea to associate myself with a double-murderer on death row.

Was That Thunder?

Priscilla (white hair), sitting in front of me;
Don Ranck at the right; at a Delaware abortuary.

Correspondence begins

My second reaction to Priscilla's letter was to remember the Lord's commendation in Matthew 25 – I was in prison and you visited me. In any case, I felt a heart-tug at this request, and toward the end of November, sent a letter to Paul in Florida State Prison.

In that first letter I spelled out two alternative courses. I was willing to carry on a light dialogue with him simply for the purpose of "visiting" (Matthew 25), but without "preaching" -- or I was willing to enter into dialogue with him on the central issue for which he stood condemned by law.

If Paul was willing to pursue the issue, then my greatest desire was to be an agent of his repentance. I felt obligated to make that clear to him at the outset. I more or less put those two alternatives for our correspondence before him. I offered to send him the long paper/booklet "Shattering the Image," my biblical manifesto about God's perspective on human death. I suggested that if he wanted to pursue the discussion, I was ready to hear his best arguments, and would try to show where they departed from scripture.

Paul elected to discuss the issue. In his reply, erroneously dated "Dec 3, 93" (It was 97), he asked that I send my paper and went on:

> ...You asked for my best arguments. ... Put simply, the 6th commandment forbids removing the defense necessary to defend the innocent; this is also reflected in the golden rule – to defend your neighbor as yourself – put roughly. Also the 1st of the Ten Commandments and the 1st Great commandment requires that the defense of life required in the 6th commandment (including lethal force if necessary) be performed notwithstanding men's prohibitions or we would put obedience to men before God and thus have another god before the one true God. That's the sum and substance of my thinking... I am ready and willing to give close consideration to your approach, Jim. ...

Our correspondence which went on over the next year, involved a total of fourteen or fifteen letters.[234]

In my next letter, 7 Dec 1997, I expressed gratitude to God and to Paul for his willingness to discuss these important issues. At the nexus of the debate were basic principles of scripture interpretation. That became the meat of my letter:

> ... As you mentioned, we both take seriously the Westminster standards – and that means we believe the Word of God to be *"given by inspiration of God, to be the rule of faith and life"* – life including all our doing as well as our thinking and talking.

---

[234] I have no copy of one of mine to which he refers.

Was That Thunder?

We look to the Bible for clarity in formulating what we believe and what we tell others to be true. We also look to the Bible for clear direction about what we ought to do in all circumstances. God has given it to us with this object, secondary only to the gospel of Jesus Christ himself – which is the heart and the central subject of all scripture.

> *The whole counsel of God, concerning all things necessary for his own glory, man's salvation, faith, and life, is either expressly set down in Scripture, or by good and necessary consequence may be deduced from Scripture: unto which nothing at any time is to be added, whether by new revelations of the Spirit or traditions of men. . .*

. . . God gave the law in the Old Testament <u>first</u> as the revelation of his will . . . we see . . . that God anticipated the disobedience to His law which is sinful man's response to it.

Second, therefore, God not only gave The Ten Commandments, but much detailed application of them in specific circumstances where they appeared to have been broken – such that these criteria could be used by the "civil courts," the elders meeting in the gates . . . to judge specific cases. In the case of the commandment "Thou shalt not kill" or "Thou shalt not commit murder," many specific qualifications and definitions are included in God's revelation so that human judges could determine whether a particular killing of a human being was a murder as prohibited in the commandment, or something else.

And then I turned to my central point:

> In other words, God, knowing the fallen human heart and condition, knew the bare words, "Thou shalt not kill" were not enough to be effectively used in difficult human judgments. . . .

> The process of "sifting" through the specific criteria should follow God's own process to the best of our ability. He gives a commandment, "Thou shalt not kill," but he qualifies it – "except . . . in just war, in self-defense, in defense of innocent others, or in capital punishment". The exceptions themselves are qualified further, however – and this is where you made the same mistake as the pacifists, etcetera – you failed to carefully assess the principle of defense of others in light of the particulars of God's word. You made an absolute, where it is a qualified principle.
>
> Those exceptions to [the requirement for] defense of innocent others are "deductions" made "by good and necessary consequence." They might be stated: "except where otherwise forbidden in God's law . . . for example where defense of others would involve deliberation and lying in wait."

The letter was a long one and went on to lay out the specifics of biblical categories of "justifiable homicide" versus those of "murder". In the end, I said that what Paul himself had done involved deliberation, "lying in wait," and the use of a deadly weapon brought to the scene specifically for the purpose of killing a particular man – all of which the Bible specifies as belonging to the biblical category of murder.

I added that "mitigating" circumstances in most cases made me opposed to the execution of women who had aborted their babies, and likewise, to Paul's own execution, but that I nonetheless believed he had justly be found guilty of murder.

I challenge him to be intellectually honest and keep separate the three categories of defense, just war, and capital punishment, rather than mixing them all up as some advocates for the use of lethal force were doing. I reminded him I had asked for his best arguments, and he had replied solely in terms of the defense of innocent others.

I ended by saying I believed God had called me to write this letter – and to call him to repent of his sin. I also said I loved him in Christ and would pray for him.

Was That Thunder?

John Brown of Harper's Ferry fame, sometimes held up as a model by those defending the abortionist shooters.

Paul's answer to this letter was dated 16 Dec 1997. He thanked me for my letter and my scriptural and impartial approach. He affirmed that the exercise of Matthew 18 was a good thing and that the church needed more of it. He went on:

> Now, cutting to the heart of your argument you say, "The key point at which you departed from scripture was in trying to stretch a biblical defense of others into an action that could be deliberate, and involve the goal of a planned killing of a particular man at a particular time." You say, "The key point at which your actions were at odds with a biblical description of legitimate defense was in your <u>deliberation</u>."
> You rightly quote several passages where lying in wait to kill an innocent person is condemned. This "lying in wait" is contrasted with no previous hatred or intent to do so if we lay in wait for the man killed.

Thus, the point being made by these scriptures is not to condemn someone for defending an innocent person against an unjust aggressor by preparing to meet the aggressor at the best place to end his murderous career; rather, the point is that while a totally accidental killing of an innocent person is not to be punished as "murder" if the one who kills the innocent person has lain in wait, it was obviously not accidental and thus not justifiable. You quote Ex 21:12 "He that smiteth a man, so that he die, shall be surely put to death. And if a man lie not in wait, but God deliver him into his hand; then I will appoint thee a place whither he shall flee."

The point is not that this killing would have been justified if he had not lain in wait but the fact that he laid in wait proves it wasn't accidental but intentional. This doesn't speak to either an individual or a policeman intentionally killing a known murderer.

It is granted that if it is wrong to kill someone, it is also wrong and made more heinous to kill with deliberation and premeditation.

Clearly premeditated murder is wrong – but is premeditated prevention of murder also wrong? . . .

. . .Jim, please speak to this issue for me Do all the qualifications for individual lethal defense of another you mentioned also apply to the police?

Do you object to the police waiting for an armed bank robber with a hostage to come out of a bank so a sniper can shoot him between the eyes and end the conflict and danger? Please tell me whether these principles [apply] to individuals but not to police. . . .

Paul concluded cordially, and emphasized "I am certainly not 'refusing to listen to you'. Matt 18."

The arguments here, though both ultimately specious, were no more sloppy than most being bandied about on the topic. The difference was this brother had done a lot more with his sloppy arguments than argue. His first point, that "deliberation" was not necessarily a proof of murder, was simply begging the question. But the "example" of the police sniper was certainly confusing – to the degree that many law enforcement officers are also unclear about what they may ethically do. The simple fact is that the Bible makes no allowance for <u>any individual</u> to lie in wait with the purpose of deliberately killing an innocent other.

As tempted as we are to use complicated law enforcement situations or wartime extremities as case examples, these justify nothing, especially on the level of the personal and private ethics. But I too was confused on this, and had to go back and wrestle with the "justification" for the kinds of extremes among law enforcement agencies we were unfortunately familiar with in recent decades. I could find no justification for "official assassination" anywhere. The Bible nor traditional jurisprudence offer any. Ruby Ridge and Waco were tyrannous and ungodly, not at all derived from biblical ethics.

When I was in the army, a fellow I knew showed me two unmarked, but remarkably well-made "assassination pistols," which he claimed had been given to him by someone else in the army, who had been issued them in Vietnam. If this was true, and the US government was indeed authorizing and equipping its agents for such deeds, then God stood in condemnation of the US government and/or the officials who authorized it. The biblical data reaffirmed me in that conclusion, though I once would have dismissed it as a "liberal" red-herring. [235]

The Arguments

I answered Paul in a letter dated 23 December. I thanked him for taking our correspondence seriously, and

---

[235] I waited until I got out of the army and naively sent a letter addressed to President Nixon describing the incident above in general terms. Three months later I got a letter from ATF saying that if in fact such a weapon existed and if in fact it were brought into the continental US, it might constitute a violation of US firearms law! End of story. A decade or so later I saw a photo of identical weapons in a childrens' book on firearms!

added that it was an honor to discuss such things with someone who obviously had more to gain or lose from the discussion than a theoretician. I affirmed that I too valued the pursuit of Matthew 18. I also mentioned my disappointment that pro-lifers had not dedicated themselves to biblical discussion on this topic six or seven years ago.

I went on to say I believed the tendency to private interpretation of scripture was one of the scourges of American evangelicalism, quoting 2 Peter 1:20, "Knowing this first, that no prophecy of scripture is of any private interpretation." (KJV)

> ... Against the tendency to private interpretation we have several safeguards: the understandings reached by others (which we all too often dismiss, as you rightly pointed out, through our own sinful inclinations); the testimony of the saints down through the ages – particularly in the conclusions of councils and solemn assemblies (thus our great respect for the Westminster standards); and always chiefest – other scriptures ("God is his own interpreter").

I explained I had not sent the long paper yet because much of it addressed wider issues, while the specific issues of our present discussion seemed to me more important. I wrote:

> In reply to my statement about deliberation/lying-in-wait being the key point at which you acted at odds with scripture you raise several objections. They might be summarized under these headings:
> 1/ Doesn't "lying in wait" (deliberation) apply simply and only to proving intentionality?
> 2/ Can the "lying in wait" (deliberation) qualifications be ignored in cases of defense?
> 3/ Wouldn't premeditation be acceptable, even a "plus" in cases of defense?
> 4/ Question of duration in regard to premeditation.

Was That Thunder?

5/ Question of distinction between individual and magistrate in regard to deliberation.

I have thought of several ways of re-stating the biblical arguments in regard to your questions. I will try to leave none of them unanswered, but I think maybe the best way to address them is to focus on the central question of what constitutes biblically justifiable "defense".... Now consider this scenario:

Joe tries to get along with Bill, but Bill is a hateful, spiteful fellow always looking for a brawl. One day, Joe accidentally runs over Bill's dog. Bill vows that he will kill Joe. "I'm going to shoot you next Sunday when you come home from church," he said, and Joe is utterly convinced he means it. So Joe deliberates, and decides that the best thing he can do is shoot Bill Saturday night when he's coming home from the bar!

What's wrong with that picture? Well, your first objection might be that Joe couldn't proceed as he planned because Bill wasn't a known and proven killer. Your second objection might be that Joe could have gotten police protection – indeed under our current law he might have successfully gotten Bill put away for "terroristic threats". You might further object that Joe could have made a whole lot more effort to explain what happened with the dog, and talk Bill out of it.

Suppose I answer all three objections and say Bill was a proven and known killer, that Bill's relatives ran city hall and the police department, which refused to do anything to protect Joe, and that Joe had spent days trying to convince Bill that he only ran over his dog by accident. <u>Now</u> can Joe go ahead and shoot him? Indeed, is there any variation on this description that gives Joe the moral right to take pre-emptive lethal action?

My answer for which I find plenty of scriptural support and no scriptural opposition is – no, there is never a biblical justification for an individual "pre-emptive" or "preventative" killing in the name of self-defense. Neither is there any biblical justification for pre-emptive or preventative killing in the name of defending others.

What Joe could do 1/having exhausted getting the civil authorities to intervene, 2/determined that Christ would be better served by not risking martyrdom, would be 3/head for the hills, 4/arm himself and be prepared for Bill to make the first aggressive move – at which point he might respond with equal force. If (to cite Exodus 22) Bill broke into his house at night, Joe might well be justified in shooting first. But at no point (even as he pulled the trigger then) could his heart motive, his spiritual or moral goal or intention be the death of Bill. Rather his intention must remain God's glory, Bill's good, and his own defense (as a subheading of the other two – the Great Commandments).

I went on to specifically address each of the "objections" I had culled from his letter. I asked him if by any chance he regarded the "avenger of blood" [236] as a normative and operative moral category. I said I could find no evidence of an occasion after the time of the Judges when such an avenger was recognized as legitimate.

I also pursued the possibility that he was confusing the term "deliberate" (on purpose) with "deliberation" (planning beforehand) based on his remarks on "accidental" versus "with deliberation" in the previous letter. I said:

> As Numbers 35:22-24 points out, one may do something "on purpose" (shove another, throw something, drop a rock,) without purposing or intending as a consequence or goal – the injury or death of a person. Deliberate murder refers to the intention to kill, not the intention to throw the rock or

---

[236] Discussed in Exodus in the context of the "Cities of Refuge".

swing the ax, etcetera. A justifiable defense, as best I can read the scripture, involves a complete lack of intention to kill the person – even as one pulls the trigger! In other words the actual death of an assailant in justifiable homicide in defense is an "accident," an unplanned and unintended result of using equal force to repel an attack.

Looking back at that argument now, although I think it is biblical and accurate, I see it involves more subtle distinctions than I made explicit, and was very likely confusing to Paul. I did go on, however to say:

Since human courts (ecclesiastical or civil) can only read outward actions and not hearts, it is probable that many "defenders" have indeed "hated" or intended the death of their assailants at the moment they killed them, but it must wait for God's court to deal with them. However, when a man can be proven to have planned and carried out a plan to "lie in wait" and kill someone, a human court has the evidence necessary to rightly judge him a murderer.

I also tried to answer the other "objections," before closing cordially and hopefully. I thought Paul was indeed listening and addressing what I had written him, albeit without yet getting past his misunderstandings.

Disappointing Replies

Paul replied to me in a letter dated 10 January 1998. He had received my long paper and said he was about half way through it. He thanked me for my "thoughtful and unobjectionable letter of Dec 23," saying he had written to his wife that my letter was free of the sort of personal attacks many debates generate into.

But what followed was disappointing. It was a hotch-potch of arguments that went back to his private ethical category which cannot be said to exist in scripture. He wrote:

> I believe a distinction must be made between someone maliciously killing an innocent person, on the one hand, and a bystander killing a known murderer who is about to kill the innocent, on the other. . . . these two are opposites. The character, motives, goals and objective standards of the aggressive murder are vastly different from the defender. The one act is a reprehensible murder, the other is a praiseworthy and sacrificial prevention of murder.
>   . . .The Bible clearly condemns the one and clearly justifies the other.

Then Paul turned back to Exodus 22, to try to establish that his two categories were validly distinguished:

> . . . it would be a misuse of scripture to take these declarations that one may not lie in wait with an object to apply to a self defense (or home defense) situation such as you find in Exodus 22:2 They are entirely different situations. Numbers 35:16-21 clearly says if you kill someone with an object you're a murderer. But Exodus 22:2 says if a thief is struck so he dies there is no bloodguiltiness – it is justified. Why is it that striking and killing in one instance is called murder and in another is called justified? Because they are almost antithetical circumstances. In one a guilty man kills the innocent, in another an innocent man kills a guilty aggressor to save the innocent. You can't take the prohibition to lying in wait or killing with an object in one circumstance and apply it to the opposite circumstance.

He bolstered this distinction (between premeditated murder and "premeditated lethal defense") by drawing a parallel between adultery and marital sex:

> Premeditated adultery is forbidden and condemned

by scripture but, though the physical act is the same, adultery must not be confused with marital sex. Marital sex is good. Premeditated sex is often better. The fact that premeditated adultery is forbidden does not mean all premeditated sex is wrong, neither does the fact that premeditated killing is wrong. The one does not necessarily follow form the other. On the contrary, in general, if God does not forbid something we may not presume to forbid it – whatever is not forbidden is permitted.

The rest of the letter was largely the same begging of the question. Paul asserted a number of times that the burden was on me to prove that "defensive force must be unintentional to be justified."

He concluded:

. . until you can prove that defensive force – as distinguished from accidental killing – must be unintentional to be justified, I dare not accept your assertion that it is so. I don't want to add to God's word. God's word says anyone who lies in wait to kill the innocent or strikes and kills the innocent is a murderer, but this is clearly not in the defensive context. Since in a defensive context God's word justifies striking and killing – the very thing forbidden in the other context – I may not assume lying in wait is forbidden in a defensive context.

God put no such restrictions on the avenger of blood or the defending homeowner. Dare we put such restrictions on these duties apart from God's Word? I think not.

What do you think?

In His Service, Paul

Paul did refer several times to "the avenger of blood" in his arguments, but also wrote, "Please notice, I am not trying to justify my actions by claiming I acted as the avenger of blood."

It seemed to me that the tone of this letter indicated Paul was "wrought up" and defensive. As to content, rather than replying to me, he was retrenching himself in his preconceived categories. He continued to protest that they were scriptural, and that therefore I was on the defensive -- that I had to prove something.

I was discouraged, and also aware that my response to rising emotion was often hasty anger, so I did not reply, as it turned out until that sad anniversary of the Supreme Court's Supreme Folly, without which Paul and I would never have heard of one another, nor had this correspondence. I wrote my next letter on 22 January 1998:

> I did not plan to wait until today to write to you – I have been working on a number of other projects, and things that have come up, so it took me this long to get to working on a reply. I am trying to be careful and thoughtful in replying, so I may not finish today, but as you see, I'm not in Washington at the March, or even downtown in Philly, where the pro-life community is having a rally. I am meeting with my brother on death row in Florida. That's where God wants me today.

> I started out reiterating what I thought were Paul's two biblical reference points for his category of "premeditated lethal defense": the first was the "avenger of blood" passages in Exodus, and the other was the Exodus 22:1-4, more specifically verses 2-3a. I quoted Calvin at length concerning the avenger of blood, emphasizing that this was a category God tolerated for a time, rather than a category he established or approved. Paul had already explicitly stated he did not claim to be acting as an avenger of blood. However I covered this topic at more length, because he had referred to it several times in his letter as biblical evidence for this "premeditated lethal defense" category. [237]

---

[237] Of course there was nothing defensive about what the "avengers" did, but Paul's point seemed to be that since God did not condemn them outright, they must not have been murderers,

Was That Thunder?

On the avengers I concluded thus:

...Certain pagan cultures have always had customs of private vengeance. There are remnants of it continuing among us today even in this country. But in a biblical framework, the first place we see it is in Cain and Lamech – not very good models for godly behavior, I think you will agree.

It is on this basis that I reject your argument for legitimate premeditated or deliberate killing and / or lying-in-wait based on the avenger of blood. The "office" was not legitimate. The only mentions of it we have in God's law are in His efforts to eliminate it by superseding it with due process. That he stipulates it will not be punished under certain circumstances should not be taken to the conclusion that it can serve as a model.

I then go back to my proposition that deliberation/premeditation and lying-in-wait, where proven, are sufficient grounds for conviction of murder (where the rest of the rules of due process are followed, of course). I again state the complimentary proposition that [I should have inserted "apart from capital punishment" here] no killing of a human being which is intended and planned can be justified.

Having already said that I believe the deliberate killing of a person to be ipso facto (by that very fact) murder, I will not repeat what I have already written to you. Instead I will try to go to the single passage which deals with defensive killing and show you where I think you are wrong in finding it to support "lying-in-wait" or deliberation as part of a legitimate defense.

Here I quoted Exodus 22:1-4 – (see this chapter's epigraph.)

This passage is "about" stealing, but, as in all ethical

---

despite their "premeditation" and "lying in wait," and therefore it was possible to have these two characteristics without murder.

matters in a fallen universe, questions of theft are complicated by other questions having to do with other kinds of sin. Among those complicating questions are these: 1) what if the thief kills someone? 2) what if someone kills the thief? 3) what if the thief injures someone? and 4) what if someone injures the thief? The answers to the first and third of these questions are fairly clear – since God gives us passages dealing with simple murder and assault (Numbers 35, Deuteronomy 19, 21, 24, 27, etcetera), which would possibly be "aggravated" by other wrong-doing (such as breaking in and stealing), but certainly in no way mitigated. But injuring an evildoer while defending oneself or ones family (or ones neighbor) against an evildoer is more complicated, we must agree.

Notice the implicit question in verse 2 and 3a – it is, in effect, 'should we treat the killing of a thief as murder?' God wouldn't say "there shall no blood be shed for him," unless someone is liable to suppose blood should be shed for him. As I have said before to you, all discussions of "strong (potentially lethal) defense" in the Bible are carried on as subordinate to the issue of murder. Calvin and all the Reformers sum up all elements of the moral law under subheadings of the ten commandments. The law is "hierarchical" – it has order, it can be outlined and arranged in a manner that makes it clear and applicable to life's situations – to our individual moral decisions, to ecclesiastical judicial process, and to public "civil" judicial process.

When the Bible is talking about property, it is immediately talking about the eighth commandment. (Calvin arranges these four verses under that general section – for obvious reasons). When the Bible embarks on a discussion of the killing of a human being, however, it is immediately talking about the sixth commandment. (And so the implied question regarding capital punishment/shedding of blood is made central to the discussion, even though capital punishment was nowhere specified as punishment for simple transgressions of the eighth commandment.) Whenever we discuss moral questions, at each specific point we are dealing with a specific commandment. That is what we find here.

Under the general question about how to deal with theft, verse 2 and 3 of this passage ask about murder: 'if a thief is killed, should his killer be executed as a murderer?' In order to answer that question two distinguishing details are brought in. <u>First</u>, it is specified that the thief is "breaking up" or "breaking in," as we would say. The <u>second</u> detail has to do with whether it is night or day, dark or light. There would be no need for these further details if the answer were simply 'yes, the killer of the thief ought to be executed' or 'no, the killer of a thief ought to be found innocent of murder'. <u>Since the further qualifications are necessary, we may legitimately deduce that under some circumstance a killer of a thief is to be treated as a murderer and under some circumstances he is not.</u>

The first detail makes it a requirement that the thief be breaking into a dwelling. If he is not breaking into a dwelling, then we are back to the simple commandment against murder. Anyone killing him deliberately in other circumstances than breaking into a dwelling is a murderer.

The second detail makes it a requirement that he be breaking in at night (in the dark). This is important enough that God is not willing to leave it as a strong inference, but states it explicitly in vs. 3. If the thief[238] be killed during the day (even though he is breaking in) his killer is to be treated as a murderer – blood for blood, life for life.

The passage leaves us then with clear directives that a thief may not be killed by a private person under any

---

[238] Calvin makes a point of saying this guy is a thief, not a robber, by which I think he means one (probably unarmed) who steals from houses, not one (probably armed) who steals directly from persons. . . .

circumstances except those of a night-time break-in to his home.

Now teachers and commentators assume God may have a little more to tell us in this passage, that there are things which may be "by good and necessary consequence deduced from" this scripture with wider application than just how to treat thieves breaking in – even though that is the primary application.

So godly men have asked these questions: 1) what is important about the fact that the thief is breaking into a home? 2) what is important about the night/day distinction? And 3) what is special about the combination of these two factors that makes for an exception to the sixth commandment?

Much of our doctrine of self-defense is derived from this passage and the answers to these questions. And, as you know, our doctrine of the defense of innocent third parties is based on the same principles as that of our self-defense.

What then are the answers to these questions?

Calvin says of verse 2-3a: . . . ."the intention of God is by no means ambiguous, viz., that if a thief should be killed in the dark, his slayer should be unpunished; for he can then hardly be distinguished from a robber, especially when he proceeds with violence; because he cannot enter another man's house by night without either digging through a wall or breaking down a door. The Twelve Tables[239] differ slightly from this; for they permitted the killing of a thief by night, and also by day if he should defend himself with a weapon. But since God had sufficiently repressed by other laws murders and violent assaults, He is silent here respecting robbers who use the sword in their attempts at plunder. He therefore justly condemns to death those who have avenged by murder a theft in open day." (p. 142)

His conclusion is that the combination of the night-time setting and the breaking-in activity of the thief

---

[239] early Roman law code, c. 450 BC.

make him indistinguishable from an armed assailant. In the day, the householder could see the thief was unarmed, and could distinguish more clearly what the thief was doing, so that a distinction between a definite assault and a mere attempt at burglary could be made.

Breaking that down into answers to the three questions I asked above: 1) the breaking in is important in that it is an act of violence against a dwelling which might under some circumstances be part of an assault against the persons living there, 2) the night and day distinction is important because what may be clearly distinguished in the day often cannot be distinguished at night, and 3) the combination is important because the fact that the victim was engaged in indeterminate violence at a time when clear distinction could not be made between violence toward property and violence toward persons adds up to an exception (or a defense) to murder.

Does any of this support a deliberate plan to kill some one? No, it doesn't. The night/day distinction makes that abundantly clear. If it is murder to "defend oneself" against an unarmed thief in the day by killing him – even though the thief was breaking into your house, then no exception may be based on this passage to justify a "planned" or deliberate killing. For if a little daylight makes a thing a crime, a little deliberation makes it all the more so."

After another excursus in which I used the analogy of the gradation of grammar rules with their exceptions, to God's law and its "exceptions" (defenses), I summarized thus:

> Abortion is murder because none of the efforts of its advocates to justify it meet biblical tests. Deliberately lying in wait to kill an abortionist is murder because it fails to meet the test of the biblical exceptions. <u>Call it killing a thief breaking in by day, if you wish, but you cannot call it killing a thief breaking in by night.</u>

I also quoted several pages from Calvin's treatment of the Sixth Commandment in his Harmony of the last four books of the Penteteuch.

I then got a little more personal:

> Paul, when I stated originally that your error was in deliberation and lying-in-wait, I was referring to the outward evidence which make your actions murder to the best of my understanding of scripture. However, to the extent that we refer to the heart as the ultimate seat of action, and our heart motives or primary intentions as the foundation where sinful actions are grounded, I would say your error was hatred. Calvin says the two sides of the Sixth Commandment are love of neighbor and hatred of neighbor ("love is contrasted with vengeance"). One is commanded, the other is prohibited. Nor does he allow for the Pharisaical distinction between "neighbor" and "enemy" which lies behind the question "Who is my neighbor" and the older question, "Am I my brother's keeper?"

Gandalf -- wiser than most of us.

Was That Thunder?

I then quoted from *Lord of the Rings*, Gandalfs' reply to Frodo's assertion that Gollum deserves death:

Deserves it! I daresay he does. Many that live deserve death. And some that die deserve life. Can you give it to them? Then do not be too eager to deal out death in judgment. For even the very wise cannot see all ends. I have not much hope that Gollum can be cured before he dies, but there is a chance of it . . .

And after preaching a little about how when it comes to deserts, we all deserve condemnation and hell, I wrote:

No, hatred is out – even hatred of the abortionist. You have amassed a lot of self-protective arguments to convince yourself that someone could be practicing "defense" in killing an abortionist, but the Bible cuts through all that. Show me this category "deliberate killing in defense" in the Bible. Show me where it is remotely possible to plan to kill someone, arm oneself to kill someone, go out to kill someone and in that premeditated manner actually kill someone as "defense". . . .

The simple fact is that any pre-emptive killing is an act of vengeance. It comes out of a heart that hates. At the moment of doing the deed, the intent was not saving anybody from anything – it was killing someone. The heart intention is "vengeance" as you labeled it in regard to the killing of the adulterer . . . The deed is murder, and the scripture classifies such an intention and such a deed under no category other than murder.

I'm not saying the man shooting an abortionist doesn't hope real lives might be saved. Nor would I say a man shooting an adulterer doesn't hope real marital unity and faithfulness might be restored. But that hoped-for result is only an excuse, seen from a biblical framework. Results never justify actions. One's immediate motives, intentions, goals, are the things by which an action is judged moral or immoral, godly or ungodly.

Looking back over this letter, which goes on for 3 more pages (to a total of 14) I see it was a mistake to try to address all the points Paul had raised in his previous one. Perhaps I only increased his confusion, and would have done better to have edited it to ¼ of its length, with only one point and one passage discussed. Hindsight! In any case I concluded:

> I don't know all of what I am asking you to do in calling you to repent of these things. I do know, however, that the Grace of Jesus Christ is sufficient for you. The greatest condemnation in the New Testament (Romans 1) is against those who lead others into doing what is wrong. You are peculiarly well-placed to do the opposite of that – to declare you have been wrong and to call others to do only what is right.
> I pray for the Spirit to lead and comfort you. Please pray the same for me. Your brother in Christ, Jim.

How much more was there for us to say to one another? At times I wondered what it would take for me to reconsider and recant, were I in Paul's position. Despite my apparent failure to influence him, I was convinced the game was worth the candle – for him, his family, and the cause of the unborn.

"Honeymoon Over"

On 8 February 1998, Paul wrote back:

> As I anticipated shooting and probably killing the abortionist I was, and remain, convinced I had a moral obligation to use the means necessary to defend the ones he intended to kill that day and also use reasonable means to ensure he didn't kill in the future. The idea that you have presented – that is OK to kill in defensive

situations without premeditation, but its murder to kill with premeditation in defensive situations has no effect on my conscience. I find no support for this in God's word. This consideration – since it is wrong – should not keep people from defending the innocent. Do you mean to say that all the individual, police, soldiers, bombadeers, and operators of heavy lethal military explosives known to kill – were transformed from doing a honorable and highly commendable duty to being murderers and guilty of severe penalty if, in their minds, while killing or dropping a lethal bomb in the midst of men they knew it would kill – they intended to do what they knew full well would result in death? To me this is unreasonable. One guy is a hero and another is a murderer though they both did what they knew would kill. The difference between the hero and the murderer is the hero knew he would kill but somehow mentally denied he intended to kill. To me this is very unreasonable. I doubt a jury, or the police or the armed services or many other people would agree with you.

If the lives of hundreds of innocent people depends on a soldier igniting a huge explosive that will certainly kill the enemy – if he can't kill without intending to kill is he to allow the aggressors to kill the innocent? I tell you this – I would not want you in a fox hole next to me. I would not want you to be responsible for my bodily defense. Now, on the contrary – I would like you[r] theory very much if I were an abortionist.

In short, Jim, I can't see your point. At this point I think we have likely benefited from each others point of view as much as can be expected.

If you want to respond – that's fine, but I don't want to make unwise use of your or my time.

I do appreciate your zeal and the integrity of your intentions and manner of discussing this.

To be very honest, just as you see me to be guilty of doing wrong – as I'm sure you suspect, I think you are adding to God's word a man made commandment which serves to annul a very weighty and necessary duty – using the means necessary to defend life.

So that's where we are at. I appreciate your time but respectfully disagree and wonder how profitable beating this horse is going to be.

God bless you.

Let me know what you think Jim.

Paul

The honeymoon was certainly over! It crossed my mind after this letter with its rambling logic and grammar to wonder if Paul was being sedated. I know when we were in jail the rumor constantly recurred that there was drugs in the water.[240] Do prison managers regularly use mood-altering drugs on their death-row inmates? I don't know. Paul was evidently coherent in his interview with Life Dynamics the day before his execution.[241]

Paul interviewed the day before his execution.

---

[240] The scuttlebutt was that this was added to dampen sexual drive. But that was a favorite rumor in the army, too.

[241] Three-part Life Dynamics interview, seeYoutube.

At any rate I did not feel I had the right to quit at this point. I wrote back on February 17:

> So you're fed up with me! Well, I can understand that. Other people have said the same thing – notably my wife! You have the luxury she does not. You don't have to reply – but since you made the mistake of replying this time, I will keep on keeping on.
>
> I don't think you're listening.
>
> I can understand that. I'm not sure I would be listening in your position. You have literally staked you life on an idea, a viewpoint, a way of understanding God's will, and it's well-nigh impossible for you to seriously consider that idea or viewpoint to have been a mistake. In a sense, you feel that to say "I was wrong" would be to say "I've wasted my life." Beyond that, for you to say "I was wrong" would not only feel like saying "I wasted my life," but it would also involve saying you wrongly ended two other lives. In essence, for you to say "I was wrong" would be to say "I threw away three lives." That is not a pleasant prospect for anyone to contemplate.
>
> Personally I struggle a great deal with a sense that I have wasted or am wasting one life – and I constantly have to come back with naked faith and cry out to God for a child-like heart that rests in him. A book came out recently called *Perilous Pursuits*, which is about American Christians' obsession with significance. So much of the time I feel frustrated because I am not significant. I think I shared with you that in writing you part of my struggle is my flesh wanting to make it a quest for significance rather than real fellowship and part of the coming of the kingdom.
>
> What is it that really makes a life insignificant – that makes for a "wasted life" – from God's perspective? Is it lack of great accomplishments? It is making mistakes? Is it sinning? Or is it something else? In any case, I have a deep sense of how hard it must be to talk about these things and carry on civil dialogue (which you

have!) with this "wasted life" sword hanging over your head (and me swinging it back and forth!).

Nevertheless, I believe the gospel adequate for this difficulty. The gospel never calls us to defend the past – it only calls us to face the present reality. Jesus is Lord. Jesus is Savior – for sinners. No one had more clearly wasted his entire life than the believing thief, yet his whole life was redeemed in the hours of faith and repentance at the end of it.

When I say you're not listening, I am referring to the things I have presented out of the scriptures – in response to your arguments for "premeditated lethal defense". While claiming a scriptural basis, you are able to present none. You refer to the thief-breaking-in passage again and again, but refuse to deal with half of that passage – the part which limits such "lethal defense" to a nighttime situation. Why does God say we <u>cannot</u> do likewise in the day?

I went on to more or less cover ground already gone over in other letters, but I added something which had come out of the discussions of the colloquium years earlier – the exceptional complexity of the abortionist situation over against most models related to justification defenses:

As gut-wrenching and awful as the abortion situation is, it does not fit the biblical description of a strong defense situation. An abortionist cannot be treated as an assailant because he is never more than half an assailant. No abortionist on this planet* kills by himself. [note: *Of course this is only true where abortion is voluntary – in China's forced abortion regime, the mother is not one of the co-conspirators. There are others instead, and she is often a pure victim along with her child.] He is indeed a contract murderer, but his chief accomplice pays him to do what he does.

She, alone, <u>wills the murder</u> which she engages him to perform. <u>Her will alone can stop the murder.</u> Her will alone – not his alone. He is never a thief breaking in at night assaulting a child – because she holds the child out the window for him to kill. Justice strictly speaking would involve the execution of both of them – they are co-conspirators to murder.

When evil leaders have passed an evil law allowing the two of them to kill a child, there is a third party to the evil – the state itself. Justice would involve severe punishments to all three. Those evil leaders were appointed by other high leaders who are also co-conspirators. Justice would involve punishments for these, too. The voters of the United States elected those high leaders who appointed those other high leaders, who allowed the two murderers to kill the child. Justice involves punishment for all five. In other words, Justice demands that we all be punished. Can you mete out that kind of justice?

If a day comes when you hear these things, Paul, what might you do? What would I do if I were in your shoes? First of all and most importantly, I think I would get on my knees and ask God's forgiveness. You've done it many times before. You know how simple and hard it is.

Putting myself in your shoes, I suppose the second thing I would do would be to talk to my wife and try to tell her in simple terms what I have come to. Third, I think I would write a straight-forward public statement – and maybe check it with my lawyers . . . I believe (and this is no prophetic word) that you should address the pro-life activist community first and foremost and maybe the American church secondarily.

Finally, I would steel myself for the fact that the secular powers – press and proabort propaganda would try to "make hay" out of my statements. This simply means getting ready to ignore the kind of baloney the press would put out.

But your last letter makes it clear you aren't there yet . . .

You hint that you have other things to do with your time. Based on my brief stays in penal institutions, I imagine correspondence is your chief labor – and I know that can be a lot of work. So I am very willing to suspend our communications as long as you wish. I would hope, however, that every now and then you would read through my letters and reassess what I have written over against the scriptures. Where you find me to be wrong, I would like to hear about it. If I'm mishandling the Word of God, I would like to know it. Anytime you write, I will write back.

Paul's reply was dated 7 March 1998. Thus far his arguments had been based on the dubious category of "premeditated lethal defense," which he had treated for the most part as a further variation on self-defense and the defense of innocent others. But in the last letter and even more in this one, he tried to move the arguments to those very different categories of just war and law enforcement:

> As for premeditated personal defense I see no more need for a passage specifying that lethal defense may be premeditated (and should be where possible) than there is a need for specifying this in the case of lawful war or public justice. There is no more need for a specific passage saying lethal defensive force may be premeditated than there is a need for a specific passage saying non lethal force may be premeditated – as in rescue. If non lethal force may and should be premeditated, if possible, the same is true of lethal force.

Four very different things all jumbled together in one paragraph! There is part of me that would like to believe that Paul Hill was simply not too bright. But at this point I think he was more culpable than that. This is obfuscation. He was capable of listening and reading, of thinking. Here he is flinging out random bolts in order to avoid thinking.

And what a low blow this last "justification" for abortionist shooting he raises here – rescue! If it's all right to plan to sit in front of an abortion clinic, then it's also all right to take a shotgun there and kill the staff! On the face of it, this would certainly seem to debunk our claims that there was no connection between rescue and violence. In Paul's mind, at least, there seemed to be!

Then he fell back to something he had not explicitly quoted before, but which he indirectly referred to in his first letter, and which was foundational doctrine to the arcane set of proof-texts which made up his apologetic:

> The rules for the right understanding of the Ten Commandments assert this truth. Q. 99, 6: "that under one sin or duty, all of the same kind are forbidden or commanded; together with all the causes, means, occasions, and appearances thereof, and provocations thereunto." ([Westminster] Smaller Catechism)
>
> One necessary means, often, for using both lethal and non lethal defense is premeditation. It's hard to have an effective rescue unless it is carefully premeditated. The same is true of lethal rescue. . . .

Now shooting an abortionist has become "lethal rescue" ! He goes on to say that "common sense" dictated the use of premeditation for the "necessary duty to use lethal defensive force." He went on:

> I don't mean to pick over words but one of your statements struck me as false. On the second page of your Feb 17 letter you begin a paragraph. "Where then are the Bible passages justifying lethal defense"? Nowhere. There aren't any. The only Bible justification (to be arrived at by any good and necessary inference) for use of strong force in self-defense and defense of others is the commandment against murder itself."
>
> I don't mean to be straining knats [sic] but Q. 136 of the Catechism justifies "taking away the life . . . of others . . . in case of . . . necessary defense". The proof text printed in the authorized version for "necessary defense" is Exodus 22:2. In light of this in your next letter will you explain you above quote statement [sic]. It appears to me to directly contradict the Catechisms

text for justifying "necessary defense".

And again, the last lines of text in the letter,

> . . . Please clearly prove from the Bible that lethal force is only justified if unpremeditated. Do you feel you have borne the burden of proof? Do you accept the burden of proof? Also, do you deny that Ex 22:2 justifies lethal "necessary defense" as you appear to do?

It was as if the previous letters had never reached him. I may not always be nearly as lucid as I think myself, but what was going on here was not primarily about my inability to communicate. All of a sudden I thought of his poor fellow presbyters who must have gone through this same sort of thing back when Paul was being examined by the Orthodox Presbyterian denomination, to the ultimate conclusion of his being defrocked as a pastor.

There have been other people in my life with personalities very like Paul's. Their great temptation is to lock onto "a position," be it some private view of baptism or the "illegitimacy of all divorce," after which no mere Bible passage makes a dent in this belief. They are hard-headed and hard-hearted -- because not in submission to the word of God. Like the Pharisees, their claims are to a higher standard – higher than God's! I suppose there have been many times when I was one of them. But the fundamental tragedy is they claim the scripture as authority, while persisting in being impervious to its actual contents.

On 12 March 1998, I tried a different tack. I sent Paul a fantasy dialogue between a Martian and a Presbyterian which began:

> If you were a Martian and I was a Presbyterian and we were talking about the Bible and Christian morality for the first time the conversation might go something like this.
> M. So you humans are infected with this "original sin" and it keeps you from doing what God says you

should do, even though you know what he wants you to do in your hearts. I'm surprised you haven't all annihilated each other and the planet, too!

P. Yes, I guess the only reason we haven't is that God's grace continues to restrain the whole human race at the same time as his saving grace is working to really change quite a few of us, so that through faith in Jesus Christ, we not only are forgiven of past sin, but are made increasingly able to resist and overcome sin and do what is right.

M. You mean God has two different programs – one for those of you he wants to save and one for the ones he doesn't?

P. That seems to be the necessary conclusion to a number of things in the guide-book God gave us, the Bible, but it is important to keep in mind that he doesn't have two sets of rules about what is right and wrong. Furthermore, there is no way for any of us to know which category any other person is in. It is only the grace of God that lets any one of us know that he himself is saved. Therefore we each have to act toward all the others in as careful and godly a way as possible – speaking the truth to them, which may help them get saved, and demonstrating righteousness, which might either help them get saved or help them grow in righteousness.

This was a ten page letter, but was meant to present the "big picture" in relation to the issues we had been discussing, in a more prosaic and less confrontational manner. It got down to the nub on page nine:

M. Isn't there any kind of defensive effort that can be planned ahead of time?

P. Well, you might argue that building a house and putting locks on the door is a defense planned ahead of time – or that burglar alarms and floodlights and such are pre-meditated defenses. A machine gun set up to go off when someone breaks through your door, however, is illegal and immoral, because it will kill the thief breaking in by day as well as the probable assailant breaking in at night. A contingency plan for defense is fundamentally different from a premeditated attack in that 1/the contingency plan has as its primary intention the <u>prevention</u> of something which <u>might happen</u>, and 2/it will only go ahead when the thing to be prevented has begun to be an immediate reality. A premeditated attack, on the other hand 1/has as its primary intention the wounding or killing of a particular victim, and 2/it will go ahead when the perpetrator has the opportunity to begin his attack. Another way to put it is that, so far as heart intentions go, the "contingency" plan or preparation for possible eventualities is <u>not a fixed intention</u>, while the premeditated attack has been "determined," or decided on, or <u>fully intended</u> – before the fact of being carried out.

    M. But isn't this "rescue" movement Christians have been involved in – the peaceful, prayerful blocking of an abortion clinic door – a premeditated defense?

    P. No, it is correct to say it has been planned or "premeditated," but it is not correct to say it is a defense. Rather it is an extreme appeal. It is not a defense, because it is not a response to direct assault. Furthermore, as many have pointed out, it lacks the element of being "likely to succeed," at least as measured statistically. It is in fact an appeal – chiefly to the chief co-conspirator in a murder – the mother of the child about to be killed. It is also, secondarily, an appeal to the other co-conspirators to murder, the abortionist and his/her staff. It is also an appeal to the officials, the community and the society in general made to the extent of going to court and jail to demonstrate by personal sacrifice that this is not merely a political issue or a matter of personal opinion. And in some sense, it is an appeal to God. But it is not a pre-meditated defense".

    M. But aren't there other non-lethal defenses?

    P. The idea of "non lethal defense" pre-supposes the

idea of "lethal defense" – both are equally distant from Bible principle. Both terms miss the point in legitimate defense that the degree (the strength or intensity of power of the particular means) of the defense depends on the degree of the assault. Thus the prosecution of the man who shot at kids who threw snowballs at him a few years ago. There is no "gun defense" and no "snowball defense" in the Bible, only appropriate defense, which means it is a direct response to a particular assault using means equivalent to those being used by the assailant.

It ended with the Presbyterian asking the Martian how things were on his planet. The Martian replied, "On Mars we don't kill each other at all." In closing I told Paul, "I think I've hit most of the points you asked me to address, although probably not in quite the form you expected! What have I missed? Next time I promise to just write a plain letter. Yours in Christ, Jim". [242]

Perhaps I was too whimsical or too didactic in my dialogue between the Martian and the Presbyterian, but Paul's answer again seemed to give little serious consideration to my letter. He wrote:

> Dear Jim, Greetings in our Lord. I hope all is well with you and your loved ones.

---

[242] Although I tried to avoid discussions of capital punishment and just war in my letters to Paul, the issues were covered in my longer paper on "Human Death in the Bible". Summarized in brief, I found actions such as Paul's cannot biblically be regarded as capital punishment because there was no "due process," as we call it, no objective or disinterested legal procedure. Obviously Paul had no standing as a civil authority who could mete out punishment, except as a member of a jury, but even if he'd been a judge or a policeman, he could not have done what he did.

Just war involves five or six requirements or prerequisites, including pursuing alternatives, declaring war, and waging war under legitimate authority, as discussed briefly in the Afterword, below. Obviously this did not apply to Paul's situation, either.

I am making good progress on a paper formerly titled "Does the PCA Endorse Anti-Abortion Force?" It has grown into quite a treatise. I plan to include it as an appendix to my forthcoming book, *Freedom from Abortion*.

Thank you for your letter of March 12.

I think both of us are simply doing a lot of restating of our beliefs.

One new idea came to mind as I reread your treatise. As I remember, you previously took the position that all force would be justified if the would-be murderer were in the act of murdering (or <u>very</u> close to it). But if you think of the situation in Ex 22:2, the man justifiably killed was not in the process of murdering – He is identified as a thief – not a murderer. Since he was struck so he died while breaking in – he most likely is outside the house. He just appeared to be presenting a threat to the people inside. He didn't have a knife at their throat.

I think you can reasonably deduce from this that you need not wait until the last seconds before murder before you can be justified in using lethal force.

There was a degree of obliviousness or obtuseness indicated here that fascinated and still fascinates me – because I desperately wanted and want to understand it. Exodus 22:2-3 is not that complicated. What Jewish commentators, Calvin and myriads of other Christians have said about it is not that complicated. So what kept Paul from being able to simply absorb this understanding? Some elements of his responses made me think he was mixing me up with some other correspondent – or with others who had opposed him in the past. But when all was said and done, I was brought to the conclusion that he was simply hardening his heart.

Paul ended his short letter with this postscript:

P.S. Dead abortionists don't return to kill but wounded abortionists have been known to do so. If in doubt as to whether the wounded abortionist will return to kill the benefit should go to the 100s of innocent people he may kill (considering his occupation and past history). The benefit of the doubt should not go to the known murderer (though his intended victims are seldom seen and their lives are often not weighted with as much care as the habitual murderer).

It is possible to be so very concerned about not killing a attacking soldier or a attacking abortionist that you spare his life at the expense of many innocent people.

It would be vastly better for every abortionist and all their accessories to be immediately struck dead than for them to be allowed to kill even one more unborn child.

To call a defender of the innocent a murder [sic] because he carefully planned his defense is to sin by calling good evil.

Paul here tells me I am sinning "by calling good evil." This letter brought me to the point of conviction that all I had left to do was state the converse as strongly as I was able – that he was continued in deadly sin by calling evil good.

Concluding Arguments

My next and essentially my last letter [243] was a little more than four pages long, and dated 1 July 1998

Here is the text of my July letter in full :

Dear Paul,

In response to your May letter, I must agree that what I hear is a repetition of previous arguments. The only thing which seems new to me is the conclusion to your postscript which says "To call a defender of the innocent a murderer because he carefully planned his defense is to sin by calling

---

[243] I did send Paul one more letter beyond this one, apparently dated Nov 24, as mentioned below.

good evil." I will try to respond to that carefully, to make sure what you intend by saying it I will respond in two stages. The first stage is to reaffirm the basis of our discussion. The second stage is to apply the basic principles to the specifics of your statement.

First stage: basis for our discussion: First, there is no sin except before God. Second, there is no good except before God. Third, there is no definition of evil except before God. Fourth, we can determine the specifics of God's will, what is good, what is evil and what is sin from the Bible -- not from any other authority -- not from experience, not from observed results, not from others' political theories, not from our feelings -- not from anywhere but the Bible.

Second stage: application of principles to your statement: First, I find no basis in the Bible to ever call a defender of the innocent a murderer - the two terms are mutually exclusive. I have said before the term "lethal defense" meaning deliberate killing is at head-on odds with the Bible. Second, the Bible concludes those who premeditate, plan, and carry out a particular killing "from ambush" to be murderers and not "defenders". Third, to call such a one a murderer, to say he has committed sin and done evil, and to call him to repentance is an obligation, most especially when that one names the name of Christ. I have said so from the beginning of our correspondence, and although I have carefully read your letters over, I have found no argument from scripture in them to sway me from that practice and that purpose. Finally, that you regard my doing so as sin only seems to me evidence of a hard heart.

I know that you have been repeating these same ideas for a number of years, and that you have been opposed by a number of other Christian men. I am sure that they, like me, were sinners and that they may have run roughshod over your heart and your arguments at times. I know that it is difficult for you not to lump us altogether as men who have "sold out" to ease and comfort and to the various idols of our culture. I even suspect that you may have a life-long history of feeling isolated and alone, and that this debate and your actions based on your conclusions continue to make you feel isolated and alone - the one true prophet. But with great respect for all of these things, I come inevitably to the conclusion that in addition to the effects of the sins of others, your own hard heart is keeping you from hearing what God says about murder.

You are indeed a defender, but the things you defend are your own acts of murder. You claim a biblical basis for your action, but the force of your arguments comes from somewhere else -- a commitment to a course of action which you have taken. To turn back from this course of action could only come with a huge about-face, a public statement of error and sorrow. This is what you fear. I am, to the extent I know my flesh, very sympathetic with that reluctance. But that does not excuse either of us from repentance -- repentance is the bravest act, the holiest act, and the only act, in this case which can glorify God and do good to your fellow men.

Paul, I don't know if this is true in other areas of your life and doctrine - but you are not a very good student of the scriptures. Your strings of logic are knotted and broken. I'll give you some examples from the first part of your last letter in a minute but first I want to ask you to consider this as evidence that your heart is hard about these things - and your mind and eyes consequently blind to what God has said and required of us. I am willing to bet you are sharing the gospel with some of your fellow inmates -- and that you do this winsomely and clearly. I am willing to bet you have often been a good shepherd and teacher to your wife and family and your congregations in many of the most important matters about which the Bible teaches us. Why is it then that you generate such a fog of faulty exegesis, illegitimate terms and wrong conclusions in regard to this matter we have been discussing? I pray that the Spirit of God may allow you to step back from yourself and answer that question honestly.

That you have a few others who continually "support" you and tell you you are a hero and have done something wonderfully holy, I am also sure -- but ask yourself if these indeed are the "wise" or have come to love what they see as "justice" more than Christ. These are blind guides, Paul. What a horrible thing to be so dedicated to the innocent that we become reprobate ourselves. We were not put in this world with an absolute command to defend the innocent at all costs -- we were put here, or at least called here to have one unswerving devotion -- to Christ and His Kingdom.

If the unborn become an idol for us, so that we are willing to disobey Christ "for their sake" we have turned Matthew 28 on its head. We are no longer doing it "for the least of these my brethren," because we are not doing it "unto me [Christ]". Turn, Paul, turn from the obsession and idolatry of committing murder for Christ - turn to Christ, who let himself be murdered for us. To the extent that you persist in calling murder "good," you murder Christ again.

Here, in order, are several sections from your last letter:

> One new idea came to mind as I reread your treatise. As I remember, you previously took the position that all force would be justified if the would be murderer were in the act of murdering (or very close to it). But if you think of the situation in Ex.22:2, the man justifiably killed was not in the process of murdering -- He is identified as a thief -- not a murderer. Since he was struck so he died while breaking in -- he most likely is outside the house. He - just appeared to be presenting a threat to the people inside. He didn't have a knife at their throat
>
> I think you can reasonably deduce from this that you need not wait until the last seconds before murder before you can be justified in using lethal force.

I went through the Exodus 22:2-3 passage at length in the last two letters, and I cannot think that you even bothered to consider the details of what they say in light of the rest of scripture. I repeat, the big question in regard to "justifiable homicide" in Exodus 22 is what distinguishes verse 2 from the first part of verse 3? When you have answered that, you have learned God's will concerning the distinguishing point between "justifiable homicide" and murder. Was the sun shining on your two victims? If it was what you did was not just defense, but murder.

I quite agree that there are some times when, in war, it is better to shoot to wound rather than to shoot to kill -- but there are also many instances in which the best strategy is to aim and shoot at the spot most likely to kill the man so he doesn't possibly survive to shoot again from a wounded posture. Dead men don't shoot back but wounded men may.

Also, I totally agree, that in "normal" circumstances -- when defending someone you should just try to subdue the would be killer - not kill him -But in extraordinary circumstances such as legalized murder -- where a wounded murderer may be healed and restored to his murderous practice - intentional lethal force is reasonable.

There is not room for a discussion about whether to "shoot to kill" or "shoot to wound" until one has determined whether it is legitimate to talk about shooting at all.[244] That is the single issue which you continually jump over. Your efforts to correlate your actions to those of soldiers in war or law enforcement officers are without warrant. You are neither. I was willing to discuss the ethics of those situations to enumerate the categories of human killing in the Bible and to emphasize how highly God emphasizes the sacredness of human life. But they have no direct bearing on our present options or past actions. The whole Bible is about "extraordinary circumstances". Sin is what made the Bible necessary. It addresses all of our dilemmas and ethical difficulties.

You enter again into the extremely cold-blooded discussion of deciding to kill or not on the basis of whether it will be effective ("whether he will go back to his murderous

---

[244] *The concept of shooting to wound an abortionist was not one I had ever heard argued, but apparently it was indeed what Jim Kopp was attempting when he killed Bernard Slepian in October 1998. That's what Jim said in his confession several years later. Perhaps this was also Shelley Shannon's intention.

practice", etc.) which is completely outside the pale of Christian ethics. The end never justifies the means -- we may never say 'let us do evil that good may result'.

> Obviously -- under "normal" circumstances known murderers, if not killed, are restrained from ever killing again. The gov. does this. The gov. doesn't assume they will never kill again but assumes they might and goes to great expense to prevent it. In the same way - one of my main reasons for intending to kill and not just to wound the abortionist I killed was not because I knew if I wounded him I would never be able to do so again and there was a good chance he would return to murder as I sat in jail.
> Thus, if it is justified to kill in defense of others when the offender would be restrained in the future if wounded - How much more was it justified to kill under the circumstances that existed when I killed.

That, Paul, simply put, is a clearcut confession to murder as the Bible defines it. Furthermore, it completely exposes the hypocrisy of the "defense" language which the hardy band of pro-murder "pro-lifers" insist on using. The Bible recognizes no defensive act which does not have the immediate purpose of keeping <u>particular</u> victims of assault from being seriously harmed or killed. Your words here demonstrate that it is not the babies to be killed that day that you are concerned about, but rather the general run of babies everywhere anytime.

That may sound grand to you, but if we are to begin killing people to prevent what we deem to be great harm to general mankind in the future, why stop at abortionists? Wouldn't it be just as valid to go after liberal politicians and pornographers and who knows who else!? No, you were not operating as a defender in any sense the Bible defines. You were a self-proclaimed agent of God's vengeance meting out death sentences. That didn't come from the Bible - it came from a proud and sinful heart.

Was That Thunder?

Plus, just as murder by abortion is extremely heinous due to several aggravations -- so defense against murder is very virtuous due to several argmenters (sic).

If many people are saved, if the gov. forbids it and threatens to punish the defense -- if others are likely to imitate the defense act. All this makes the defense more virtuous in God's eyes.

You speak blasphemously. You claim something as virtuous in God's eyes, which is contrary to the explicit statements of God's revealed will -- and that makes you a false prophet. Furthermore you reveal that you are motivated by a number of strange perspectives -- first, that good results (and who would deny that it is good in itself when even one baby's life is saved) justify evil means. It is a common argument, a good Marxist argument, a fine pragmatist argument, an existentialist argument . . . but not a biblical argument.

Second, it is far from a biblical principle that there is something more virtuous about doing something the government forbids. First of all -- the rulers of America are ours -- we put them there - we "the people". If they are perverted -- it is we, the people's fault. We, the people could impeach any or all of them in a couple months if the people were righteous. Shall we shoot the people? But beyond that, even in an evil dictatorship, there is nothing "more virtuous" about opposing that government.

Finally, raising up imitators is not a legitimate motive and certainly does not make ones acts "more virtuous" even when those acts are in themselves good -- we do all things unto Christ -- we never play to the crowd. Our righteous acts are to be done in secret -- but this is all beside the point, because you have gone off the deep end here in trying to create a cloud of illusions behind which to mask the simple fact of your sin. It isn't a question of "more virtuous," it's a question of sin or not. The Bible has one answer -- you have another. Who is right?

If you persist in your hardness of heart, you will

indeed have a legacy. The most immediate legacy will have to do with your first and foremost stewardship -- of your own life -- a pathetic throwing away of what God gave you. The second legacy will have to do with your second stewardship -- that of your wife and children. You have put a burden on their lives which will affect them deeply for a long time to come. The sins of the fathers come down in many ways. The very best thing you can do for them is repent. If you do not, I cannot prophesy the results, except that they will be so much harder for them than if you had repented.

Will there be imitators? Possibly. But if you think the killing of an abortionist and his bodyguard has kept immoral men from pursuing the very lucrative abortion business, what do you think the effect of your execution will be on Christians? Do you think they will be more likely to pursue an immoral deliberate "martyrdom"? And do you think the day of judgment will not include your accounting for any additional murders that your act causes - by "imitation"?

Paul, I am speaking as directly as I know how. I began this discussion hoping and praying that you were open to biblical persuasion. I now am forced to conclude your heart is hard against the Word of God. I love you more now than when we started writing, but I am no longer able to merely trade arguments. I call you to confess the godless murder of two fellow human beings and to bring forth whatever actions are proper to that repentance.

I continue to pray for you. I would be glad to hear from you, but I will reply in the same vein as this letter. I believe your hard heart is in the way of much that God wants to bring about -- including the end of abortion in America.

Your brother in Christ, Jim Trott

In October 1998, abortionist Barnett Slepian was murdered in his New York home, shot in the shoulder through his kitchen window by an unknown assailant. I got a call from a local radio station that morning, asking for a statement. I tried to make a strong statement against the murder on behalf of pro-lifers, at the same time as I emphasized abortion was also tragic.

Was That Thunder?

About half an hour later the station called back and played my statement back to me. I was horrified to realize that one-too-many parentheses made it susceptible to a darker interpretation – as though there might be some justification for the shooting. In fact, their second call was to ask me if I wanted to modify it. I decided not to, because I felt the right interpretation was the one people would hear. They played only part of it through most of the day, but did use the whole thing a few times that evening. Nevertheless I was reminded once more, as I had found in writing to Paul, one can never be too careful of his words.

Within a month or so the FBI announced it was seeking James Kopp for questioning in connection with the Slepian killing. At that time, not one among us who knew Jim believed for a second that he had been responsible. And when it became apparent he had gone into hiding, we all assumed he was doing so because he was afraid of being framed.

The photo of Jim Kopp circulated by the FBI.[245]

---

[245] Another question mark in the FBI pursuit of Jim Kopp was that the photo they circulated did not look like him – indeed when I saw it, I did not think it was him at all. The same photo was

Furthermore at least one defender published articles quoting other pro-lifers who claimed to be a witnesses to Jim's alibi for the supposed time of purchase of the rifle used.

Paul did not respond to my July letter until the 22nd of December. At that point his reply was most immediately to another short note I had sent him in November, asking permission to publish our correspondence. He responded to my request thusly:

> As to your request to use my letters to you in your book – I am going to decline your request. As you have pointed out to me in your letters to me quoting me – my letters are filled with errors.
> I am talking to you strictly off the top of my head and making no effort to write printable stuff. As you know it is one thing to write sloppy personal letters to someone off the top of your head – it is quite another to write stuff to be published. I assure you my writing that is intended to be published is quite different from what you read here. For this reason I am sure you will understand why I deny permission to print any of my letters to you – I'm sure you will agree – they are pretty bad as letters and are nowhere near in printable form.

---

used on the wanted poster put up in post offices across the country. An article published online offers an explanation.

"The photo is indeed of Kopp, but it is a mug shot taken following a pro-life 'rescue' at which Kopp had been physically assaulted and maced by police. It also shows him without his extremely thick eyeglasses. The question is why the FBI and the media would choose to distribute a photo that looks almost nothing like the person being sought. The FBI had other photos, and on their website they displayed two others that far more accurately depicted Kopp. So if the FBI wanted the public's help in catching him, and the media was truly interested in accuracy, then why did they purposely choose to distribute the one photo that looked nothing at all like him? [Because} . . . it projected an image of Kopp they [the FBI's political bosses and the media] wanted the public to have." (freerepublic.com)

Was That Thunder?

Paul went on to re-hash what I had come to recognize as his mantra on "lethal defense" citing the Westminster standards, the 6th commandment and that it "was sinful to neglect the means necessary for the defense of the innocent (including lethal force)." Once more he claimed Exodus 22:2 as foundational! He asked for my thoughts on all this!

He also explained his lack of response to my July letter:

> The reason I did not respond to your letter of July was it was filled with personal attacks and harshly judging motives. I found out a long time ago that if I start attacking people personally as opposed to objectively trying to expose their sin from God's word – being careful not to judge the heart, they usually are not anxious to continue the discussion. Besides, personal attacks are usually not necessary if one has the truth on his side. If I begin to indulge in such a mindset myself I find that my objectivity is effected [sic]. You declared your intent to continue in this vein and I really don't want a part of it myself Jim. I prefer to treat you with respect – things seem to go much better if I treat people with respect. Your letter of Nov 24 didn't contain any of the personal attacks. Thank you, Jim.

He told me he was still working on his book, but was about ready to start looking for a publisher. And finally, he gave a further explanation for not giving me permission to publish our dialogue:

> Jim, the way I feel about my letters is similar to the way you feel about the manuscript you sent me, except more so. You realize that the manuscript you sent me has errors in it and it was obviously something carefully considered and typed up. My responses to you in my letters were almost all very superficial and I would likely take a very different approach if I were writing to be published. My letters here have been strictly late nite

off the cuff junk not fit to be printed (as I'm sure you would agree.)

I suppose I had grown pretty hardened to rejection by Paul at this point. Nevertheless, in looking back at this letter and postscript I realize it was one more crucifixion, in that it essentially said our correspondence had meant nothing, that he hadn't really given it much thought, that he had never taken it seriously. It was "off the cuff junk" and "sloppy" and "off the top of [his] head." It was particularly ironic in light of his claim to prefer "to treat people with respect." (And the strangest irony of all, "personal attacks are usually not necessary if one has the truth on his side.")

I don't know if there were other things that might have been at work here. I don't think there were still legal processes going on which might have been affected by our dialogue being made public. What I'd read elsewhere gave me the impression he had never cared much about the legal processes, and in fact seemed quite content to let them roll on to his execution with little or no hindrance. Perhaps his own desire to publish made us "rivals" in this.

But I had given myself enough excuses for him. I had given him my prayers, my time, and quite a few of my best brain cells. I wrote no more.

I make no apology about including parts of his "sloppy personal letters" here.[246] A man who shoots two people on principle has no right to say he doesn't want his written statements of those principles put into print! Regardless of what he said in this letter, they were his real thoughts, his real arguments, and honest statements of his "philosophy". Parts of the things Paul was writing (his "book") with other statements of his are available online. They present the same arguments.

It is difficult to talk about this man, whom I think of as a lost friend, even now years later. One of the effects of being part of an urban church is an idolatrous nation is that deep

---

[246] I have included but a fraction of what he wrote and none of his letters in full.

disappointment becomes all too regular a phenomenon – on every hand. The same was often true in the rescue movement. It seems one of the worst forms of suffering comes with finding a comrade has abandoned what you had in common in Christ.

Nonetheless we continue to love and we continue to feel. I have prayed for his family in their peculiar kinds of suffering -- and for other people who shared his delusions regarding God's will in "defense" of the unborn. But his lostness and his loss are mine, like scars that emit a dull pain.

A pro-life prayer vigil – this kind comes out by prayer and fasting

CHAPTER TWELVE -- EASING OFF (1998)

> Thine hands have made me and fashioned me together round about; yet thou dost destroy me. Remember, I beseech thee, that thou hast made me as the clay; and wilt thou bring me into dust again? Hast thou not poured me out as milk and curdled me like cheese? Thou hast clothed me with skin and flesh, and hast fenced me with bones and sinews. Thou hast granted me life and favour, and thy visitation hath preserved my spirit. And these things hast thou hid in thine heart: I know that this is with thee.
> -- Job 10:8-13

January 1998 was the 25th anniversary of Roe. Estimates put the number of babies aborted in the United States by then at about 36 million. Was it Stalin who said one death is a tragedy, but a million deaths is a statistic?

Our Sunday School classes at church included Roseann's update on various dimensions of the pro-life, pro-family battles. I shared my reflections on ten years of involvement. The following week we had several women and men share testimonies about their own abortions and how the Lord had met them with forgiveness. The next week one of our doctors, Chuck Parker, (one of the first men to rescue from our church) led a class on "Birth Control and Abortion."

Abortion and American Idolatry

These days "American Idols" means amateur performers who break through into the big time via a television talent show. But America's idolatry in the more basic sense had come to be one of my preoccupations. So on the last week of our Church's classes, I spoke about "Abortion and American Idolatry." The themes of which had been slowly crystallizing out of a nagging set of questions.

When I first got involved in rescue, I thought we were the first wave of what would become a tsunami of Christian activism, which would in turn bring an end to legalized abortion in fairly short order. But after a while, as we were continually frustrated in recruiting, I realized it wasn't going to happen -- at least not as quickly as we had hoped. There had been barely the smallest hints of a rescue movement for the first ten years after Roe and only a small movement from '83 to '88. Even at its greatest levels of participation ('88 – '92)[247] a tiny percentage of the church was involved. I was increasingly puzzled about the causes of this apathy. Why were American Christians so oblivious to this great evil and so little involved in resisting it?

I was compelled to go back and ask why the same thing had been true with racial slavery. The men who wrote our Constitution "compromised" on racial slavery, and agreed not only to continue slavery, but to count slaves as less than full persons, without any of the rights guaranteed to other people.

As a penultimate cause of the Civil War, the Supreme Court under Chief Justice Taney rejected the Dred Scot case, and confirmed the "non-personhood" of Black slaves in federal law.

Roe had done the same thing for unborn persons. What else did these watershed events have in common? These decisions were made on behalf of "convenience" and "prosperity". A great many Christians had gone along with making convenience and prosperity paramount in both cases – was this chiefly because they had such a share in them?

Among many ramifications of this, I began to look at the Bible and history books in tandem. The real conflict was as old as mankind – the "choice" between God and Baal, between God and Mammon. It was personal pleasure, convenience, fulfillment and prosperity over against holiness. And American history was full of examples of this conflict.

Despite starting with a politically conservative and

---

[247] 40,000 people "risked arrest" said one 1990 publication.

evangelical perspective on American history, my reading of early documents and accounts brought a sea-change. I could not escape the conclusion that the early Indian wars, the Salem witch trials, slavery, jingoism, then sexual "freedom" (immorality), no-fault divorce, and now abortion, were founded on basic idolatries flourishing behind a veneer of Christian values.

Chief Justice Roger Taney of the Dred Scot decision

I had been early struck that women going into abortion clinics had three main motives: personal reputation, personal prosperity, and personal convenience. If the life of most American Christians was centered around these same three idols, what could we say to these women? Our "standing," our bank accounts, and our comfort yoked us unequally to the idolatry around us. We were serving other gods, too.

For the first time, largely through the issues raised through rescue, I was ready to say loud and clear "The unquestioned goals which American evangelicals share are not defensible! They are a mixture of idolatrous and godly values. Since no man can serve two masters, the American church does not represent or honor its titular Lord."

The order of the day was an unprecedented call for the church's repentance. But because we all have been steeped in this plan-A/plan-B spiritual schizophrenia for three hundred years, it is no easy task figuring out what repentance would look like, much less how to do it. All I was or am able to say is we're in it together and need to learn to repent together.

Meanwhile the worldly powers in our nation were and are going in the opposite direction, calling us to give up God and be more single-minded in our dedication to the idols! The media hype in 1998 was the "great hope" offered in "research" suggesting fetal tissue implants might cure Parkinson's disease or Alzheimer's or whatever. [248] Let's see if we can live forever! One more attempt to create heaven on earth, raise up a Tower of Babel, and be like gods – by sacrificing babies.

Partings and Messages

On January 17th, a very good friend who was far outside our church or prolife worlds, Dr. Patricia Van Burgh Alison, died of cancer. She and I had met over, and shared a love for fungi, her academic specialty. My family and I had shared time with her on many occasions over the years. Her obituary was published in the *Inquirer* on that other anniversary, January 22nd. She gave a million dollars to a local art museum, and honored Roseann and me by giving us her kitchenware and books. Among those books were a number of college magazines, one of which contained this poem she wrote during her college days:

---

[248] Yet another argument for abortion – harvesting tissue! Despite the hype, even by 2007, no one had demonstrated any real evidence that fetal stem cells can do this better than stem cells available from other sources.

A Memoir of Pro-life Rescue

Elegy
by Patricia Van Burgh

No words for this one.
No sonnets in tribute.
It was swift,
And bright beyond memory's daring –
And very thorough.
It has no song,
Only a child's small voice wailing
From a darkened staircase somewhere
And echoing. [249]

I already felt much sorrow over Patricia's death, and to read this very personal poem about a "child's small voice wailing" on top of it was doubly hard.

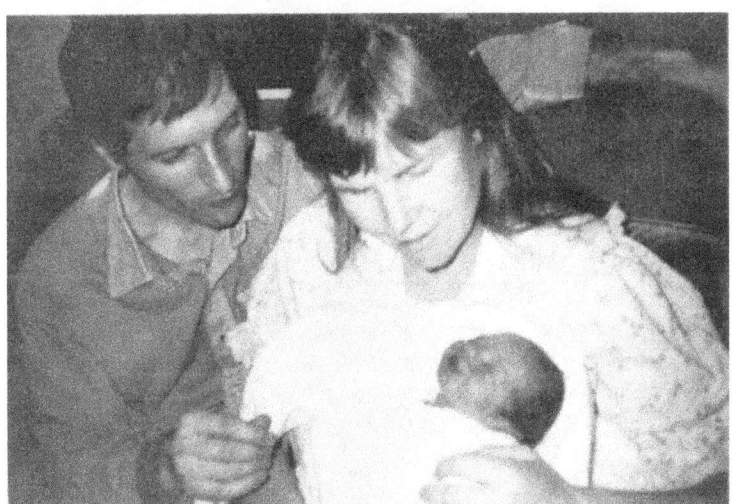

Chris, Joan and baby, Mary, Bell

On the 15th of January, Joan Andrews Bell, went back to jail in Pittsburgh for 3 to 23 months. Judge Novak jailed her again on the basis of the 1985 protest for which she had already spent 2 ½ years in jail, but for which she had failed to

---

[249] In *Gifthorse*, 1948: A Yearbook of Writing, Association of Graduate Students in English, Ohio State U., 1947-8, p. 13.

keep the probation requirements – which is to say she rescued again. True to her principles, Joan went limp in courtroom after sentencing, and was carried out.

This case was entirely about "probation conditions," which Joan had not accepted in the past and would not accept now. After the FBI arrested her in Sep 97, the judge did give her a couple of months to complete the adoption of one of her children before sending her back to jail – perhaps a sop to his own conscience, but also a reminder that children are a blessing.

Also in January, Pennsylvania's Senator Rick Santorum shared the moving story of the birth of son, Gabriel Michael, with a pro-life group, People of Life, in Erie. The child had a fatal abnormality, which meant that he lived only two hours after he was born

Rick Santorum with daughter Bella, born 2008 with a genetic disorder.

The actively pro-life senator shared how he and his wife had dealt with this knowledge beforehand, and how they and the rest of their family gave God thanks for the child, and rejoiced over this brief life.

In February, a federal judge found a handful of Philly

rescuers guilty of violating 'the civil side" of FACE. Meanwhile the FACE suit in which Kimiko and I were named for our part in Englewood rescues went forward. Among many others named were Joan Andrews, Bob Brothers, Tina Krail, and Jim Kopp.

In April 1998 the first Oregon "assisted suicides" were killed under the new law there. It appeared that while some of us were going to live forever supplemented by baby stem cells, we were going to eliminate those whom we didn't fix. As we mentioned the language used in the bill was taken from Casey – postmodern gobbledygook about no one knowing what constitutes life, etcetera.

A Pittsburgh woman was sentenced for "involuntary manslaughter" for killing her child born secretly. She wrapped the child in t-shirts and stuffed it under her bed, the next day putting the bundle in a trash bag and throwing it into a trashbin near the bank where she worked. Another unwanted child was suddenly deemed human by the courts! But why this one, and not the other 35 million?

Then the news was trumpeted through the liberal press that Joe Scheidler,[250] the venerable Chicago pro-life activist leader, with Timothy Murphy and Andrew Scholberg was found guilty by a federal jury on RICO charges.

The court granted $85,962.92 in damages, which was automatically tripled under RICO. Many of us had been named years earlier in this case, but subsequently dropped from it. Nevertheless the Delaware clinic was one of the parties claiming damages – which meant poor old Joe was being held liable for a place he had never seen, so far as I know. A few of our favorite local pro-aborts were witnesses in the case, which involved many aborturaries.[251]

---

[250] I had the blessing of meeting Joe in the early 90's while in Chicago for a pro-life conference.

[251] According to Ed Martin's *American Rescuer*, Randy Terry signed an agreement in order to get out of the 1986 NOW v Schiedler case, the one from which this case originated, to the best of my knowledge. Randy was running for congress in upstate NY and was willing to say he had no plans to engage in any unlawful

Was That Thunder?

Joe Scheidler, faithful Chicago-based leader

Sandy Vito, head of NARAL in Pennsylvania called the verdict "a great victory for women." She said:

> Violence against reproductive health centers continues to be extremely high . . . Here in Philadelphia, I'd have to say clinic blockades aren't as frequent as they once were because of the Rendell administration zero tolerance policy. But this verdict will go even further to discourage such acts.

It was true, Rendell's "zero toleration", plus FACE, plus confusion over violence had pretty much halted rescue.

However, a lot of activist energy was being contributed to political campaigns. The Peg Luksik campaign went forward through 1998, probably with as much sweat

---

activities against abortion clinics or abortion providers for the next 12 years. But by then few of us did!

and enthusiasm as savvy.

In September the "emergency contraceptive" Preven was made available. Despite the Clinton administrations efforts, RU486 was still not available, but this other abortifacient was released on the public, using double-speak that showed something of the progress we were making. Truth in advertising would have indicated a label like "pharmacological abortificient," but "emergency contraceptive" was just a lie. "Contra" means "against" and "ceptive" comes from a word meaning "beginning," as in "conception". A contraceptive prevents conception. But this thing, in much the same way as the third mechanism of the "pill," made sure the "conceptus," that is the child already conceived, did not live.

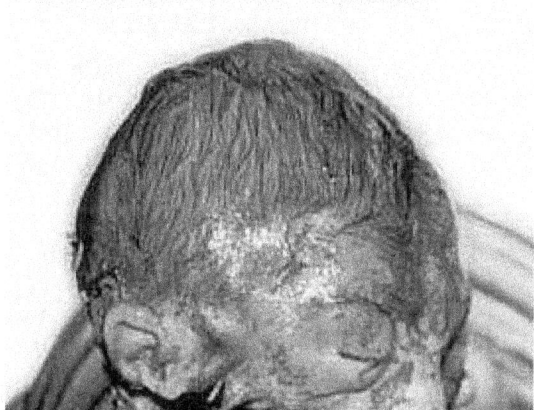

Tell the Truth Tour poster

In October, prolifers took the Tell the Truth Tour posters to a high profile evangelical event, the Promise-Keepers Conference in DC. The signs, many of them

Was That Thunder?

photographs of aborted children, were variously received. "Letting the children tell their own story" is effective.

That same month, as mentioned in the previous chapter, New York abortionist Bernard Slepian was murdered in his home. At first most pro-lifers thought it the work of radical pro-aborts trying to bring further repression on pro-life efforts. Rumors circulated that Dr. Slepian had been on the verge of giving up abortion, and perhaps even ready to oppose it. It was several years before the truth emerged.

Closer to home, a young couple in our church had been going through much the same struggles and spiritual triumphs which Senator Santorum and his wife had faced in the birth of a severely handicapped child. On December 15, Abigail Elizabeth Badorf was born amidst a great deal of prayer. She lived 4 days. A memorial service 16 Jan 2000 gave honor to this small person and to the God in whose image she was made. The whole church pitched in, and we felt honored that the Badorf's shared their daughter with us.

Abigail Badorf - In Memoriam

Abigail Elizabeth
Ordained by the laying on of hands:
The yet to be born by the elders'--
The unseen by the whole visible church --
And secretly while machines declared a tangle,
By Greatest Knitter's hands of all.

Large prayers were answered,
Granting us a working week
Before you went home to prepare for your family,
Leaving us too long to long, and to conclude
Some of the best are women preachers.

Destined for death
Come to die,
Proclaiming Christ
In softest sigh.

A Memoir of Pro-life Rescue

AFTERWORD 1999 – 2007

"To be pro-life is to be enveloped by a desperate, agonizing moment in history. An awareness of injustice grips you, you cannot free yourself and it is suffering. Here was terrible loneliness. I felt alienated from the world, from my culture, my society. I even felt alienated from my own country. Words like "liberty and justice for all" didn't seem real to me. I had a sense of painful separation. I had thrown my lot with an unwanted people – and felt rejected with them. The unborn and I were one in the night of their abandonment. I felt the burden of being aware that a whole segment of the human family was denied their right to live. "   Monica Migliorino Miller, *Abandoned*

Jim Kopp after his extradition from France.

In December 1998, Jim Kopp's car was discovered abandoned at Newark airport. Police were openly seeking him "as a material witness". In April 1999 the FBI discovered the gun which had killed Dr. Slepian buried in the woods near the Slepian home. After May, Jim Kopp was sought, no longer as a material witness, but as a suspect. In June, when they were pretty sure he had fled the country, the FBI placed him on their ten most wanted list, along with another new name, Osama Bin Laden.

Nevertheless at that point most of us who knew Jim did not believe he had done it. We were just paranoid enough ourselves to think him innocent and yet to rationalize his flight. In fact, many felt a sort of grudging admiration for him in being able to evade arrest so long. It later came out he traveled from Mexico to Scotland to Ireland and to France.

Last Thoughts On Violence

On the 7th of February 2000 I was surprised to get another note from Paul Hill, and on seeing the envelope I felt a flutter of hope. He wrote:

> I came across one of your letters today and decided to write. I would like to apologize for my last letter to you Jim. I sort of "went off on you" (to use a jail house term) and was not as respectful as I should have been. Please forgive me for my indiscretions in my last letter to you.
>
> I do appreciate your interest in the issues for which I stand, and your willingness to consider the issues in question. I also appreciate all the thought you have put into this matter, Jim.
>
> You wrote previously that you were committed to writing me as long as I responded. I agree with you that iron sharpens iron, and that if two regenerate men – (especially those who agree on the Westminster Standards) have a disagreement, if they are willing to submissively consider the Scripture together (especially on an issue like this) that the truth should become apparent.
>
> A short piece (about 30 pages) of mine is on the internet. You may want to take a look at it . . . .
>
> All is well here. I continue to work on my writings.

Also I am in the midst of reading John Piper's *Desiring God*, Multnomah books. If you haven't read it yet, you absolutely must drop everything immediately and drive to your nearest store (or order it) to get it. I'm not kidding Jim, this book is a wonderful blessing.

Also, you asked about permission to quote me in your previous letter. If you are really interested in a particular quote send it to me to check over and edit etc. I'm sure you understand my not wanting my sloppy personal letters in print.

Thanks for your fellowship in Christ.

Was our fellowship in Christ? My wife pointed out to me the New Testament tells us that (unrepentant) murderers shall not enter the kingdom. Not abortionists or abortionist-shooters -- unless they repent and seek God's forgiveness. That of course seems to be part of the logic behind the anathema against suicide – through suicide one is nearly certain to die an unrepentant homicide. Nevertheless, I am unable to say Paul was not a Christian, no matter what else I might say about him. And as I do for others standing on doubtful ground, I prayed that he would repent before he faced his Maker and Judge.

I perhaps ought to add that Paul Hill's arguments, while they comprehend most, do not include all of the arguments put forward by advocates for "lethal defense". Mike Bray is quoted as citing that other good Lutheran, Dietrich Bonhoeffer, who in turn apparently relied upon Reinhold Neibuhr's thoughts about the place of force/violence at the extremes of Christian ethics. Bonhoeffer, of course, was executed for his part in a plot to kill Hitler.[252] It's hard to take away the high ground from anyone who gave his life to stop Hitler – but traditional Christian ethics would not attempt a justification for that plot or action in any category but that of just war. Bonhoeffer, as

---

[252] Adam von Trott was also executed for his part in this plot. So far as can be determined, he was not a relative of mine despite sharing the name.

an ally of Hitler's enemies, as a loyal member of a German underground led by "lesser magistrates," as it were, was perhaps justified in using the means of war against the Nazi regime, and that enemy's generalissimo.

Dietrich Bonhoeffer, an ethical challenge.

But to use Bonhoeffer as an ethical model, one must answer a few questions. Are the circumstances analogous? Which is the unjust regime, and which regime is the ally of those who would use this ethic to justify shooting abortionists? In other words, what powers wage this war and what is the nature of the conflict? It's fine to use war as a metaphor for the great divide between pro-abortion and pro-life agendas, but if we are talking about the doctrine of "just war," we must use "war" more precisely, and the current status does not fit the bill.

It's true we've had more than 50 million deaths by abortion and many hundreds of women killed by legal abortion, thousands physically injured, and millions emotionally and spiritually devastated, as demonstrated in suicides and murders by moms and pops known to have been involved in abortion. [253] Nonetheless, the steps to "just war" have not been completed. In *Shattering the Image* [254] I listed them briefly:

   1/War is to be employed only as intervention in the most grievous wrongs,
   2/it is to be a last resort even in these causes,
   3/it ought to be openly declared,
   4/it ought to be declared by and led by magistrates/civil leaders on behalf of the people,
   5/ it ought to be prosecuted expeditiously toward the end of subduing the enemy,
   6/ it ought to involve no unnecessary violence, especially as regards non-combatants and neutrals (no rape, pillage, murder, etcetera). [That category seems to be the result of ethical projections of the rules against murder, etcetera, in normal circumstances. You can only wage war against those who are consciously waging war against you.]
   War is to be prosecuted under the aegis of him who "bears the sword," that is the magistrate. It may have a "vengeance" aspect (dealing with ongoing wrongs) but not primarily a "deterrent" aspect (preventing future wrongs). Since a nation at war is far more ponderous and slow-moving than an individual, a war can scarcely be said to deal with "imminent harm" in the same sense as self-defense or defense of an helpless or innocent person under deadly attack, yet it cannot be waged against either ancient or merely potential wrongs.
   War is akin to capital punishment in that it is the

---

[253] It has always seemed to me more reasonable to link the many other forms of violence in our cities and country with the cheapening of life through abortion than to blame handguns. To paraphrase a current saying, 'Guns don't kill people – people hardened to the killing of people kill people.'

[254] *Shattering the Image* –unpublished manuscript by James H. Trott, 1999. Subtitle: On Human Death : Destruction of the Image of God -- An Exposition and Meditation on Bible Passages Dealing with the Death of Human Beings.

result of prior deliberation or adjudication [by those in authority, magistrates], if you will. It is a response to real evil and an effort to "cleanse" or prevent blood-guilt, but it does not (usually) focus on the death of one person as the goal. Its goal is rather forcing the cessation of some kind of serious transgression or oppression or, to those ends, the overthrow of the regime responsible for it.

Another class of justifications for "lethal defense" arguments is more elusive. Nobody calls it by name, yet if you listen carefully, and seek the sources for the rhetoric, it appears to be Marxist. It's true "the system" and "empowerment," "oppressed" and "liberated," may merely be assimilated terms, but for those motivated by the ideology and "principles" they espouse, the origin of such terms is significant – and in this case Marxist.

Many of the earliest pro-life activists had roots in the civil rights and Vietnam peace movements. The Civil Rights movement was certainly not essentially Marxist [255] but the "revolutionary" rhetoric that characterized some of the late (post-MLK) ideology borrowed deeply from Marxist perspectives.

Similarly, in Latin America especially, adherents of "liberation theology" (chiefly Catholics at first) also borrowed a great deal from Marxist thought. Some elements of the Vietnam peace movement had strong connections to Marxist doctrine, if not among the rank and file, then certainly within the leadership.[256] Central to Marxist/ Leninist/ Maoist thought is the war of the classes, the oppressed against the oppressor and the oppressive "system," resulting eventually in revolution.

For these political ideologies, terrorism is not merely an occasional outcropping, but an important tool. Modern

---

[255] Despite what is said of J. Edgar Hoover's suspicions.

[256] I got to hear Maoist ideologues at first hand in the late '60s as they called the tunes at Harvard during the riots and "student strike" there.

terrorism owes a very great deal to Lenin et al. "Stirring up" or "shaking up" or "breaking up" are seen as necessary preliminaries to revolution and social change. [257]

They caught Jim Kopp in March of 2001 in France though a money order. It turned out the FBI had tapped into an e-mail communication line he and two friends were using. He was extradited in May 2002, after the US agreed not to seek the death penalty against him (a universal French demand in extradition proceedings).

Meanwhile not only had he been indicted for the Slepian murder, but it was rumored Canadian officials suspected him of wounding an abortionist there.

At first Jim's public statements indicated he wanted to come back to the US to clear himself. But in November 2002, in an interview with a Buffalo paper, Jim stated he had indeed killed Dr. Slepian, although his intention had been to wound and not kill him. He said part of his reason for confessing was that he felt bad about all his pro-life friends defending his innocence. The prolifers I knew were shocked. I suppose we shouldn't have been. At least I shouldn't have been. After all I'm supposed to be a Calvinist. Nonetheless I was. I had to face another betrayal by a fellow-rescuer. It was sobering in a different way than my dialogue with Paul Hill. I had only corresponded with Paul after he had gone round the ethical bend, while I had known Jim before.

I had one phone call, from someone purporting to be Jim Kopp, that still mystifies me. It confused me at the time, and I made no record of it, so I'm not even sure exactly when it was, except that I think it was sometime between mid 1997 to late 1998. I say that because I at first thought he was calling about the four Englewood cases, in which we were all grouped together through the FACE charges. Thus he and I were both named in the same defendant list. [258]

---

[257] Several of the convicted abortionist shooters, including Paul Hill, seemed to use this paradigm – the idea they would serve as spark plugs and examples to inspire further acts like their own.

[258] Curiously too, the wanted poster that was eventually hung in US post offices billed his chief crime as a violation of FACE. I doubt that many other FBI "most wanteds" were charged with

Was That Thunder?

I cannot reproduce the phone conversation exactly, but to the best of my recollection it went like this. When the call came through I said "hello" and he said, "Who is this?" "I said this is Jim Trott. Who is this?" And he answered, "This is Jim Kopp. Do you know me?" "Jim! " I said, "How are you? Sure I know you. We met in Atlanta." And then I think he laughed – not a pleasant laugh, but possibly the kind of laugh someone laughs when they just caught someone in – or by -- a deception. To the best of my recollection, whoever it was then hung up without saying anything further.

I was left with the definite feeling that either this was somebody pretending to be Jim Kopp in order to find out if I was in league with him or this was indeed Jim Kopp and he was suspicious of me. If it was he, he sounded like he was pursuing some paranoia or other. He certainly did not sound like the Jim Kopp whom I would have called a friend until then.

What I remember most about him back before anyone thought about shooting abortionists was talking once, perhaps at that big Dobson rally in Washington, or perhaps overnight in a DC jail, and finding out he was a George MacDonald fan, as I am. He told me he had been in Edinborough once, and came upon a book seller with piles of MacDonald novels dirt cheap.[259] He'd bought up a bunch and shipped them back to the states. He had expressed a wistful desire to find a nice Christian girl to marry. Jokingly, he asked me if I didn't know some nice Evangelical girl who was looking for a husband. If I had, from all I knew of him at the time, I might have recommended him to her. [260]

---

unconstitutional crimes! Of course Jim was also charged with murder.

[259] Bob Brothers tells me he has been corresponding with Jim in prison, and that Jim is still a big George MacDonald fan.

[260] Jim Kopp was found guilty on the basis of his confession, and after various appeals regarding the charges and sentencing, he was sentenced to life imprisonment plus 10 years for illegal use of a firearm, on June 20, 2007.

A Memoir of Pro-life Rescue

Roots of Our National Idolatry

The Justice Department had spent considerable effort in trying to get substantial judgments against all of us on the Englewood FACE list. Between our lawyers and the even-handed judge on the case, all their efforts netted them a sum total of $5000 in fines covering all the people and all the "incidents". None of us seemed inclined to pay anything, but some anonymous donor apparently felt differently. Both Kimiko and I, along with twenty or so others, were thus found guilty on the civil side of the FACE bill, although we experienced no repercussions. We were never prosecuted by the local authorities who had kept us in jail in Bergen County.

My Salem witch trial novel.

In late 2001, out of what was at first only a mild interest, I began to do deeper research into the Salem Witch trials. This culminated in my writing a novel centered about Rebecca Nurse, who turns out to have been my ancestress. Somehow this research and writing became a summing up for me. Through it I recognized how deeply early America, and Puritan New England in particular, were rooted in self-serving and materialism – not the pristine Christian faith evangelicals so often like to claim. The good old days weren't so good after all. Our forefathers were often as benighted as their descendants in our times. A Calvinist should know that, too.

I learned that in 1692, as it is now, science was a sacred cow, and that among the three false witnesses of science, superstition, and selfishness, the law of love was suppressed in Salem as it has been so often since throughout our nation. In 2002, I put out a small edition of the novel on my own. Thirteen years later a new revised edition is available online. [261]

From 1999 through 2007, pro-life month at our church became less and less emphasized. Perhaps it was a measure of our success. Most years we still presented the basics during Sunday School a week or two in January. Many from the church continued to teach about their own active ministries: crisis pregnancy counseling, foster care, adoption, ministering to post-abortion people, abstinence education, political awareness, etcetera. My own contributions varied between presenting the abundant biblical data for the humanity of the unborn to speaking against our cultural and political idolatries. In 1999 other classes were run parallel with the pro-life ones.

In 2002, we had no pro-life classes at all, to the best of my memory, but I had the opportunity to address a church in Wilkes-Barre on the subject of our confused commitments as American evangelicals. It was not a sermon, but an excursus – a reflective ramble which others were welcome to join, in hopes we might see a glimmer or two amidst our dilemmas.

The 2003 Sunday class I taught focused on an article from *First Things* magazine in which the authors put together a mega-study of American attitudes toward abortion. The main conclusion they came to was that Americans fall into predictable categories of inconsistency and hypocrisy on the issue. People on both sides of the issue claim certain

---

[261] *A Gallows Set Upon a Hill.* James H. Trott. A new edition available on Createspace, 2015.

"beliefs," but the decisions and actions of most do not appear to be tied to the beliefs claimed.

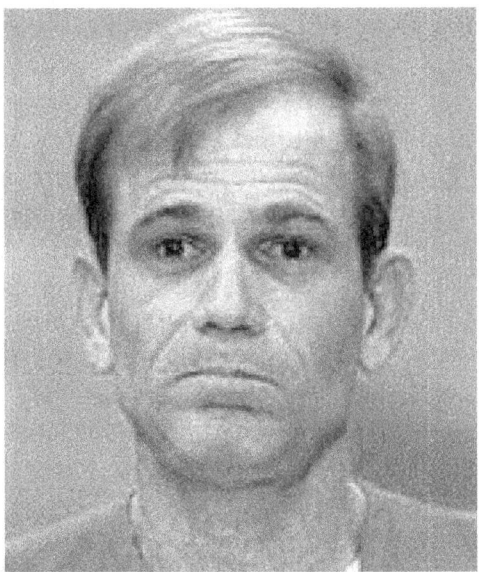

Paul Hill on Death Row.

On the 3rd of September 2003, Paul Hill was put to death by lethal injection. It was another nexus of sorrow.

Nonetheless, a few of his stalwart defenders were still saying things like "…I believe that when abortion is outlawed, as it surely will be, future generations will view Paul Hill as the sanest and bravest man of our age." Philadelphia rescuers, on the other hand, were united in rejecting the arguments for violence and Paul's violent actions.

In January 2004 I spoke to our Sunday School on group responsibility, making special reference to the Salem trials, abortion, and our 300 years of idolatry. Despite the worship of individualism in our nation, we are up against the fact that God deals with groups. Not only blessing, but judgment comes on groups. Groups are held responsible. Presbyterians of all people should know this – but we don't. We can say the words "covenant relationship," with hardly a notion of what that means. Groups can begin to export righteousness only when they are humbled before their God in their own hearts and homes. As long as babies are dying in America, we have little basis upon which to call the world to account. Nor have we any right to fine-tune things like the environment as long as we coldly murder our children.

In 2005, if I recall, one of our well-meaning staff accidentally got a Sunday School speaker whose chief message seemed to be that prolifers were hypocrites. I would be willing to agree, but am inclined to believe they are less hypocritical than most Christians, who I hope are less hypocritical than most people. On the other hand, my father-in-law used to answer people who said the church was full of hypocrites like this, "There's always room for one more!" But seriously, one might cogently argue that all policemen and soldiers are hypocrites, but would we argue they ought to quit doing their jobs for that reason? Rather lets see if we can get rid of our hypocrisy!

Also in 2005, a federal district judge in Texas ruled the FACE Bill was unconstitutional, but a 5th Circuit Appeals court soon reversed this. I wrote Kimiko, who was working with a Christian mission to Southeast Asians in London, to inform her we had joined the elite number of those convicted of crimes under unconstitutional laws. But the Supreme Court seems to have continued unwilling to review the constitutionality of this bill of attainder.

In 2006, we had no adult prolife Sunday School classes. It sometimes looks like the inclination toward a "seamless garment" pro-life agenda in many of our churches will diminish concern about abortion. A "pro-life" position which makes preserving the ecology and getting decent wages for third world workers equal in importance to stopping abortion seems to me based on a false equation, since abortion is murder. Those other issues may involve issues of stewardship, justice, and repentance, but murder will always be of greater weight. As long as the American church tolerates abortion, which means for instance voting for politicians who favor it, God's judgment will hang over us.

Where the greater injustice is tolerated, no efforts to redress lesser injustices will be rewarded. I am personally opposed to our involvement in foreign wars only in this: that

I can find no biblical reason to believe God will reward a nation that tolerates the unrighteousness of abortion in efforts to establish righteousness elsewhere.

Among Philadelphia's best known Protestants is Tony Campolo, once briefly in the national press as a spiritual adviser to President Clinton. Tony loved to claim that he holds basic evangelical Christian positions on homosexuality and abortion.[262] However, he usually went on to argue that such perspectives are old-fashioned and not exclusive of the opposite positions! A dynamic speaker, he seems to me to be chiefly in love with the sound of his own voice. One of my worst fears is that more and more evangelicals are losing their ability to simply read and reason from the Bible. Tony epitomizes for me what a post-modern church could end up looking like. Salt with absolutely no taste. And many similar voices sound forth from what passes for Christian academia.

The inability of Christian teachers and leaders to foresee and prepare for the crises of our nation and church is so outstanding as to appear the rule rather than the exception. The responses of Massachusetts Bay colony to Baptists and Quakers, the Indian wars, the equivocation which allowed the Salem Witch trials to drag on fatally for nearly a year, the slave trade, institutionalized racial prejudice and Roe v. Wade were all major failures of the church to seek God's face in the midst of major spiritual battles. It's easy for the non-Christian or anti-Christian to explain these things, but what are Christians to say?

Complacency

In my experience amidst the abortion rescue movement, I saw this same "syndrome," this same failure to humbly and earnestly seek God's face. This took place:
1) in the inability of the church (particularly the Protestant church) to address the issue biblically in the years

---

[262] This year, 2015, Tony has finally admitted publically his true position on homosexual practise – that it is not sin after all!

leading up to (1967-1971) and immediately following Roe (1971-78);

2) in the inability of contemporary church leaders to understand or even listen to biblical arguments for "rescue" (usually "civil disobedience" or "law-breaking" were the foremost issues in their minds);

3) in the inability of the pro-life rescue community to adequately understand the "force" issue in terms of the Bible, the whole counsel of God; and

4) more recently, in the waffling of the evangelical church in losing track of the centrality of abortion in the political battle. In all four cases the failures were very serious in their consequences, and certainly retarded the awakening of the American church to God's condemnation of abortion. Our repentance could conceivably have come before Roe, and even before legal abortions were allowed in a few states (Colorado, Oregon, North Carolina).

The church could have turned out en masse in front of the clinics at least by 1988, with the national emergence of Operation Rescue. Biblically founded leadership could have completely discouraged violence among prolifers well before the first abortionist was shot. And we could have been more consistent in campaigning for and electing pro-life executives, legislators and judges before and after Roe v. Wade. As all but the biggest dullards know, the judicial appointments made by elected pro-aborts have continued to perpetuate this fundamental violation of basic God-given rights.

It is amazing God can be so patient with us. It is remarkable that he grants repentance to a people who are so complacent.

Indeed complacency is the underlying reason we do not go hungrily to the scriptures and feed there until our hearts and minds are conformed to Christ.

Complacency is the reason our thoughts and actions do not grow out of meditating on what God has said and done.

It's the reason we are content to pursue the Great American Dream rather than the Great Christian Hope.

Complacency is the reason we tolerate the extreme

injustice called abortion-on-demand.

The Idolatry of Prosperity

De Tocqueville said of America in the early 1800s, that its chief preoccupation was prosperity. He saw this in churches as well as outside them – in fact the sermons he heard seemed to him to be as much about prospering as about spiritual matters.

> Not only do Americans practice their religion out of self-interest, but they often even place in this world the interest which they have in practicing it. Priests in the Middle Ages spoke of nothing but the other life; they hardly took any trouble to prove that a sincere Christian might be happy here below.
> But preachers in America are continually coming down to earth. Indeed they find it difficult to take their eyes off it. The better to touch their hearers, they are forever pointing out how religious beliefs favor freedom and public order, and it is often difficult to be sure when listening to them whether the main object of religion is to procure eternal felicity in the next world or prosperity in this. [263]

The more things change the more they stay the same. The "prosperity movement" that has preoccupied much of the American evangelical church for decades is not new. In some ways it is only a more honest statement of what American Christians have always believed. "Name it and claim it" may be a relatively new motto, but it an old idea.

De Tocqueville also said Americans would never have great art, nor would we ever have our best men for our leaders. In both cases, he saw these as results of the universal preoccupation with prospering. But he did not realize our nation could not sustain even a semblance of obedience to a

---

[263] De Tocqueville, *Democracy in America*, pp. 529-30.

Holy God because of the same preoccupation.

Christians in the 1970's who heard from a few prophets that Roe was a terrible and destructive attack on God's law were shocked – not at Roe, but at the suggestion such a thing could happen right under our superior American noses.

The negative reaction of many Christian leaders who were invited to participate in or encourage rescue, was the same sort of shock – that anyone could suggest we missed the boat so badly that "lawbreaking" might be legitimate in "the land of the free". [264]

The unwillingness of key people in the rescue movement to do the hard work of applying the scriptures to the issues of violence against abortionists, was also born out of shock – at the suggestion that their "hearts," their "gut reactions" and those of their friends could be entirely wrong. Complacency is just another name for original sin, for pride. Were it not for that complacency, the church would have mobilized at all three crisis points, and come away re-united in humble submission to God's will.

No Ears to Hear

For all the lofty claims of "sola scriptura" among Protestants and Reformed Protestants in particular, there is very little love or respect for the Bible among us. [265] We do not really believe the Bible has the answers for life's dilemmas. Like Dostoevsky's "Grand Inquisitor," we see

---

[264] How thoroughly tired I am of hearing Christians say or pray that they are so thankful to be living in free nation or in a nation where they may practice their religion freely. What are we saying or praying! Can we call ourselves free when so many innocent are dying? Not to mention the increasing restrictions place on the "practice" of our religion and expressions of our faith and morals in public arenas, etc..

[265] Nationally prominent Catholic politicians seem to think American Catholics are not any better at submitting to their professed authorities.

God failing at his job and substitute our own better ideas about how to do it right. Professional "pastors" include many who fit into two broad groups – falling off a proper balance on one side or the other.

First there are those who have so little exposure to real people in their need that they think of the Bible as a by-the-numbers "rule book." For example a well-known and much respected pastor in our area preached and wrote his way through the Book of Romans during the rescue era. When he came to Romans 13, he stated unequivocally that this chapter required Christians to submit to those in authority on all occasions. He essentially treated this derivative and much-qualified instruction as though it were among the Ten Commandments.

No serious biblical-theological study should ever end with this conclusion, but having little pastoral involvement with those who wrestle with this issue, he was more inclined to find rules than seek wisdom for life's hard decisions in scripture. It's a shame the third world church, through its more difficult experience, should know so much more on this subject than an highly educated American churchman.

The other kind of pastor is often a man who starts out "evangelical" and full of official respect for the Bible, but through intensive pastoral involvement, gradually lets "compassion" erode that respect. The Bible seems to have too many corners to fit in the rounded holes of life. Soon unchecked compassion is liable to make us into antinomians and relativists. Thus some "evangelical" and "reformed" pastors would not teach against abortion in their churches, and rumors abounded of ministers or their wives who actually encouraged parishioners to seek abortions!

Neither the rule-seeker or the relativist truly believes God speaks through his word. The coming of the kingdom isn't the central business they are about. They, too, are preoccupied with "other" things. Is it any wonder that the leadership of the rescue movement seldom came from pastors and church leaders?

Was That Thunder?

The Privilege of Participation

I remember reading an interview with Malcolm Muggeridge many years ago, not too long after he was inspired by Mother Teresa. In it he said he had come to have very little expectation for our age – that we seemed to stand among the ruins of a culture. But at the same time he said he was more hopeful than ever – only his hope was not founded in this world.

In a similar way, I feel the years "lost" in rescue were of infinite gain insofar as gaining insight. I feel I see a bleaker picture much more accurately, and am forced by that vision to found my hope more thoroughly in Christ. I feel privileged to have had a small part in events through which lives were saved and lives were changed.

In her interview with Bridgehead Radio[266], Cheryl Conrad of California said,

> Rescue changes people – I didn't know what Christianity really meant until I was involved in rescue. I did the church stuff, but when you have to live it out it changes who you are -- it's not about me and my life and a nice home and having those goals, but living for Christ.

And Jeff White added:

> ...The core was repentance – God forgive me, abortion exists because I participate, I ignore, I do nothing to oppose it – so have mercy on me. Second aspect of it was obedience – if you believe its murder ...that required an action. It's difficult today – we were privileged – there was a straight forward way to do something It was a blessing because it was so clear-cut. It's much easier to die for Christ than to live for Christ. Much more difficult to live day after in obedience to

---

[266] A history of rescue in five parts, Bridgehead Radio with Jonathan Vanmaren of Canada, 2015. See Youtube.

God day after day.

People now want to have a conversation – want to talk to evil. That's not how it's overcome. The challenge is how to convince young people that we are not supposed to be friends of the world. The biggest problem today with the prolife movement is that they want to be liked.[267]

But abortion is still legal. Immorality rages and rules. Euthanasia has become "legal" and the efforts will increase to spread it. The Supreme Court of the United States has stated that homosexual marriage is legitimate. The murder rate rises in Philadelphia and the nation and the politicians blame it not on the commonplace cheapening of life through abortion and euthanasia, but on unlicensed handguns!

As long as babies are being killed how can we speak of having gained anything? God have mercy. Christ have mercy. God have mercy on us.

After debating various alternatives with the help of my family, I chose my ambiguous title[268] because God has not revealed the end of the storm – the end of the story – that is, he has not revealed to us the outcome of American or world history. Perhaps we are indeed Sodom and Gomorrah, or "Babylon the Great," as so many other nations have begun to call us. If so, our persistence in aborting babies will be the loudest charge brought against us. Or perhaps we are Ninevah – and will turn in repentance at the eleventh hour. What would such a national repentance look like? The rumblings of God's judgment are ominous, but we cannot interpret them fully.

However He has made many things clear – that there is real forgiveness in Christ for those who repent – that there is real eternal life and eternal death beyond this life – and that he will bring about justice in his final judgment. Those of us who have heard the thunder know we must ourselves repent and we must then act in faith and love. I learned to do those

---

[267] Bridgehead Radio interviews
[268] Revelations 11:4 – see title page.

things during my blessed years as a rescuer. As Joe Wall said, it was a gift and privilege to have done the right thing on a few occasions -- and to have known it for sure.

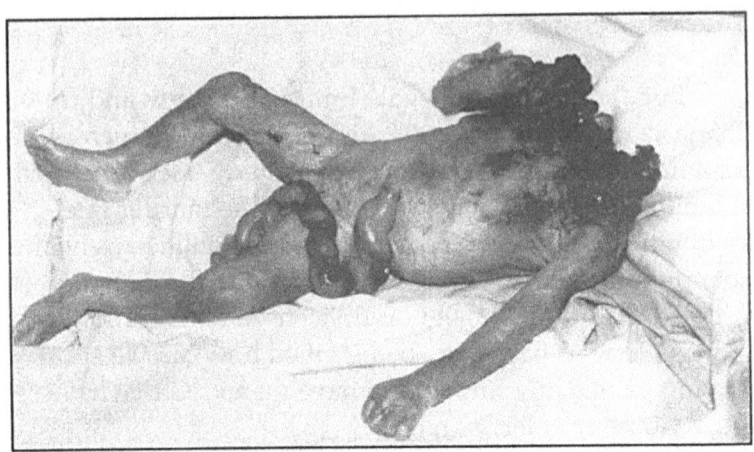

Baby David, one of the children
tortured and murdered by "legal" abortion[269]

---

[269] Baby David was aborted at 28 weeks at a clinic. The 16-inch pre-born child underwent a D&E abortion, during which his head and arm were ripped off his body. Pro-life activists retrieved his body from the abortion clinic and photographed the child, but when photo developers and police saw the pictures, they believed a terrible crime had been committed, and searched the activists' home until they discovered the truth. – Priests for Life website.

A Memoir of Pro-life Rescue

APPRECIATIONS

All of the errors in this memoir are my own. Each human being has peculiar abilities and weaknesses. I think different people remember different kinds of things in different modes and with varying degrees of accuracy. On several occasions I have discovered my imagination is far too good for me to claim a perfect memory. As early as junior high school I could distinctly remember details of events that did not happen, or were transposed. Alas, I know this because other witnesses spoke to the contrary.

My shorthand excuse is that my imagination cannot stand blanks, and so it fills up the gaps in memory. I think I have a very good memory for some things, however. I hold onto faces very well and I also have a geographical memory, which is to say I can remember things in terms of their settings. However several events in the same place are easily mixed for me. And similar places sometimes slide together, too.

My mind includes a great lumber room full of impressions. These are not movies or even photo albums, but rather dog-eared notebooks, snapshots and scraps with a few lines jotted on them. They are records of mood and atmosphere, color and tone. And the archival librarian is dozing more and more.

These are some of the reasons I have needed other people to help me avoid writing fiction instead of a memoir. My wife Roseann is the chief auxiliary memory. We compliment one another's amnesia in most important areas. My children have also contributed. Kimiko and Joshua went beyond the call of duty in reviewing and giving me the benefit of their skills.

For stirring up details of the rescue years, old letters and reports from Mike McMonigal, Joe Roach, Jack O'Brien, Bob Lewis, Patty McNamara, and others in the Philadelphia rescue community have been invaluable. These people served as unforgettable examples of servant leadership, and my debt to them is very deep and goes far beyond mere recollection.

Andy Burnett, early rescuer and editor
of the Oregon-based *Life Advocate*

In addition to these my memory has been jogged by printed letters, leaflets and videos from Operation Rescue and Operation Rescue National, Randy Terry, Joe Foreman, Keith Tucci, Art Tomlinson, and others. I have referred to various pro-life publications: *Voices of the Unborn, The Rescuer, The American Rescuer, The Boston Rescuer, The Missionary, Action News, Life Lines, Crossing Over, Pro-Life Action News, The Advocate/ Life Advocate*, and to publications of Prisoners of Christ, Watchmen on the Walls, Advocates for Life, National Right to Life and many smaller and local organizations. Ed Martin's newsletter has always been an inspiration. Denny Green's and Steve Osborne's ministry newsletters and emails have been an encouragement.

The people who corresponded with me in the "colloquium" seeking biblical answers to the questions about "use of force" widened my perspective and spurred me to examine scriptures I thought I understood more carefully. In the same way, many people in our own church blessed me by asking questions and challenging my complacency as I taught pro-life classes.

I could not possibly name all these here. I think in the pro-life movement as in most things, the unsung heroes are the greatest heroes. I used to say that the single moms were the biggest heroines. I still say they are heroines – along with other moms and also dads who take responsibility. Beyond them there are huge numbers of heroes and heroines doing sidewalk counseling, crisis pregnancy counseling, foster care, adoption, and the drudgery of political work.

Chuck Depoy, Sue Laurito, Joy Fesi, Don Ranck, Bill and Nancy Devlin, Chuck Parker, Stanley Kalbach, Jill Paige, Jody Wilson, Dotty Free, Penny Freeman, George and Tina Krail, and, later, Betty Jean Wolfe are some of the church friends who an objective observer would say did much to bless my personal pro-life labors – because these, along with many others, labored ahead of or beside me.

One of the things that strikes the would-be memoir-writer is that there are many stories that cannot be told, even dimensions of our lives that are too delicate to be told or told more fully. There can be no complete account short of heaven.

Manuscript readers who contributed important kinds off insights, both of the "good news" and "bad news" variety in addition to my son and daughter were: cousin Jay Alan Trott, daughter-in-law Sarah Griffin Trott, sister Laurie Bumgarner, fellow rescuers Bob Brothers and and Joe Wall. These last two contributed each his respective expertise – Bob helped particularly with some copy editing and his suggestion of more use of photographs.

Again I come back to Roseann who has given the most, not only as I have worked on this manuscript, but during those many years and jail-widow nights, when she gave me freedom to stretch our resources beyond what I had any right to expect. She has often been Christ's vicar to me.

After that the list of those who have contributed becomes not twenty more people, but two hundred more, and then I would still be grossly unfair to many . But to all of you, thanks, and as you have often said to me:

Was That Thunder?

Roseann, my wife and backbone

Remember the babies.

                                                            Jim Trott
                                                            Philadelphia
                                                            Thanksgiving 2015

BIBLIOGRAPHY
(Alphabetical by author)

Reflection - "Bright, Shining Moments" by Joe Wall. Taken from *Voices of the Unborn*, Philadelphia, PA. August 1999.

****

"Brother Andrew" (Andrew van der Bijl) *The Ethics of Smuggling*, 1974.

"Brother Andrew". *God's Smuggler*, with John and Elizabeth Sherrill, 1964.

Alcorn, Randy. *Christians in the Wake of the Sexual Revolution Recovering our Sexual Sanity*. Multnomah Press, 1985.

Alcorn, Randy. *Does the Birth Control Pill Cause Abortions?* Eternal Perspective Ministries, 1997.

Alcorn, Randy. *Is Rescuing Right: Breaking the Law to Save the Unborn*. Downers Grove, Illinois, InterVarsity Press, 1990.

Alcorn, Randy. *ProLife Answers to ProChoice Arguments*. Multnomah Press, 1992.

Alcorn, Randy. *Why Pro-Life?: Caring for the Unborn and Their Mothers*. Eternal Perspective Ministries, 2004.

Allen, William B., chairman of the U. S. Commission on Civil Rights. *Wall Street Journal* article on violence against rescuers. 18 August 1989.

Andrews, Joan, with Richard Cowden Guido. *You Reject Them, You Reject Me*. American Life League, 1988. (and other editions)

Barkun, Michael. *Millennialism and Violence*. Cass Series on Political Violence. Frank Cass, London, England; Portland, Oregon. First published 1996, Frank Cass & Co, Ltd, Oxford, Great Britain, and Frank Cass, New York, NY. Transferred to Digital Printing 2005.

Beckwith, Francis J. *Defending Life: A Moral and Legal Case Against Abortion Choice*. Cambridge University Press, 2007.

Boldt, David. *Philadelphia Inquirer*, 18 July 1993, commentary, "The Dirty Business of Abortion".

Calvin, John. *Institutes of the Christian Religion*.

Dabner Jack Duane, director. *The Silent Scream* video. Narrated by Bernard Nathanson. (with early ultrasound). 1984. Donald S.

Was That Thunder?

Smith. Brunswick, OH: American Portrait Films. SEE: www.silentscream.org/video1.htm

De Tocqueville, Alexis. *Democracy in America,* 1835-40. (Based on his 1831 trip to America)

Demark, Michael A., Director. *Operation Rescue – Documenting the Pro-life Movement,* video. Copyright 1989, Operation Rescue Incorporated. Producer: Christopher D. Rogers, Gary Leber: Project Coordinator, Consultant: Eric Holmberg. Produced by CDR Communications, Inc.

Dostoevsky, Fyodor. "The Grand Inquisitor," Book Five, Chapter Five, in *Brothers Karamazov.*

Foreman, Joseph Lapsley. *Shattering the Darkness: The Crisis of the Cross in the Church Today.* Cooling Spring Press, 1992.

George, Robert P. and Christopher Tollefsen. *Embryo: A Defense of Human Life.* Doubleday, 2008.

Grant, George with Alan Keyes. *Our Character, Our Future: Reclaiming America's Moral Destiny*, 1996.

Grant, George with Mark Horn. *Legislating Immorality: The Homosexual Movement Comes Out of the Closet*, 1993.

Grant, George. *Grand Illusions: The Legacy of Planned Parenthood.* 1988, '93, '98, 2000.

Grant, George. *Killer Angel: A Biography of Margaret Sanger.* 1995, 2000, 2010.

Grant, George. *The Legacy of Planned Parenthood.* 1989.

Grant, George. *The Quick and the Dead: RU-486 and the New Chemical Warfare Against Your Family,* 1991.

Grant, George. *Third Time Around: History of the Pro-Life Movement from the First Century to Present.* 1990, 2010.

Grant, George. *Immaculate Deception: The Shifting Agenda of Planned Parenthood.* 1996.

Grant, George. *The Family Under Siege: What the New Social Engineers Have in Mind for Your Children.* 1994.

Green, Melody. *Why I Got Arrested in Atlanta.* (tract) Last Days Ministries, 1988.

Greenway, Roger. "I Saw My Students Arrested". *Presbyterian*

Journal, 26 Dec 1984.

Hill, Paul, interview. September 2003. *Life Dynamics.* Youtube.

Hill, Paul. *Freedom From Abortion: Proclaiming the Duty to Defend Life.* (Projected publication) Publication data unknown.

Holmberg, Eric. *Brutal Truth* , video. American Portrait Films, 1989.

Holmberg, Eric. *God's Law and Society*, video. With study guides. Includes 16 speakers (George Grant, Rousas Ruchdooney, Gary DeMar, R.C. Sproul, Jr., Randy Terry, Doug Wilson, etc.) American Portrait Films, 2009.

Holmberg, Eric with Greg Cunningham. *The Hard Truth* video. American Portrait Films. June 9, 1991. Available on Youtube.

Holmberg, Eric, Director. *Massacre of Innocence,* video. American Portrait Films, July 9, 1988.

Kasun, Jacqueline. *The War Against Population.* Ignatius Press, 1988.

Kerouac, Jack. *The Town and The City,* 1950. *Dharma Bums,* 1958. *On the Road,* 1957.

King, Martin Luther, Jr., *Letter from the Birmingham Jail.* Open letter written 16 April 1963.

Krauthammer, Charles. *Philadelphia Inquirer* opinion, March 1997. Article on Partial Birth Abortions.

Lawler, Philip F. *Operation Rescue: A Challenge to the Nation's Conscience.* Our Sunday Visitor Books. Huntington, Indiana, 1992.

Leo, John. *US News and World Report* article on police violence against rescuers in East Hartford. 6 August 1990.

Miller, Monica Migliorino. *Abandoned : The Untold Story of the Abortion Wars.* Saint Benedict Press, Charlotte, NC, 2012.

Padawer, Ruth . "The facts on partial-birth abortion: Both sides have misled the public". *Bergen County Record*, September, 1996.

Percy, Walker. *Lost In the Cosmos: The Last Self-Help Book.* Farrar Straus & Giroux, 1983.

Piper, John. *Desiring God.* 1986. Multnomah edition, 2011.

Prontnicki, Louis. *Brief History of The Beginning of the Pro-Life Movement Among Evangelicals in the Philadelphia Area: The Start of the Urban Family Council/The Philadelphia Christian Action Council.* Four page typescript, May 2008.

Rathburn, Bruce. "A Weekend Witnessing in Jail". *Presbyterian Journal* , 24 Apr 1985.

Roach, Joseph. *Rescuing During the Cultural War.* 2001.

Santorum, Rick, with Karen Santorum and Elizabeth Santorum. *Bella's Gift: How One Little Girl Transformed Our Family And Inspired A Nation.* Thomas Nelson, 2015.

Schaeffer, Francis, Sr. and C. Everett Koop. *Whatever Happened to the Human Race?* film series, 1979,. Also book by same title, Good News/Crossways, 1983.

Scheidler, Joseph M. *Closed: 99 Ways to Stop Abortion.* Pro-Life Action League, 1985. (Updated edition 1993)

Solzhenitsyn, Aleksander. *Gulag Archipelago, 1973.*

Solzhenitsyn, Aleksander. *In The First Circle,* 2009 (First truncated version, *The First Circle,* published in 1968)

Solzhenitsyn, Aleksandr. *From Under the Rubble,* Collins and Harvill Press, London 1975.

Stowell, Joseph M. *Perilous Pursuits: Overcoming Our Obsession with Significance.*, 1994.

Ten Boom, Corrie, with John and Elizabeth Sherrill. *The Hiding Place,* 1971.

Terry, Randall. *Accessory to Murder: the Enemies, Allies and Accomplices to the Death of Our Culture.* Brentwood, Tennessee: Wolgemuth & Hyatt, 1990.

Tolkien, J.R.R. *Lord of the Rings, 1954-55.*

Trott, James Howard. *Prisoners' Pardons,* 1992, 1993, 1998. Republished, see *Conceptions and images.*

Trott, James H. *Shattering the Image* – unpublished manuscript. Subtitle: On Human Death : Destruction of the Image of God -- An Exposition and Meditation on Bible Passages Dealing with the Death of Human Beings. 1999.

Trott, James H., editor. *A Sacrifice of Praise: Christian Poetry in English from Caedmon to the mid-Twentieth Century,* Nashville, Cumberland House, 2nd edition, 2006.

Trott, James Howard. *Conceptions and images: Pro-life poems with Prisoners' Pardons, revised.* Oak and Yew Press 2015. Available online at Createspace ebookstore.

Trott, James Howard. *A Gallows Set Upon a Hill : An Historical Novel*, 2015 edition available online at Createspace, ebookstore.

Van Maren, Jonathon, host. *The Bridgehead Radio*, Interviews, A five part series, "The Rescue Movement". . . May 1, 2015. See Youtube.

Vernon, Bob. *Peacemaker in Blue*, 1977.

Verny, Thomas, MD, with John Kelly. *The Secret Life of the Unborn Child*. Dell Publishing, 1982.

Wall, Joe. "A Brief History of Rescue", unpublished typescript.

Weddington, Sarah and Ron. (Co-counsels in Roe v. Wade). *A Question of Choice*, 1992.

Williams, Daniel K. *Defenders of the Unborn: The Pro-life Movement Before Roe v. Wade*. Slated for publication in 2016 by Oxford University Press. Author Associate Professor of History at the University of West Georgia. He is also author of *God's Own Party: The Making of the Christian Right*.

Wills, George. Article on LAPD's violence, *Philadelphia Inquirer*, 14 March 1991.

Was That Thunder?

SOURCES OF PHOTOS & ILLUSTRATIONS

An effort has been made to properly attribute photographs used, including licensing those from commercial sources and listing attributions for each.

In cases where no source could be found, the photos are listed "**UCH/CCL/PD**", which means "unknown copyright holder/ possibly under Creative Commons license/ or in the Public Domain." Copyright should be assumed.

Mary and Charles Gindhart

By far the chief contributor of photographs here has been **Charles Gindhart**. To him and his wife Mary I can only express extreme gratitude. His faithful visual records of Philadelphia rescue are of tremendous value. Other local photographers of note were Charles Maffei and Bob Brothers.

Other important sources of photos were videos, most of them made by or in association with Eric Holmberg and American Portrait Studios, including the *Operation Rescue* video, *The*

A Memoir of Pro-life Rescue

Hard Truth and **The Brutal Truth**. Other stills were captured from Bernard Nathanson's **The Silent Scream,** and from Charles Gindhart's rescue videos.

The photos are listed here by abbreviated captions, except for a few portraits, for which context supplies the name.

PHOTO CAPTION	SOURCE	PAGE
Joe Wall Bob Brothers	Prefatory Meditation	no p. #
Jack and Rosemarie Miller	John Tolsma	page 2
James... and Lucille...Trott	J. E. Trott	5
Striking students... Harvard	UCH/CCL/PD	7
...Japan after Kimiko's birth	Roseann Trott	9
Rescue... Blackwell...4/1991	Charles Gindhart	11
...Graven...palms of my hands	J. H. Trott	16
Rabbi Yehuda Levin ...	OR video	18
John Cavanaugh O'Keefe	UCH/CCL/PD	22
My friend, Stanley Kalbach...	J. H. Trott	24
A "youthful" Randy Terry...	OR video	26
Joan Andrews, an inspiration...	Charles Gindhart	27
Randy... 1st New York Rescue	UCH/CCL/PD	28
Adele Nathanson	OR video	31
Nellie Gray	OR video	32
Doug Nagy (with beard)...	Charles Gindhart	34
Tredyferin Township officer...	OR video	36
Faithful rescuers...in rain...	Charles Gindhart	39
...Chuck Depoy...Joy Fesi	OR video	40
Brother Andrew... law-breaker	UCH/CCL/PD	42
Corrie ten Boom... law-breaker	UCH/CCL/PD	43
Aleksandr Solzhenitsyn... prophet	UCH/CCL/PD	46
Chuck Parker and... daughter	Michelle Parker	47
Mayor Andrew Young...	UCH/CCL/PD	49
Joseph Foreman	OR video	52
Chet Gallagher... dedicated...	Life Advocate	56
Dr. MLK, Jr. arrested...	UCH/CCL/PD	58
Bishop Austin Vaughan	OR video	59
Susan Odom	OR video	61

Was That Thunder?

Pain compliance... Atlanta...	Brutal Truth video	63
"Atlanta crawl"... --like babies	UCH/CCL/PD	65
Major Burnette, ...Baptist deacon.	UCH/CCL	66
Glen Kaiser of Jesus People...	Cornerstone	70
Melody Green...well-known...jailed...	OR video	71
...Source..."Maxwell Smart" line	UCH/CCL/PD	73
Joe Foreman, self-sacrificing...	UCH/CCL/PD	76
Civil rights... Hosea Williams	UCH/CCL/PD	78
Hosea Williams... MLK... Selma	UCH/CCL/PD	79
George Krail, former biker...	Charles Gindhart	81
Pat Mahoney...	UCH/CCL/PD	87
Father Norman Weslin	Life Advocate	89
Joan Andrews	OR video	92
Rescue...Crozer-Chester...MLK...	Charles Gindhart	93
Howard Walton...	Charles Gindhart	97
Patricia McNamara...	Charles Gindhart	98
Maryann... wheelchair...	Charles Gindhart	99
Brian Woznicki...on wheels	Charles Gindhart	100
Jack Klotz... pro-football player...	Charles Gindhart	101
Anita Brothers... steadfast helpmeet	Bob Brothers	102
Nat Hentoff...novelist...writer...	UCH/CCL/P	106
Michael McMonagal... spelled wrong...	OR video	109
Rev. Daniel J. Little	OR video	110
Rev. Jesse Lee	OR video	110
Chuck Depoy... early rescuer...	UCH/CCL/PD	112
One... innocent...abortion killed	UCH/CCL/PD	114
...Civil Rights leaders in Selma...	UCH/CCL/PD	118
"Baby Face" – Would this child...	Hard Truth video	119
...Young people... prayer vigil	Charles Gindhart	121
Brenda Caley and Susan Odom...	Charles Gindhart	122
Jim Caley... pro-life activist	Charles Gindhart	123
Joe O'Hara's baby model...	Charles Gindhart	125
John Stanton...	Charles Gindhart	127
Pat Stanton...influenced...	Charles Gindhart	129
Margaret Sanger, eugenicist...	UCH/CCL/PD	130
Arrested..."bad weather" rescue...	Charles Gindhart	131
...Pittsburgh... holding baby model	Charles Gindhart	136
...Fairly accurate baby model	UCH/CCL/PD	137
Young people...rescue...NEWC	Charles Gindhart	140

Jeff White... California	UCH/CCL/PD	143
I turned out...a push-over	Charles Gindhart	144
Jack O'Brien... faithful... servant	Charles Gindhart	146
Bill Devlin, Presbyterian elder...	UCH/CCL/PD	147
Clergy rescue, ...rain, ...jail.	Charles Gindhart	149
Art Tomlinson, Operation Rescue	OR video	152
Roseann and Mike...Vets Rescue...	Charles Gindhart	153
...Dave Miller and George Krail	J. H. Trott	156
High school girls... rescue	Charles Gindhart	158
Mary and Elizabeth, greetings...	UCH/CCL/PD	160
Annual March for Life...	UCH/CCL/PD	169
Former... pro-lifer Jesse Jackson	UCH/CCL/PD	171
...Women's Rescue ... daughters	Charles Gindhart	174
Randy Terry, not first rescuer...	UCH/CCL/PD	176
Huge crowd Blackwell...	Charles Gindhart	178
Joshua praying among crosses	J. H. Trott	179
Abortion Survivors...	Life Advocate	181
...Logo for Survivors' Rescue	J. H. Trott	182
"Ordinary Friday..."	R. McIntosh, CH10	183
Dave Miller carried by police...	Charles Gindhart	185
Steve Osborn...Paoli...	Charles Gindhart	187
Phil Beachey, dragged...Cherry Hill	Charles Gindhart	192
Men taking responsibility	Charles Gindhart	193
Tina Krail... worship...Pittsburgh	Charles Gindhart	194
Denny Green...poured out his life...	Charles Gindhart	200
George Grant, pastor, author...	UCH/CCL/PD	203
Alan Keyes, courageous voice	UCH/CCL/PD	205
William B. Allen... Civil Rights	UCH/CCL/PD	207
LAPD's Bob Vernon	UCH/CCL/PD	209
Jim Kopp burdened by Pittsburgh...	UCH/CCL/PD	218
Jerome Lejeune... Modern Genetics	UCH/CCL/PD	220
Jim Owens... gentleman and lawyer	Charles Gindhart	223
Bernard Nathanson's... "Silent Scream"	video	227
Kids from Milwaukee join us...	Charles Gindhart	230
Father's Rescue at Blackwell...	Charles Gindhart	231
Mike McMonigal talks...rescuers...	Charles Gindhart	235
Hallway... B, B, & K.	Charles Gindhart	239
Abu Hayat... "Butcher..."	UCH/CCL/PD	240
Sherry Neal (with Roseann) ...	Kennedy, AM Phil	243

Was That Thunder?

Linda Ronning and daughter	Charles Gindhart	245
Josh... custody... Comly Road...	Charles Gindhart	248
Rev. Johnny Hunter of Buffalo	UCH/CCL/PD	253
Dr. Alveda King, niece of MLK	UCH/CCL/PD	254
Rev. Paul Schenk	OR video	255
Joe O'Hara... Kissing Bandit	Charles Gindhart	257
Franklin Graham	UCH/CCL/PD	259
Mike and Ceil McMonigal	Charles Gindhart	260
...Daughter Tory at prayer vigil...	Charles Gindhart	264
...Bob Casey last pro-life Democrat	UCH/CCL/PD	265
Mike McMonigal, ...candidate	Charles Gindhart	266
State police...rescuers... Allentown...	Charles Gindhart	268
John, Linda Ronning ...daughter	Charles Gindhart	269
Walt Gies... young leader	Charles Gindhart	270
Elijah.. under... juniper bush	UCH/CCL/PD	272
Michael Griffin, first... shooter...	UCH/CCL/PD	275
Phil Donahue... Paul Hill...	UCH/CCL/PD	276
Paul Hill.. supported Griffin...	UCH/CCL/PD	276
Joe Roach gave countless hours....	Charles Gindhart	278
Cities of Refuge... Genes Epps...	Charles Gindhart	280
Steve Freind, Pro-life Legislator	UCH/CCL/PD	281
Joe Rocks, Pro-life Senator	UCH/CCL/PD	282
Rev. Keith Tucci	OR video	283
Arrested...Brandywine...Delaware	Charles Gindhart	286
...Streets Rescue, downtown Philly	Charles Gindhart	289
Bob Lewis, Baptist Pastor...	Charles Gindhart	290
Arrest, end of Streets Rescue	Charles Gindhart	292
Fr. Pigeon and Fr. McFadden...	Charles Gindhart	296
Gene Kreuger... servant-leader...	Charles Gindhart	297
The forbidden baby model	UCH/CCL/PD	298
...Joe O'Hara... Paoli Rescue	Charles Gindhart	303
Dynamic duo...Jack...and Brian	Charles Gindhart	304
Arrest... Center City Philadelphia...	Charles Gindhart	307
Fr. John McFadden	OR video	308
Bob Lewis... front of clinic	Charles Gindhart	309
Reading Bible to fellow rescuers...	Charles Gindhart	311
Surg.-Gen. Koop... indistinct...	UCH/CCL/PD	313
...Leaders... rescue in New Jersey	Charles Gindhart	316
...Prayer vigils at clinics...	Charles Gindhart	317

A Memoir of Pro-life Rescue

Michael Bray	UCH/CCL/PD	321
Rachelle "Shelley" Shannon	Life Advocate	324
Flip Benham, Norma McCorvey	OR National	325
Terry Sullivan in 2012...	UCH/CCL/PD	327
Fr. Frank Pavone, Priests for Life	Priests for Life	331
Paul Hill in prison garb	UCH/CCL/PD	332
Rick Santorum... openly pro-life	UCH/CCL/PD	334
John Salvi...deeply disturbed	UCH/CCL/PD	338
Twenty-eight... block PP... 1995	Charles Gindhart	340
...Chester... wheelchair rescuers	Charles Gindhart	342
Frame from "Hard Truth"	*Hard Truth* video	343
Pastor Wegert... article	Hamburg paper	346
Dr. Beverly McMillan...	UCH/CCL/PD	347
Dr. Bernard Nathanson Ob-Gyn...	*Silent Scream*	349
"Show the Truth"... poster	UCH/CCL/PD	353
Pat Carroll	Charles Gindhart	356
Partial Birth... illustrated	Life Advocate	363
Gianna Jessen...survivor...	UCH/CCL/PD	365
Bill Calvin...with John Hegarty...	Brutal Truth video	369
1st Arrest, January 1997, Englewood Record, "Ed Hill, staff photographer," BUT responsible agency, ie., North Jersey Reprints and Permissions unable to trace	Photo in *Bergen Co.* UCH/CCL/PD	371
Barry Howell trophy of Christ...	Charles Gindhart	373
Second arrest with Bob Brothers to Associated Press, but AP unable to trace...	NYTimes/attributed UCH/CCL/PD	380
Bob Lewis carried away...	Charles Gindhart	394
Priscilla... at Delaware abortuary	Charles Gindhart	396
John Brown of Harper's Ferry...	UCH/CCL/PD	400
Gandalf, wiser than most of us	UCH/CCL/PD	415
Paul...before execution (from video)	Life Dynamics	419
Photo...Jim Kopp... FBI	UCH/CCL/PD	438
Pro-life prayer vigil	Charles Gindhart	442
...Roger Taney of Dred Scot...	UCH/CCL/PD	445
Chris, Joan... Mary Bell	The Rescuer	447
Rick Santorum, daughter Bella	book: *Bella's Gift*	448
Joe Scheidler... Chicago-based...	UCH/CCL/PD	450
"Tell the Truth" poster	UCH/CCL/PD	451

Was That Thunder?

Jim Kopp after... extradition...	UCH/CCL/PD	453
Dietrich Bonhoeffer, ...challenge	UCH/CCL/PD	456
Salem witch trial novel	J. H. Trott	461
Paul Hill on Death Row	UCH/CCL/PD	463
Baby David... legal abortion	UCH/CCL/PD	472
Andy Burnett...rescuer and editor...	*Life Advocate*	474
My wife, Roseann	Dora Demoss	476
Cover -- *Conceptions and images*	J. H. Trott	481
Charles and Mary Gindhart	Source unknown	482

A Memoir of Pro-life Rescue

www.ingramcontent.com/pod-product-compliance
Lightning Source LLC
Chambersburg PA
CBHW060816190426
43197CB00038B/1618